T0301553

INTEGRATING PROGRAM MANAGEMENT MANAGEMENT AND SYSTEMS ENGINEERING

INTEGRATING PROGRAM MANAGEMENT AND SYSTEMS ENGINEERING

Methods, Tools, and Organizational Systems for Improving Performance

Eric S. Rebentisch, Editor in Chief

With Foreword by

Larry Prusak

WILEY

Library of Congress Cataloging-in-Publication Data is Available

ISBN 9781119258926 (Hardcover)
ISBN 9781119259145 (ePDF)
ISBN 9781119259152 (ePub)

Cover image: © VLADGRIN/Getty Images
Cover design: Wiley

Printed in the United States of America

10 9 8 7 6 5 4 3 2 1

To the program managers, chief systems engineers, project managers, systems engineers, and reformers in academia, corporations, government, professional societies, and research institutions who are helping to advance integrated approaches to successfully deliver value through well-executed complex programs.

EDITORS

Eric S. Rebentisch
Marvin R. Nelson
Stephen A. Townsend
Edivandro Carlos Conforto
Virginia A. Greiman
Eric S. Norman
Elizabeth "Betsy" K. Clark
Tina P. Srivastava
Kenneth M. Zemrowski

CONTRIBUTORS

Akio Mitsufuji
Alan S. Harding
Bohdan Oppenheim
Brian Maddocks
Bryan Moser
David Pearson
Deborah Nightingale
Dennis Van Gemert
Eric Nicole
Guruprasad C. Vasudeva
Josef Oehmen
Kambiz Moghaddam
Mark A. Langley
Michael O'Brochta
Stanley I. Weiss
Thomas Paider
Timothy Wiseley

CONTENTS

PART I: IN SEARCH OF INTEGRATED SOLUTIONS   1

1 TOWARD A NEW MINDSET   3

2 THE ENGINEERING PROGRAM PERFORMANCE CHALLENGE   17

3 THE FEATURES OF SUCCESSFUL INTEGRATION OF PROGRAM MANAGEMENT AND SYSTEMS ENGINEERING   37

5 KEY CONCEPTS IN INTEGRATION   79

PART II: BUILDING CAPABILITIES TO EFFECTIVELY EXECUTE ENGINEERING PROGRAMS   97

6 HOW INTEGRATION WORKS IN PROGRAMS   99

11 INTEGRATION THROUGHOUT THE PROGRAM LIFE CYCLE 217

12 THE IMPACT OF EFFECTIVE INTEGRATION ON PROGRAM PERFORMANCE 237

PART IV: A CALL TO ACTION 341

16 CALLS TO ACTION 343

AFTERWORD: TOWARD AN INTEGRATED FUTURE 365

GLOSSARY 371

INDEX 381

LIST OF FIGURES

LIST OF TABLES

FOREWORD: PRACTICES, KNOWLEDGE, AND INNOVATION

Documented knowledge and associated practices exist as far back as the earliest civilizations. Some of the first written documents are speculations about what is known and what isn't. However, because of the way the English language works, the word "knowledge" stands for a fairly large variety of "things." We talk about mathematical theorems and computer algorithms as being knowledge essential to math and computer science. But we also talk about the knowledge of a skilled surgeon or carpenter—a type of knowledge that is quite a different thing than formulae and completely codified signals.

Philosophers, beginning with Aristotle, marked this distinction by breaking the word knowledge into two distinct categories: know-what and know-how. The former focuses on knowledge that is self-contained, codified, and cheap and easy to transmit from one knower to another. The latter is about the type of knowledge that is much closer related to skills, expertise, talents, and practices. This latter type of knowledge is much more contextual than know-what, is difficult and sometimes impossible to codify, and is expensive and time-consuming to transmit, if it can be done at all.

Most of the knowledge we work with in our daily lives is know-how. It spans such mundane tasks as getting to work to the actual tasks and work we perform as part of our career activities. However abstract it may seem, all these activities are embedded in practices. So what does this actually mean? Simply that know-how does not stand alone. It becomes embedded in our habitual ways of acting and working, and is embodied in our memories, habits, and psychological pathways. Practices are composed of vocabularies, work habits, accumulated historical stories, interfaces and entanglements with technologies, and our deep understanding as to the best way to do things.

This shared jumble of activities and words, emotions, and tacit memories allows practitioners in the same field to rather quickly understand one another and allows them to work together in ways that would be almost impossible if practices were not to some extent similar. I have seen many examples of this in my work as a consultant focused on knowledge development and transmission. For example, I once worked with oil riggers working in the North Sea who were being temporarily transferred to the Gulf of Mexico in order to teach the workers there some new methods they had developed. Vast distances in culture, language, and physical appearances melted away when it came to discussing and doing the actual rig work. Both groups' oil rig practices were enough alike to allow this transfer to be accomplished with little friction.

On the other hand, people working in different areas of practice probably won't be as fortunate as the oil rig workers in transferring knowledge. Tacit knowledge is "sticky" within its own arena and can be expensive and difficult to share outside of its arena. That is a primary challenge with knowledge work in general, and the particular challenge addressed in this book. How do you successfully bring together two (or more) different ways of knowing and doing to accomplish an important task?

Moreover, practices do not, and should not, stand still. New technologies and new accumulated knowledge of various types are continuously being developed that have the capability to alter and improve practices. Sometimes entirely new practices emerge from the absorption of these new techniques. Other times, older practices evolve into newer ones without any central force acting upon them—not wildly dissimilar to biological evolution. Think of how the field of cybernetics, developed during World War II, has evolved in the past 75 years or so, losing its name and transforming into several different and distinct practices, one or two of which are the focus of this book.

My own field of knowledge management was primarily the synthesis of information management and process management mixed in with the emerging personal computer technology tools in the late 1980s. This was a heady mix leavened with the ideas of Peter Drucker, Alvin Toffler, Daniel Bell, and several other popular prognosticators of the blossoming "knowledge age." There was a need to develop a new practice to synthesize these tools and ideas, and this new practice, knowledge management, quickly developed. It brought forth eager practitioners who were quick to mix cases from business schools, journalist's stories, and consulting advice. This was melded with various methods and frameworks to help organizations get started, along with metrics, technologies, incentive policies, and all the other tools that make practices applicable and workable. Within a decade of getting underway, the practice was established in over 300 organizations and it is still, as I write, a lively and established activity.

But it, too, will evolve by incorporating new ideas, perspectives, and tools to remain relevant to society and the economy. Practices in the past that failed to evolve, or fought off any attempt at change, almost always disappear eventually, although not without serious costs to those concerned.

Many practices, like the more formal disciplines found in universities, do not exactly embrace substantive change to the core assumptions. Every professor knows the perils of doing cross-disciplinary work, and students pay the price by not being taught what could best help them to understand the world and its ways. Economics is a good field to look at in this regard. The field was very slow to bring the insights of psychology and sociology into its models, to say nothing of considering knowledge as a factor of production. Even now the standard textbooks shy away from these types of insights even though two Nobel prizes in economics have gone to non-economists (Herbert Simon and Daniel Kahneman) who have forced the field, through the power of their ideas, to adapt somewhat to them.

So, with these challenges, this book has taken on the task of helping two important practice areas work together in a more seamless fashion. Program management and systems engineering have each existed as formal disciplines for less than a century. Each has extensive bodies of know-what in their standards, publications, and tools with structured certification processes that take practitioners years to demonstrate mastery. But even more importantly, they are critically dependent upon deep reserves of know-how that is embodied within their most experienced and skilled practitioners. The difference in capabilities between the experienced "A" team and the less experienced "B" team or even whether a few high-performing individuals are available to contribute can quickly determine whether a complex program will be a success or a failure. Transferring this know-how from one generation to the next within each practice area can take the substantial part of a career—despite the fact that they are in the best cases using the same practices, speaking in the same terms, and working on the same problems. Imagine the challenge of transferring know-how when the know-what is still fuzzy and perceived differently across the discipline. The merging of know-how between the two disciplines around a common challenge is even more imposing—but ultimately necessary to success.

"Nothing comes from nothing" the philosophers proclaim. All new ideas build upon other, older ideas. New knowledge emerges from orderly processes such as science or more typically from the fusion, merging, fighting, or embracing of older knowledge. It eventually becomes codified into know-what and new practices are then built upon it. It has always been so and will likely continue this way as long as this remains an inherently social process.

This book is a wonderful attempt to see what two established and valuable disciplines have to offer to one another, to their customers, and to society. What may come out of it has the potential of bringing a harmonious understanding of how to deliver better solutions more successfully. This could be a great blessing to all concerned so let us congratulate the authors of this first attempt and hope for its success.

Larry Prusak

PREFACE

In 2011, International Council on Systems Engineering (INCOSE) and Project Management Institute (PMI) allied to enhance, foster, and enable collaboration between program managers and systems engineers. Our organizations believed that the two disciplines had developed silos between them that inhibited collaboration and that we needed to change mindsets to remove such barriers. We issued a call to action through a joint whitepaper, *Toward a New Mindset: Bridging the Gap Between Program Management and Systems Engineering* (Langley, Robitaille, & Thomas, 2011), that identified the following challenge:

> While program management has overall program accountability and systems engineering has accountability for the technical and systems elements of the program, some systems engineers and program managers have developed the mindset that their work activities are separate from each other rather than part of the organic whole (p. 24).

Regardless of who was in authority, whose inputs were more respected and accepted, or who better understood the path forward, the whitepaper put forward the proposition that silos focused each discipline on advancing its own approach toward delivering solutions to meet customer needs. The whitepaper went on to say:

> Historically, program managers and systems engineers have viewed the stakeholder problem entirely from within their own disciplinary perspectives.... As a result, the two groups have applied distinctly different approaches to the key work—managing the planning and

implementation, defining the components and their interactions, building the components, and integrating the components (Langley et al., p. 25).

Since the whitepaper's publication, our subsequent engagements with stakeholders have anecdotally confirmed the existence of the issues we identified to varying degrees. That led our organizations to formally evaluate the level of integration and collaboration between program managers and chief systems engineers. Partnering with MIT's Consortium for Engineering Program Excellence (MIT CEPE), our organizations conducted a series of studies over three years exploring the following questions:

- How integrated were the practices, tools, and approaches used by chief systems engineers and program managers? Did critical links exist where they were needed? Were common practices, such as risk management, managed in intersecting or parallel paths? Were practices, tools, and approaches evaluated and benchmarked to identify opportunities for improvement?
- How formalized were the roles, responsibilities, and competencies of each discipline? Did each discipline perform unique functions or were there functions that both disciplines performed?
- How well did the chief systems engineer and program manager collaborate with each other? Did any tension exist in their relationship and, if so, how did that tension affect their ability to work together?
- In organizations with strongly integrated practices and low levels of interdisciplinary tension, what distinguishing characteristics could be identified? How did the disciplines achieve integration and collaboration?
- In organizations with weakly integrated practices and high levels of tension that affected collaboration, what distinguishing characteristics could be identified? What were the barriers to achieving integration and collaboration?
- Does integration and collaboration demonstrably impact program performance?

The research helped to validate the need to move toward a new mindset:

> This new mindset recognizes that there cannot be two separate views of the stakeholder problem, but rather a single one that incorporates all elements of the program.... What emerges is an understanding that all of the work is relevant to both groups, and that the delivery of stakeholder value requires an appropriate contribution from both areas of professional expertise (Langley et al., 2011, p. 26).

Our research and our stakeholder engagements have uncovered active efforts to move toward this mindset. Efforts are starting at the program level as individual program managers and chief systems engineers join forces to improve their program outcomes. These efforts are often not deliberate though. As two colleagues—one a program manager and one a chief systems engineer in the same company—shared at the 2015 INCOSE International Symposium, "dumb luck" helped them uncover that each had a piece of the solution that the other needed. The relationship they forged brought about change that established better alignment, integration, and collaboration. But as one of them left the organization, they feared that the change they started did not have sufficient roots beyond their relationship to be sustained. In other words, alignment, integration, and collaboration had not become embedded in the organizational culture, processes, and systems as critical components. Alignment, integration, and collaboration were not measured or reported to senior leadership, and thus their value to the organization was hidden from top leadership.

So beyond the premise and beyond the abilities of the two disciplines to change on their own, senior executives within corporations and government also must change their mindsets. They must see the connections between strategy, benefits, performance, and capabilities, and work within their organizations to remove gaps and improve performance. They must recognize the value their organizations could gain from even incremental efforts to reduce wasted investments due to poor program execution. They must ensure their organizations learn from examples of success and failure, such as those presented in this book, and utilize that learning to continuously improve their own practices. Most importantly, they must stand with their program managers and chief systems engineers and lead the change toward a new mindset—the focus of this book.

Alan Harding, President, International Council on Systems Engineering
Mark Langley, President & CEO, Project Management Institute

Reference

Langley, M., Robitaille, S., & Thomas, J. (2011). Toward a new mindset: Bridging the gap between program management and systems engineering. *PM Network*, *25*(9), 24–26.

ACKNOWLEDGMENTS

This book results from a significant collaborative effort involving many individuals and institutions during the course of the last five years. The comparison of this collaborative effort to a program is appropriate. It has defined objectives, many stakeholders, and a stream of benefits generated over time. This book is but one project producing benefits for the overall effort.

Like any program, multiple stakeholders operate in a number of different functions to produce the overall benefit. Each plays a unique role that collectively produces something that they individually could not produce. Some of the contributions are managerial, some are technical, and others are enabling. Upon reflection, over the course of the last 16 months during which this book has been in various stages of development, many have contributed. This is an attempt to acknowledge their efforts in what has become a fairly dynamic project. Some of those who started the project were unable to complete it or completed their parts early and went on to other things. Others joined partway through, or even close to the completion. Others have been part of the project from start to finish. They represent participation from a broad spectrum, and truly exemplify the spirit of this book: bringing together multiple perspectives to create something unique and noteworthy. It is not intentional that anyone who contributed to this effort would not be recognized, and all contributions and involvement have been deeply appreciated whether acknowledged here or not.

The overall effort was directed through the PMI/INCOSE/MIT Alliance team, which included Randall Iliff (INCOSE lead), Stephen Townsend (PMI lead), and Eric Rebentisch (MIT lead), with Tina Srivastava, Kenneth M. Zemrowski, Jack Stein,

Ashok Jain, Richard Gryzbowski, and Eileen Arnold, all from INCOSE, and Keith Rosenbaum from PMI. This group helped to define the vision for the book, helped organize and enable the research activities that supported the knowledge base for the book, organized the dissemination of the findings at conferences and other venues, and assisted with the development and publication. They also helped to identify and recruit the numerous contributors to the book from within their respective professional communities. Both PMI and INCOSE mobilized their network of chapters and chapter leads to solicit subject matter expert and practitioner participation and contributions to this book. Notably, Jean-Claude Roussel, the INCOSE EMEA Sector Director, Claes Bengtsson from the INCOSE Swedish chapter, and Jack Stein from the INCOSE Michigan chapter helped to recruit contributors to this effort.

Playing central roles in creating the knowledge foundation for this book were Maria Pacenza from PMI Market Research, who conducted the first integration survey and presented the initial findings. Edivandro Conforto and Monica Rossi performed in-depth analysis of the first integration survey data, and followed up with additional interviews and synthesis of findings to clarify what is meant by integration between program management and systems engineering. Thomas Reiner and Lucia Beceril conducted follow-on confirmatory research as part of their graduate studies to further refine and validate the concept of integration. Additional perspective in shaping and directing the book content came from Randall Iliff, Jeffrey Thompson, Ann Bachelor, Claude Baron, Samuel Boutin, and Tomoichi Sato. PMI and INCOSE members Heinz Stoewer, James Armstrong, Brian Maddocks, Jeffrey Thompson, Randall Iliff, and Tina Srivastava helped to build awareness of program management and systems engineering's potential through their conference presentations, as did presentations by MIT researchers Josef Oehmen, Edivandro Conforto, and Eric Rebentisch.

The editors and contributors have been acknowledged in lists in the front of the book. They had formally designated roles in creating the content of this book. The editors created chapter drafts that form the basic structure of the book. The contributors provided significant and important content for those chapters. Their roles are in fact not so easily defined, as many of them filled in and took on the work that needed to be done to produce the book. While all their contributions provide the substance of this book and are greatly appreciated, two individuals played an outsized role and deserve additional mention for their contributions. Marvin Nelson filled the role of principal co-editor of this book. In addition to writing chapters in the book, he also edited and integrated the entire manuscript of the book and did much of the detailed technical work that is necessary when publishing a book. Stephen Townsend wrote or played a significant role in writing a number of chapters in the book. Additionally, he provided essential leadership in shepherding the manuscript through the many steps and around potential pitfalls in the process to getting a completed manuscript. Both were critical to the completion of this process, and whose contributions are not adequately captured by their appearance in the lists above.

As the manuscript was taking shape, many subject matter expert reviewers from both PMI and INCOSE helped to review an early draft of the manuscript and provide feedback on its strengths, weaknesses, and omissions. Over one thousand comments were provided by these experts from North America, Europe and Asia, who provided good ideas, important insights, and in some cases the awareness of the need to change course or redo some sections. They were Bryan Pflug, Brigitte Daniel-Alle, Alain Roussel, Jean-Claude Roussel, Gary Smith, J. Robert Wirthlin, Med Ahmadoun, Laurie Wiggins, Liew PakSan, Linda Agyapong, Clement Yeung, Kambiz Moghaddam, Claes Bengtsson, Magnus Cangard, Timothy H. Wiseley, Dennis Van Gemert, Jörg Lalk, Cecilia Haskins, Timothy Ferris, Arie Wessels, Kenneth Zemrowski, Virginia Lentz, Joseph Dyer, Eduardo Flores, Heather Ramsey, Michael Morgan, and Garry Roedler.

Others provided essential support for this effort by enabling connections to people, content, or in the form of knowledge of how to write a book. Donn Greenberg (PMI Publications Manager) helped to facilitate initial contacts with Wiley and offered valuable advice on structuring agreements between the parties. Barbara Walsh (PMI Publications Department) facilitated the graphics design work for the book. Holly Witte and Bob Kenley from the INCOSE Publications Office provided assistance in enabling access to INCOSE content and in the formal INCOSE review process. Paul Schreinemakers (Technical Director), Mike Celentano (Deputy Technical Director), and Kenneth Zemrowski from the INCOSE Technical Operations Team helped with the review and approval of the final manuscript by INCOSE. Margaret Cummings (Executive Editor at John Wiley & Sons) was an invaluable source of guidance and support throughout this project and was able to effortlessly identify a path forward through all potential challenges.

Because of the multistakeholder nature of this project, legal expertise proved to be essential. Elizabeth Levy (MIT Office of General Counsel), Marjorie Gordon (PMI Counsel), and Gita Srivastava, Stephanie Tso, and Laura Kalesnik (from Norton Rose Fulbright, INCOSE's Counsel) played key roles in structuring the legal frameworks for the book project and related collaborative agreements needed to allow the collaborative work to proceed. Peter Bebergal (MIT Technology Licensing Office) and Catherine Viega (from PMI) helped in making the intellectual property from their respective organizations available to the team to produce the final manuscript. Thanks also to Benjamin Lindorf, General Counsel, Institute for Defense Analysis, for his help in making the content of Chapter 7 readily available for this book.

Others provided essential enabling support to the project. Craig Killough (PMI Vice President, Organization Markets) supported the participation of Stephen Townsend and Marvin Nelson in the production of the book, which proved critical to its completion. Cindy Anderson (PMI Vice President, Brand) signed off on the co-brand license with Wiley. David Long (Past INCOSE President) did the same for INCOSE. Jordon Sims (PMI Organization Relations Director) helped with engaging Larry Prusak to write the Foreword. Thanks also go to David Long (Past INCOSE President) and John A. Thomas (Past INCOSE President) for their enthusiastic support of the PMI/INCOSE Alliance and the origins of this particular project. Seemingly simple things can often make a big difference in the progress of a project. In this case, being able to meet as a team periodically to discuss, take stock, and make plans was very important to being able to maintain progress toward the end goal. Thanks to Jillian Moriera and the Sociotechnical Systems Research Center at MIT, Stephen Townsend at PMI, and Randall Iliff at BB7 each for hosting these important meetings of the team.

Last, but far from least, not a few families and those close to the authors and contributors were inconvenienced by "the book project" as writing was underway, and particularly around key deadlines. A special thank you goes to them for their patience and support during this project.

This is the product of many hands. As the saying goes, many hands make light work. In a complex project involving the coordination and reconciliation of a diverse set of inputs, that doesn't always seem to be the case. However, in the case of this book, it is correct to say that many hands make superior work—that is the message (and the experience) of this effort. Any errors or omissions, however unintentional, are the sole responsibility of the editor in chief.

INTRODUCTION

The core message of this book is that bringing people together from diverse perspectives will dramatically improve their ability to produce valuable outcomes. This is not necessarily a new idea. The value of working this way is axiomatic in fields as diverse as science, politics, or industrial management. This book specifically explores how a close working relationship between program managers and chief systems engineers in complex programs can significantly improve the resulting benefits to their stakeholders. Indeed, this book is the product of that very approach to working. Representatives from program management, systems engineering, and academic communities worked collaboratively to pool, merge, and synthesize their collective insights into something of potentially great importance to not only their respective disciplines, but also to an array of industrial sectors, government, and to society.

The Origins of an Important Collaboration

This publication results from a collaborative journey underway for five years as of this writing. The journey began with two separate efforts that shared common interests, participants, and institutional sponsors. In 2011, Project Management Institute (PMI) and International Council on Systems Engineering (INCOSE) formed a strategic alliance to advance the integration of the systems engineering and program management disciplines. That alliance was driven by the vision that better integration of these two disciplines would lead to the delivery of better solutions for organizations and their stakeholders.

Also in 2011, a gathering of researchers and partners from a number of industrial firms (primarily aerospace) met to explore the application of Lean principles to program management. This group would eventually coalesce around what would come to be called the Consortium for Engineering Program Excellence (CEPE) at the Massachusetts Institute of Technology (MIT). Many of the initial participants were experienced program managers or systems engineers (or both). Some of them were also members of PMI and INCOSE. Through these initial interactions and the mutual connections between them, both initiatives began to become more involved at an institutional level. The first major outcome of this collaborative working relationship between industry, professional societies, and academics brought together research and practical experience to produce *The Guide to Lean Enablers for Managing Engineering Programs* (Oehmen, 2012). The creation of this joint publication not only developed working relationships, but also created the formal agreements for collaboration and sharing necessary to produce a joint publication and established a community of diverse perspectives focused on addressing issues of shared interest.

Subsequent collaborative efforts within the community produced expanded online content for the *Guide*. In 2013 it was awarded the Shingo Research and Professional Publication Award in recognition of its contributions to the understanding of Lean and operational excellence. Perhaps the most important outcome of the collaboration was the development of a means for two important professional disciplines and academics to work together and bring their unique perspectives to bear to address common problems.

Creating a Knowledge Foundation through Exploratory Research

The research basis for this book unfolded through four distinct phases over a period of nearly three years. It combined survey research, interviews, literature reviews, statistical analysis, and simulation modeling methods. The data were drawn from sources geographically dispersed and included a diverse array of industrial sectors and government. Supporting evidence was drawn from other published research in this area and was used to shape and confirm the insights that emerged from the analysis. While largely exploratory in nature, the evolution of the study included formal definition and testing of several hypotheses about integration. The combined insights from these numerous methods form the knowledge foundation of this book.

In October 2012, PMI and INCOSE conducted a joint survey to better understand the roles of program managers and chief systems engineers and to gauge the level of their integration. MIT CEPE researchers provided research support in analyzing, reviewing, and summarizing the survey results with PMI and INCOSE. The results were subsequently presented to audiences at PMI Global Congresses and INCOSE International Symposia, as well as to working groups of professionals from both organizations and other industry participants.

The initial results from the analysis of the survey data were informative, but raised more questions than they answered. The initial findings just scratched the surface

	Phase I	Phase II	Phase III	Phase IV
	October 2012	July–Sept 2013	Nov 2013–Mar 2014	June 2014–Feb 2015
Focus	Exploratory survey to understand how program management and systems engineering are integrated within the organization.	Investigation of practices in companies without unproductive tension.	Investigation of practices in companies facing unproductive tension.	Survey to gather data and test the Integration Framework.
Methodology	Online survey with a global sample of 694 usable surveys (340 current program managers, 222 current chief systems engineers, 132 functioning as both).	Interviews with survey respondents (9 program managers or chief systems engineers) to characterize what their organizations did to integrate program management and systems engineering.	Interviews with survey respondents (7 program managers or chief systems engineers) to characterize what their organizations did to integrate program management and systems engineering and to better understand unproductive tension.	Online survey with a global sample of 157 usable surveys (program managers and systems engineers) representing 18 industry sectors. Validation through statistical analysis.

Table 0-1: The program management and systems engineering integration knowledge base was established over multiple phases of research.

of what appeared to be an important but largely unaddressed area. New questions were formulated, and additional investigation was begun by the researchers at MIT CEPE. With each new cycle of investigation, new questions would arise. Through this process of evolving questions and studies to find answers, a multiphase research program emerged. The four distinct phases of the research and their objectives are explained in the following table, with additional detail on the studies to follow in subsequent chapters.

Phase I Study

The invitation to participate in the joint PMI and INCOSE survey in 2012 was sent to approximately 3,000 INCOSE members (systems engineers) and 5,000 PMI members (program managers). Usable responses were received through a web-based survey from almost 700 participants spread across the globe. The respondents were restricted from participating in the survey unless they were either a current program manager (the one who has the ultimate authority and accountability for the overall program consisting of multiple related projects), a current chief systems engineer (the one who has ultimate technical authority and accountability for the product or system being developed), or currently functioning as both.

The survey was constructed to better understand how program management and systems engineering are integrated within organizations. It posed questions about:

- Common job skills and responsibilities between the two roles
- The level of interaction and integration between the two roles

- The interactions between the use of standards, integration, formalization, level of effectiveness, and degree of unproductive tension between program management and systems engineering
- Ways that INCOSE and PMI could collaborate to better align systems engineering and program management practices

The survey provided helpful first insights about the state of interactions and integration between program management and systems engineering. Because the survey spanned a number of diverse topics, it did not dive into great detail in any one of those areas. In addition to integration, unproductive tension between program managers and systems engineers emerged as an important factor to help partition the responses into different groups that suggested differing levels of performance. Unproductive tension was defined as any issue between the two disciplines that might negatively affect program performance with a focus on practices, tools, and techniques, as well as job descriptions and responsibilities. All of the responses to the question about unproductive tension, with the exception of "No unproductive tension," reflected a spectrum with varying degrees of negative impact on the program's performance. The data underwent extensive statistical analysis to understand the circumstances under which integration and unproductive tension occurred. While a number of useful insights emerged from this analysis, the connection between integration, unproductive tension, and overall program or organizational performance remained unclear at this stage. The action mechanisms for enabling greater levels of integration were likewise unclear.

Phase II and III Studies

The survey provided a good starting point to understand the high-level issues associated with integration of program management and systems engineering. In order to clarify the mechanisms of integration and the impact of integration on performance, additional information about how integration actually occurred in organizations was needed. Fortunately, the survey allowed the respondents to indicate that they were willing to answer follow-up questions related to the study topic. This provided an opportunity to learn more about how organizations managed integration between program management and systems engineering. Those who indicated that they were willing to engage in further discussion were also most likely to have indicated that their organizations experienced little or no unproductive tension between program management and systems engineering. Consequently, Phase II of the research focused on those organizations that experienced little or no unproductive tension. The respondents were asked to describe what they understood about integration, unproductive tension, the characteristics of their teams, the relationship between program management and systems engineering, and other related factors that might explain why they indicated that their organizations experienced lower levels of unproductive tension between program management and systems engineering.

To provide a basis for comparison, a separate sample of respondents that indicated high levels of unproductive tension in their organizations was identified from the initial group of survey respondents. Interviews with this sample comprised Phase III of the research. The respondents were asked to answer the same questions used in Phase II. Additionally, they were asked to describe what they perceived to be the primary sources of unproductive tension between program management and systems engineering in their organizations. The responses from each phase were compared and the contrasts were used to better define integration, unproductive tension between program management and systems engineering, and to understand the factors that might contribute to or mitigate either.

To complement the findings from the Phase I study and the interviews, published research, including case studies, on the topic of integration in general and specifically between program management and systems engineering was reviewed. Exploration of these and a number of peripherally related topic areas revealed that apparently little research had been done in this area previously. While case studies focusing on program management or systems engineering alone were available, very few case studies were found that focused specifically on the nature of the relationship between program management and systems engineering and how the characteristics of that relationship affects program outcomes.

Without a strong research precedent or empirical base to build on, this study became largely exploratory, or in the "observe, describe, and measure" stage of theory development (Christensen, 2006). This means that the study was inductive, with effort primarily focused on identification of the key factors or constructs that drive the overall behavior, and how those factors relate to one another. Once the primary constructs and relationships between them have been identified by a study (i.e., a model of the system is developed), deductive or confirmatory analysis where specific hypotheses can be tested and the strength of relationships established becomes available.

With model development and testing as the objective then, the analysis of both the survey and interview data were used to draft a practitioner-oriented framework to help organizations understand integration and possible areas for improvement. The analysis of the interviews also produced more formal definitions of integration and unproductive tension. The definitions, framework, and research results were presented at a number of conferences and workshops with both program management and system engineering audiences, and were additionally scrutinized by subject matter experts from each domain, helping to further refine the working definition of the integration constructs.

Phase IV Study

From the practitioner-oriented framework a more formal research integration framework was created. This included formal definition of variables and hypothesized relationships between the variables. Using this framework, a survey was created to measure each of the variables in the framework consistent with accepted research standards and practices. This was then hosted online and invitations to participate in the survey were sent to a sample of program managers and systems engineers drawn from the same general populations as the Phase I survey. The data produced by the new survey were used to formally test the Integration Framework and provide additional insights into the relationships between the various elements of integration.

The online survey sampled 157 participants from around the world and included program managers and systems engineers. The resulting dataset enabled a more rigorous and systematic analysis of the data to validate the concepts that had been identified previously using advanced statistical analysis and modeling methods. The results provided a better understanding of what factors contribute to integration in programs, as well as a better estimate of the impact of integration on program performance. With the detailed empirical data about the integration elements, a simulation model was developed to help test the nature of integration between program management and systems engineering under a range of different circumstances.

Strengths and Limitations of the Research Foundation

This overview of the research presents not only the empirical basis for the ideas presented in this book, but also highlights its limitations. Research on the integration of program management and systems engineering should be considered at this point in the early stages of theory development and understanding. A general rule of thumb in research is to keep collecting data until no significant new insights emerge from the analysis of that data. The data used as the basis of this discussion is certainly more extensive than what had been uncovered at the beginning of this effort. But new insights emerged with each additional sample, suggesting that research in this domain is still in the exploratory phase.

The ideas presented here, therefore, may best be considered as reasonable approximations of how program management and systems engineering can be better integrated. They may be useful for practitioners and researchers alike, but much yet remains unknown. Some of what is hinted at by the research so far likely provides only an incomplete perspective at this point. Other ideas or activities presented here may only address symptoms rather than the underlying issues and root causes associated with the impact of poor integration on program performance. To address these limitations, more research on these topics is not only welcome but warranted. So, this book is not meant to provide the last word on integration between these disciplines. Rather, it should be considered an initial invitation to open active discussion and investigation about a critical topic.

Integrating Practitioner Knowledge with Research

The results of the multiple research phases, and particularly the Integration Framework, frame the flow and presentation of information, examples, and ideas in this book. Excerpts from the analysis appear in various chapters throughout the book. The analysis resulted in papers that went through the academic peer-review process and were targeted toward academic audiences. It also resulted in practitioner-focused publications and presentations with discussions that gave a "reality check" to the findings. The exposure of these ideas to multiple perspectives has hopefully improved them with each iteration of the review process, and made them more relevant and accessible in this book.

The ideas and concepts identified in the research also provided a roadmap for the content that was contributed by practitioners and collaborators on this project. Opening up the potential number of contributors and perspectives not only greatly enhances the strength and applicability of the ideas, but it also makes the book more readable and interesting to a wider array of potential readers. Moreover, it provides additional observations and examples to help overcome the limitations in the size and scope of the dataset as described previously.

As noted earlier, not many case studies were found that focus specifically on the relationship between program management and systems engineering. Case study examples are useful to illustrate complex concepts and to make the text more readable and memorable. Case studies written to illustrate the specific points of the Integration Framework were used whenever they could be identified and were available. Published, research-based case studies were generally preferred as they would have been required to adhere to a scientific standard of verification of evidence. In other instances, case examples drawn from the popular press were used to illustrate specific points. In those instances, all efforts were made to find corroborating evidence from different sources in order to increase confidence that the points being represented were accurate. In all cases, the standard for deciding whether to use material in this book is that examples should be documented in a verifiable way and be consistent with findings from this or other systematic research.

Finally, a mature draft of the manuscript of this book was reviewed by subject matter experts drawn from the PMI, INCOSE, and academic communities. Over 30 reviewers read parts or all of the draft manuscript and provided over a thousand comments to address the accuracy, relevance, and tone of the content, or to suggest alternative or new considerations regarding the integration of program management and systems engineering. Their feedback included considerable thought and in some cases new content that strengthened and improved the text overall.

This book is, therefore, an amalgam of a diverse array of preliminary evidence about why the integration of program management and systems engineering is important to the practice of both disciplines and, ultimately, valuable to the beneficiaries of their programs. The hope is that by bringing this content together now, practitioners may derive some near-term benefit and others may be inspired to continue the investigation and documentation of this important area. Through the normal operation of the scientific method, gaps, errors, and incomplete elements may hopefully be addressed in the future.

Overview of the Book

This book is partitioned into four parts, as outlined below. Part I makes the case for why integration between program management and systems engineering is important—**why** the reader should care about this topic. The progression of ideas in each chapter takes the reader from the initial recognition that there is great opportunity to improve the performance of programs through better integration of the program management and systems engineering disciplines, to an understanding of the underlying barriers to integration, and the potential benefits that might come from better integration.

Part II describes in greater detail the practices and methods that enable greater integration between the program management and systems engineering disciplines—**what** to do to have more integrated program execution. The chapters are organized around the major elements of the Integration Framework. Each includes research findings from the study discussed here, complemented by examples drawn from other studies and from practitioner experience.

Part III addresses the challenge of how to create sustained change toward a new way of operating in a more integrated state—**how** to make integration a reality in programs. Change is difficult, and transformational change is even more challenging because of the complexity introduced by the various factors. The chapters in this part describe these challenges and how to overcome them, supported by examples of successful change.

The book concludes in Part IV with a call to action. The ideas presented in the first three parts are oriented toward programs and the organizations that immediately support them. Programs, however, exist in an environment that practitioners often are not able to effectively control, but which may exert considerable influence on the program itself and the practitioners' ability to operate in an integrated fashion. The challenges to integration posed by various elements in the program's operating and resource environment are addressed here with recommendations for changes that are intended to enable programs to operate in a more integrated fashion.

Finally, the focus of this book is on programs and their context. Many readers may work primarily in a project environment, and may conclude that these ideas are not relevant for their work. PMI (2013) defines programs as "a group of related projects, subprograms, and program activities that are managed in a coordinated way to obtain benefits not available from managing them individually" (p. 4). Projects differ from programs in that they tend to have a tightly defined scope of work, along with a fixed budget and timeframe within which the output is to be delivered. While the focus of this book is on programs, the principles and practices of integration discussed in the chapters should be applicable to both programs and projects. In either case, some tailoring of the principles to the requirements of the immediate setting likely will be needed.

References

Christensen, C. M. (2006). The ongoing process of building a theory of disruption. *Journal of Product Innovation Management, 23*(1), 39–55.

Oehmen, J. (Ed.). (2012). *The guide to Lean enablers for managing engineering programs, version 1.0.* Cambridge, MA: Joint MIT-PMI-INCOSE Community of Practice on Lean in Program Management. URI: http://hdl.handle.net/1721.1/70495

Project Management Institute (PMI). (2013). *The standard for program management* (3rd ed.). Newtown Square, PA: Author.

INTEGRATING PROGRAM MANAGEMENT AND SYSTEMS ENGINEERING

Part I
IN SEARCH OF INTEGRATED SOLUTIONS

Part I explores the importance of complex programs for society and the positive impact they can have when they perform well, as well as the downsides when they do not. Some of the challenges and causes of poor program performance, as well as factors that contribute to program success, are examined. There are a number of common elements that begin to explain the range in program performance, including the functions performed by the program management and systems engineering disciplines and their approach to working together. The section concludes by identifying a way to mitigate or avoid many common program challenges—the concept of integration.

Chapter 1 uses the example of SpaceX Corporation to illuminate the difference in performance that can result from a unique approach to managing engineering programs. It explores how performance outcomes may result from a combination of factors, but ultimately are rooted in the capabilities that organizations build to be both innovative and efficient. Key players in creating the conditions for success or failure in these programs are the program management and systems engineering functions.

Chapter 2 illustrates the different challenges that programs face, often rooted in the complexity of tasks and how that complexity is navigated. Poor handling of these challenges results in poor program performance, as illustrated in three case examples. These challenges are well-known, yet many programs still suffer the negative consequences of not identifying and dealing with them appropriately. The chapter argues that an integrated management framework that brings together program management and systems engineering may produce better outcomes for these complex programs.

Chapter 3 examines effective or high-functioning programs to better understand the factors that contribute to their success. Higher levels of program performance are achieved through what is referred to as "integration"—increasing the ability of all program participants to collaborate, communicate, and bring their respective contributions to bear in addressing challenges. Better collaboration and integration between systems engineering and program management functions can overcome program challenges and improve overall performance.

Chapter 4 explores the fields of program management and systems engineering to understand their history and evolution, the roles played by their respective practitioners, and their orientations toward work tasks. Large, complex programs rely on high performance on the technical side and exceptional management overall. Both program management and systems engineering disciplines contribute critical benefits to the program, but can often work at cross purposes. Both possess unique and specialized sets of knowledge capable of creating significant benefits independently, but, more importantly, even greater benefits when working together. However, they are also susceptible to being trapped within their own local mindsets to the detriment of overall program performance.

Chapter 5 explores integration between program management and systems engineering to identify its role in program success. Properly defining and understanding integration across the organization is paramount to improving performance in large programs. Integration may manifest itself in a number of different ways depending on the setting. This chapter conveys an expansive definition of integration in operational terms and how it is manifest in specific organizations across many sectors.

1

TOWARD A NEW MINDSET

1.1 Striving for Perfection in Complex Work

A once relatively common expression in the United States was "if we can put a man on the moon, why can't we <insert complaint>?" It conveyed a sense that the country, its technical experts, its government, and its people were capable of amazing things if they put their minds to it. There was another term that went along with it—"rocket scientists." Those were the clever people who made those miraculous things happen so that they seemed commonplace. Given enough rocket scientists, one imagined, just about any problem, no matter how complex, could be solved. Perhaps those expressions are locked in a certain time and place—the late 1960s and early 1970s—when the United States was routinely putting men on the moon, less than seven decades after people first took to the sky in the dawn of powered flight.

The same expression simultaneously conveyed a sense of frustration that things don't always work as hoped or planned, no matter how clever or skilled we might appear or how much thought we put into the plans. Why is it that despite having advanced knowledge, tools, and capabilities, and even having demonstrated that it is possible to do something amazing, best efforts sometimes end in disappointment or failure? Many other human activities that don't involve the complexities of spaceflight but are in their own way complex (think energy, infrastructure, transportation, public health) nevertheless invoke the same question. This book tries to answer that question in the context of complex programs.

The effort to send men to the moon and bring them back safely was a huge program that was itself embedded in the U.S. national space program, and was linked with other programs that served U.S. national strategies and priorities during the Cold War. The Apollo program comprised many individual, highly complicated engineering projects, but also other program activities that touched research, education, defense, and ultimately commercial products. The management challenges were significant, and so, of course, were the engineering challenges. To address these technical challenges, a new discipline called systems engineering rose to prominence. The marriage of systems engineering with program management approaches proved to be critical to the Apollo program's success.

As successful as it was, though, it was not sustained or repeated in quite the same way. The last human to walk on the moon, Gene Cernan, stepped into his spacecraft and left the surface of the moon on December 14, 1972. Humans have not returned since, nor left low earth orbit (LEO) for that matter. Of the 12 people who ever walked on the moon, only seven survive today. The passage of so much time has left those remaining elderly.

However often it might appear that the capability to accomplish important and inspiring things is diminishing, counterexamples seem to appear. It has been over four decades since people last set foot on the moon after the United States mobilized a national-level effort to accomplish that task. But a small U.S. company is defiantly working not only to recapture those capabilities, but to significantly exceed them. The Space Exploration Technologies Corporation, better known as SpaceX, during its relatively short existence has not only accomplished many important and inspiring things, but has done so in a way that significantly outperforms all competitors, both government and private, and seems poised to create a renaissance in the space sector.

1.2 Boldly Going Again Where People Have Gone Before

The founder of SpaceX, Elon Musk, is a successful entrepreneur with a tendency to disrupt business-as-usual in a surprising array of business sectors, including finance (PayPal), energy (Solar City), transportation (Tesla Motors), and of course space transportation (SpaceX). His long-term vision and the impetus for starting SpaceX was to make humans a multiplanet species by enabling them to settle on Mars, and more quickly than the perpetually slipping timetables of government space agency plans. Based on what SpaceX has accomplished so far, that vision seems achievable (Vance, 2015). Perhaps as compelling as the impressive launch hardware and support systems that SpaceX has created is the way that it has been able to assemble teams of, yes, rocket scientists, and to design a work system that enables them to be incredibly productive and produce complex systems quickly. The following case study describes how SpaceX has been able to accomplish this.[1]

Since its inception in 2002, SpaceX has accomplished more in a short period of time than any of its competitors. SpaceX has logged over 30 successful flights and has achieved certification for NASA and United States Air Force launches. SpaceX has developed about 100 major flight-proven products in 14 years. These include the development of five engines (Merlin, Merlin Vacuum, Kestrel, Draco Thruster, Raptor), three launch vehicles (Falcon 1, Falcon 9, and the full-thrust Falcon 9) and Dragon and Dragon 2 spacecraft, an autonomous spaceport drone ship to enable landing reusable rockets, along with associated modern ground test, launch, and mission facilities. At the time of this writing SpaceX is completing development of the most powerful rocket since the Saturn V moon rockets, the Falcon 9 Heavy. It continues to fine-tune the propulsive landing reusable first stage of its Falcon 9 booster, and a reusable propulsive landing version its Dragon 2 spacecraft.

The development time and cost of these products are several times smaller than the competition. A NASA analysis of commercial space launch alternatives used a historical cost-based cost estimating tool to predict the development costs for space hardware systems. It predicted that using a traditional NASA approach to develop a new launch vehicle would cost US$4 billion, but using a more commercial approach would cost about US$1.7 billion. It verified that SpaceX developed both the Falcon 1 and Falcon 9 vehicles for a total of US$390 million (NASA, 2011). United Launch Alliance (ULA), an incumbent launch services provider and SpaceX competitor, has acknowledged that developing a new engine has typically cost about US$1 billion and a new rocket development about US$2 billion (Ray, 2015).

The reduced costs directly impact the marketplace for launch services. SpaceX is the only launch provider that publicly lists the price of its launches. It quotes launch costs of US$62 million on its website; by comparison the cost of a ULA launch on an Atlas V is about US$164 million (Ray, 2015). For many years, the cost of launching a kilogram of mass to LEO hovered around US$14,000/kilogram, a benchmark in the industry. This cost had not changed much for the industry incumbents. Incremental improvements over time, particularly in the face of new competition, have lowered the cost per kilogram for LEO to between US$10,000 and $13,000. The Falcon 9 has reduced that cost to about US$4,000/kilogram. The Falcon Heavy is priced at a cost of US$2,200/kilogram to LEO (Stackexchange, n.d.), and is projected to achieve a cost of US$1,000/kilogram if all first stages are recovered and reused. SpaceX launch prices are so low that even heavily state-subsidized rockets like China's Long March family cannot compete with them on price (Vance, 2015). Its low costs allow SpaceX to enjoy comfortable profit margins on each launch.

Its other activities illustrate the kinds of efficiencies that SpaceX is able to achieve in its operations. For example, the launch operations team for the Falcon 9 comprises eight people in the Launch Control Center. By comparison, the Space Shuttle launch control team comprised approximately 200 people (NASA, 1995). Similar differences in efficiency of operations are observed in a wide range of other activities.

SpaceX's operational record is not perfect. It has experienced a few failures during testing, system development, and operations. The initial Falcon 1 experienced three anomalies, "rocket scientist" speak for vehicles that are lost during a launch, sometimes spectacularly. The Falcon flight 19 failed in June 2015 because an externally purchased structural strut that was supposed to be tested and certified by the vendor was not and failed in flight. A Falcon vehicle and its payload were lost during a fueling exercise on the launch pad in September 2016, with the cause of that accident under investigation at the time of this writing. Several tests of propulsive landing of the Falcon 9 reusable first stage failed during the initial testing. The Falcon flight 20 landing was successful, and a string of successes followed both on land and at sea on the autonomous spaceport drone ship. Landing a rocket booster intact after flying a typical orbital mission profile was unprecedented. Since the alternative to attempting to land and recover them was to let them fall into the ocean, these attempts are best thought of as low-cost add-on experiments to develop new technologies and operations models that would otherwise be too expensive to pursue independently.

This approach to using operational systems as test beds to learn, improve the product, and develop new technologies is intrinsic to the SpaceX development process. Most impressive is that with a complex and unforgiving technology, SpaceX has managed to build an organization that is capable of rapid learning. In addition to developing new products rapidly, it has demonstrated that it can identify faults and corrective actions rapidly. The return to normal flight operations occurred only six months after the Falcon flight 19 loss, with Falcon flight 20 also marking the first successful intact landing of a Falcon 9 first stage. Return to flight after accidents involving other launch systems typically has taken longer—often two years or more.

How has SpaceX been able to accomplish this? A number of factors have played a role:

- **Focus on simplicity in the design.** SpaceX's approach to rocket design revolves around the core belief that simplicity is the precursor to both reliability and low cost. From the very beginning SpaceX has designed its Falcon rockets with commonality in mind. Both of the Falcon 9 stages are powered by rocket-grade kerosene and liquid oxygen, which allows the use of a common engine. Both stages are the same diameter and are constructed from the same material, reducing the tooling and processes to significantly reduce costs in manufacturing. The Falcon 9 was designed from the beginning to be human rated, which increased the focus on producing a reliable system. Using nine smaller, common engines for the first stage rather than fewer (or one) large engines enabled the use of a few common engine models. This improves reliability since the rocket can tolerate an engine failure in flight without catastrophic failure or aborting the mission. It also helps drive up manufacturing volume to reduce costs through learning effects. It allows continuous product improvement efforts to focus on one engine instead of across a number of different engines. This has resulted in reducing the number of parts and increasing its power and efficiency. The Merlin 1D production model for the Falcon 9 has the highest thrust-to-weight ratio of any rocket engine ever made, and is designed with a service life measured in tens of missions (Chaikin, 2012).

- **Colocation.** SpaceX has avoided the practice of spreading its development activities geographically and outsourcing a significant portion of its product to suppliers. The original motivation for Musk to start the company was that by controlling much of the process from raw materials to flight hardware, he could dramatically reduce the cost of launch compared with existing providers. This is accomplished by tight colocation of most activities (engineering offices, test infrastructure, mission control, a complete factory for all products, logistics, management, and administration) in a single, one-million-square-foot building in Hawthorne, California (see Figure 1-1), where most of the approximately 4,000 people work. The floor layout in the facility is quite open. Everyone works in open cubicles, from the most junior intern to the CEO (the exception being job functions that require privacy, such as human resources). Only propulsion and large-scale structural testing is done at test facilities at McGregor, Texas. SpaceX uses or is planning to develop four launch sites in the southern United States. All of the sites are linked to Hawthorne by modern internet tools so that engineers at Hawthorne have a virtual presence at these remote sites. This colocation has vastly simplified communication and coordination, and enabled SpaceX to produce the results that it has.

- **Vertical integration.** SpaceX quickly learned in its early development efforts that suppliers in the launch sector were accustomed to the practices of their existing customers, particularly the long lead times and tolerance for high prices. It found

Figure 1-1: The SpaceX facility in Hawthorne, California, USA brings together people and nearly all processes from design through launch into one location.
SpaceX

that it could often build what it needed in-house much more rapidly and for lower cost than by procuring it from outside vendors. It had the added benefit of keeping the expertise in-house, which enabled rapid responses to changes and continuous improvement. The company buys raw materials and develops, builds, assembles, and tests in-house all engines, rockets, and spacecraft, and a variety of support systems such as ground support equipment and remote tracking stations. Most of the components for these systems are manufactured in-house too, including parts normally procured from specialty subcontractors such as tank domes, stage tanks, flight computers, engine controllers, batteries, engines and thrusters, turbopumps, valves, star trackers, Lidars, radios, composite overwrap pressure vessels, and numerous other smaller items. Vertical integration enables efficient and frequent system development, testing, and integration activities.

■ **Mission assurance embedded in routine operations.** SpaceX relies on extensive system optimization and testing in all phases of development, production, and just-before-the-flight in the "what you fly" condition. Since testing is a pillar of SpaceX mission assurance, the company created a unique, highly modern, and advanced design-testing-manufacturing-integration-IT infrastructure for rapid, repeatable, advanced, and inexpensive testing over the entire life cycle: from prototype to design, qualification, integration, preflight, and flight testing. The focus is on assuring quality and performance with powerful and efficient system-level optimization and portfolio optimization. The optimization is performed by trading off major system-level parameters such as mass, orbit, and flight characteristics. In order to permit testing of all components, subsystems, and the system, all parts must be reusable, including a restartable engine and stage separation devices. The company designates individuals responsible for the different aspects of development and integration during the system and mission life cycle. The highly coveted position of a "responsible engineer" comes with complete "horizontal" responsibility for the timely development, testing, acceptance, production, integration, and performance of an assigned component throughout its life cycle, including all coordination with any and all applicable individuals and departments. Vertical integrators assure the integration of elements into subsystem and the overall system. Vice presidents assure development and performance of major subsystems (propulsion, structures, avionics, etc.). Payload managers assure payload-vehicle integration. Mission managers assure the mission life cycle. These individuals coordinate with all relevant stakeholders efficiently, fully documenting their decisions and agreements using specialized software. All together, these individuals constitute a well-designed matrix of mission-assurance activities.

- **Culture.** Arguably the most important pillar of SpaceX is the culture that promotes very high levels of teamwork, mutual support, coordination, and communication in the spirit of pushing the boundaries. Employees are encouraged to continuously seek better solutions. Senior employees are selected on the basis of experience and accomplishments. Junior employees are selected on the basis of competence, but also unusual interests, passion, and a "spark in the eye." Information technology is regarded as a critically important activity supporting efficient execution of all other activities and extraordinarily efficient communication, coordination, and approval tools.

To be sure, SpaceX is not the only innovative company working in this area making the vision of expanded human presence in space a reality. There are a number of startups that are making inspiring progress in a number of different areas. SpaceX does, however, provide a good example of what can be accomplished using the right approach. In the end, a significant part of this success comes down to a new way of working together that SpaceX has pioneered, at least in this sector. It combines management practices, engineering practices, product strategy, organizational processes and tools, and a leadership climate that encourages responsibility, innovation, learning, and high performance. Perhaps this is a fitting return to the practices seen in the early days of the space industry. This example illustrates more than just the reinvigoration of a single sector. It demonstrates that organizations can bring together diverse skill sets to overcome challenging problems, and ultimately make miracles seem commonplace. This book argues that these behaviors are not just confined to SpaceX, but can be achieved in a wider array of settings where management and technical disciplines learn to work together seamlessly in order to create the benefits needed by their customers and other stakeholders.

1.3 Strategy Realization Requires Good Management

Program managers and chief systems engineers lead efforts like those within SpaceX to implement a strategy to realize its associated benefits, both tangible (e.g., financial, market share) and intangible (e.g., new knowledge). They lead teams of individuals who take strategy—a vision or idea of what can be—and translate that strategy into products, services, or capabilities that are real and beneficial for customers, employers, and other stakeholders through collaboration, skill, and disciplined approaches. The *Guide to Lean Enablers for Managing Engineering Programs* (Oehmen, 2012) made a strong case for why engineering programs are vital to society and to organizational strategy:

> Taking on large-scale engineering programs is one of the most difficult, risky, and—when done well—rewarding undertaking[s] a government or company can attempt. It not only pushes the envelope of what is possible, but defines a new envelope. It generates capabilities, technologies, products, and systems that are innovative and unique, and generates tremendous societal benefits— from hybrid cars to a trip to the moon, from road networks to GPS navigation, and from carbon-neutral electricity sources to the "smart" city (p. 3).

One might argue that this is just about developing the right strategy. But the Economist Intelligence Unit (EIU, 2013) report, *Why Good Strategies Fail: Lessons for the C-Suite*, pointed to the need for linkages between strategy development and strategy implementation. Strategy implementation represented the collective organizational effort to execute strategy by investing in the right initiatives to deliver desired business benefits. The study found that organizational leaders recognize that there is a critical gap between what they want to accomplish and the ability of their organizations to successfully deliver.

Organizations depend on the professional capabilities of program managers and chief systems engineers to deliver strategy and amazing results. Recent examples include:

- The Big Dig that unsnarled traffic between Boston, Cambridge, and other cities in Massachusetts and created opportunities for new economic development.
- The 2012 London Olympics sponsored by the United Kingdom government that constructed new competitive venues with the deliberate intention of repurposing the infrastructure for ongoing commercial activities after the Olympics.
- The Airbus A380 and the Boeing 787 Dreamliner, planes with longer range and higher fuel efficiencies.

There have been many other successes that have not captured headlines or garnered broad attention for the unsung individuals who led, facilitated, and contributed to results that delivered benefits to their customers and their employers.

The engineering programs that fail, and even many of the successes, experience performance challenges. The Big Dig cost over US$14 billion and will not be fully paid for until about 2038 at a full price tag of about US$24 billion, which is US$22.6 billion more than it was projected to cost (Hofherr, 2015). When the London Olympics Authority experienced cost overruns related to some of the Olympic venues, the Authority had to obtain money from the U.K. government, not all of which has been recovered (Kortekaas, 2012). Boeing and Airbus have had to do substantial rework on different components of their planes at significant cost to those organizations and to their customers (Botelho, 2015; Flottau, 2015; Hamlin, 2015). So although some programs ultimately deliver something vital, the delivery path is often painful.

PMI's *2016 Pulse of the Profession®* study (PMI, 2016) found that for every US$1 billion invested in strategic initiatives, organizations waste US$122 million due to poor performance. Many of those strategic initiatives also fail to meet their original goals and business intent; fail to deliver within allocated budget parameters; or are delivered late. Other data points seem to bear this out. In 2009, the U.S. Department of Defense's 96 largest engineering programs generated a cumulative cost overrun of nearly US$300 billion and an average schedule overrun of more than two years (GAO, 2009). The United Kingdom's National Audit Office (2014) estimated that in 2014 at least £112 billion of major investments was at risk due to program performance issues.

In all fairness, many of today's engineering programs represent leading-edge breakthroughs. The innovativeness, technical risk, and complexity of these endeavors cannot be overstated. Airbus and Boeing translated the dream of long-range and highly fuel-efficient aircraft into reality. Boston's Big Dig ultimately reduced travel times and created new economic opportunities for areas of the city while sustaining the day-to-day commuter flow of thousands of people and vehicles. That is why INCOSE's (2014) *A World in Motion: Systems Engineering Vision 2025* specifically calls out complexity as a growing factor that will continue to confront systems engineering professionals and require a new skill set to manage. But the perceived financial, social, and political pain among stakeholders in achieving those breakthroughs is most often what receives attention, inside and outside of organizations.

Despite the perceptions and realities related to program performance, one of the underlying challenges is building the will within organizations to invest in improving engineering program capabilities. Many executive leaders often do not view programs within their companies as being strategic, and activities that are not strategic often do not receive executive-level attention.

Enhancing engineering program capabilities must start with a better understanding of the linkages between engineering programs and strategy among executives. Highlighting the linkage between engineering programs and strategy also needs to make the case that investing in strengthening such capabilities could help to reduce the millions of dollars at risk from poor performance. Achieving these objectives necessitates an organizational culture that links talent management with strategy along with ongoing investments to improve workforce capabilities and enabling systems, structures, and process.

1.4 Workforce + Organizational Capabilities = Competitive Advantage

The increasing requirement for deeper knowledge by organizations emphasizes and rewards specialization. With increased specialization comes the potential to create barriers to sharing and collaboration as objectives, tools, and even syntax become more unique to each field. Rooted in the same historical and professional context of the Cold War, the arms race, and the race to the moon, the program management and systems engineering disciplines have advanced along similar paths. Both show the hallmarks of traditional professions:

- Each has a unique body of knowledge that is codified, but continues to evolve to reflect good practice.
- There are professional certifications that demonstrate whether individuals can apply their knowledge and experience to effectively utilize tools, techniques, and practices to address challenges they are presented.
- Professionals from both disciplines have a broad range of professional development options to keep them abreast of evolving practice, build their skills, and help them to educate others.
- Academic, industry, and government research helps to inform and evolve practice, competence, and capabilities.
- Each has a community of like-minded professionals with whom to network and exchange information.

Despite having the same roots and following similar paths to professionalism, the two disciplines have experienced somewhat divergent evolutions. Program management has become much more defined within some organizations than systems engineering, particularly in the government sector. Program manager roles, responsibilities, and authority have become formalized and documented, and clear career paths for the role have sprouted. Program management processes and procedures have evolved, some by statutory requirement, some unique to the types of programs being managed, and others through the evolution of the practice. Most engineering programs have an assigned program manager from the very start, but a chief systems engineer may not be assigned before elements of the program requirements are defined. Today, elements of this divergent evolution appear to be impacting the ability of the two disciplines to effectively align their work practices and collaborate. This is a critical area where organizations need effective workplace cultures that guide the way people and groups work with each other.

In addition to potentially competitive issues between the two disciplines, organizational systems, or the lack thereof, also inhibit effective engineering program management and performance. Often, the lack of aligned practices is blamed when program disruptions occur. For example, the Professional Services Council (2013) report, *From Crisis to Opportunity: Creating a New Era of Government Efficiency, Innovation and Performance* noted:

> ...the services acquisition process is often driven by a loose amalgamation of regulations (Federal Acquisition Regulation and agency/component supplements) and a growing body of legislative and executive branch policy pronouncements that are at times ineffective and/or in conflict with one another. They often fail to align what is being acquired to a real strategy and are exceptionally difficult to implement consistently, even within a single government entity.

Effective practices are critical for integrating efforts to deliver results in program environments. Engineering program environments require good planning approaches, proactive risk management, stakeholder engagement, and other, similar capabilities. The Professional Services Council (2013) report captured the challenge very effectively:

> In an era when "collaboration" is increasingly recognized as a central operational component in the best of private sector organizations, and a critical element of their success, it is in worrisome decline within the government itself and such decline has frequently been cited in Government Accountability Office (GAO) studies as a contributing factor in underperforming government programs, duplication and fragmentation. Disconnects between the policy, human capital, mission, technology and acquisition communities have improved only marginally at the leadership levels and almost imperceptibly, if at all, at the operational levels. This stovepipe approach leads different components within an agency to pursue different immediate goals, often to the detriment of the desired overarching mission outcome.

Interestingly, while the report indicated that there is stronger collaboration in the private sector, the new research for this book on integration and collaboration found similar challenges in both sectors (Conforto, Rossi, Rebentisch, Oehmen, & Pacenza, 2013).

Every day, organizational leaders, systems engineers, and program managers are tackling these tough challenges. This book intends to capture some of the valuable lessons from their experiences in hopes of supporting their efforts to find approaches that yield better results.

1.5 Rays of Hope

All is not doom and gloom for two reasons. First, this book highlights successful engineering programs along with key integration elements that played a role in that success. For example, the Prairie Waters program discussed in Section 3.2 adopted a highly integrated teaming approach that aligned various program participants from various governmental bodies, contractors, and subcontractors. This book will share some of the innovative ways that Boston's Big Dig program enabled stronger collaboration from which new best practices emerged. Second, learning from failure is absolutely critical to advancing engineering program performance. This book features examples from the National Aeronautics and Space Administration (NASA) and explores how NASA transitioned into a more collaborative and integrated organization.

1.6 Trekking toward a New Mindset

This book blazes a new path by focusing on approaches for better enabling collaborative work between program managers and systems engineers. While there is plenty of published material focused on enhancing the performance of each individual discipline, very little published matter spotlights how the two disciplines align their efforts and work collaboratively. This book intends to help close that gap by:

- Uncovering how engaged people working within living systems called "engineering programs" align their efforts to deliver results. This book identifies potential insights from the experiences of interdisciplinary teams that may be useful to program managers and systems engineers facing similar challenges. The case examples are not limited to program management and systems engineering, but all contain applicable insights that are discussed in the context of how those insights relate to engineering program management.

■ Shining a light on enabling factors that support engineering programs. This book presents new research and a framework for integration to help program managers, systems engineers, and their executive leaders enhance joint effort, joined thinking, and common language. This examination yields insight into factors that either enable collaboration or create barriers to integrated approaches. While some of the case study examples in this book may be well known from an engineering or program management perspective, this book will objectively assess those case studies through the lens of interdisciplinarity to offer new insights. Prescribing specific practices for integrated systems engineering and program management is neither the intent nor focus of this book.

■ Sparking further research to advance understanding of dynamics of interdisciplinary collaboration. Given the scant content—scientific studies, case studies, articles, etc.—exploring interdisciplinary challenges among teams collaborating on large-scale programs, this work attempts to fill that gap and to encourage further research and content in this important area.

This book is an amalgam of a diverse array of preliminary evidence about why the integration of program management and systems engineering is important to the practice of both disciplines, and ultimately to beneficiaries of their programs. The hope is that by bringing this content together now, practitioners may derive some near-term benefit, and others may be inspired to continue the investigation and documentation of this important area.

Because clearly defined terminology is critical to understanding, it is important to note here how the terms "program" and "project" are used in the context of this book. Readers will find that there are a range of definitions for these terms and, in some instances, the terms are used interchangeably. A program is "a group of related projects, subprograms, and program activities that are managed in a coordinated way to obtain benefits not available from managing them individually" (PMI, 2015). A project, on the other hand, is "a temporary endeavor undertaken to create a unique product, service or result" (PMI, 2015). In the specific context of this book, references to "programs" should be understood to mean the program and its subordinate projects that produce outputs required for the program and the realization of targeted benefits.

This book also uses terminology to identify key roles in the program environment, and those roles are defined as follows:

■ *Program manager* refers to the job position that has the ultimate authority and accountability for the overall program.

■ *Chief systems engineer* is used specifically in reference to research undertaken for this book and refers to the job position that has ultimate technical authority and accountability for the product or system being developed by the program.

■ *Project manager* refers to the job position that has ultimate authority and accountability for project deliverables.

While program managers and chief systems engineers lead and integrate efforts at the program level, project managers and systems engineers drive delivery of project-level outputs for the program. Some case studies and examples in this book highlight project-level considerations that also have applicability or impact at the program level.

As part one of the book will show, integration and collaboration are critical in coordinating complex work, which ultimately advances organizational strategies or missions. It is important to understand the organizational dynamics and challenges that frame elements of interdisciplinary integration and collaboration that will be further elaborated upon in the remaining chapters of the book.

1.7 Summary

Engineering programs are challenging, but there are interventions that organizational leaders, program managers, and systems engineers can utilize to address those challenges. The key enablers include recognizing the linkages between programs and strategy, and supporting program leadership in enabling alignment and collaboration within the program team. Companies like SpaceX are pioneering methods for tackling tough engineering program challenges using these key enablers. This book provides additional insights and approaches that support realizing the benefits from such objectives.

1.8 Discussion Questions

1. On programs on which you have worked, were there any mechanisms that helped the team establish a sense of "collective consciousness?" Were those mechanisms formally structured in some way or informally developed by team members themselves? Did you observe any difference in the use of formal versus informal mechanisms to enable the team?

2. Identify a program that you felt had strong connections to strategy and one that did not. If applicable, identify any distinctions between those programs and the level of executive involvement. If applicable, how would you explain the differences?

3. How does your organization's approach to talent management and development enable or hamper integration between program managers and systems engineers? What enhancements or changes do you think would better support integration?

1.9 References

Botelho, G. (2015, May 5). *FAA finds Boeing Dreamliner could lose all power, issues maintenance mandate*. Retrieved from www.cnn.com/2015/05/02/us/boeing-787 -dreamliner-faa-directive/

Chaikin, A. (2012). Is SpaceX changing the rocket equation? *Smithsonian* January 2012. Retrieved from www.airspacemag.com/space/is-spacex-changing-the-rocket -equation-132285884/

Conforto, E. C., Rossi, M., Rebentisch, E., Oehmen, J., & Pacenza, M. (2013). *Survey report: Improving integration of program management and systems engineering.* Presented at the 23rd INCOSE Annual International Symposium, Philadelphia. Retrieved from www.pmi.org/~/media/PDF/Business-Solutions/Lean-Enablers/PMI-INCOSE-MIT -Integration-Study.ashx

Economist Intelligence Unit (EIU). (2013). *Why good strategies fail: Lessons for the c-suite.* Retrieved from www.pmi.org/~/media/PDF/Publications/WhyGoodStrategiesFail _Report_EIU_PMI.ashx

Flottau, J. (2015, October 29). Report card: Airbus A380 after eight years in service. *Aviationweek.* Retrieved from http://aviationweek.com/airbus-a380/report-card-airbus -a380-after-eight-years-service

Government Accountability Office (GAO). (2009). *Defense acquisitions: Assessments of selected weapon programs.* Washington, D.C. Retrieved from www.gao.gov/new.items/ d09326sp.pdf

Hamlin, G. W. (2015, February 9). Viewpoint: An Airbus A380neo makes no sense. *Aviationweek.* Retrieved from http://aviationweek.com/advanced-machines-aerospace -manufacturing/viewpoint-airbus-a380neo-makes-no-sense

Hofherr, J. (2015, January 5). *Can we talk rationally about the Big Dig yet?* Retrieved from www.boston.com/cars/news-and-reviews/2015/01/05/can-talk-rationally-about -the-big-dig-yet/0BPodDnlbNtsTEPFFc4i1O/story.html

International Council on Systems Engineering (INCOSE). (2014). *A world in motion: Systems engineering vision 2025.* Retrieved from www.incose.org/AboutSE/sevision

Kortekaas, V. (2012, August 19). Project management: Lessons can be learned from successful delivery. *Financial Times.* Retrieved from www.ft.com/cms/s/0/57d92e9c -d7df-11e1-9980-00144feabdc0.html#axzz4C8vX47N9

National Aeronautics and Space Administration (NASA). (1995). *The space shuttle launch team.* Retrieved from http://science.ksc.nasa.gov/shuttle/countdown/launch-team .html

National Aeronautics and Space Administration (NASA). (2011). *Commercial market assessment for crew and cargo systems.* Retrieved from www.nasa.gov/sites/default/files/ files/Section403(b)CommercialMarketAssessmentReportFinal.pdf

Oehmen, J. (Ed.). (2012). *The guide to lean enablers for managing engineering programs, version 1.0.* Cambridge, MA: Joint MIT-PMI-INCOSE Community of Practice on Lean in Program Management. URI: http://hdl.handle.net/1721.1/70495

Professional Services Council. (2013). *From crisis to opportunity: Creating a new era of government efficiency, innovation and performance.* Retrieved from https://issuu.com/ professionalservicescouncil/docs/2013_psc_commission_report

Project Management Institute (PMI). (2015). *The PMI lexicon of project management terms* (version 3.0). Newtown Square, PA: Author.

Project Management Institute (PMI). (2016). *Pulse of the Profession®: The high cost of low performance: How will you improve business results?* Retrieved from www.pmi.org/ learning/pulse.aspx

Ray, J. (2015, April 13). ULA unveils its future with the Vulcan rocketfamily. *Space-flightnow*. Retrieved from http://spaceflightnow.com/2015/04/13/ula-unveils-its-future-with-the-vulcan-rocketfamily/

Stackexchange. (n.d.). Retrieved from http://space.stackexchange.com/questions/1989/what-is-the-current-cost-per-pound-to-send-something-into-leo

Vance, A. (2015, May 14). Elon Musk's space dream almost killed Tesla. *Bloomberg Business*. Retrieved from www.bloomberg.com/graphics/2015-elon-musk-spacex/

Endnote

1. Contributed by Bohdan Oppenheim, Professor of Systems Engineering, Loyola Marymount University.

2

THE ENGINEERING PROGRAM PERFORMANCE CHALLENGE

2.1 Introduction

Exploring lessons learned from past activities forms the foundation for making improvements in future activities. Understanding the reasons why some approaches may work better than others under certain conditions and then further enhancing solid processes or techniques leads to continuous improvement and better performance.

This chapter explores engineering program examples to highlight challenges that often affect complex programs. Not all of the examples used formal program management and systems engineering approaches, and where relevant, that fact is highlighted. However, central to each example and its applicable lessons is the view that an integrated approach including program management and systems engineering may well have produced different outcomes.

There are no "silver bullets" or perfect solutions that work in every circumstance. The individuals working on complex programs must be adaptive and responsive to the unique characteristics of their programs and the challenges encountered throughout the program's life cycle.

2.2 Making White Elephants Extinct

Merriam-Webster (n.d.) defines a "white elephant" as "something that requires a lot of care and money and that gives little profit or enjoyment." Its usage within complex programs can refer to aircraft and weapons systems that have outlived their usefulness but continue to be maintained; stranded infrastructure that no longer serves any useful purpose; and technology that has become obsolete and is no longer supported by its developer. White elephants exist in almost every industry sector and geographical location around the world.

At the start of the 2016 Olympic Games in Rio de Janeiro, Brazil, the world's eyes were fixed not only on the actual sporting events, but also on how Brazil, the host country, would perform. Brazil is the first country in South America to host a modern Olympic Games. Expectations are always high for such a global spectacle, but the stakes were higher for the first country in the region hosting the Games. Leading into the Games Brazil's economy had shrunk by 27% in the previous year and national politics were unsettled by scandals. That was in stark contrast to the economic strength and national confidence that Brazil displayed during its bid to host the games some nine years earlier. Among the promised benefits of hosting the Olympic Games were the improved infrastructure, roads, public transportation, and so forth that remain after the Games conclude. Also of interest was the hope to leverage the investment in the facilities to promote economic growth. As a result of the deterioration of the Brazilian economic and political situation, funding was scarce for many of the infrastructure improvement projects, potentially undermining the delivery of the long-term benefits from hosting the Games. Would Brazil be left burdened with stranded assets or "white elephants" as has often been the case with similar events?

Facilities that directly supported or were critical to the delivery of the Games were finished by the start of the Games, but in some cases only just barely. Olympic teams arrived to housing with significant plumbing, electrical, and other problems (Phillips, 2016a). Officials scrambled, but finished work on an extended subway line to transport participants to key venues, conducting limited operational and safety tests using sandbags instead of human passengers (Phillips, 2016b). Other promised infrastructure improvements failed to materialize as funding and time ran out. For instance, promised sewage treatment for the highly toxic Guanabara Bay where many of the water events were to occur was not delivered at all (Connors, 2016).

Despite the concerns and gloomy predictions beforehand, the delivery of the Games themselves was generally considered to be successful, with only a few minor operational issues that would naturally be expected in any complex undertaking. Nevertheless, the fear remained that after the Games, Brazil's investment in the associated facilities and infrastructure would produce "white elephants" (Pearson, 2016). It can take many years to assess the impact of Olympic Games on the host country, so it is still too early to comment about the long-term benefits of the Rio de Janeiro Olympic Games when considered as a complex program. The hope is that lessons were learned and applied from the 2014 World Cup experience.

The 2014 World Cup games in Brazil provide cautionary evidence of how early hopes of a productive legacy from major sporting events can fail to produce the promised benefits. An investigation a year after the World Cup games found that R$11 billion (US$3.5 billion) worth of the 35 projects budgeted in 2010 were not complete or had been abandoned (Rapoza, 2015). Manaus is home to a US$600 million stadium that was used for four World Cup games and is now rented out for private parties and similar events. Brasilia's US$900 million stadium seats 72,000, but the home Brasilia club barely draws 5,000 people to its games. The city is using the facility to park some 400 buses in the vast, unused parking lot (Stromberg, 2015). Several of the big projects, such as light-rail systems in São Paulo, Cuiabá, and Fortaleza, still are not close to being finished. Only 21.4% of the promised public transportation infrastructure was complete a year after the games (Rapoza, 2015).

By way of comparison, the London 2012 Olympic Games is considered among the more successful of these events at creating a legacy of sustained benefits to its host country. Judging whether the promised benefits were delivered can be challenging, especially since only four years have elapsed. By the most basic measure, whether residents are using the facilities or have abandoned them, London seems to have succeeded. The venues, including the massive Olympic stadium, are being updated, repurposed, and used more or less as intended. Local residents are moving into repurposed and new housing. Four million square feet of new commercial and office space is approved for construction and is expected to bring many new professional jobs to a formerly neglected and underdeveloped area. Some of these developments were underway prior to the Games, but the preparations for the London 2012 Games helped to significantly enable, accelerate, or expand the overall development of the area (Hill, 2015; White, 2015).

What explains this apparent success in an endeavor that has challenged so many others? The London 2012 Olympic Committee adopted a management approach that demonstrated application of core systems engineering and program management principles with an emphasis on integration and collaboration.

- **Clear Vision/Goals and Benefits:** There were two key goals that governed every aspect of planning, execution, and management: delivery and legacy (ensuring the new or enhanced infrastructure remained usable after the Games). The Olympic Games were successfully delivered and there are varying levels of the use of legacy infrastructure and of new investments in the region (Guskey, 2016).
- **Governance:** The Olympic Delivery Authority (ODA) integrated the various governmental bodies and agencies that needed to be involved into a "single governmental interface with planning authority" (Kortekaas, 2012). "From the outset, the ODA instituted processes and systems, meeting structure and delegations to ensure strategic direction, performance management and value for money" (Kintrea, 2012).
- **Management Approach:** Organizers maintained an integrated systems view over all aspects of the Games and leveraged program and project management to maintain alignment and integration. "At the programme level additional processes were required to manage the cross-project interfaces to ensure the consequential impacts were identified and programme priorities applied in resolution" (Kintrea, 2012).
- **Integrated Planning and Risk Management:** With a constant eye on critical path, integrated planning incorporated "dependency management (schedule logic/construction sequencing), design management (coherent and compatible solutions), physical integration (for example, two or more projects need the same place at the same time) and [scope] change management (consequential impact of scope or schedule changes particularly across project/organizational boundaries" (Kintrea, 2012).
- **Customer and Stakeholder Management:** The ODA maintained proactive customer and stakeholder engagement and communications at both the project and program levels (Kintrea, 2012).

■ **Scope and Requirements Control:** Organizers realized that over the five-year development, delivery, and management life cycle for the program, various changes within and outside of the program would impact its scope. They established a change control system to manage "requirements creep," risk, and necessary trade-offs to achieve program-level objectives. The program also incorporated verification and testing processes into the program schedule with sufficient time to address any defects well in advance of the Opening Ceremonies (Kintrea, 2012).

Viewing the management challenge through a systems-oriented lens, Olympic Games are complex programs. They are very comparable in scale, required interfaces, and complexity to complex programs like those in the aerospace, medical device, and automotive industries. Of course, Olympic venues and associated infrastructure can be fairly specialized and are not always able to be used as extensively as was anticipated in the original bids to host the Games. However, the London Olympics example showed how applying program management and systems engineering approaches to complex systems can support strong performance. That performance can be much more effective when interdisciplinary alignment and collaboration also exist, as the London Olympics example also demonstrated.

2.3 Large Engineering Programs Are Complex

The Guide to Lean Enablers for Managing Engineering Programs (Oehmen, 2012a) noted that in an organization whose workforce has developed among the most mature engineering program management capabilities—the United States Department of Defense—the underperformance of its engineering programs was astounding. The accumulated cost overrun of the largest 96 engineering programs had reached nearly US$300 billion when assessed in 2009. Engineering-related costs represented almost half of the expense increases associated with those programs (see Figure 2-1).

Most of those programs were at least two years late in their delivery. Recognizing that such underperformance is not sustainable, the *Guide* identified approaches to help counter the challenges that affect performance.

For the purposes of this work, it is important to define some key terms that will be used throughout the book to describe properties associated with some projects and programs. The term "complicated" generally means that "the interactions between the many parts are governed by fixed relationships. This allows reasonably reliable pre-diction" (INCOSE, 2015). On the other hand, the term "complex" generally means that "interactions between the parts exhibit self-organization, where local interactions give rise to novel, nonlocal, emergent patterns" (INCOSE, 2015). The key distinction is between elements that demonstrate predictable behaviors and those in which expected or unexpected behaviors may emerge. In project and program environments, com-plexity is a characteristic that is difficult to manage due to human behavior, system behavior, and ambiguity (PMI, 2014). The Cynefin Framework (Snowden & Boone, 2007), developed by David Snowden and depicted in Figure 2-2, provides a graphical representation of these and related contexts. Being able to characterize the different

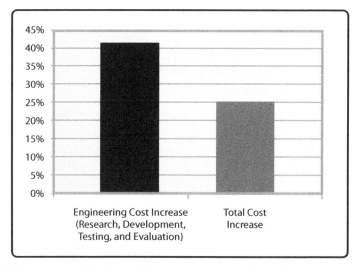

Figure 2-1: Cost increase of the largest 96 acquisition programs of the U.S. Department of Defense
Oehmen, 2012a. *The Guide to Lean Enablers for Managing Engineering Programs, Version 1.0.* Massachusetts Institute of Technology, 2012. Copyright and all rights reserved. Material from this publication has been reproduced with the permission of MIT.

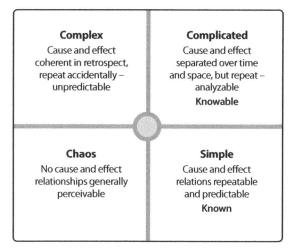

Figure 2-2: Cynefin framework illustrating the dimensions of program characteristics
Adapted from De La Rue, 2008.

regions of complexity with their associated characteristics and challenges can enable program managers and chief systems engineers to tailor their approach to better suit a given set of circumstances and to increase the likelihood of program success (Kemp, Beasley, & Williams, 2015).

Following are three specific examples that illustrate the complex array of issues that make complex programs challenging. The examples pull out scenarios from complex, multiyear programs to identify how specific challenges evolved over time and impacted the program. They are simple vignettes that are not intended to reflect the full program, fully analyze "root causes," or detail all of the factors that challenged performance.

2.3.1 A White Elephant: Denver International Airport Baggage Handling

The experience of the Denver International Airport automated baggage handling system provides insight into challenges of integrated planning, stakeholder management, requirements management, and technical scalability. Growth in and around the Denver metropolitan area coupled with the need to accommodate newer airplanes signaled that the region's Stapleton International Airport was obsolete. Stapleton was also infamous for flight delays (de Neufville, 1994). Despite resistance from United and Continental, the largest airline carriers serving the area, city and state officials decided to proceed with the program, believing they would eventually convince the airlines to embrace the program (Kerzner, 2006). So from the start, program stakeholders had divergent expectations about the new airport (GAO, 1994).

The new airport was expected to handle close to 20 million passengers by 1995, two years after its scheduled opening. It was also planned to house more airline gates than Stapleton and incorporate newer technologies to make traveler services more efficient. The program's projected cost in 1989 was close to US$2 billion (Bryant, 1994). Having secured funding from the U.S. federal government and municipal governments, the program to build Denver International Airport (DIA) began in December 1989 (Bearup, 2015).

Program planning began with the assumption that each individual airline would be responsible for baggage handling between the concourses and airplanes. An early feasibility study for implementing an integrated baggage handling system indicated such a system would be too complex and costly (Calleam Consulting, 2008). At Stapleton, airlines managed their own baggage handling using carts and trolleys, so designs for DIA did not incorporate any considerations for centralized baggage handling capabilities (Calleam Consulting, 2008). Since the airlines were not committed to the program, they were not involved in the airport's initial design. That fact, coupled with the lack of a strong change control process for documenting, evaluating, considering alternatives, or prioritizing requirements changes would soon create major issues for the program (Calleam Consulting, 2008; INCOSE, 2016).

Two years into the program, United and Continental signed on, and United decided to implement an automated baggage handling system that would speed up airplane turnaround times in its main concourse. The company hired BAE Systems to design and implement a solution. A few months later, DIA officials contracted with BAE to design the baggage handling system for airport-wide implementation. DIA would then lease the centralized system to the airlines for a fee (Kerzner, 2006).

Other airports around the world had been using some elements of the baggage handling system Denver authorities planned to deploy, which made the design change appear to be easy. However, no other airport had a system on the same scale as that planned for DIA (de Neufville, 1994; Langnau, 2000). The baggage system had to be designed around the fixed building construction plans, which included several sharp, angled turns (de Neufville, 1994). The baggage handling system design was very complicated. The system would incorporate six miles of conveyors that would carry luggage to and from over 4,000 radio-controlled luggage carts traveling over close to 17 miles of track between airline terminals and planes with very limited human intervention. The system was intended to deliver bags at a rate of 60 bags per minute, allowing loading and unloading of planes within 20–30 minutes (de Neufville, 1994; Swartz, 1996).

The baggage handling project struggled from the start. The compressed timeline for planning, development, testing, and deployment placed significant pressure on BAE Systems to deliver results. Based on postdelivery reports of the project, there seemed to be little risk management planning applied and mitigation utilized (INCOSE, 2016). So the project team was forced to react to situations as they occurred. Some of the situations included:

- DIA authorities committed to an automated rail-mounted cart system even though the existing baggage handling tunnels were not designed to accommodate such a system. This change occurred more than a year into the development and construction of the luggage system (de Neufville, 1994).
- Engineers failed to consider important design elements for the airport's system. First, luggage queues vary based on the number of passengers, number of flights arriving and departing at a particular time, and other related factors. As luggage traffic increased, some conveyors did not have any empty carts into which bags could be loaded. This issue was not identified within the project until late 1993 (de Neufville, 1994). Second, system design did not adequately consider the interactions between luggage weight, the cart's tilting design, speed, and sensors that controlled bag loading. Therefore, when sensors allowed too much luggage to be loaded into carts, the tilting carts tossed bags as they sped down the tracks. And sensors did not stop the carts if there were bags on the tracks (de Neufville, 1994; Swartz, 1996).
- As test after test showed that the fully automated system would not function properly, the project team reported that there was no back-up plan for baggage handling. As one assessment pointed out, "Remarkably, the design of the fully automated baggage system at Denver [DIA] did not include a meaningful back-up system. The planners provided neither a fleet of tugs and carts that could cope with the level of baggage expected, nor even access roads between the check-in facilities and the aircraft" (de Neufville, 1994, p. 4). So in cases of power failures, software glitches, or other issues affecting baggage handling the airport risked having to shut down because it had no alternative baggage handling capability.

The baggage handling system resulted in program delays and delayed the ultimate objective—the airport's opening and its attendant benefits. The delays cost the airport authority about US$33 million per month, and cost the airlines about US$50 million. An alternative baggage handling system using tugs and carts was implemented so the airport could finally open for business—two years behind schedule. The change to a manual system cost an additional US$75 million to implement (de Neufville, 1994) on top of what was being spent to continue work on the automated system. After several years of struggling to get the automated system to work effectively, the system was eventually decommissioned in 2005 (Bearup, 2015; Calleam Consulting, 2008).

This case highlights several issues that affect engineering program performance:

- **Lack of planning for an integrated airport system.** The program plan did not incorporate an integrated systems view of the airport from the beginning.
- **Ineffective governance and stakeholder management.** City officials committed the program to several major changes, including the baggage handling system, without consideration to impacts on scope, cost, schedule, technical risk, feasibility, or alternatives (INCOSE, 2016). This gap opened the door to an uncontrolled stream of changes to convince critical stakeholders—the airlines that would operate out of the new airport—to support the program in progress.
- **Failure to apply systems engineering.** The late decision to implement an integrated baggage handling system would have benefited from application of systems engineering. Such application could have identified trade-offs early in the process that may have delivered a less complicated but working system. It likely would have identified needed redundancies and back-ups in case of failure in any of the primary systems.
- **Ineffective risk management.** Making the other challenges more intense is the fact that risk management was not integrated at any level—program or project. Despite the shortened planning time, the program and project leadership failed to mitigate the baggage handling project risks in any way.
- **Reactive management.** All of these challenges made the program and project teams highly reactive to situations that flared up. It is highly likely that this reactive approach affected collaboration among the program, project, and engineering leadership.

2.3.2 Learning While Failing: Future Combat Systems

Another example comes from the United States Army and its Future Combat Systems (FCS) program, which evolved over a 10-year period before its cancellation in 2009. The FCS exemplifies many of the challenges and opportunities associated with engineering programs. It yielded some new best practices as well as many important lessons learned.

To maintain twenty-first-century military superiority, U.S. Army leadership envisioned a response force that could deploy within days and provide rapid-strike capability. To achieve the level of efficiency and coordination required for such superior strike performance, the Army would need a highly sophisticated technological interface to support soldiers in the field. While the concept had been evolving with the U.S. Department of Defense (DoD) and military branches for years, the idea became a strategic goal in October 1999. The FCS program evolved from that strategy. Its objective was to develop and deliver digitally linked battlefield vehicles, sensors, and communications equipment and improve their interoperability (GlobalSecurity.org, n.d.).

Another key goal for FCS represented a significant breakthrough in the way the DoD approached developing major new technologies. Army officials realized the program would require a massive workforce with diverse management, technical, analytical, contracting, and other capabilities. But it also needed that workforce to operate as "one team," which became the cornerstone for the program. Because of the significant technical interfaces, Army officials also understood that design and development required "system of systems (SoS)" integration (Pernin et al., 2012). So from the beginning, integration and collaboration were central program themes.

The Army initially partnered with the Defense Advanced Research Projects Agency (DARPA), an agency within the DoD responsible for research into breakthrough technologies for national security. However, neither organization possessed the workforce scalability or the full range of skills required for such a complex program. Officials decided to contract with a Lead Systems Integrator (LSI), a single contractor responsible for developing and integrating SoS capabilities within budget and schedule parameters (Pernin et al., 2012). LSIs had been used on smaller programs in the past, but there was no understanding of how its application would work within a large-scale, revolutionary program like FCS. Army officials selected the consortium of Boeing/SAIC as the LSI in March 2002. The contract identified key LSI objectives as shown in Table 2-1.

Also under the LSI agreement terms, the Army provided program management leadership while the LSI served as the integrating interface between program management and the various program teams (Pernin et al., 2012).

The FCS program management approach attempted to revolutionize established program practices while remaining aligned with the "one team" and SoS objectives. The program tested new acquisition approaches like the LSI that allowed for innovation, streamlined business management, and unique government/industry collaboration. It implemented collaborative tools like the Advanced Collaborative Environment (ACE), a one-stop-shop for important information and resources associated with the program that was accessible to all program team members. It attempted to adapt planning, management, and control tools like those for earned value management and risk assessment and mitigation for the unique program environment. Some of the innovations like ACE were deemed highly successful while others, including adapting program tools and piloted approaches that produced important insights, were considered less successful (Pernin et al., 2012).

Table 2-1: Lead Systems Integrator objectives stated in the U.S. Army's contract with the FCS program partners	
Collaboration	■ Maintain a collaborative environment throughout the program's life cycle ■ Have a "one team" operation that facilitated teamwork and partnership
Performance	■ Achieve program affordability ■ Leverage existing technology to minimize development cost and maintain schedule
System Requirements and Integration	■ Design and plan for the continuous integration and insertion of new technological capabilities over the lifespan of the FCS ■ Ensure consistent and continuous definition of requirements
Workforce Capabilities	■ Develop the government acquisition community's capabilities ■ Create opportunities for highly skilled talent within industry to participate in the program

Adapted from GAO, 2007

According to postcancellation assessments, the "one team" philosophy and integrated team culture change had mixed results. Senior-level officials felt strongly that the program culture had high levels of collaboration, teamwork, and open discussion. "Government officials working at the first and second tiers in the structure reported they had good working relationships and generally achieved consensus on key program decisions" (Pernin et al., 2012). At lower levels within the program, though, the feelings were not as positive. Team members reported being reluctant to or discouraged from escalating critical issues up the program leadership chain. There was tension between Army staff and staff working for the LSI—LSI staff were perceived as having greater authority than the Army staff. Army staff also felt unclear about their responsibility for oversight and critical decision making versus that of the LSI staff (Pernin et al. 2012; GAO, 2007).

FCS did have strong executive sponsorship. Those leaders impacted the program in various ways. Executive leadership within the Army and DoD championed the program, and their support was instrumental in its rapid start-up in 2000. Leadership set the tone for innovation and experimentation within the program. Executives, however, also created some challenges for the program. The initial program schedule set the first major milestone for concept testing and design out six years from the program's start. But top Army officials pushed for a more accelerated schedule. After receiving a positive assessment of technological readiness to achieve the accelerated schedule from the Army's Chief Engineer, leadership reduced the six-year milestone to two years (Pernin et al., 2012).

Shortly after the accelerated schedule was approved, the U.S. Government Accountability Office (GAO, 2007) identified major risks associated with the Army's ability to deliver based on the accelerated schedule.

> The FCS program's complexity and aggressive schedule is unprecedented for the Army. As we have reported, the program was not near ready for starting the system development and demonstration phase when it did, primarily because the majority of the needed technologies were immature. The Army not only went forward with FCS, it did so with a planned schedule less than that of a single new system.

A retrospective review of the program provided further insight into the reasoning behind the GAO's assessment:

> The FCS consists of [18] individual systems, including manned and robotic ground and air vehicles, software radios, and satellites, as well as an overarching network and operating system tying those components together. Developing such enormous "systems of systems" poses technical and management problems that are neither well defined nor well understood. The software alone—95 million lines of code for the FCS, at last count—poses a daunting challenge. Nobody has yet figured out a way to develop reliable, secure software for much smaller projects (Charette, 2008).

Initial FCS requirements started to evolve immediately after the program's start and before some of the key management and operational components were in place.

The rush to quickly advance requirements immediately placed three major constraints on the program:

- Initial requirements were designed for conventional warfare and did not anticipate nonconventional military conflicts.
- Initial requirements were not "properly evaluated for technical feasibility," which caused significant rework, schedule slippage, and increased cost throughout the program's life cycle.
- Requirements failed to balance competing objectives for small and light systems on one hand and survivability and lethality on the other (Pernin et al., 2012).

Program leadership had contracted for components before systems engineering and architecting (SE&A) work was completed on initial requirements. So companies received contracts for requirements and technical specifications for the SoS and its components before the program ensured the specifications could be harmonized (Pernin et al., 2012). "Ultimately, there was serious 'misalignment' between the concurrently developed SoS and product specifications, and no good mechanism for adjudicating the disconnects.... The government's shortfall in personnel with SE&A experience and expertise also contributed to the problem.... senior leaders—driven by schedule demands—chose to authorize just enough SE&A to launch the program" (pp. 149–150).

At various levels, program requirements and priorities shifted significantly in response to external pressures. The Al-Qaeda terrorist attacks on the World Trade Center and Pentagon on September 11, 2001 led to the United States and its allies fighting simultaneous wars in Iraq and Afghanistan. Instead of fighting the military of another country in conventional warfare, allied forces were fighting insurgents using nontraditional tactics. The course of the wars and real-time adaptations to a different type of warfare quickly added pressures to the FCS program. When the program hit its first major milestone in 2003, the total number of systems to be included in FCS dropped from 18 to 14 due to cost and prioritization considerations. But a year later, the number of systems was restored to 18 and the program was expected to "spin out" new capabilities, meaning "producing and fielding systems as their technologies matured" to provide allied forces with tactical advantages as quickly as possible. Spinning out capabilities required assigned program team members to shift their focus from SoS activities to support tasks related to deployment and support of fielded technologies. With a tight schedule and a complex system still under development, this change considerably interrupted SoS workflows (Pernin et al., 2012).

By 2007, Congress began to intervene in the FCS program. GAO audits and other reports indicated that the program's technology was still very immature and questioned whether continued investment was warranted. Congress responded with significant reductions in funding and hearings to determine the program's feasibility. Eventually, Congress mandated a "go/no go" review to determine the program's final fate (Pernin et al., 2012).

The funding impacts and obvious risks that the program might be cancelled pushed executive leaders to break the single program into eight "program elements" focused on delivering specific capabilities. This approach allowed for shifting funding and resources as priorities and requirements changed. And if the full program were cancelled, some of the program elements might be shifted to other active programs. This particular change greatly undermined the "one team" and SoS integration goals set at the program's start (Pernin et al., 2012).

By 2008, the FCS team completed the "go/no go" review of the program's feasibility. The following year, Army officials announced that the program was cancelled (Pernin et al., 2012). Some program elements remained active after the program's cancellation, but few of the developed technologies remain in use today (GlobalSecurity.org, n.d.). The total cost of the program, including cancellation costs, is estimated at about US$20 billion, with very little resulting warfighting capability to show from that expenditure (Freedberg, 2012). In addition to the lost investment from that program, FCS was a large enough part of the Army acquisition budget that it displaced or delayed other programs competing for funding in the acquisition portfolio. Finally, the component elements of FCS still represented capabilities that were needed and had to be addressed through new or restructured programs, resulting in years of delay in fielding those capabilities.

This case is complex because it goes against the grain of programs being classified as either significant failures or unqualified successes. It demonstrates that there is a lot of gray space in which programs may deliver benefits, products, practices, or learning that can be used and improved upon by other programs even though the program may not fully achieve its original goals. It also highlights the following important points:

- Systems engineering is critical from the beginning and throughout the deployment phases for programs requiring high levels of technical integration.
- Program leadership needs the ability to adapt and perhaps even revolutionize program management approaches, particularly when managing programs that are both novel and complex.
- Program teams should collaborate to develop or adapt tools to facilitate their work, collaboration, or reporting.
- Executive leadership can play important enabling roles that remove barriers, set expectations about program culture, and ask tough questions of program leadership that need answers. They can also make decisions that can derail the programs they sponsor or add to scope, cost, and schedule.
- Talent management is critical for organizations sponsoring technical programs, particularly for government agencies that are often reluctant to invest in staff training and development. For government programs, guidance may be needed for effective workforce scaling practices, particularly when programs grow from 250 people to more than 10,000 over the life of the program (Pernin et al., 2012).
- Although study after study has identified the vital importance of effective requirements engineering and management approaches, it remains a key vulnerability for programs and projects.

2.3.3 What Does Ethics Have to Do with Integration? Volkswagen's Emissions Scandal

Private industry is also not immune from program challenges as Volkswagen found with its attempt to circumvent emissions testing laws. Volkswagen's case reflects a system in which the failure of program leadership to stand firm against detrimental executive decisions have damaged the organization's brand and reputation globally.

Volkswagen reportedly had a culture that looked the other way to avoid telling superiors the truth. That may be because long-standing chief executive Ferdinand Piech created a culture of fear that did not tolerate failure (Smith & Parloff, 2016). According to a first-hand account, Piech related how he used fear and intimidation to get results:

> I called all the body engineers, stamping people, manufacturing and executives into my conference room. And I said, "I am tired of all these lousy body fits. You have six weeks to achieve world-class body fits. I have all your names. If we do not have good body fits in six weeks, I will replace all of you" (Lutz, 2015).

In the early 2000s, Volkswagen had ambitions to be the world's most profitable automotive company. To achieve that objective, the company had to increase its share of the U.S. market, which stood at only 2% at the time. The problem was that U.S. clean air standards targeted the type of pollution from oxides of nitrogen that diesel engines like those in Volkswagen vehicles produced. So until the company could find a way to reduce those emissions to acceptable levels, it could not crack the U.S. market (Smith & Parloff, 2016).

Then came "clean diesel." According to the Diesel Technology Forum (n.d.), "Today's ultra-low sulfur diesel fuel, advanced engines and effective emissions control combine to achieve near zero emissions that is smoke free." A Volkswagen engineering program team was charged with developing a vehicle that could run on clean diesel and meet U.S. emission standards. Despite the team's best efforts, they seemed unable to produce a satisfactory result. That increased the pressure since failure was not an option (Smith & Parloff, 2016).

As the team was working on the challenge, the U.S. standards became stricter in 2009. Based on investigations that are still ongoing at the time of this writing, it appears that the team decided to find a way around the problem since the team could not resolve the problem. Software engineers were tasked with developing a "defect device" that could sense emission testing conditions and "put the vehicle into a sort of safety mode in which the engine ran below normal power and performance" (Hotten, 2015), which would mask the actual emission output that would be produced under normal driving conditions. The software did the trick, and the engineering team reported success to Volkswagen executives.

Volkswagen spent millions rolling out its "clean diesel" fleet of automobiles. Steadily, the company's sales began to climb, and sales figures from the United States started to show ongoing improvement. The "clean diesel" cars won all kinds of awards and received positive news coverage. For six years, Volkswagen continued to produce and sell its high-performing cars around the world (Smith & Parloff, 2016). Then the truth came out.

News reports indicated that an internal whistleblower notified a senior company official of the use of the "defect device" as early as 2011. Then, engineers at the International Council on Clean Transportation (ICCT) were testing car emissions in Europe using both stationary and on-road testing. Their tests identified that Volkswagen vehicles did not perform the same during both tests. ICCT shared its results with the California Air Resources Board (CARB), and they decided to conduct similar tests in the United States. They partnered with West Virginia University's Center for Alternative Fuels, Engines and Emissions, which found similar results in its tests to those of ICCT. The information was shared with the U.S. Environmental Protection Agency (EPA) in 2014 (Raby, 2015).

When the EPA notified Volkswagen of the findings, Volkswagen initially claimed that it was a minor error that required fixing and issued a limited recall. But internally, damage control efforts had started (Smith & Parloff, 2016). After the recall, CARB continued exploring why the stationery and on-road tests were different and finally determined that the autos had some type of trigger device. EPA officials continued to believe that there was a larger issue. Finally, in July 2015, when the EPA and CARB refused to approve any of the company's 2016 models for sale, Volkswagen officials admitted that the company had installed the "defect device" in its cars since 2008 (Raby, 2015).

The Volkswagen emissions scandal cost the company its reputation, and the financial damage is still being tallied. The company likely faces upwards of US$20 billion in fines and penalties. There will likely be lawsuits from car owners, dealers, and shareholders seeking to recover various damages they have incurred (Barrett, 2015). Government officials in Germany, Italy, the United Kingdom, France, South Korea, and Canada have started investigations (Hotten, 2015).

Volkswagen executives and engineers are also at risk. The board chairman, CEO, two executive engineers, and the head of brand development were forced out. The U.S. Justice Department has opened criminal investigations into whether there was a conspiracy within the company to perpetuate the fraud (Barrett, 2015). It seems that failure is possible at Volkswagen.

In this case, highly authoritarian leadership and organizational culture harmed a company with a solid reputation for quality. Program leadership was so afraid to tell executive leaders that their requirements could not be met that they instead engineered a potentially criminal device to circumvent emission regulations. It is possible that executive leaders did not become aware of the device until external investigations revealed the testing irregularities. However, the lack of objective governance at the corporate level removed any potential checks and balances between the demands of top executives and engineering program staff. And the fact that staff willingly participated potentially undermines integrity, which is foundational to trust, collaboration, and, ultimately, integration.

2.3.4 Typical Engineering Program Challenges

The issues affecting engineering program performance and the professionals who lead them have not changed. The team that developed *The Guide to Lean Enablers for Managing Engineering Programs* (Oehmen, 2012a) undertook extensive research to learn why engineering programs are so challenged. That research uncovered several major challenges that affect engineering program performance, as documented in Table 2-2.

Ask any program manager or systems engineer who is unfamiliar with this research, and they are likely to cite similar issues and challenges. So we know what can go wrong and we have roadmaps like the *Guide* to help chart the way. So what more is needed?

2.4 We Need a Better Solution

The scope of programs, now and into the future, requires strong performance and outcomes. The World Economic Forum estimates that the world's infrastructure needs require investment of US$5 trillion per year for the next 15–20 years (World Economic Forum, 2013, p. 12). Such investment would deliver energy generation and delivery systems; water and sewage services; roads, airports, ports, and bridges; and telecommunications services. Subjecting such investment to the cost and schedule delays associated with today's program performance could more than triple the price tag. Something must change.

As with the challenges, there are known solutions. The solution begins with organizational culture that values people and their capabilities. That culture engages executive leaders in governance roles to provide oversight, decision making, and support to engineering program teams. Those executive leaders empower program managers and chief systems engineers as collaborators to deliver complex programs by balancing management considerations, technical requirements, and customer needs. Program managers and chief systems engineers guide their teams to plan, develop, test, and manage program elements as a cohesive unit of subject matter experts. Processes, methods, tools, techniques, and systems support individuals in completing their tasks, handing off work, addressing emerging issues, and engaging the right people. Ongoing training and development ensures that individuals gain and enhance their knowledge, experience, and capabilities, and begin to work in a collaborative, integrated way if integration concepts and practices are included in the training.

2.5 Summary

Challenges to program performance are well documented and known. From poor planning to ineffective requirements management to lack of effective stakeholder management, many programs reflect a situation of history repeating itself. The current

Table 2-2: Engineering program challenges	
Typical Program Challenges	Description
Firefighting—Reactive Program Execution	The lack of careful and collaborative planning, coordination, and management results in programs being executed in a reactive mode. Rather than effectively coordinating planned activities, program teams spend their time firefighting, focusing their efforts on fixing urgent problems instead of preventing them. The underlying issues can be caused by interpersonal issues (e.g., there is no coherent leadership team); lack of required skills (e.g., insufficient program risk management capabilities); ineffective management (e.g., competing resource requirements); or lack of executive engagement (e.g., differing priorities within collaborating organizations).
Unstable, Unclear, and Incomplete Requirements	Inadequate requirements management represents one of the highest contributors to program and project failures. For products and services that have to be highly adaptive and responsive to human interfaces, it can be extremely challenging for potential customers to clearly articulate all of the functions, capabilities, situational applications, and details they may need. It can be equally challenging for a designer or requirements specialist to properly capture what the customer states, including appropriate reflection of the associated nuances and interpretations. There may also be a lack of appreciation for the complexity of the requirements. As a result, engineering program requirements may change frequently, be unclear, and/or be incomplete. Since the requirements determine what is built and how, unstable or inaccurate requirements affect efficient and effective execution of the program delivering them. If there are multiple customers involved, one customer's set of requirements may conflict with or create a mismatch with the other customer's needs. In the end, it is possible that both customers' needs may not be fully met.
Mismanagement of Program Culture, Team Competency, and Knowledge	Some programs lack appropriate expertise and knowledge associated with management of complex engineering programs among individuals, teams, and within the organization at-large. Either individuals do not have the necessary skills and experience or there is ineffective knowledge transfer from experienced employees and team members to new employees. Additionally, knowledge and experience captured from lessons learned are not translated into improvements that could enhance program performance and management.
Insufficient Alignment and Coordination of the Extended Enterprise	The complex network of organizations and departments involved in delivering the program value is not aligned with its priorities. This includes the alignment and optimization of strategic priorities and portfolios.
Unclear Roles, Responsibilities, and Accountability	The roles, responsibilities, and accountability of individuals, teams, staff functions, and line functions are not clearly defined. There is lack of alignment and integration between program management and systems engineering exacerbated by incentives that inhibit or discourage collaboration. There may be power struggles over who has accountability for plans and outcomes and over who is empowered to make decisions.
Insufficient Program Planning	There is a lack of detailed and integrated planning at the program's start. Uncertainties are not adequately recognized and incorporated into early planning, leading to unrealistic expectations and plans.
Lack of Proactive Program Risk Management	Budgetary and time constraints can lead to limited or no risk management activity by the program team. The program team attempts to function without clear off-ramps and mitigation approaches. Ownership of risks is ill-defined.
Poor Program Acquisition and Contracting Practices	Time constraints lead to inadequate quality of the request for proposal or contract bid. Legal and regulatory requirements, improper management of immature technologies, and insufficient leadership exacerbate this challenge. The request for proposals is issued before customer requirements have sufficient clarity and stability. There is no adequate process for maturing program technologies, and trade-offs are difficult to negotiate.

Adapted from Oehmen, 2012b. *Working session: Lean enablers for managing engineering programs.* Massachusetts Institute of Technology, 2012. Copyright and all rights reserved. Material from this publication has been reproduced with the permission of MIT.

situation is not sustainable, particularly as societies around the world require the benefits that only major engineering programs can deliver.

Fortunately, there are principles that, if applied, can make a difference. The principle of respect for people strikes at the heart of what is important—creating structures, systems, cultures, incentives, tools, processes, and capabilities that help people work together more effectively. Program managers and chief systems engineers play important roles in making that principle come to life. By helping to foster integration and collaboration, these leaders can drive team efforts focused on reducing developmental cost, cycle time, and risk. And that means stronger program performance. This book captures these lessons along with research findings to suggest a better way to manage complex programs—through effective integration of program management and systems engineering disciplines.

2.6 Discussion Questions

1. In a single day, how many individual elements of organizational infrastructure do you interact with? How many of those system elements function as well as they should? What happens if they fail?
2. Think of an example of a program failure. Was that failure due to poor execution of an otherwise sound plan, bad planning that was otherwise flawlessly executed, or some combination of both?
3. Which is more important, the engineering ability to define the development destination or the execution ability to actually get there?
4. Is ethics an important consideration for collaboration? Why or why not?
5. With additional information following the completion of the 2016 Olympic Games, evaluate the Rio 2016 Olympics using the framework provided for the London Olympics. What are some key differences? Did Rio provide any new insights associated with the program characteristics evaluated for London's Games?

2.7 References

Barrett, P. (2015, September 22). Putting a price on Volkswagen's emission-fraud mess: It's going to cost them billions. *Bloomberg*. Retrieved from www.bloomberg.com/news/articles/2015-09-22/putting-a-price-on-volkswagen-s-diesel-emission-fraud-liability

Bearup, B. (2015, March 5). *Denver International Airport: A 20-year history* [Web log post]. Retrieved from http://airwaysnews.com/blog/2015/03/02/denver-international-airport-a-20-year-history

Bryant, A. (1994, May 11). Denver's new airport still a "field of dreams." *New York Times*. Retrieved from www.nytimes.com/1994/05/11/us/denver-s-new-airport-still-a-field-of-dreams.html?pagewanted=all

Calleam Consulting. (2008). *Case study: Denver International Airport baggage handling system—an illustration of ineffectual decision making.* Retrieved from www5.in.tum.de/~huckle/DIABaggage.pdf

Charette, R. N. (2008, November 1). What's wrong with weapons acquisitions? *IEEE Spectrum.* Retrieved from http://spectrum.ieee.org/aerospace/military/whats-wrong -with-weapons-acquisitions

Connors, M. (2016, January 11). *Rio 2016 faces a carnival of unusual problems.* Retrieved from www.wsj.com/articles/rio-2016-faces-a-carnival-of-unusual-problems-14525 58081

De La Rue, K. (2008). *Understanding complex organizations: The Cynefin model.* Retrieved from /www.slideshare.net/kdelarue/keith-de-la-rue-cynefin-03-presentation

de Neufville, R. (1994). The baggage system at Denver: Prospects and lessons. *Journal of Air Transport Management, 1*(4), 229–236. doi:10.1016/0969-6997(94)90014-0

Diesel Technology Forum. (n.d.). *What is clean diesel?* Retrieved from www.dieselforum .org/about-clean-diesel/what-is-clean-diesel

Freedberg, S. J. (2012). *Total cost to close out cancelled Army FCS could top $1 billion* [Web log post]. Retrieved from http://breakingdefense.com/2012/06/total-cost-to-close-out -cancelled-army-fcs-could-top-1-billion/

GlobalSecurity.org. (n.d.). *Future combat systems (FCS).* Retrieved from www.global security.org/military/systems/ground/fcs.htm

Government Accountability Office (GAO). (1994). *New Denver airport: Impact of the delayed baggage system.* Retrieved from www.gao.gov/assets/80/78935.pdf

Government Accountability Office. (2007). *Defense acquisitions: Role of lead systems integrator on future combat systems program poses oversight challenges.* Retrieved from www.gao.gov/new.items/d07380.pdf

Guskey, J. (2016). *London continues to use Olympic facilities.* Retrieved from http:// mediaschool.indiana.edu/london2016/2016/05/27/london-continues-to-use -olympic-facilities/

Hill, D. (2015, July 23). London's Olympic legacy three years on: is the city really getting what it needed? *The Guardian.* Retrieved from www.theguardian.com/cities/ davehillblog/2015/jul/23/london-olympic-legacy-three-years-on-2012-games

Hotten, R. (2015, December 10). Volkswagen: The scandal explained. *BBC.* Retrieved from www.bbc.com/news/business-34324772

International Council on Systems Engineering (INCOSE). (2015). *Systems engineering handbook: A guide for system life cycle processes and activities* (4th ed.). D. Walden, G. Roedler, K. Forsberg, R. Hamelin, T. Shortell (Eds.). Hoboken, NJ: John Wiley & Sons.

International Council on Systems Engineering (INCOSE). (2016). *Guide to the systems engineering body of knowledge (SEBoK),* v. 1.6. San Diego, CA: Author.

Kemp, D., Beasley, R., & Williams, S. (2015, July 13–16). *Suits you sir! Choosing the right style of SE before tailoring to fit: Using functional failure modes and effects analysis to guide selection of the right systems approach.* Presented at the 25th Annual INCOSE International Symposium, Seattle, WA.

Kerzner, H. R. (2006). *Project management case studies* (2nd ed.). Hoboken, NJ: John Wiley & Sons.

Kintrea, K. (2012). *Learning legacy: Lessons learned from the London 2012 games construction project.* Olympic Delivery Authority. Retrieved from http://learninglegacy .independent.gov.uk/

Kortekaas, V. (2012, August 19). Project management: Lessons can be learned from successful delivery. *Financial Times.* Retrieved from www.ft.com/cms/s/0/57d92e9c -d7df-11e1-9980-00144feabdc0.html#axzz4C8vX47N9

Langnau, L. (2000, August 1). *Lessons from an engineering fiasco* [Web log post]. Retrieved from http://machinedesign.com/linear-motion/lessons-engineering-fiasco

Lutz, B. (2015, November 4). One man established the culture that led to VW's emissions scandal. *Road & Track.* Retrieved from www.roadandtrack.com/car-culture/ a27197/bob-lutz-vw-diesel-fiasco/

Merriam-Webster. (n.d.). Definition for "white elephant." Retrieved from www .merriam-webster.com/dictionary/white%20elephant

Oehmen, J. (Ed.). (2012a). *The guide to lean enablers for managing engineering programs, version 1.0.* Cambridge, MA: Joint MIT-PMI-INCOSE Community of Practice on Lean in Program Management. URI: http://hdl.handle.net/1721.1/70495

Oehmen, J. (2012b, May 6). *Working session: Lean enablers for managing engineering programs.* Presented at PMI Global Congress EMEA, Marseille, France.

Pearson, S. (2016). Rio's Olympics building spree fails to enthuse. *Financial Times.* Retrieved from www.ft.com/intl/cms/s/0/ccf26ccc-0dfd-11e6-b41f-0beb7e589515 .html#axzz4BHwleGYq

Pernin, C. G., Axelband, E., Drezner, J. A., Dille, B. B., Gordon IV, J., Held, B. J., et al. (2012). *Lessons from the Army's future combat systems program.* Rand Corporation. Retrieved from www.rand.org/content/dam/rand/pubs/monographs/2012/RAND _MG1206.pdf

Phillips, D. (2016a, August 1). "Please fix my toilet:" Olympic teams suffer through problems at Rio's athletes' village. *Washington Post.* Retrieved from www .washingtonpost.com/news/worldviews/wp/2016/07/27/olympic-teams-are -complaining-about-the-pathetic-state-of-rios-athletes-village/

Phillips, D. (2016b, August 1). Rio's long delayed Olympic metro line opens in the nick of time. *Washington Post.* Retrieved from www.washingtonpost.com/news/ worldviews/wp/2016/08/01/rios-long-delayed-olympic-metro-line-opens-in-the -nick-of-time/

Project Management Institute (PMI). (2014). *Navigating complexity: A practice guide.* Newtown Square, PA: Author.

Raby, J. (2015, September 29). *West Virginia University that exposed VW emission scheme did it before* [Web log post]. Retrieved from www.claimsjournal.com/news/southeast/ 2015/09/29/266000.htm

Rapoza, K. (2015, June 7). A year later, Brazil's FIFA World Cup infrastructure still not built. *Forbes,* Retrieved from www.forbes.com/sites/kenrapoza/2015/06/07/a-year -later-brazils-fifa-world-cup-infrastructure-still-not-built/#5b0c330b2fae

Smith, G., & Parloff, R. (2016, March 15). Hoaxwagen: How the massive diesel fraud incinerated VW's reputation—and will hobble the company for years to come. *Fortune*. Retrieved from http://fortune.com/inside-volkswagen-emissions-scandal/

Snowden, D., & Boone, M. (2007, November). A leader's framework for decision making. *Harvard Business Review*.

Stromberg, J. (2015, May 12). Brazil's $900 million World Cup stadium is now being used as a parking lot. *Vox*. Retrieved from www.vox.com/2015/5/12/8592805/brazil-world-cup-stadiums

Swartz, A. (1996). Airport 95: Automated baggage system? *Software Engineering Notes*, *21*(2) 79–83. Retrieved from www5.in.tum.de/~huckle/swartz_DIA.pdf

White, A. (2015, July 25). Olympic Park legacy starting to fulfill its huge expectations. *The Telegraph*. Retrieved from www.telegraph.co.uk/finance/property/11762954/Olympic-Park-legacy-starting-to-fulfil-its-huge-expectations.html

World Economic Forum. (2013). *The green investment report: The ways and means to unlock private finance for green growth*. Retrieved from http://reports.weforum.org/green-investing-2013/

Additional Resources

Alexander, I. F., & Beus-Dukic, L. (2009). *Discovering requirements: How to specify products and services*. Hoboken, NJ: John Wiley & Sons.

Checkland, P., & Scholes, J. (2001). *Soft systems methodology in action*. Chichester, England: John Wiley & Sons.

Eisner, H. (2008). *Essentials of project and systems engineering management* (3rd ed.). Hoboken, NJ: John Wiley & Sons.

National Aeronautics and Space Administration (NASA). (2007). *Systems engineering handbook*. Washington, D.C.: Author.

THE FEATURES OF SUCCESSFUL INTEGRATION OF PROGRAM MANAGEMENT AND SYSTEMS ENGINEERING

3.1 A Major Engineering Program Failure?

Success related to engineering program management is often very narrowly defined in terms of cost and schedule performance, and this can be to the detriment of delivered value. If either or both measures fall outside targets but the program delivers the desired result, the entire program may nevertheless be deemed unsuccessful. While these measures are convenient to assess and report, they provide only a limited perspective. They do not account for the full range of value and benefits that these programs are intended to deliver, and consequently do not provide a full accounting of the program, its benefits, or its degree of success or failure. In short, the more complicated the program objectives, the more complicated it is likely to be in providing a full accounting of its outcomes and, ultimately, its success.

Boston's Central Artery/Tunnel (aka the Big Dig), like other major infrastructure programs such as the English Chunnel and San Francisco/Oakland Bay Bridge, is an example of a program that accomplished a complete restructuring of Boston's central roadways, which greatly improved the flow of traffic. The program also opened up areas of the city for new development. But the constant media barrage of articles and reports of schedule delays, out-of-control costs, and allegations of major corruption cemented a mindset among many stakeholders that the program had failed. Elements of that perception still linger today. Thus, engineering programs such as this may always risk being deemed failures if they are evaluated simply on measures of cost and schedule.

When the definition of success is expanded with more of a focus on benefits realized, programs may be seen in a different light. Benefits metrics such as reduced traffic, economic growth opportunities, client satisfaction, customer retention, future business enabled, and program team capability development better demonstrate the degree to which desired business or mission goals may be realized. Ten years after completion of the Big Dig, a *Boston Globe* (Flint, 2015) article highlighted significant achievements:

> "Rush hour brings what radio reporters refer to as heavy volume. But the traffic moves and for 1.5 miles through downtown Boston, it moves out of sight, underground.... Getting to and from Logan Airport has never been easier" (Flint, 2015).

> When the program started, Boston's Central Artery roadway carried about 200,000 commuters. It now carries about 536,000 commuters each week day. "Bottlenecks are minimized through the use of the add-a-lane design, where onramps become a permanent additional lane, requiring less merging" (Flint, 2015).

> "the greatest success of the Big Dig is this: It established a new landscape for the city to flourish all around it.... Numerous reports have chronicled big jumps in property values.... All kinds of previously nondescript buildings are being redeveloped and turned into lofts and office space—buildings that had little value when they overlooked an elevated highway and are now suddenly on a gold coast" (Flint, 2015).

Part of the challenge with perceptions of success related to the Big Dig is that perceptions started to solidify during the development and implementation periods when cost and schedule were about the only solid, trackable metrics. Opinions could not wait for the full program to conclude to evaluate the degree to which desired objectives had been achieved. With only part of the program visible and looking through the cost and schedule lenses, it became impossible to see anything positive resulting from the program. Only after the passage of 10 years and subsequent experience associated with the program have its benefits led some to revisit their perceptions of its successes.

The technical elements of success are often evaluated based on design elements and technical risk management that ultimately affect cost and schedule. Although there are leading indicators of technical success, true success is often only measurable at the end of a program or long after its completion. Referring back to the Big Dig program, engineers received credit for applying the best technologies and practices on the program. However, managing construction underneath a major city while daily work and life above ground occurred as usual was a substantial feat in and of itself. But the program also presented tough problems that required significant replanning and redesign in real time. Some of the technical risks were known to the federal and state officials advocating for the program, but the cost and schedule implications were downplayed to get the program authorized. As a result, state officials and the primary contractors took heat as costs increased and the schedule was extended months and months into the future. As with program performance, negative perceptions of technical performance colored views of the program's success, despite the innovative approaches that became new best practices in major infrastructure programs. And as with program success, perceptions of technical success can change when the sum value of all optimization decisions become visible at the end of the program. The *Boston Globe* (Flint, 2015) article highlighted the value delivered by optimization decisions during the Big Dig:

> "The joint venture team of the state, Bechtel/Parsons Brinckerhoff, and lead contractor Modern Continental had to act like Matt Damon and his NASA team in *The Martian*, continually confronting problems and figuring out ways to solve them on the fly" (Flint, 2015).

> "A set of tunnel boxes for the I-90 connector...needed to match up exactly in the murky waters of Fort Point Channel; engineers deployed an elaborate jacking system that was unprecedented in its use and inflatable devices to float the giant sections into place" (Flint, 2015).

New best practices and unprecedented approaches to engineering major infrastructure programs meant little to taxpayers, media representatives, or opponents of the program, who watched the meter run and the distance to the finish line stretch out further and further. In the end, the article summed up the risk associated with major engineering programs: "The architects of infrastructure are expected to get everything 100 percent right, but tragically, some realities only become apparent by way of failure" (Flint, 2015).

Individual definitions of success vary wildly from stakeholder to stakeholder and can evolve over time. As when seeing a movie, no still image can ever serve as a true measure of success—individuals need to see the entire movie to offer a truly informed review. Even then, each individual's own biases and perceptions will color the conclusions. Nevertheless, observations from what have been designated as successful engineering programs can provide insights on the drivers of success.

In the case of the Big Dig, there were unpredictable organizational, political, operational, and technical challenges that had to be overcome by the program management team. The program faced a diverse set of steep technical challenges and had to have world-class experts in each of those areas, and those experts had to work together effectively to ensure that the overall system functioned and delivered the benefits for which the program was created. The program management team (comprising both program management and systems engineering leads) applied best available technologies and practices, encouraged innovation to create new best practices where existing ones were inadequate, and continually confronted problems and figured out ways to solve them as they arose. Exactly how they did this is explored in greater detail in Chapters 11 and 14. The overarching point is that the management team went to great lengths to ensure that the program and project managers, systems engineers, and technical experts were coordinated and aligned in their efforts on this very complex program.

Like the Future Combat System example in Chapter 2, this case and the others presented in this chapter are relevant to the exploration of integration and collaboration between systems engineers and program managers. First, there is a direct tie between program and technical activities and benefits realized from the program's outputs. As noted above, the Big Dig tested new practices and approaches for tackling tough problems in real time, just as systems engineers and program managers must do as they encounter novel challenges. Such experimentation is absolutely necessary, but comes with the potential of failure, added cost, and schedule impacts. Second, how leadership on any engineering program handles stakeholder expectations, including communications with the public through media, particularly on major programs that impact a broad group of stakeholders has a significant influence on perceptions. In the Big Dig and London Olympic Games examples in Chapter 2, both programs undertook extensive media and community engagement activities, albeit with different outcomes. Most importantly, the key point is that the roles of chief systems engineer and program manager are much broader than they may appear. They are scientists and pioneers discovering new ways. They are problem solvers who overcome new challenges. They are networkers who facilitate and enable multiple branches of communication and connection. They are leaders who champion a vision, direct the course, and engage others in support.

3.2 Bridging Boundaries to Foster Program Success

The Prairie Waters program (Oehmen, 2012; PMI, n.d.) was considerably less complex than the Big Dig. On its merits, it is relatively easier to call it a successful program (it was formally recognized and awarded the 2011 PMI Project of the Year Award), but that recognition is related to how it approached the unique challenges it faced. Those challenges and ultimate evaluation of success will be different for every program. However, the case provides useful insight into attributes and practices that can support achieving successful program outcomes.

A massive drought from 2002 to 2003 depleted the water supply in the city of Aurora, Colorado, to an all-time low, falling to just 26% of its total capacity. The city was left with a nine-month supply of water for its citizens—far less than the three- to five-year supply it prefers to keep. Officials decided to implement a program that would prevent future drought-related shortages. In August 2005, the Aurora City Council launched the Prairie Waters project, which called for the construction of nearly 34 miles (55 km) of 60-inch (1.5 m) pipeline, four pump stations, a natural purification area, and one of the world's most technically advanced water-treatment facilities, handling 50 million gallons (189 million liters) per day. The project was to deliver full operational capability by the end of 2010.

C2HM Hill won the prime contract for the Prairie Waters program and six key subcontractors supported various elements of engineering design, construction management, and legal management. From the outset, C2HM Hill and its subcontractor partners established the foundation for strong program integration within a team comprised of about 5,000 individuals.

The Prairie Waters program fostered professional excellence regarding behavior. Not only did program leadership clearly communicate what behavior was expected, they also asked their management to role model these behavioral characteristics. For example, the team established a culture of "what is right" and not "who is right," emphasizing the fact that everyone was encouraged to share their ideas and that those ideas would be heard and treated equally, regardless of their position in the organization.

The program had 11 very clearly defined benefits it aimed to achieve, and the core program focused exclusively on those outcomes. All additional activities had to undergo review and approval. This practice ensured that the program team did not get carried away with side projects that did not add value. The program team established a set of critical success factors such as budget, schedule, environmental protection, and proactive communication. These success factors were continuously tracked and displayed in a dashboard making the current status highly visible. These top-level metrics were broken down for every bidding package to track contractors' performance.

The Prairie Waters program used a number of approaches to ensure efficient and collaborative decision making. During a process called chartering, the team developed a delivery or value stream map, exploring the best path to achieving the program goals. Within that system, each workflow was broken down on a process level that facilitated assigning responsibilities, defining the format of the task output, and assessing the time available for completion. The chartering workshops also established the foundations for efficient decision making throughout the program. For example, the organizational structure was adapted not only to foster collaboration, but also to speed up decision making. Operating procedures also ensured that the right information required to make decisions was available and up to date.

The program team developed a manual to serve as a guidebook for team members. It outlined standard operating procedures as well as roles and responsibilities for key tasks. It covered communication flows and protocols outlining rules for information dissemination and quality. Since the program incorporated multiple organizations under its umbrella, for each key organization the program designated specific individuals as direct points of contact between organizational and functional counterparts, which proved to be a major facilitator of direct and efficient communication and decision making.

Because the program had a very tight deadline and multiple concurrent project activities, it needed to leverage significant innovation and improvisation with the team and the subcontracted organizations. Contractors were incentivized to propose ideas to reduce costs. In cases where the ideas proved valid and were selected for realization, the savings were split evenly. But, even more challenging was the need to draw upon expertise in a number of disciplines to work together collaboratively rather than just contribute individual skill sets to objectives of their portion of the program.

Another critical management element based on the program's constraints was effective risk management. Program leadership leveraged the team to develop a detailed risk management plan and mitigation strategies. The potential impact of every risk was analyzed and weighted by the potential impact the risk could have on the program. Responsibility for monitoring, tracking, and reevaluating risks was pushed to the appropriate management level along with the accountability for taking any necessary mitigation actions.

The benefits realized from the Prairie Waters program include the ability to supply about 3.3 billion gallons of water per year and treat about 50 million gallons of water every day. The outcome of the program serves more than 300,000 people in the city of Aurora, and is expected to meet the water needs of the city until 2030 (Kable, n.d.).

So how did the Prairie Waters program do it? Some of the practices employed are (or should be) standard for any program. These started with having a common vision for the objectives of the program that was shared across the program team, with clearly defined benefits and critical program success factors on prominent display. Other practices aimed to improve communication, collaboration, and efficient decision making. Program leaders were expected to model collaborative behaviors to set the climate for the program. Roles and responsibilities for key tasks were defined with standard operating procedures so everyone knew how they contributed to the program. Program participants were incentivized to propose ideas to reduce costs to the program through innovative alternative solutions. What emerges from this case is a picture of a program management team that was very collaborative and encouraged the full engagement of all program participants. But were these actions characteristic of just Prairie Waters, or can they be found in general across many successful, high-performing programs?

3.3 Contributors to Success in Action

Engineering program success requires contributors to combine their skills and abilities effectively to deliver the desired business benefits. The following examples will show briefly two examples of programs deemed successful, and how the joint contributions of systems engineering and program management contributed their underlying capabilities to deliver results.

3.3.1 Accelerated Excellence

Lockheed Martin's Skunk Works still stands today as the symbol of how innovative programs should operate after decades in existence and a long list of category-defining aircraft programs. The term "skunkworks" is now a part of business vernacular. Although many of its definitions focus on the process, structural, or mechanical aspects of the model, few focus on the most important element of what made the model work and sustains it as the symbol of innovation—the people. Urban Dictionary's (n.d.) definition of skunkworks captures the critical people-side of the equation:

> a group of people who, in order to achieve unusual results, work on a project in a way that is outside of the usual rules. A skunkworks is often a small team that assumes or is given responsibility for developing something in a short time with minimal management constraints. Typically, a skunkworks has a small number of members in order to reduce communications overhead.

As the U.S. War Department prepared for the land invasion of Europe during World War II, rumors circulated that the German government had developed a leading-edge airplane capable of very high speeds. Trying to remain ahead of the enemy, the War Department engaged Lockheed Martin to design and build a plane in total secrecy in six months or less that could reach speeds of 600 miles per hour. Lockheed assigned

Clarence L. Johnson to lead the effort. More than a month ahead of schedule, Johnson's team delivered Lula Belle, the P-80 Shooting Star prototype that later became the F-80 fighter plane.

Johnson and the program leadership applied approaches to the assignment that today carry labels such as "lean" and "agile." Program team members were selected for the specialized skills the program required. This fact alone, however, had the potential to create unproductive tension as each specialization would tend to see the "problem to be solved" through their own specialized field of expertise.

The team was relatively small for such a major endeavor, growing quickly from 60 to 80 people as planning and design shifted into development and production. Team members from design to production were located in the same building so they could quickly collaborate to resolve emerging problems. Team members and program leadership held daily meetings to resolve problems and keep workflows moving. These daily meetings served more than just to resolve problems. It also provided for an environment where the program manager, project managers, and the engineering team worked in concert to integrate their expertise and processes to achieve the higher goal of the program as a whole. Team culture valued cooperation and collaboration, but also encouraged "creative tension" where team members challenged each other's ideas to improve upon them (Wilson, 1999).

For decades more, Lockheed's Skunk Works continued to perform miracles that other organizations strove to replicate for themselves. Having others copy one's approaches is not only flattering, but also reflects that others recognize that those approaches lead to successful outcomes.

3.3.2 The Consistent Engine that Could

One of the most comprehensive reviews of an organization's overall engineering program capabilities was published by the National Aeronautics and Space Administration (NASA) in 2008 (Bilardo et al.). Rather than exploring how individual programs succeeded, the study focused instead on an organizational assessment of success—which capabilities within NASA were critical for effective engineering program management. This view provided important perspective because it examined the complex relationships associated with professionals—designers and builders—whose interests could sometimes be diametrically opposed. Looking at how the engineering program system diffused opposition and forged collaboration illustrates an organization that has leveraged its key success contributors as a strategic competency.

NASA formed its Organization Design Team (ODT) to "investigate organizational factors that can lead to success or failure of complex government programs, and to identify tools and methods for the design, modeling and analysis of new and more efficient program and project organizations" (Bilardo et al., 2008, p. 1). The ODT team started in 2003 following the launch of NASA's Next Generation Launch Technology Program. That program's goal was the development of new technologies that would reduce cost, improve performance, and maximize safety. ODT was one of several teams formed to conduct research related to practices, tools, etc. However, ODT's task included an assessment of the impact that "program, project, and technical line organizations have on the space launch 'system of systems'" (Bilardo et al., 2008, p. 3). To accomplish its tasks, the ODT brought together representatives from various disciplines who had worked on 25 major programs over the past 50 years for a series of workshops on organizational effectiveness. The workshops identified a series of principles that staff members felt were instrumental in the success of their programs. These principles equate to the key success contributors identified earlier in this chapter:

■ **Vision:** Effective program leadership set a vision and kept the team focused on program goals. When U.S. President John F. Kennedy declared that the United States would put a man on the moon and bring him back safely, all of NASA's efforts focused on achieving that mission. As stated in the report, "there remained little doubt among NASA and industry personnel about what every meeting, every proposal, every budget discussion, or every decision was ultimately intended to accomplish" (Bilardo et al., 2008, p. 5).

■ **Continuous block and tackle:** Program sponsors and leadership played both offensive and defensive roles as program protectors. Given the long life cycle of programs, changes in organizational leadership or priorities represent constant threats that must be anticipated and managed, like most risks. So NASA program sponsors and leadership helped to sustain executive-level support for the program by actively and regularly engaging stakeholders. Such engagement not only sustained support, but was also vital for securing top talent and insulating programs from disruptive changes like requirements changes that necessitated replanning. The report cited a real example of what could happen when protectors disappeared from one specific program. When President Bill Clinton came to office, his administration cancelled the Strategic Defense Initiative started under President Ronald Reagan after all of the program's key executive sponsors had been replaced.

■ **Building empowered, collaborative teams:** At their inception, all of NASA's programs benefited from strong leaders capable of building solid foundations for success. They started with establishing the right program culture. Leaders not only influenced the culture but through their behaviors, reflected the right way of doing things. Within NASA, strong program leaders would "hire people smarter than [them] and give them the responsibility and resources needed to accomplish the task" (Bilardo et al., 2008, p. 9). These leaders pushed decision-making authority to the responsible people while maintaining overall accountability for performance. They ensured that roles, responsibilities, and deliverables were clearly defined and empowered individuals to chart their own paths to success. At the same time, leaders and managers created an environment where individuals from different disciplinary approaches, perspectives, and roles knew how to collaborate, negotiate, and accept decisions once they were made.

■ NASA leaders also utilized standards for managing program cost and schedule that required regular program reviews with critical program personnel and stakeholders. Serving as a level of program governance, the review meetings represented important gate checks to ensure that the program remained aligned with mission objectives.

- **Smooth engineering management:** NASA representatives understood the important connection between the effective alignment of program management and technical management: "Good systems engineering starts with good requirements and good management practices that will result in clear, stable program objectives" (Bilardo et al., 2008, p. 22). As an example of solid alignment and collaboration, the report cited the Joint Strike Fighter program which used a "strategy-to-task-to-technology approach to prioritize needed technologies" (p. 18). Once program leadership, including the program manager and chief systems engineer, approved operational capabilities, they empowered their teams to collaborate to "identify and prioritize mission-enabling technologies" (p. 18). The leadership discouraged practices that simply represented following standard practices or processes, instead emphasizing approaches designed to enhance value and improve the product.
- NASA's most effective programs established an environment where everyone on the team held each other accountable for program performance. A key mechanism for doing so involved an integrated program baseline, "consisting of requirements, system concept, budgets, schedules, and risks, then rigorously controlling that baseline as the program moves forward through its lifecycle" (p. 19).

3.3.3 Creating "Collective Consciousness"

Performing, producing, and delivering what organizations need in a competitive market to satisfy customers is what program managers and systems engineers do. The ability of program managers and systems engineers to succeed requires combining their efforts. When they do, they can achieve significant results together as avionics manufacturer Rockwell Collins demonstrates.

Rockwell Collins often utilizes a unique team workshop approach at the outset of its planning process that has delivered substantial savings across the life of a program. In June 2011, Rockwell Collins signed a contract with Boeing to provide a range of advanced avionics and mission equipment for KC-46 aerial refueling tankers being built for the U.S. Air Force. A key part of the program was the development of a state-of-the-art remote vision system that uses technology to guide refueling capabilities during midair operations. Previously, refueling operations were conducted by a boom operator lying in the back of the aircraft and flying the air-refueling boom by watching it through a small window. The system developed by the Rockwell Collins team would allow the operator to guide the boom using a computer screen that offers a view of the boom and the other aircraft. Rockwell Collins also provided the flight deck, aircraft networks, surveillance and air-traffic management equipment, and communications and navigation gear.

To ensure the program went smoothly, the program team relied on Rockwell Collins's lean engineering accelerated planning (LEAP) team, an internal group dedicated to helping program teams apply lean principles to program planning. Deborah Secor, LEAP's principal project manager, stated, "LEAP helps project and program managers focus on the dependencies between tasks. By helping team members understand how their actions impact the preceding and following tasks, they are able to make more efficient choices" (Gale, 2013).

The LEAP team moderated a kickoff meeting with all key stakeholders across the life cycle of the program, including engineers, program managers, and factory teams. Because some of the biggest challenges occurred during the transition to manufacturing, everyone involved in the program needed to be engaged as early as possible, and before critical decisions were locked down. The integrated team created a 13-foot (4-meter) value stream map that laid out every task and decision leading up to the transition, along with deadlines and exit criteria. This step helped ensure that nothing was missed, and that decisions important for operations and testing were evident. For example, in the meeting, team members identified the need to mandate standardized screws so the manufacturing line wouldn't have to change out tools.

Once they mapped out the steps, the team set deadlines for each task and decision. According to Brett Stephenson, principal program manager at Rockwell Collins, "The secret sauce is knowing when decisions need to be made in order for engineers to incorporate them into their designs" (Gale, 2013). For example, if design engineering, test engineering, and operations plans are not concurrently executed, minor updates, such as adding a test point or changing to a preferred part, could drive rework or requalification. These forms of waste can be avoided through simulation, 3D modeling, and by including critical stakeholders in design reviews (Gale, 2013).

In the end, the value-stream mapping exercise took only six hours, but it resulted in measurable savings across the program. Stephenson noted, "In the beginning people worried, 'How can we afford to put all these resources into lean planning?' But I was able to show that it doesn't take a lot of resources to get results" (Lucae, 2014).

The LEAP workshops capture a number of important elements for a detailed program plan that will evolve over its life cycle:

- Action items, due dates, milestones, needed resources, and responsibilities
- A RACI (Responsible-Accountable-Consulted-Informed) matrix that documents communication needs between different functions and program contributors
- Risks and opportunities
- Traceable and vetted assumptions

And after the initial workshop, some teams use the workshops for iterative planning between phases (Lucae, 2014). For example, after a critical milestone is achieved, the team would again use the workshop to plan the next period in greater depth. Frequent stand-up and cadence meetings are used to check if everyone stands by his or her commitment and to keep track of potential risks, assumptions, and other identified issues. After a planning workshop, other workshop formats may be used for adjacent topics (e.g., risk management planning, business process training, tool training).

Rockwell Collins has established integrated systems, supported by organizational components such as culture, to drive strong program team performance. This pervasive integration creates the "collective consciousness" that helps teams work together to deliver stronger results to customers.

Some of the points above are fundamental underpinnings of any program or project. But a few are worth noting that go beyond just good program management.

In fact, in some cases, good program management techniques in isolation may actually lead to contention rather than success. But what appears striking is the degree to which the teams understood, or realized through lessons learned, the need to bring together their individual capabilities and perspectives in a way that forged an integrative team rather than star contributors pursuing their own agenda. The unified vision assists in focusing the team members on the purpose, but it is the downstream processes where each team member understands the need to integrate his or her approach with others on the team in pursuit of that common vision.

3.4 Summary

Program success is more than just meeting cost and schedule budgets. It is also about the benefits delivered, which may take years to fully realize, as in the case of the Big Dig. Like all good business management, it is about the benefits gained—both tangible and intangible. But that does not mean that all successful programs must have a positive ROI from a strictly financial perspective. The benefits must have been deemed to have been worth the investment (time and cost) to achieve them. Program payback can take years and even decades, and be difficult to quantify—the Big Dig being a case in point. However, successful programs focus on maximizing the benefits while managing cost and schedule, and do so through the collaborative and integrative contributions of team members.

There are a number of recurrent themes observed in successful programs. These include, but are not limited to:

- **Teaming:** The good of the whole (the outcome) is valued more than the individual disciplines separately, as demonstrated on the Prairie Waters program.
- **Communications:** Maintaining clear visibility into all aspects of the program as it progresses so that all stakeholders (both internal and external) are presented with a single point of view of the details throughout the program life cycle and understand how any contribution they make fits within the whole, as seen in the Big Dig program.
- **Collaboration:** The contribution of all disciplines is valued and information is shared openly. This was exemplified in the NASA case where they drove to build a common vision with supporting management and empowered teams.
- **Alignment:** The intended outcome of the program as a whole avoids the tendency to optimize components at the expense of the integrated whole. The good of the program's result is the intent and not optimization of individual components that can jeopardize the overall results.

These characteristics of successful engineering programs can be achieved through integration, specifically the disciplines of systems engineering and program management. What one will notice in the following chapters is that successful integration really boils down to the intentional actions of team members to achieve a new way of working together. To do so, both the chief systems engineer and the program manager must understand the particular lens through which they view the challenge.

Chapter 4 provides insight into the mindset (lens) that each discipline brings to the task. Chapter 5 then looks at defining what integration looks like when these two disciplines better understand their own lens as well as the lens of others. As you read, ask yourself, "How are my actions contributing to or inhibiting the realization of good integration of program management and systems engineering in my organization or sphere of influence?"

3.5 Discussion Questions

1. What comes to mind when you think of a successful program? What aspects of the program do you associate with success? What trade-offs do you imagine were involved?
2. Now think of an unsuccessful program. What was missing?
3. Which points from this chapter have relevance to integration and collaboration between chief systems engineers and program managers? How are the points directly relevant to the two roles?
4. What questions related to the examples in this chapter would provide greater insight into integration and collaboration? On programs in which you are involved, are the answers to such questions publicly accessible for review and evaluation? Why or why not?

3.6 References

Bilardo, Jr., V. J., Korte, J. J., Branscome, D. R., Langan, K., Dankhoff, W., Fragola, J. R., et al. (2008). *Seven key principles of program and project success: A best practices survey*. Retrieved from http://ntrs.nasa.gov/archive/nasa/casi.ntrs.nasa.gov/20080021182.pdf

Flint, A. (2015, December 29). 10 years later, did the Big Dig deliver? *Boston Globe*. Retrieved from www.bostonglobe.com/magazine/2015/12/29/years-later-did-big-dig-deliver/tSb8PIMS4QJUETsMpA7SpI/story.html

Gale, S. F. (2013). Lean into savings. *PM Network, 27*(6), 29–35.

Kable. (n.d.). *Prairie Waters Project, Aurora, Colorado, United States of America*. Retrieved from www.water-technology.net/projects/prairie-waters-project-aurora-colorado-us/

Lucae, S. (2014). *Improving the fuzzy front-end of large engineering programs: Interviews with subject matter experts and case studies on front-end practices*. Diploma thesis, Nr. 1392. Retrieved from http://cepe.mit.edu/wp-content/uploads/2014/04/SL_Improving-the-fuzzy-front-end-of-engineering-programs_print.pdf

Oehmen, J. (Ed.). (2012). *The guide to lean enablers for managing engineering programs, version 1.0*. Cambridge, MA: Joint MIT-PMI-INCOSE Community of Practice on Lean in Program Management, http://hdl.handle.net/1721.1/70495

Project Management Institute (PMI). (n.d.). Submitted documentation for PMI Project of the Year application. Copy in possession of Project Management Institute, Inc.

Urban Dictionary (n.d.). *Definition of skunkworks*. Retrieved from www.urbandictionary .com/define.php?term=The+Skunkworks

Wilson, J. (1999, December). Skunk works magic. *Popular Mechanics*. Retrieved from http://me372.groups.et.byu.net/recreation/documents/skunkworks.pdf

Additional Resources

Gooch, J. (2005). The dynamics and challenges of interdisciplinary collaboration: A case study of "cortical depth of bench" in group proposal writing. *IEEE Transactions on Professional Communication, 48*(2). Retrieved from www.utd.edu/~jcg053000/ Gooch_IEEE_June2006.pdf

National Aeronautics and Space Administration (NASA). (2007). *Systems engineering handbook*. Washington, D.C.: Author.

Stockman, B., Boyle, J., & Bacon, J. (2010). *International Space Station systems engineering case study*. Air Force Center for Systems Engineering. Retrieved from www .nasa.gov/externalflash/iss-lessons-learned/docs/design_ISS_SE_Case_Study.pdf

4

THE CASE FOR INTEGRATING PROGRAM MANAGEMENT AND TECHNICAL MANAGEMENT

4.1 The Roots of Nonintegration

The systems engineering, project management, and program management disciplines evolved from similar roots during World War II (Levitt, 2011; Cooke-Davies, 2012). Technologies for aircraft, submarines, navy ships, and weapons systems were evolving at an increasingly rapid pace as the Allied and Axis powers struggled to gain dominance on the battlefield. Mission management focused on bringing "order and discipline to large teams of specialists" facing time-pressured delivery of solutions (Levitt, 2011). Technical management needed to oversee development of systems with complex interfaces across many technologies. Those systems were then expected to perform consistently during human interactions. Because the war had to be won, cost was not the driving consideration at the time. Mission managers and technical managers often struggled over whose considerations were primary, but urgency required the leaders in both disciplines to negotiate a middle ground or cede the larger goal. There were cracks in the interdisciplinary relationship, but the cracks were generally contained.

The rebuilding of Europe and Asia, the Cold War, and the Space Race that followed contributed to a "win at all costs" mentality for engineering program management. So speed and innovation remained critical factors while cost was less important. A crisis point came in the 1970s when the accumulated costs of war and space exploration, resistance to increased taxation, and the energy crises along with rising inflation exerted pressure on world governments to improve utilization of monetary resources. Cost quickly replaced speed as a primary consideration in engineering program investments, and unstable or poorly defined requirements became a key contributor to increased cost and budget overruns.

Efforts to control requirements and reduce cost spawned more intensive management and oversight. Laws and regulations mandating practices and approaches surfaced. In the defense sector, government and industry often became adversaries rather than collaborators as each attempted to shift financial risk to the other (Oppenheim, 2015). Within industry, tightening profit margins led to more internal controls to avoid further profit erosion. As management and control efforts within industry and government became more formalized, the focus shifted away from accomplishing the mission. Mission now had to be achieved within the constraints of cost, schedule, and expected performance. This new paradigm expanded the crack that existed between mission management and technical management that continues today.

The focus on controlling cost, schedule, and performance also spawned professional societies whose missions targeted advancing practices that could help produce better results within the domains of specific disciplines. In 1965, the International Management Systems Association, which later became the International Project Management Association (IPMA), formed in Switzerland to advance application of the Critical Path Method (CPM). According to IPMA, "CPM showed a way to manage large projects with international sponsors, uncertain results as well as with complex influences and dependencies from different technical disciplines" (IPMA, n.d.). The Project Management Institute (PMI®) followed in 1969 with a mission to:

> foster recognition of the need for professionalism in project management; provide a forum for the free exchange of project management problems, solutions and applications; coordinate industrial and academic research efforts; develop common terminology and techniques to improve communications; provide interface between users and suppliers of hardware and software systems; and to provide guidelines for instruction and career development in the field of project management (Toth, 1996, p. 473).

The world of systems engineering evolved a bit differently. Because systems engineering is by its very nature multidisciplinary, many long-standing engineering associations had elements of systems engineering practice and application under their umbrellas. Associations representing mechanical, electrical, civil, and other engineering branches developed resources and information about systems engineering for their members. The American Society for Engineering Management (ASEM), founded in 1979, served an instrumental role in establishing systems engineering as a discipline (Wikipedia, n.d.). It was through ASEM that the founders of what would become the National Council on Systems Engineering (NCOSE) gathered. In 1990, they formed NCOSE to advance systems engineering as a unique discipline. NCOSE changed its name to the International Council on Systems Engineering (INCOSE) in 1995 (Honour, 1998).

4.2 Program Management and Systems Engineering Are Different

Programs are initiated to create something new; and technical programs generally involve a high degree of engineering. It is not uncommon for these programs to involve multiple contributors, have a high degree of ambiguity or uncertainty, and a large number of interfaces within the program components and the environments in which they will function—in other words, these programs exhibit a high degree of complexity (PMI, 2013c). Defining the solution then becomes a chicken-and-egg challenge in that the best solution is not known at program initiation and the technical requirements cannot be fully known. Thus, the challenge is one in which the chief systems engineer is attempting to describe and define the optimal solution while at the same time the program manager is attempting to determine the necessary work components and develop the program implementation plan.

One might be tempted to jump to the conclusion that the best solution to the dilemma presented by these interrelated and interdependent needs is to have one person fill both roles. However, this tends to oversimplify the issue as one individual is limited by available time and experiential knowledge—not to mention that the solution does not tend to scale well. As noted above, the two disciplines of program management and systems engineering began to develop specialized knowledge along independent paths. The amount of information generated would be difficult, if not impossible, for one person to acquire in a lifetime. While having one person fill both roles might be the right answer for smaller organizations or programs with low complexity or limited scope, it is not surprising that industry faces challenges associated with the integration of these two important disciplines in complex programs, which first requires that each discipline understand at least the fundamentals and value contribution of the other.

A cursory understanding of each other's discipline begins with an understanding of how each discipline evolved with different measures for success. Bringing the two disciplines together with a common success measure requires the integration of functions within programs. The starting point for improved integration, then, is a foundational understanding of each discipline and the standards that inform the practice of the discipline. As will be seen, tension between the two disciplines has its roots in the specialized practices and standards that are highly role-specific and often have different measures of success. This does not mean that integration is not possible—difficult perhaps, but very much doable. The following sections briefly review the definition and standards associated with program management and systems engineering published by the various professional bodies that support each discipline.

4.3 Program Management

The term program management does not yet carry universal meaning. Often the term's meaning is defined by the background and job responsibilities of the practitioner. Unless formally attached to a common, agreed-upon definition or articulated in context, the intended meaning can be, and often is, misunderstood.

A reliable source of practices, tools, and techniques for program management is the published standards that reflect the broad body of knowledge in program management. PMI publishes one such standard, *The Standard for Program Management* (PMI, 2013a). According to PMI, the standard:

> provides information on program management that is generally recognized as good practice for most programs, most of the time. "Generally recognized" means that the knowledge and practices described are applicable to most programs most of the time, and there is general consensus about their value and usefulness. "Good practice" means that there is general agreement that the application of these activities, skills, tools, and techniques may enhance the chances of success over a wide range of programs (p. 2).

4.3.1 Program Management as Defined by PMI

PMI's definitions for "program" and "project" detailed in this chapter serve as the reference point for how those terms, their management, and the associated roles should be understood in the context of this book. The *PMI Lexicon of Project Management Terms* (PMI, 2015) defines a program as, "A group of related projects, subprograms, and program activities that are managed in a coordinated way to obtain benefits not available from managing them individually" (p. 8). A group of unrelated projects centrally managed is simply a portfolio of projects. A program, however, initiates a number of related projects and other related operational activities, and collectively manages them as components of a larger initiative to achieve a defined benefit or set of benefits. Herein lies the value contribution of program management. *The Standard for Program Management* (PMI, 2013a) defines program management as "the application of knowledge, skills, tools, and techniques to a program to meet the program requirements and to obtain benefits and control not available by managing projects individually." The focus of the program is on delivering benefits for the sponsoring organization or the beneficiaries of the program's outcome. This does not mean that the required components of the program are clearly defined and understood at the outset. Often the means to achieving the outcome are not well known or even clearly definable at the outset.

Unlike a project where the focus is on producing a specific output based on a defined scope, a program begins with a desired benefit or set of benefits. The exact means by which the outcome is to be achieved is often ambiguous at the outset of the program and is thus often termed the "fuzzy front-end." The initiation of a program originates from a set of objectives or goals delineated during the development of an organization's strategic plan. This then leads to the commissioning of a program as part of a portfolio of investments. It is up to the program team to determine the best way to achieve the benefits. *The Standard for Program Management* (PMI, 2013a) captures this idea:

> Programs are a means of executing corporate strategies and achieving business or organizational goals and objectives. Program benefits may be realized incrementally throughout the duration of the program, or may be realized all at once at the end of the program (p. 5).

As the program progresses, the means by which the program will achieve the benefits (i.e., the contributions required by specific projects and operational activities) begins to take shape. However, as the program progresses, there are a number of decisions that must be made. There is an aspect that remains "messy," and this uncertain space can generate unproductive tension—tension that produces conflict and works at cross purpose with program success—among program team members. What remains consistent throughout the program life cycle is the target objective of the program—the benefits to be delivered.

Program management consists of phases of activities through which the work progresses. The three phases of the program management life cycle are program definition, program benefits delivery, and program closure. Projects and other work initiated as part of the program occur during the program benefits delivery phase. The program manager does not typically manage any of the projects directly, but is often the sponsor of the projects and monitors the activity and progress of the projects with a view to meeting the program objectives within schedule and cost. The project manager, on the other hand, is responsible for successful completion of the project and its deliverables. A chief systems engineer may also monitor project activity, but with a different focus and objective. Rather than managing for benefits delivery, the systems engineer is often concerned with optimizing the components, for instance in a product development program, to deliver an outcome that maximizes user experience and optimizes the final product delivered. If these roles are not working together closely, the result is often contention and conflict. Table 4-1 reflects the integrated nature of the disciplines within a program environment.

4.3.2 Distinctions between Projects and Programs

Given the commonality of terms and the connection between program performance domains and project processes, it is not surprising that the terms "program" and "project" are often used in ways not consistent with the definition in the standards. However, there are important differences, as highlighted in Table 4-2. Programs consist of one or more projects initiated to supply specific outputs necessary for realizing the collective benefits of the program. Projects differ from programs in that they tend to have

Table 4-1: Integration of program management, project management, and systems engineering disciplines

Integrated Program View		
Domain	Representation of the "Stakeholder Problem"	Example: New Aircraft Development
Program Management	Benefit	Global market leadership in hub-to-hub connections
Project Management	Deliverable	Deliver engine for $16 million on May 10
Systems Engineering	Functionalities including requirements	Optimization of the entire system such that optimization of the individual components does not lead to suboptimization of the whole. The process produces the requirement: The new engine must have over 300kN take-off thrust, weigh less than 6 tons, must be designed for manufacture on existing assembly lines, cost no more than $15 million to produce, and be FAA certified by May 9

Adapted from Oehmen & Norman, 2012. Applying lean principles to program management: Results from a joint study by PMI, International Council on Systems Engineering and MIT's Lean Advancement Initiative. Massachusetts Institute of Technology, 2012. Copyright and all rights reserved. Material from this publication has been reproduced with the permission of MIT.

Table 4-2: Comparison of program and project activities		
	Projects	**Programs**
Definition	A project is a temporary endeavor undertaken to create a unique product, service, or result.	A program is a group of related projects and program activities that are managed in a coordinated way to obtain benefits not available from managing them individually.
Scope	Projects have defined objectives. Scope is progressively elaborated throughout the project life cycle.	Programs have a scope that encompasses the scopes of its program components. Programs produce benefits to an organization by ensuring that the outputs and outcomes of program components are delivered in a coordinated and complementary manner.
Change	Project managers expect change and implement processes to keep change managed and controlled.	Programs are managed in a manner that accepts and adapts to change as necessary to optimize the delivery of benefits as the program's components deliver outcomes and/or outputs.
Planning	Project managers progressively elaborate high-level information into detailed plans throughout the project life cycle.	Programs are managed using high-level plans that track the interdependencies and progress of program components. Program plans are also used to guide planning at the component level.
Management	Project managers manage the project team to meet the project objectives.	Programs are managed by program managers who ensure that program benefits are delivered as expected, by coordinating the activities of a program's components.
Monitoring	Project managers monitor and control the work of producing the products, services, or results that the project was undertaken to produce.	Program managers monitor the progress of program components to ensure the overall goals, schedules, budget, and benefits of the program will be met.
Success	Success is measured by product and project quality, timeliness, budget compliance, and degree of customer satisfaction.	A program's success is measured by the program's ability to deliver its intended benefits to an organization, and by the program's efficiency and effectiveness in delivering those benefits.

The Standard for Program Management, 3rd ed. (p. 8), Project Management Institute, Inc., 2013; *A Guide to the Project Management Body of Knowledge (PMBOK® Guide),* 5th ed. (p. 8), Project Management Institute, Inc., 2013. Copyright and all rights reserved. Material from this publication has been reproduced with the permission of PMI.

a tightly defined scope of work, along with a fixed budget and timeframe within which the output is to be delivered. The PMI (2015) *Lexicon of Project Management Terms* defines projects as, "A temporary endeavor undertaken to create a unique product, service, or result" (p. 8).

Again, there is commonality between the program phases and the project process groups, as shown in Table 4-3. The commonality of concepts, however, does not mean that the work is the same. But it does demonstrate why programs at times are referred to as projects. This will be seen in several of the case studies throughout the book. Projects have a definitive beginning and end, but this does not mean that the duration is necessarily short. A project may well extend over months and years. The work is often broken down into smaller chunks, some of which may run in parallel. A program, on the other hand, has delivery of benefits as its primary objective, and while a program may deliver a product, the focus is on the realization of the benefits the product is intended to produce. Producing the desired benefits requires the coordination of multiple projects to deliver the whole.

Table 4-3: Comparison of program process phases and project process groups	
Program Process Phases	**Project Process Groups**
Program Definition	Initiating
	Planning
Program Benefits Delivery	Executing
	Monitoring and Controlling
Program Closure	Closing

The Standard for Program Management, 3rd ed. (p. 19), Project Management Institute, Inc., 2013; *A Guide to the Project Management Body of Knowledge (PMBOK® Guide),* 5th ed. (p. 50), Project Management Institute, Inc., 2013. Copyright and all rights reserved. Material from this publication has been reproduced with the permission of PMI.

In the early stages of managing a program, the desired outcome is further elaborated as part of the program scope statement. The scope statement may include a number of high-level requirements, but these requirements evolve through further elaboration as the program progresses in an effort to uncover the best solution within the constraints of time and budget. Sopko and Demaria (2013) portray the program management process and its initiation of related projects as a "Vee" diagram elaborated from *Managing Successful Programmes* (AXELOS, 2011), as shown in Figure 4-1. Specific projects and other work activities are initiated to build out components of the solution. The breakout of work into component projects is intended to enable parallel work streams with dedicated expertise applied to each undertaking. However, the result can be an increase in complexity and can lead to conflicting objectives. The role of the program manager is to ensure that each project is optimized for the delivery of

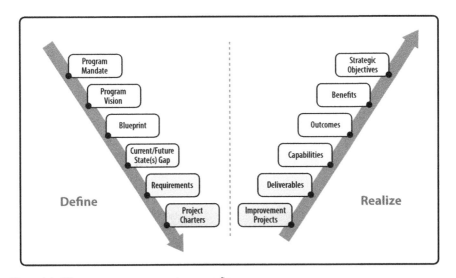

Figure 4-1: The program management process flow
Sopko & Demaria, 2013. Siemens Corporation, 2013. Copyright and all rights reserved. Material from this publication has been reproduced with the permission of Siemens Corporation.

its contribution to the program objectives, and this is often another potential point of unproductive tension with the systems engineer who is following a similar, but different Vee process (see Figure 4-3).

To summarize, programs begin with a conceptual strategic objective or outcome to achieve envisioned benefits. The best way to obtain the outcome is often unknown at the outset. The program manager begins to identify specific outputs needed to achieve the intended benefits and authorizes projects to produce outputs that in turn contribute to the realization of the intended benefits. These projects and other work move forward under the oversight of the program manager who is focused on managing the components collectively to gain maximum benefit and to resolve conflicts or contention between component projects, and to do so within the specified budget. The program manager is, therefore, focused primarily on business processes and outcomes.

4.3.3 Program Management as Defined Worldwide

As a profession develops, practitioners often come together to solidify the practice of the discipline in standards of practice and then develop certifications that recognize mastery of the practice. PMI members developed *The Standard for Program Management*, now in its third edition (PMI, 2013a), as a consensus-based standard detailing the common practice of the profession and building on internationally published practice and research. Each revision of the standard is exposed globally for practitioner comment and balloted as reflective of good practices within the discipline. In 2007, PMI released the Program Management Professional (PgMP®) credential to certify mastery of the knowledge and practice experience related to managing programs. The certification content is built upon the findings of a global role delineation study of existing practitioners and is supported by an evaluation exam containing questions that align with respected publications in the market. While PMI does not publish a specific role-based competency profile, the core competencies necessary for good program management are contained within the exam content outline as summarized in the Sidebar: Program Manager Competencies. It is not surprising, therefore, to find that certified program managers align their approaches with the standards and literature. While it is quite possible and desirable to integrate with systems engineering processes, it is helpful to understand this lens through which the program manager sees the program.

Program Manager Competencies

PMI's program management credential is based on a Role Delineation Study that utilizes standardized best practices for assessing practitioner competence and for determining the level of salience, criticality, and frequency of each of the knowledge, tasks, and skills required to perform in the role of a program manager (PMI, 2011). There are five domains of practice in which a program manager should demonstrate competence.

Domain #1: Strategic Program Management. Identifying opportunities and benefits that achieve organizational strategic objectives through program implementation.

Domain #2: Program Life Cycle. Performing activities related to:

1. Initiating. Defining program and constituent projects, and obtaining agreement from stakeholders.
2. Planning. Defining scope and developing the program, including all constituent projects and all activities that occur within the program.
3. Executing. Performing work necessary to deliver program objectives and benefits.
4. Controlling. Maintaining progress, updating the program plan, and managing change and risk.
5. Closing. Finalizing all program activities, including constituent projects, executing the program transition plan, archiving, obtaining approvals, and reporting.

Domain #3: Benefits Management. Defining, creating, maximizing, and sustaining benefits from the program.

Domain #4: Stakeholder Engagement. Capturing stakeholder needs and expectations, gaining and maintaining stakeholder support, and mitigating/channeling opposition.

Domain #5: Governance. Establishing processes and procedures for maintaining proactive management oversight and decision-making support for the applicable practices and policies across the program life cycle.

In addition to *The Standard for Program Management* (PMI, 2013a), there are other complementary standards and practice guidance for program and project management in the market. For example, the Project Management Association of Japan publishes *A Guidebook of Project & Program Management for Enterprise Innovation* (PMAJ, 2014), which comprises practices, tools, and techniques related to different levels of program and project management, and to enterprise management. IPMA publishes the IPMA Competence Baseline (ICB) (IPMA, 2013), which provides a comprehensive list of competencies for professionals working in projects, programs, and portfolio management. The Office of Government Commerce (OGC), an agency of the government of the United Kingdom, originated *Managing Successful Programmes* (AXELOS, 2011), which comprises a set of practices, principles, and processes for managing programs.

Organizations also use program management models and practices that they form for their own unique community of practice. This is particularly true in the military and aerospace markets. While there are subtle differences in how each group defines the program management processes, there is common, underlying agreement. Specifically, all of the groups see program management as a process for authorizing and managing component work in pursuit of specified benefits. Still, there are subtle differences and it is worthwhile to understand the motivation of each publishing organization and the unique approach they take with respect to details of what constitutes good program management.

4.3.3.1 International Organization for Standardization

In 2007, the International Organization for Standardization (ISO) began work on a series of international standards for project, program, and portfolio management with the intent of identifying a common understanding and definition of each discipline to which all member contributors agree. As such, the standards focus on baseline definitions and practice, but do not go into detail on the underlying knowledge and application. ISO 21500:2012 (ISO, 2012) defines the discipline of project management and is now published. ISO 21504:2015 (ISO, 2015a) is also published and focuses on portfolio management. ISO 21503 will address program management, but is still in committee with an anticipated release in 2017.

4.3.3.2 UK Office of Government Commerce

The UK Office of Government Commerce (OGC) initiated the development of *Managing Successful Programmes* (MSP) as a guide for managing programs based on best practice. As such, it is not technically a standard in that it has not been subjected to review by a standards organization. However, it has been adopted by organizations and government, particularly in the United Kingdom and Australia, as a de facto standard for the development of organizational processes around program management. MSP defines a program as "a temporary, flexible organization created to coordinate, direct, and oversee the implementation of a set of related projects and activities in order to deliver outcomes and benefits related to the organization's strategic objectives" (AXELOS, 2011, p. 5). The MSP framework is "primarily designed to cater to leading and managing transformational change" (p. 10). The framework consists of: principles, governance themes, and transformational flow.

The program is initiated based on an accepted business case for change that defines the value intended related to the organization's strategic plan. The details of how the benefits will be delivered are often ambiguous at the outset and part of the program management process is moving from ambiguity to certainty over the life cycle of the program. MSP describes a transformational flow that begins with the program mandate from the strategic vision and moves through a process to arrive at the program definition. The definition is subject to change as the program initiates component activities and evaluates benefit contribution from the outputs. This is an iterative process that continues throughout the program life cycle until the program is either terminated or closed. Thus, managing the transformational change as a program is valuable in that the focus remains on the whole (the intended benefits) and not on the components as isolated endeavors.

4.3.3.3 Association for Project Management

APM does not produce standards. Rather, it develops products and services based on OGC and ISO standards. APM is one of the federated members of IPMA based in the United Kingdom and offers certifications for project managers aligned with the IPMA levels of certification. APM also publishes the *APM Body of Knowledge* (APM, 2012) covering information related to project, program, and portfolio management.

4.3.3.4 Project Management Association of Japan

The Project Management Association of Japan's *Project and Program Management for Innovation* (PMAJ, 2014) places heavy emphasis on mission profiling as the most important process, and one that should be conducted as the first step of program formulation. It consists of analyzing the business strategies, clarifying the program mission to carry out the strategies, and developing multiple scenarios showing how to reach "what the program should be" from "what it is" now. Program design involves designing the program architecture or structure of plural projects based on several scenarios as a result of the mission profiling. Each of the constituent component projects and the relationships among them are designed so that the program mission can be achieved. The roots of this perspective on program management grow out of the adaptation of program management to its cultural context. Background on how the standard came about is discussed in the Sidebar: PMAJ Program & Project Management and it exemplifies the need for adapting the program management approach to the cultural context within which it is undertaken.

PMAJ Program & Project Management

The Japanese Ministry of Economy, Trade, and Industry (METI) set up a committee in 1999 to create a new methodology that could change Japanese industry after having suffered through 10 years of stagnation. The committee published in 2001 the Program & Project Management for Enterprise Innovation, abbreviated as P2M and now in its third edition (PMAJ, 2014). It represents a combination of systems engineering and project management elements from the West and Japan tailored to Japanese circumstances and culture. The P2M standard focuses more on emergent programs (those with a high degree of uncertainty and unknowns) than do other standards, as shown in Figure 4-2.

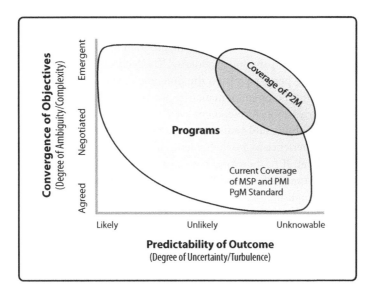

Figure 4-2: The relative focus of P2M compared with other standards

Adapted from *Program management*, Thiry, M, © 2015, Gower Publishing Limited. Reproduced by permission of Taylor & Francis Books UK.

(*continued*)

> The P2M approach differs in that rather than define program missions, goals, and objectives mainly through a top-down approach, it is done using a "middle-out approach" that is more consistent with a Japanese style of consensus-based decision making. In this process top management provides a vague concept in its official and unofficial communications. Middle managers try to acquire the true meaning of the communications through a process that develops a shared vision. The concept changes from vague to specific mission, vision, and strategy through mission profiling in an iterative process. Middle managers then specify program mission, goals, and objectives.

4.3.4 Understanding Program Managers

Unlike engineers whose detailed technical training and credentialing requirements forge a strong shared identity regardless of other differences, program managers may come into the profession from various backgrounds and paths. Many engineers eventually move into program management, some as part of deliberate career paths within an organization. The Phase I study on integration between systems engineering and program management found that 20% of the program manager respondents had been chief systems engineers in the past, and 49% of chief systems engineers reported they had been program managers in the past (Conforto, Rossi, Rebentisch, Oehmen, & Pacenza, 2013). Other program managers may have been project managers, business managers, or leads for other functional areas, such as finance. This diversity of paths into the program manager role is possible because the program management skill set can be added on top of experience in other fields reasonably successfully.

While there is movement toward formal degree programs in program management, today it is still much more likely that the program manager will have developed skills based in part from on-the-job experience. The feedback period between making decisions and learning personally from the outcome is very long on large programs, arguably far longer for the program manager than for engineers, whose decisions can often be verified early in the development cycle.

Just as it takes training and years of experience to become a solid program manager, it also takes experience as a stakeholder to understand and appreciate the role of program management. It is, therefore, not surprising that some stakeholders hold far more realistic views than others regarding what program management can reasonably be expected to accomplish.

4.4 Systems Engineering

The term "systems engineer," like the term "program manager" discussed above, does not yet carry universal meaning. As with program management, unless the term "systems engineering" is formally attached to a professional society definition or articulated in context, the term can be the source of great confusion. This is particularly true in IT, where the term "systems engineer" often refers to the completely different specialty skill of network administration.

Another problem exists when defining systems engineering in that many fields have evolved problem-solving approaches, often very similar in function to systems engineering, but carrying unfamiliar names and terms. An experienced systems engineer will recognize these parallel approaches, but it is less common that someone from an unrelated field will recognize systems engineering as the universal model.

The counterpart to the program manager is sometimes designated the chief systems engineer. Similar to the program manager, the chief systems engineer has ultimate technical authority and is accountable for the technical performance of the product or system being developed. In defining the role of systems engineer, INCOSE (n.d.) states:

> The systems engineer is the primary interface between management, customers, suppliers, and specialty engineers in the system development process. While most have a background in other engineering disciplines, the career descriptor also has a lot to do with the ability and interest to think with a systems perspective. This may come from the specific and recognizable engineering fields but also from a science/math, human systems, business, or any field that develops critical and logical thinking.

To make things more complex, the role of a systems engineer varies by the type of program and the life cycle stage of that program. When the program requires a slightly different subset of the full body of systems engineering methods, outsiders can be easily misled into thinking that subset represents the whole.

> Systems engineering is concerned with the overall process of defining, developing, operating, maintaining, and ultimately replacing quality systems. Where other engineering disciplines concentrate on the specifics of a system . . . systems thinking allows the systems engineer to focus on the integration of all of these aspects as a coherent and effective system. Systems engineers bring a particular perspective to the engineering process. . . . that serves to organize and coordinate other engineering activities (INCOSE, n.d.).

This section starts by examining the definitions established by INCOSE and then acknowledges other professional bodies worldwide and their understanding of the term. A common thread in these definitions is that systems engineering applies the principles of systems thinking to engineering problems. Again, there is much variability in how systems thinking is defined, but at the root most agree that it is the process by which one attempts to look at the whole rather than the individual parts to gain a better understanding of how the parts interact and are interdependent within the larger system.

4.4.1 Systems Engineering as Defined by INCOSE

As with the definition of "program," the INCOSE (n.d.) definition for systems engineering detailed in this chapter serves as the reference point for how that term, its management, and the associated role should be understood in the context of this book.

> Systems Engineering is an interdisciplinary approach and means to enable the realization of successful systems. It focuses on defining customer needs and required functionality early in the development cycle, documenting

requirements, then proceeding with design synthesis and system validation while considering the complete problem.... Systems Engineering integrates all the disciplines and specialty groups into a team effort forming a structured development process that proceeds from concept to production to operation. Systems Engineering considers both the business and the technical needs of all customers with the goal of providing a quality product that meets the user needs.

Few systems stand alone. Sometimes, a system and its constituent subsystems can be implemented by a single program. In many cases, however, a system must exist in an environment with other systems, collectively referred to as a system of systems, which are probably at different points in their life cycle. INCOSE (2015) states:

A "system of systems" (SoS) is an SOI [System of Interest] whose elements are managerially and/or operationally independent systems. These interoperating and/or integrated collections of constituent systems usually produce results unachievable by the individual systems alone. Because an SoS is itself a system, the systems engineer may choose whether to address it as either a system or as an SoS, depending on which perspective is better suited to a particular problem (p. 8).

Schwalb (2016) adds to the INCOSE definition by pointing out:

A SoS is different from a single system. It is actually a set of components that when separated are still regarded as systems themselves. This means that each of these individual systems remain operational after the SoS they are associated with is disassembled. Further, each of these individual systems is independently managed. This means that they can and do operate as individual entities and this continues regardless of the SoS of which they are a component.

An airport is a good example of a system of systems. There will be many types of aircraft systems operated by several airlines and other operators. There will be an air traffic control tower managed by an air navigation service provider. Controllers and pilots will communicate via radio systems from a variety of manufacturers and service providers. Within the terminal there will be many systems for dealing with the passengers and their luggage. There will be ground transportation systems such as parking garages, taxi dispatchers, automobile rental, and so on. This system of systems must be integrated and interoperable, although it might be individual entities managed by multiple businesses and private individuals. While it is the responsibility of the program manager to ensure that in combination all these different systems provide the stream of benefits stakeholders have been promised, it is the responsibility of the chief systems engineer to ensure that they are capable of producing these benefits from a functional and technical standpoint while minimizing the potential for loss. This is accomplished through the functions, processes, and methods of systems engineering.

Earlier in this chapter a Vee model concept for program management was introduced. Systems engineering also adapts a Vee model to visualize the activities of defining and validating system solutions as depicted in Figure 4-3. INCOSE (2015) notes that the Vee model is:

useful in defining the start, stop, and process activities appropriate to the life cycle stages.

The Vee model provides a useful illustration of the SE activities during the life cycle stages. In this version of the Vee model, time and system maturity proceed from left to right. The core of the Vee (i.e., those products that have been placed under configuration control) depicts the evolving baseline from stakeholder requirements agreement to identification of a system concept to definition of elements that will comprise the final system. With time moving to the right, the evolving baseline defines the left side of the core of the Vee, as shown in the shaded portion... (pp. 32–34).

The Vee model is a framework by which the systems engineer goes about breaking down the whole of the problem to be solved, but does so in a way that maintains connectivity of the subcomponents to the whole solution. The framework guides the process, but does not define the details, nor does it mandate actions. As will be seen in the following definitions of systems engineering by other organizations, all of the definitions contain elements of this Vee approach or thinking as a central concept within the definitions, albeit without necessarily calling it out specifically.

In order to effectively perform all the program functions previously described, systems engineers must possess a broad range of skills and abilities. They must use systems thinking and a systems view of the components of benefits delivery in the program. They must have the capabilities to use a specific set of tools and methods as highlighted in the Sidebar: Z6 Systems Engineering Competency Framework. These required skills shape the systems engineer's perspective on program responsibilities, how the work is approached, and how challenges are managed. While the systems engineer's work is

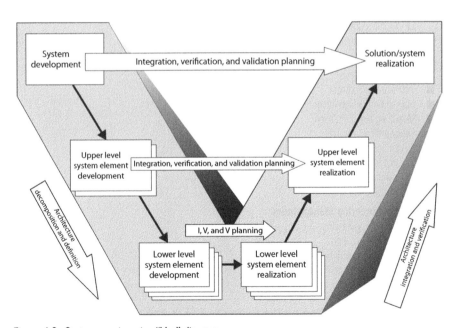

Figure 4-3: Systems engineering "Vee" diagram

integral to the success of the program and intertwined with that of program managers, the systems engineer necessarily works using a different approach with its own unique processes, methods, and tools.

Z6 Systems Engineering Competency Framework

What does a good systems engineer need to know and be able to do? The INCOSE UK chapter developed a Systems Engineering Competency Framework that describes the competencies that are required to conduct good systems engineering, consistent with the International Standards Organization ISO15288, EIA632, and INCOSE Systems Engineering Body of Knowledge & Systems Engineering Handbook. The Systems Engineering Competency Framework was adopted by INCOSE and reflects the organization's position on systems engineering competencies. The INCOSE UK acknowledges that a well-rounded systems engineer will need other competencies, knowledge, skills, and abilities tailored to the particular role or area in which the systems engineer operate. Nevertheless, these reflect a consensus position on the competencies a systems engineer should possess (INCOSE UK, 2010):

Systems Thinking
- Systems concepts
- Super-system capability issues
- Enterprise and technology environment

Holistic Life Cycle View
- Determine and manage stakeholder requirements
- System design:
  - Architectural design
  - Concept generation

Design for
- Functional analysis
- Interface management
- Maintaining design integrity
- Modelling and simulation
- Select preferred solution
- System robustness
  - Integration and verification
  - Validation
  - Transition to operations

Systems Engineering Management
- Concurrent engineering
- Enterprise integration
- Integration of specialisms
- Life cycle process definition
- Planning, monitoring, and controlling

(Z6 Systems Engineering Competencies Framework Copyright INCOSE UK, www.incoseonline.co.uk.)

4.4.2 Systems Engineering as Defined by Others

Perceptions of systems vary worldwide, so it can be expected that there would be different approaches to systems engineering. These cultural differences are associated with people, but also form the mindset associated with a profession or industry. Within almost every engineering discipline there is at least a subgroup focused on systems. Systems thinking is an imprecise and evolving concept as is the somewhat related emergence of the concept of design thinking. How the term "systems" is defined, therefore, varies widely. The efforts of the following well-known organizations to standardize the practice of systems engineering, the processes used, and the artifacts produced demonstrate the nuance of perspective and variance of definition in the market.

4.4.2.1 International Organization for Standardization

International Organization for Standardization (ISO) standards define systems engineering as an "interdisciplinary approach governing the total technical and managerial effort required to transform a set of customer needs, expectations, and constraints into a solution, and to support that solution throughout its life" (ISO, 2010). ISO/IEC/IEEE 15288:2015 defines technical performance measures; the integration of engineering specialties toward the establishment of an architecture; and the definition of supporting life cycle processes that balance cost, performance, and schedule objectives (ISO, 2015b). Kowalski (2015) points out that "This [ISO/IEC/IEEE 15288:2015] is the standard upon which INCOSE aligns the process and life cycle content in the SE [Systems Engineering] Handbook" (INCOSE, 2015).

4.4.2.2 National Aeronautics and Space Administration (NASA)

One could argue that the U.S. National Aeronautics and Space Administration (NASA) was the first to implement systems engineering widely. The NASA *Systems Engineering Handbook* (2007) defines systems engineering as:

> a methodical, disciplined approach for the design, realization, technical management, operations, and retirement of a system. A "system" is a construct or collection of different elements that together produce results not obtainable by the elements alone. The elements, or parts, can include people, hardware, software, facilities, policies, and documents; that is, all things required to produce system-level results. The results include system-level qualities, properties, characteristics, functions, behavior, and performance. The value added by the system as a whole, beyond that contributed independently by the parts, is primarily created by the relationship among the parts; that is, how they are interconnected. It is a way of looking at the "big picture" when making technical decisions. It is a way of achieving stakeholder functional, physical, and operational performance requirements in the intended use environment over the planned life of the systems. In other words, systems engineering is a logical way of thinking.

> Systems engineering is the art and science of developing an operable system capable of meeting requirements within often opposed constraints. Systems

engineering is a holistic, integrative discipline, wherein the contributions of structural engineers, electrical engineers, mechanism designers, power engineers, human factors engineers, and many more disciplines are evaluated and balanced, one against another, to produce a coherent whole that is not dominated by the perspective of a single discipline.

4.4.2.3 United States Department of Defense

The U.S. Department of Defense was an early pioneer in the development and application of systems engineering. Not surprisingly, the *Defense Acquisition Guidebook* (U.S. Department of Defense, 2016) defines systems engineering in very similar language to NASA. For the Department of Defense, systems engineering is:

a methodical and disciplined approach for the specification, design, development, realization, technical management, operations, and retirement of a system. A system is an aggregation of system elements and enabling system elements to achieve a given purpose or to provide a needed capability. The enabling system elements provide the means for delivering a capability into service, keeping it in service, or ending its service, and may include those processes or products necessary for developing, producing, testing, deploying, and sustaining the system.

SE [systems engineering] ensures the effective development and delivery of capability through the implementation of a balanced approach with respect to cost, schedule, performance, and risk using integrated, disciplined, and consistent SE activities and processes regardless of when a program enters the acquisition life cycle. SE also enables the development of engineered resilient systems that are trusted, assured, and easily modified (agile).

SE planning, as documented in the Systems Engineering Plan (SEP), identifies the most effective and efficient path to deliver a capability, from identifying user needs and concepts through delivery and sustainment. SE event-driven technical reviews and audits assess program maturity and determine the status of the technical risks associated with cost, schedule, and performance goals.

4.4.2.4 Smaller Entities

Systems engineering as a recognized discipline is often attributed to the aerospace and defense programs in the mid-twentieth century. Many other large organizations have also embraced systems engineering and established organizational standards, such as described above for the U.S. Department of Defense or NASA. However, some organizations recognize the value of systems engineering, but also consider the tradeoffs with the necessary investment. In addition, many people practice aspects of systems engineering, but would not consider themselves to be systems engineers. In many ways, smaller organizations are now at the point where many in aerospace found themselves 50 years ago—seeking common sense ways to deal with the complexity of technical programs.

As systems become larger and more complex, the control of suppliers by large systems engineering organizations, largely composed of small and micro organizations, is critical to the success of their work. Small and micro organizations are involved in schemes such as extended enterprise, groups of enterprises, and participation in innovation platforms. These schemes often induce profound organizational and cultural changes and the adoption of new engineering methodologies.

4.4.3 Understanding Systems Engineers

It takes training and years of experience to become a solid systems engineer. Systems engineers usually start out with a Baccalaureate or equivalent-level degree in an established engineering branch—mechanical, electrical/electronic, civil, or the like. For many, the next step involves meeting jurisdictional qualifications, such as registration, certification, or licensure by a state, provincial, or national body. Then there is the extensive training and experience required to develop systems engineering capabilities, including the possible pursuit of professional certification from an organization such as INCOSE. Many individuals pursue graduate or doctoral degrees in systems engineering. So unlike the program manager role, systems engineers share a common foundational knowledge associated with engineering and engineering management principles. Some systems engineers may have extensive exposure to their discipline without opportunities to develop broader management experience. This isolated professional development may contribute to unproductive tension with program managers.

As with program managers, stakeholders may not fully understand or appreciate the role of a systems engineer. That lack of understanding may be further exacerbated by the fact that the definition of systems engineering is more variable than that for program management, and the systems engineer role is less well defined in many organizations than that of the program manager.

4.5 Why Divergence Is Such a Problem

Professional disciplines demand ongoing professional development. Generally, such learning takes place only within the context of the isolated discipline. As each focuses on developing professionally within their respective fields, the danger is that they will continuously take a narrow view that only sees possible solutions through their respective lenses. These isolated mindsets have occurred in many technical programs, and the result has been lack of cooperation and integrated approaches to agreed solutions. Each often sees the solution differently, which can lead to unproductive tension regarding the optimal solution. As illustrated in Figure 4-4, each discipline often focuses on the solution from its own perspective without collaboration toward the optimal solution.

One of the dimensions investigated in the Phase I research was the level of unproductive tension that existed between the two disciplines. Survey respondents rated the degree to which unproductive tension between program managers and system engineers existed in their organization.

Creating a stream of benefits from a program requires ongoing integration of contributions from a team of individuals from various specialized domains. The degree of specialization and diversity of sources only increases as the program and associated benefits become more complex. Each specialized knowledge domain brings a different

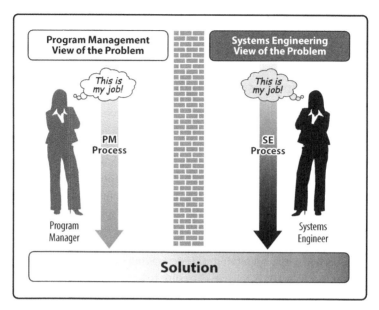

Figure 4-4: The current view of the application of program management and systems engineering to developing a solution

and distinct perspective regarding the solution to the problem to be solved. This diversity of disciplinary perspectives creates tension within programs, particularly as the different perspectives come together and clash in the back-and-forth exchange of ideas. This tension can be productive if it forces the different disciplines to share, collaborate, create common understanding, and make tradeoffs in the pursuit of a common set of solutions. Innovation often results from the collision of different perspectives as new ideas are introduced as possible solutions to a challenging problem. However, the tension can become unproductive if, rather than seeking a joint solution, the parties retreat into the security of their own perspectives, dig in, and reinforce themselves with their own facts about why they are right. Such approaches create battles with others to establish whose perspective is the superior one and which perspective will ultimately lead to the preferred solution.

The Phase I research (Conforto et al., 2013) explored this concept of unproductive tension in respondents' organizations without providing a specific definition of unproductive tension to ensure the capture of all perceptions of the tension and its causes. Individuals were asked about the extent to which they had experienced unproductive tension between program managers and chief systems engineers. Fortunately, the majority of respondents said they did not experience significant levels of unproductive tension and 19% indicated they experienced no unproductive tension at all. However, 29% of respondents said they had experienced some or significant unproductive tension in the relationship between program managers and

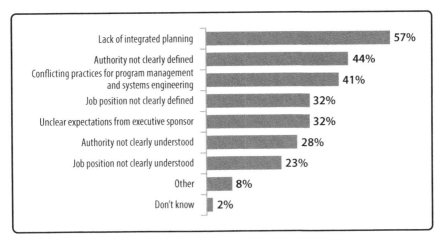

Figure 4-5: The perceived sources of unproductive tension between program managers and chief systems engineers
Conforto et al., 2013

chief systems engineers. Among the factors rated by respondents (n=177), three key factors stood out as sources of unproductive tension: lack of integrated planning, authority not clearly defined, and conflicting practices for program management and systems engineering (see Figure 4-5).

4.5.1 Lack of Integrated Planning

A lack of integrated planning was most often cited as a contributor to unproductive tension. Disjointed planning creates tension when systems engineering is engaged after key program elements have become formalized. For example, studies of federal programs by the U.S. Government Accountability Office (GAO) found that some federal acquisition rules restrict the application of systems engineering until program requirements have been established and approved (GAO, 2001; GAO, 2015). Often, by the time systems engineering is engaged and identifies issues with the documented requirements, convincing the program manager and program team to make significant changes to requirements creates conflict over the impact to cost, schedule, and program performance. The most recent GAO (2015) report highlighted that challenge:

> Another service chief stated that requirement changes made during weapon system development are often viewed as sacrificing capability rather than reconciling requirements with operational conditions. The chief was concerned that program managers too often take the view that requirements cannot be changed and avoid elevating problems to leadership before they become critical, forgoing the opportunity to make needed trade-offs (p. 18).

The view that requirements cannot be changed and that there can be no negotiation on possible tradeoffs not only affects collaboration between program managers and chief systems engineers, it also produces waste that negatively impacts program cost, schedule, and performance. Engineering programs inside and outside of the government sector have significant, unnecessary tension attributable to ineffective planning, inaccurate requirements, and lack of collaboration and trust. For example, needed tradeoffs, such as using existing, stable technology rather than relying on technology that is being developed, could keep a program on schedule and within budget parameters while still delivering mission-critical capabilities. But, if there can be no negotiation over the original requirements, the program may experience significant cost and schedule overruns trying to stabilize the new technology developed based on the requirements.

The GAO (2015) report went on to identify how organizational culture can contribute to unproductive tension. The report stated:

> We have found in prior work that characteristics of DOD's [U.S. Department of Defense] processes and incentives create pressure to push for unrealistic defense system requirements and lead to poor decisions and mismatches between requirements and resources. This culture has become ingrained over several decades and a number of studies and reforms have been directed at changing the incentives underlying the culture, without much success (p. 19).

4.5.2 Authority Not Clearly Defined

The second primary source of unproductive tension was associated with unclear definition of authority. Figure 4-6 presents the comparison of program manager's (n=469) and chief systems engineer's (n=356) self-reported responses about their respective roles and the extent to which their roles and the authority associated with each role are defined.

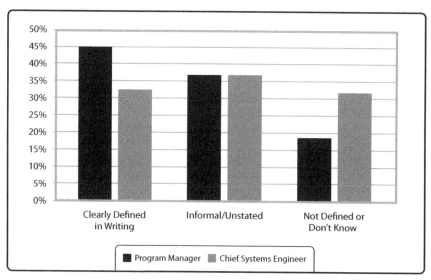

Figure 4-6: Definition of roles: A comparison between program managers and chief systems engineers
Conforto et al., 2013

Nearly half of the program managers interviewed declared that they have roles and responsibilities defined in written form compared with only one-third of chief systems engineers. Written position descriptions and defined roles are critical organizational enablers because they specify such things as:

- Areas of accountability specific to the role
- Level of authority to make decisions, commit resources, and so on
- Required competencies for the role
- Supervisory or personnel management and leadership responsibilities

Chief systems engineers were significantly more likely to report experiencing unproductive tension than were program managers, attributing the tension to unclear expectations and authority associated with roles within the program. This may result from ambiguity and uncertainty surrounding the relationships between the two functions. Decision making in an environment of ambiguity and uncertainty is a key concept in decision theory. Decision theory states that in situations of uncertainty, decisions tend to be biased and referential (Kahneman & Tversky, 1979). Rather than using an absolute reference to evaluate alternatives, options are assessed from a known or familiar state. In a strong discipline-based environment, the clearest reference point from which to make a decision is established by professional identity, which includes the knowledge base of the practitioners and the influence upon their knowledge by the standards, certifications, tools, and so on defined by the professional organizations within the discipline (Rebentisch, Townsend, & Conforto, 2015). Further, these decision processes are part of a process that is affected by factors such as perceived influence, representation, participation, power, and other factors not entirely in the control of individual disciplines. It is not surprising, then, that the reported primary sources of unproductive tension between program managers and systems engineers link back to uncertainty in the context of shared decisions and responsibilities.

4.5.3 Conflicting Practices for Program Management and Systems Engineering

The third key contributor to unproductive tension is misaligned practices. Many programs, particularly large-scale programs lasting multiple years, are like independent businesses. These businesses have executives that lead them; governance that provides oversight; dedicated resources to do the work; and financing, supply chains, and so on that help the business operate and produce things of value. Like any business, programs establish their own unique culture and approaches to managing the work. When the approaches to managing the work are informal, the connection points across the organization—whether departments or teams—may become misaligned in the absence of documented processes or practices. Similarly, when program teams do not collaborate on development of a common program methodology, each discipline may use practices, processes, and techniques specific to the discipline. As the integration study uncovered, many program managers and chief systems engineers use third-party standards in their work, but the practice is not universal. For example, over half of chief systems engineers reported using INCOSE's (2015) *Systems Engineering Handbook*.

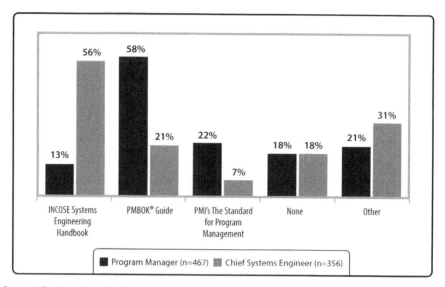

Figure 4-7: Use of standards by program managers and chief systems engineers
Conforto et al., 2013

Over half of program managers reported using PMI's (2013b) *A Guide to the Project Management Body of Knowledge (PMBOK® Guide)* and less than a quarter (22%) used *The Standard for Program Management* (PMI, 2013a).

In some instances, a specific discipline reported using more than one standard. Chief systems engineers, for example, reported using INCOSE's *Systems Engineering Handbook*, as well as guidelines from IEEE, government agency handbooks, and ISO standards. The study found that while the two disciplines in some organizations cross-referenced standards in each domain, that approach is more the exception than the rule as shown in Figure 4-7 (Conforto et al., 2013):

The program manager and chief systems engineer have unique responsibilities they must fulfill. The integration study found general agreement about elements of those responsibilities. The study also found that there were several areas where responsibilities were shared, such as life cycle planning, risk management, supplier relations, and quality management (see Figure 4-8). In those shared spaces, when each discipline approaches the responsibility from its own perspective, there can be duplicative work, critical gaps that can affect program performance, or conflicting work efforts. For example, if technical, stakeholder, organizational, and environmental risks are approached from an individual perspective instead of an integrated approach, key program-level risks could be missed or ignored.

In addition to the survey findings, in-depth interviews with program managers and chief systems engineers revealed more details associated with their experiences with unproductive tension. The most common themes from the in-depth interviews exploring the causes of unproductive tension included:

- Failing to communicate and establish a common set of objectives shared by all
- Individuals/groups focusing on achieving objectives defined by their own discipline identity and/or processes

Program Managers view their responsibilities as:	Chief Systems Engineers view their responsibilities as:	Both roles are responsible for:
• Overall results • Goals and objectives • Program and project risk • External supplier relations • Life cycle planning	• Technical requirements • Systems definition • Systems requirements • Configuration management	• Program/project risk • External supplier relations • Quality management • Life cycle planning

Figure 4-8: Reported responsibilities of program managers and chief systems engineers
Conforto et al., 2013

■ Being unable to work together to achieve the desired outcome
■ Not valuing others' roles and contributions to achieving the desired outcome

Without active approaches to develop and maintain an integrative and collaborative team, unproductive tension becomes a natural outcome of bringing different disciplines together.

4.6 Integrating Is Difficult, but Not Impossible

Program managers and chief systems engineers each have unique but intertwined roles to play in successful program outcomes. Viewed exclusively from their own professional identities, capabilities, and methods, the need to work together may not be apparent. They each have their own discipline-based measures of what problems have highest priority along with associated rewards. Sometimes their respective roles are not well-defined and may even be in conflict with one another. The opportunities and rationales for them not working together closely are manifold, and the result can be unproductive tension, or worse.

One might conclude from the forgoing that the solution for effective integration is to combine the roles of program manager and chief systems engineer into one role. As will be seen in subsequent chapters, this may introduce problems of its own. In addition, combining work tasks under one individual does not scale well and, in the final analysis, does not really solve the issue of unproductive tension across the organization. Even if these two roles are combined, there is still the need to integrate at the component level for the multiple projects undertaken as part of the program. Therefore, one must find a way to promote integration across the organization.

Integration of roles entails a mindset change for individual employees and changes to processes and procedures for the organization. The latter may require a change to organizational culture, which comes with its own set of issues as will be considered in Chapter 15. For individual employees, the change requires that program managers and chief systems engineers first understand the roles of each discipline as discussed above, and then embrace the overall goal of improved technical program performance and each practitioner's ability to contribute to that goal. Further, each must find ways to apply the specialized knowledge of their respective disciplines in a way that works to produce a sum greater than the parts. This requires vision beyond the task at hand and can prove to be extremely difficult because it requires developing new ways of looking at the challenges—a task that forces new patterns of thinking.

As the case studies in this book show, the benefits of integration far outweigh the effort required to integrate the disciplines. The payoff can be large. But it is not necessary to move from minimal integration to full integration in one step. Change begins with the first step and is sustained by determining to press on with the next step even when the going gets tough.

4.7 Discussion Questions

1. How do you define program management? How has your understanding changed as a result of reading this chapter?
2. How do you define systems engineering? How has your understanding changed as a result of reading this chapter?
3. Evaluating your organization, where do you see examples of unproductive tension? What specific steps might be taken to change this unproductive tension into productive tension?
4. Where have you seen successful integration of the disciplines of program management and systems engineering in your organization? Describe the situation and note the examples of integration and how integration helped achieve positive results.
5. In your own words, write a brief business proposal for your manager justifying the value of investing in better integration within your organization.

4.8 References

Association for Project Management (APM). (2012). *APM body of knowledge* (6th ed.). Buckinghamshire, England: Author.

AXELOS. (2011). *Managing successful programmes*. Norwich, England: Stationery Office.

Conforto, E. C., Rossi, M., Rebentisch, E., Oehmen, J., & Pacenza, M. (2013). *Survey report: Improving integration of program management and systems engineering.* Presented at the 23rd INCOSE Annual International Symposium, Philadelphia, USA. Retrieved from www.pmi.org/~/media/PDF/Business-Solutions/Lean-Enablers/PMI-INCOSE-MIT-Integration-Study.ashx

Cooke-Davies, T. (2012, July). *Systems engineering and project management: Complementary disciplines, or competing paradigms?* Presented at the International Council on Systems Engineering International Symposium, Rome, Italy.

Government Accountability Office (GAO). (2001). *Better matching of needs and resources will lead to better weapon systems outcomes.* Retrieved from www.gao.gov/assets/160/156905.pdf

Government Accountability Office (GAO). (2015). *Acquisition process: Military service chiefs' concerns reflect need to better define requirements before programs start.* Retrieved from www.gao.gov/assets/680/670761.pdf

Honour, E. C. (1998). INCOSE: History of the International Council on Systems Engineering. *Systems Engineering 1*(1), 4–13. doi:10.1002/(SICI)1520-6858(1998)1:1 <4::AID-SYS2>3.0.CO;2-M

International Council on Systems Engineering (INCOSE). (n.d.). Retrieved from www.incose.org/AboutSE

International Council on Systems Engineering (INCOSE). (2015). *Systems engineering handbook: A guide for system life cycle processes and activities* (4th ed.). D. Walden, G. Roedler, K. Forsberg, R. Hamelin, T. Shortell (Eds.). Hoboken, NJ: John Wiley & Sons.

International Council on Systems Engineering UK (INCOSE UK). (2010, March). *Z6: Systems engineering competency framework.* Issue 1.0. Series editor Hazel Woodcock.

International Organization for Standardization (ISO). (2010). *ISO/IEC/IEEE 24765:2010, Systems and software engineering: Vocabulary.* Geneva, Switzerland: Author.

International Organization for Standardization (ISO). (2012). *ISO 21500:2012, Guidance on project management.* Geneva, Switzerland: Author.

International Organization for Standardization (ISO). (2015a). *ISO 21504:2015, Project, programme and portfolio management: Guidance on portfolio management.* Geneva, Switzerland: Author.

International Organization for Standardization (ISO). (2015b). *ISO/IEC/IEEE 15288: 2015, Systems and software engineering: System life cycle processes.* Geneva, Switzerland: Author.

International Project Management Association (IPMA). (n.d.). *IPMA history.* Retrieved from www.ipma.world/about/ipma-history/

International Project Management Association (IPMA). (2013). *IPMA Organisational competence baseline: The standard for moving organisations forward.* Zurich, Switzerland: Author.

Kahneman, D., & Tversky, A. (1979). Prospect theory: An analysis of decision under risk. *Econometrica, 47*(2), 263–292. doi:10.2307/1914185

Kowalski, C. (2015, March 23). *INCOSE News.* Retrieved from www.incose.org/newsevents/news/2015/03/24/iso-iec-ieee-15288-2015-update

Langley, M., Robitaille, S., & Thomas, J. (2011). Toward a new mindset: Bridging the gap between program management and systems engineering. *PM Network, 25*(9), 24–26.

Levitt, R. (2011). Towards project management 2.0, *Engineering Project Organization Journal, 1*(3), 197–210. doi:10.1080/21573727.2011.609558

National Aeronautics and Space Administration (NASA). (2007). *Systems engineering handbook.* Washington, D.C.: Author.

Oehmen, J., & Norman, E. (2012, May). *Applying lean principles to program management: Results from a joint study by PMI, International Council on Systems Engineering and MIT's Lean Advancement Initiative.* Presented at Project Management Institute Global Congress EMEA, Marseilles, France.

Oppenheim, B. W. (2015). *Program requirements: Complexity, myths, radical change, and lean enablers*. Retrieved from www.pmi.org/~/media/PDF/learning/project-complexity/Pgm-Reqirements.ashx

Project Management Association of Japan (PMAJ). (2014). *P2M: A guidebook of project & program management for enterprise innovation* (3rd ed.). Tokyo, Japan: Author.

Project Management Institute (PMI). (2011). *Program management professional (PgMP)®examination content outline*. Newtown Square, PA: Author.

Project Management Institute (PMI). (2013a). *The standard for program management* (3rd ed.). Newtown Square, PA: Author.

Project Management Institute (PMI). (2013b). *A guide to the project management body of knowledge (PMBOK® guide)* (5th ed.). Newtown Square, PA: Author.

Project Management Institute (PMI). (2013c). *Navigating complexity: A practice guide*. Newtown Square, PA: Author.

Project Management Institute (PMI). (2015). *The PMI lexicon of project management terms* (version 3.0). Newtown Square, PA: Author.

Rebentisch, E. S., Townsend, S., & Conforto, E. C. (2015, June). *Collaboration across linked disciplines: Skills and roles for integrating systems engineering and program management*. Presented at American Society for Engineering Education Annual Conference, Seattle, Washington, USA. Retrieved from www.asee.org/public/conferences/56/papers/12512/view

Schwalb, J. (2016). From the sponsor. *CrossTalk: The Journal of Defense Software Engineering, 29*(3). Retrieved from www.crosstalkonline.org/storage/flipbooks/2016/201605/index.html

Sopko, J. A., & Demaria, A. (2013). *How Siemens focuses on benefits to accelerate value delivery*. Presented at the 2013 PMI Global Congress, New Orleans, Louisiana.

Thiry, M. (2015). *Program management* (2nd ed.). Surrey, England: Gower Publishing Limited.

Toth, R. B. (Ed.). (1996). *Standards activities of organizations in the United States*. Retrieved from http://gsi.nist.gov/global/docs/SP%20806.pdf

United States Department of Defense. (2016). *Defense acquisition guidebook*. Retrieved from https://acc.dau.mil/CommunityBrowser.aspx?id=638295

Wikipedia. (n.d.). *Engineering management*. Retrieved from https://en.wikipedia.org/wiki/Engineering_management

Additional Resources

Forsberg, K., Mooz, H., & Cotterman, H. (2005). *Visualizing project management* (3rd ed.). Hoboken, NJ: John Wiley & Sons.

McManus, H. (2005). *Product development value stream mapping (PDVSM) manual*. Retrieved from www.metisdesign.com/docs/PDVSM_v1.pdf

Oppenheim, B. W. (2004). Lean product development flow, *Systems Engineering, 7*(4).

5

KEY CONCEPTS IN INTEGRATION

5.1 Introduction

The previous chapters discussed unproductive tension between program management and systems engineering as a natural outcome of differences between the two disciplines, and a core challenge to program success. They also showed that organizations with greater levels of integration between these two disciplines exhibited dramatically lower levels of unproductive tension. Integration also plays an important role in program performance beyond just unproductive tension, which will be discussed in greater depth in subsequent chapters. However, up to this point the understanding of integration remains relatively superficial.

This chapter takes a closer look at the concept and meaning of integration. It explores integration between program management and systems engineering from multiple perspectives. It uses evidence from the research to explore what this type of integration looks like in practice, including from the practitioner's perspective. This leads to a formal definition of integration that will be used throughout the rest of the book.

5.2 Assessing Integration between Disciplines

The Phase I study of program managers and chief systems engineers explored the state of integration between program management and systems engineering. That study was exploratory and its objective was to better understand how the program management and systems engineering disciplines are integrated within organizations. The exploratory study would eventually lead to more detailed and focused research to test factors and relationships related to integration. The study and its place in the overall research that informs this book was explained in greater detail in the Introduction.

Two questions from the Phase I study were particularly relevant to this discussion of integration. The first question asked respondents about the level of integration between program management and systems engineering in their organization. The possible responses were *Fully integrated*, *Mostly integrated*, *Somewhat integrated*, or

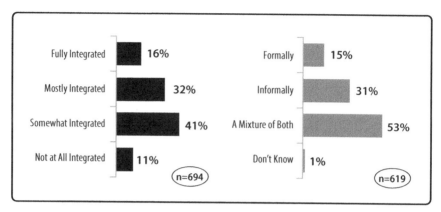

Figure 5-1: Degree of integration between program management and systems engineering, and the formality of the integration approach
Conforto, Rossi, Rebentisch, Oehmen, & Pacenza, 2013

Not at all integrated. The second question asked whether integration occurred formally (defined processes transcend the boundaries across the job position) or informally (it falls upon individuals to make the integration occur) in their organization. The possible responses were *Formally, Informally, A mixture of both,* or *Don't know.* Because the survey was exploratory, the wording of the questions was general rather than using precise language to define integration and the formality of integration processes.

Figure 5-1 shows that roughly half the respondents indicated that their organizations had either fully or mostly integrated the program management and systems engineering disciplines. Or, viewed in the negative, about half of the respondents indicated that their organizations exhibited either somewhat or no integration at all between the roles of program managers and systems engineers. Only about one in six of the respondents indicated that their organization had fully integrated the program management and systems engineering disciplines.

Figure 5-1 also shows that about half the responses were drawn from organizations that use a combination of formal and informal approaches to integrate between program management and systems engineering. The proportion of formal and informal integration approaches in organizations that use a mixture of both is unknown, so it is not clear how much the organizations relied on individual initiative versus formally sanctioned and supported methods to integrate the program management and systems engineering disciplines. Only about one in six of the respondents committed to the description that their organization used a formal approach to integrating the roles of program managers and chief systems engineers. The distribution of responses to both questions is strikingly similar, suggesting that integration and using a formalized approach to integration are related.

What does this mean? The responses indicate that the majority of organizations are using a mix of formal and informal processes for integration. The majority of organizations are also integrated to some degree. This result may be an artifact of the way the questions were asked in the survey, but it is not particularly surprising. Most organizations that are sophisticated enough to have formally defined program manager and chief systems engineer positions will likely have some degree of formalized processes for them to work together, and if they are competitive in their respective markets they will likely have some degree of successful integration of the disciplines.

The story becomes more interesting by looking at the trends in the responses. Statistical analysis showed with a high level of significance that the formality of the approach to integration is related to the degree of integration achieved between program management and systems engineering. Using an informal approach to integration results in a correspondingly declining degree of integration. Organizations that took an *informal* approach to integration were three times more likely to be only *somewhat integrated* than those that used a *formal* approach to integration. Conversely, using the *formal* approach to integration results in a correspondingly increasing degree of integration. Organizations that took a *formal* approach to integration were six times more likely to be *fully integrated* than those that used an *informal* approach to integration. The difference in effects is shown graphically in Figure 5-2. In other words, the organizations that were deliberately trying to integrate the roles of their program managers and chief systems engineers were more likely to have fully integrated them. Not surprisingly, the organizations that used informal approaches to integration and were able to fully integrate their program management and systems engineering disciplines were quite rare.

Using a formal or deliberate approach to integration is important for actually becoming more integrated. What does using a formal approach mean, exactly, when it comes to integrating program management and systems engineering? One way to answer that question is to view this from the perspective of process maturity.

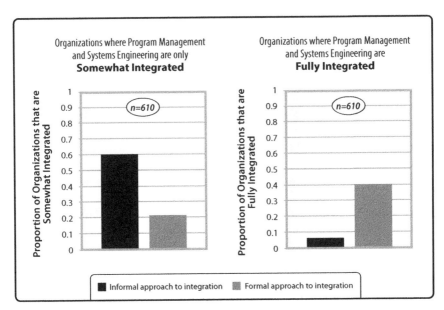

Figure 5-2: More formal or deliberate approaches to integration of program management and systems engineering result in higher levels of integration

Conforto et al., 2013

Process maturity models assume that processes are more likely to produce valuable outcomes as they become more formalized and managed. One commonly used maturity framework is Capability Maturity Model Integration (CMMI, 2010), which defines a process maturity through a spectrum ranging from 1 (Initial—processes unpredictable, poorly controlled, and reactive) to 3 (Defined—processes characterized for the organization and is proactive) to 5 (Optimizing—focus on continuous process improvement). Note that the higher maturity levels are associated with examination and active management of processes.

With increasing maturity levels, processes become more defined, applied, assessed, and improved. For a formal approach to integrating program management and systems engineering, one might expect, with increasing levels of formalization, to see greater use of standards or defined processes, and more frequent and formal assessments of whether those standards are being followed. The survey collected data related to these two points. Specifically, both program manager and chief systems engineer respondents were asked whether their organization had conducted a formal assessment of its program management or systems engineering practices and capabilities, respectively, within the last three years.

The analysis of the data confirmed significantly that greater use of standards was associated with greater integration between program management and systems engineering. Additionally, those organizations with higher levels of integration of program management and systems engineering also conducted more regular assessments. Perhaps not coincidentally, larger organizations were found to be better at formally integrating program management and systems engineering. This might be explained by larger organizations having more resources (typically "overhead" functions) to dedicate to establishing and maintaining formalized processes. Larger organizations may also need to formalize process and structure for management control, while smaller organizations may not perceive a need for formalization because they need to be agile and can rely on the experience embodied in particular responsible employees. Smaller organizations in the sample were relatively more likely to use informal or combinations of formal and informal approaches to integration.

As was the case with the level of formalization of the approach to integration, the analysis showed that organizations that had conducted formal assessments of their practices and capabilities within the prior three years exhibited higher levels of integration between program management and systems engineering. Organizations that did not conduct a formal assessment of their practices and capabilities within the prior three years were 50% more likely to be only *somewhat integrated* than those that did. Conversely, those organizations that did conduct a formal assessment of their practices and capabilities within the prior three years were almost three times more likely to be *fully integrated* than those that did not. The difference in effects is shown graphically in Figure 5-3. Note that only the analysis of the program manager responses is shown in Figure 5-3, but the results mirror the analysis of the chief systems engineers' responses.

The measures used in this initial exploration of the current state of integration were somewhat generalized. Key variables such as *integration* and *formalized* were not extensively defined for the respondents, nor were there multiple perspectives or measures of those key elements. Because this could result in potentially unreliable conclusions,

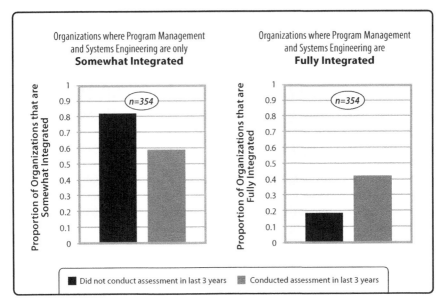

Figure 5-3: More frequent assessments of discipline processes and capabilities correlate to achieving higher levels of integration
Conforto et al., 2013

additional data were needed to triangulate and refine the definitions of these key factors in integration, as well as others related to them. This in turn prompted the additional investigation that unfolded through interviews and an additional survey. Additionally, literature from organization theory scholars was reviewed to learn what they have written about integration in complex organizations. The section that follows summarizes that investigation.

5.3 Attributes of Integration in Complex Organizations

The most appropriate generic definition of integration is "the act of combining or adding parts to make a unified whole" (HarperCollins, 2014). This definition is well suited to the combination and alignment of systems engineering, program management, and perhaps other functions in order to make a program more successful. But the same definition could also be applied to a worker building an automobile transmission, a political leader unifying scattered portions of a nation, or a child completing a puzzle. A more precise understanding of what is meant by integration in the context of complex and specialized organizations would help in creating a useful definition of integration for this book.

There are few existing studies of the integration of program management and systems engineering that define in a rigorous and detailed way the attributes and methods of effective integration of those disciplines. To gain deeper insight into the nature of integration in complex organizations one must turn to related areas of knowledge.

The field of organization theory has a rich history that includes work directly relevant to this exploration. Scholars may not have necessarily focused on integration as defined here, but their work has explored how organizations coordinate efforts across disciplines under various conditions using different approaches. As such, their findings illustrate the variety of ways that integration might be expressed in organizations and can help to bring focus to this discussion.

Thought leaders in organizational theory seek to explain how organizations function and, as a constantly evolving field of study that has existed over decades, have produced a number of explanations and approaches to organizational analysis. While these explanations are often referred to as theories, in many cases they represent ideas and understanding that is developed within a community of like-minded researchers. As such, they may not have the same formality of theories one would find in, say, the natural sciences or even other social sciences such as economics. Furthermore, they are not generally defined to the level of detail that would make them immediately useful to program managers or systems engineers, and in many cases they lack strong predictive power to say which specific outcomes might result from a set of actions. Nevertheless, they do highlight concepts that can help to frame this discussion of integration, and particularly point to areas of organizations and their processes that might be important to integration. For this book it isn't necessary to include an extensive survey of the field. Consequently, what follows is not a comprehensive overview of organizational theory, but rather selected examples that are most helpful to inform the exploration of integration in this book.

One of the earliest movements to characterize and understand how organizations conduct work was scientific management, frequently associated with Fredrick Taylor (1917) and management experts in lab coats with stopwatches shadowing workers and analyzing their movements in great detail. The focus of scientific management was to use systematic observation and analysis to improve labor productivity via process improvement. The underlying assumption was that work could be improved through the application of scientific methods using controlled experiments to the benefit of both workers and the organization. Scientific management theories addressed integration broadly through standardization and formalization of work, with measurement and feedback learning for process improvement that resulted in the design of work, methods, and processes to enable more efficient production. By deploying standardized work definitions with explicitly defined goals, experts (or, eventually, the workers themselves) could improve and optimize processes and significantly improve outcomes.

Unfortunately, the aspirations of the scientific management movement were not fully realized, in part due to the complexity of organizations, even at that time, and the social, economic, and political dynamics within organizations that were not well addressed by the early practitioners. Consequently, scientific management was viewed negatively in some circles, a perception that has largely persisted to the present. Its overall impact should not be underestimated, though. A contemporary of Taylor, Henry Gantt, along with the scientific management movement and its adherents, helped in the creation of such fields as industrial engineering, quality, human factors, operations management, and more recently six sigma and lean management. A number of these fields in turn indirectly or directly influenced the foundations of the program management and systems engineering disciplines.

Max Weber (1947), a pioneering organization theorist who was strongly influenced by Taylor and the scientific management movement, eventually developed what came to be known as bureaucratic theory. Bureaucracies were seen as a remedy to human idiosyncrasies (e.g., inconsistency, self-interested behavior, cronyism) that undermine an organization's ability to achieve its goals efficiently or effectively. Bureaucracies enable the management of integration by supporting the creation of formal organization-based offices, roles, and rules that govern who makes decisions, allocates resources, and how people interact. These require formal training and, therefore, represent the rise of professional expertise, certification, and codes of conduct. Bureaucracies are maintained by a clearly defined governance hierarchy that delineates the roles and reporting relationships.

Seen in these terms, bureaucracy sounds like an ideal solution to the challenges of unproductive tension discussed in the previous chapter. Bureaucracy, however, is often a pejorative label that has become associated with bloated, inefficient, and unresponsive organizations that appear to respond more to their own needs than those of their stakeholders. This may be explained in part because, with the formal definition of the rules, roles, relationships, and the like bureaucracy can easily be expanded (or scaled up) to address situations outside of those for which it was originally designed. If a standard solution that can be replicated easily in a new setting is not tailored to that context, the result will likely be an organization mismatched with its context that appears inflexible and unresponsive. Bureaucracies are process-oriented and tend to be most effective when tasks are routine and the environment in which the organization functions is predictable, but begin to falter when there is a lot of novelty, variety, and uncertainty.

The human relations movement emerged in part in response to some of the negative experiences of the scientific management work rationalization efforts. Its most notable foundations are from studies conducted by Mayo and Roethlisberger at the Hawthorne Works that launched the term "Hawthorne effect," a term that describes how individuals change their behavior in response to their perception of being given special attention (Mayo, 1933). The human relations movement examined the effects of social relations, motivation, and employee satisfaction on their productivity. Rather than employees being seen as merely commodity labor, the employees' psychology and fit with their organization were perceived as key factors in how productive they were. By improving interpersonal skills, communication, and motivation, workplace productivity was expected to improve. From this perspective, integration is influenced by how people in organizations interact with one another and how the organization encourages their participation and mental and emotional well-being. This includes how they are motivated (i.e., through the work itself, its design, recognition of their contributions, and, to some extent, the conditions under which they work), which impacts their level of engagement and contributions to successful outcomes.

Barnard (1968) later defined an important role for executives to create an appropriate organizational climate with clear and consistent values and purpose to help improve employee satisfaction and productivity. The human relations movement led directly or indirectly to disciplines such as organizational development, industrial and organizational psychology, and human resource management.

Adherents to contingency theory tried to overcome perceived limitations in previous movements that did not adequately describe how management style and organizational structure were influenced by the organization's environment. Integration is defined as "the process of achieving unity of effort among the various subsystems in the accomplishment of the organization's task" (Lawrence & Lorsch, 1967). In this theory there is no one best way to manage an organization, and the design of an organization and its subsystems must ideally "fit" with the environment and with themselves in the organization. Integration holds a defining position in this field since organizational fit with its environment is addressed by how its various elements relate to one another. Among the contingencies that must be considered when tailoring the organization response are structure, leadership, technology, and uncertainty.

According to contingency theorists, another contributor to overall organization effectiveness is management's ability to adapt to environmental changes. In rapidly changing environments managers must have the authority and the freedom to make decisions as required to adapt to the situation at hand. Organizational leaders can also improve fit with the environment and overall effectiveness by adjusting the alignment between the task structure and the leadership approach, and by using training to improve leader–member relations (Fiedler, 1964).

Organizational climate and organizational culture are related concepts intended to help identify elements of the work environment that significantly influence employee behavior. Organizational culture is generally considered to encompass the system of beliefs, values, and attitudes shared by people in an organization (Schein, 1992). It may include policies, rules, organization structure, and shared rituals and routines, and is potentially influenced by the product and process technologies used in the organization and by its competitive and industrial environment. Deal and Kennedy (1982) argue that organizational culture can be seen as the way that employees know how things get done successfully in their workplace.

Integration is addressed by utilizing the concept of organizational culture through the combination of elements that frame the perceptions, decisions, and actions that help people to work together more effectively. The promise of a single, strong, and cohesive organizational culture is that it helps its employees to share goals across critical boundaries, be more committed to working together toward common objectives, understand what to do when the situation is uncertain, promote more group cohesion and capability around solving problems and learning, and improve clarity around the "big picture" for the organization.

More than one unified, homogenous organizational culture may exist in organizations, which can be a source of challenges to integration. Schein (1996) identified three subcultures or occupational communities, the "operator culture," the "engineering culture," and the "executive culture," that can lead one to misunderstand another's values and objectives and can consequently cause individuals to work at cross purposes.

The executive culture and the engineering culture are significantly influenced by their respective external reference groups (occupational communities of like-minded and -trained professionals, e.g., engineering professional societies or academic disciplines). These external reference groups define value systems outside of the organization and can contribute to conflicts about how to solve problems or even how to communicate. While a strong core knowledge base enables each subculture to operate effectively and efficiently in its own domain, possible misalignment between them can result in failures of organizational learning, diffusion of innovations, and inability to change and grow at the organization level.

The term "organization" implies a coordination of activities in order to achieve an outcome that is better than could be accomplished by individual elements operating separately. Integration is an integral characteristic of organizations and has been a central part of theories about organizations for nearly a century. This review of different organizational theories has drawn highlights from the major movements in the field to identify themes that can be used to help refine the working definition of integration being developed in this chapter. It also highlights the multiple facets of integrative behavior that operate in a complex organization.

Integration in Project Management and Systems Engineering

Research specifically on project management and systems engineering has identified principles similar to those from the review of organization theory. While this research was focused on the project domain, it nevertheless provides relevant information applicable to the program domain. Eisner (2008) characterizes a high degree of integration between project management and systems engineering by:

1. Strong and effective teams
2. Commitment to "getting the job done"
3. Deep interest in the technical issues
4. Constructive problem solving
5. Corporate support for the needs of the project
6. Little or no complaining
7. Short and productive meetings
8. Rapid flow of information
9. Effective computer support
10. Involved and happy people

Eisner argues that integration can be realized on different complementary levels: managers, teams, plans, the systems approach, methods and standards, information systems, and enterprises can act as integrators. These characteristics of integration between project management and systems engineering tend to focus on behaviors and observable outcomes and do not address the integration of the work itself—how tasks are structured and performed. That criticism could also be levied against organizational and management theories. Nevertheless, the similarities between these characteristics and those found in organizational theory and in the case studies presented so far are confirmatory regarding the general characteristics and attributes to be emphasized in defining the integration between program management and systems engineering disciplines.

5.3.1 Insights from the Different Perspectives on Integration

Organizational theorists explain integration from a number of different perspectives. Because of the diversity of organizational types and instances, theories about them are often general in nature. They do not typically have the detail that is characteristic of program management or systems engineering practices. Indeed, they are often so general that they are sometimes characterized as "good leadership" or "good management." Nevertheless, the ideas and relationships covered by these theories can still help to create a richer and more useful definition of integration. The most important elements of those theories for this purpose are:

- Work toward clear and coherent goals.
- Define and standardize tasks.
- Tailor the coordination approach to the type of task being performed.
- Define roles and create professionalism through training, codes of conduct, and so on.
- Develop interpersonal skills, communication, and motivation to enable better coordination.
- Define leader decision authorities to encompass all relevant tasks and span boundaries.
- Guide decisions and behavior under uncertainty through shared beliefs, values, and attitudes.

5.4 Practitioner Perspectives on Integration

To ground attributes of integration in complex organizations, professionals with program management and systems engineering backgrounds were asked about their experience with integration during their careers and in their current organizations.

Program managers and chief systems engineers from a number of organizations around the world were interviewed subsequent to their participation in the Phase I research. These follow-up interviews were completed to clarify how program managers and systems engineers interpreted and understood concepts like integration, unproductive tension, and the approaches used in their organizations to improve the level of integration between program management and systems engineering. Because they had participated in the Phase I study, they currently filled the role of program manager, chief systems engineer, or both.

The interviews included professionals who had indicated in the survey that their organizations had either high or low levels of unproductive tension. The two levels of unproductive tension were sampled in order to gain a more complete perspective on how integration does or does not work in organizations. Because there is such a strong negative correlation between integration and unproductive tension—the higher the level of integration, the lower the level of unproductive tension between program management and systems engineering—the level of unproductive tension serves as a useful indicator of integration in these organizations. The interview questions focused on integration, integration practices, unproductive tension and its sources, and other issues related to the way the two disciplines worked together in the organization. A description of the interview methods was presented in the introduction.

The full set of interview responses were reviewed and used to develop expanded definitions of integration and unproductive tension, and to draft a framework to explain how integration between program management and systems engineering works in organizations. A sample of the responses from the interviews are presented in this section from the perspective both of what is happening when program managers and systems engineers are working together in an integrated fashion and when they are not.

5.4.1 Descriptions of Integration from Low Unproductive Tension Settings

What do the interactions between program management and systems engineering look like when things are working well? These quotes from both chief systems engineers and program managers illustrate some of the different aspects of integration from the perspective of organizations where the two disciplines work together with low levels of unproductive tension. They describe how the individual experiences integration between chief systems engineers and program managers in their organization. They are drawn from a small exploratory interview sample and are provided here to illustrate practitioners' experiences with integration. While they illustrate what worked in one organization, they do not necessarily imply that the same approach to integration would apply in all settings and circumstances.

Here is what some of the respondents reported about different aspects of the relationship between the program management and systems engineering disciplines in their organizations:

> They have shared goals. They are responsible for the whole project success. They have results to achieve.... There is not really conflict there, it is only about how you can make it happen. It is a matter of good leadership; it is people working together to make things work. It requires leadership—don't ask a follower to lead!
>
> —*Program manager, engineering consulting, U.S.A.*

> Integration is being in an environment where you will be working collaboratively, with common goals, and motivated by the same indicators of performance of the project.... The program manager and the head of engineering working side by side, reporting to a program director responsible for the overall integration of these disciplines.
>
> —*Systems engineer, shipbuilding, Europe*

> Integration is something very natural. Every project is technical, so it's about the systems engineering. We teach all the systems engineering concepts to the program manager. They are integrated because they are not considered separated. The program manager is responsible to deliver the program on cost and schedule but also responsible to deliver a proper system that meets the needs.

The program management team is accountable for all of those aspects. There is no division of duties or disciplines.

—*Chief systems engineer, U.S. government agency*

We see integration as "arising naturally from the nature of the work itself." It's then divided into professional roles to be executed. We put the project first then the roles and individual perspectives follow.

—*Chief systems engineer, commercial products, U.S.A.*

Both professionals have to understand the others' perspective. A work package that seems correct from the program manager's perspective also must be feasible from the systems engineer's perspective.

—*Systems engineer, engineering services, U.S.A.*

We typically have engineers who become systems engineers. We also have engineers that became program managers, who are more responsible for cost, schedule, and related aspects to the program. They are all located in the same office. They work together to accomplish the same goals. They are only "one team." The interactions between the program manager and the systems engineer are very frequent.

—*Portfolio manager, information systems, U.S.A.*

From a strict perspective systems engineering should be the arm of the program that directly translates the program management objectives into technical engineering actions. When a program manager sets a budget baseline and integrates the master schedule and master plan, the systems engineering group should be the one that takes ownership of the system level goals and implements the technical side on behalf of the program manager.

—*Chief systems engineer, aerospace, U.S.A.*

5.4.2 Descriptions of Integration from High Unproductive Tension Settings

The following quotes, primarily from chief systems engineers, are drawn from the interviews that focused on organizations that had high levels of unproductive tension. They illustrate how the program management and systems engineering disciplines operate in these organizations when the working relationship is challenged.

[There could be] a conflict of interest between program manager and systems engineer. We had a project where it was not possible to meet the customer's budget for executing the project. We tried to cut cost. We reviewed the requirements, reduced or simplified some requirements in order to meet the customer's budget. Then, the program manager didn't accept any of the proposals; the design that was proposed was more important than meeting the requirements.

—*Systems engineer, aerospace, Europe*

As you get driven to smaller teams to be more cost efficient, nimble, you still have to have a very strong program manager and systems engineer roles. Management often demands that a single individual does both roles. That is a recipe for trouble with just one person doing both roles. That person can be very good at setting customer expectations, talking to them, defining needs, selling, etc., but he or she will need a different set of skills to communicate all this information to the team.

—Program manager and chief systems engineer, precision instruments, U.S.A.

One problem is when you have a program management team that does not use systems engineering to implement the technical and programmatic requirements and simply focuses on managing the business side of the program and leaves the product teams that are doing the different subsystems to own the major technical programmatic goals.

—Chief systems engineer, aerospace, U.S.A.

[Y]ou fail to give systems engineering the ability to control the process. You give systems engineering a small domain of activities, some requirements, and don't force the product development teams to accept the leadership role of systems engineering. The problem is lack of authority and responsibility for the systems engineer and lack of use of systems engineering group to implement the programmatic objectives.

—Chief systems engineer, aerospace, U.S.A.

Systems engineering has been viewed by the management as almost a "fad." They had one contract for a new development program [but the scope of the contract was cut significantly]. They ramped up systems engineering to about sixty people. Before that, there was previously one other systems engineer. They are now down to twenty-five systems engineers in the company. A number of people that used to be systems engineers have moved on to other positions or jobs.

—Chief systems engineer, shipbuilding, U.S.A.

5.4.3 Comparing Perspectives on Integration

Various attributes of integration heard repeatedly across the interviews were compiled and a comparison of the attributes from organizations with greater and lesser levels of integration, respectively, are shown in Table 5-1. The characteristics and practices of organizations with greater integration are shown in the right column, while the characteristics and practices of the organizations with lesser integration are shown in the left column. Note that the text shown in Table 5-1 paraphrases the points made in the interviews rather than providing quotes, as did the previous sections.

Because Table 5-1 is constructed from analysis of the interview responses, the issues are consistent with the selected quotes in Sections 5.4.1 and 5.4.2. However, there is also consistency and overlap between the practices shown in Table 5-1 and the insights gained from organizational theory summarized in Section 5.3, and from the case

| Table 5-1: Comparison of characteristics and practices between organizations with greater and lesser integration ||
Organizations with Lesser Integration	Organizations with Greater Integration
■ Challenging to keep the same program manager and systems engineer working together from the beginning ■ Lack of process ownership, autonomy to make decisions from the systems engineering perspective ■ Conflict of interests. The program manager prioritizes schedule and cost over product aspects ■ Lack of transparency between program management and systems engineering ■ Do not understand or recognize the value of systems engineering ■ Lack of culture of integration; divergent or unclear goals and objectives ■ Cultural differences between program management and systems engineering seen as barriers ■ Lack of trust/respect for each other's discipline/role	■ Keep the same professionals working together from the proposal definition ■ The program manager is involved in the technical aspects of the program ■ Prioritize product quality, performance, then cost and schedule ■ Have the program manager and systems engineer working in the same location ■ Collaborative decision making, team-based working environment ■ Shared responsibility toward a common goal ■ Understand the differences, culture, background, and behavior of the disciplines ■ Have a good working relationship between the program manager and systems engineer

Source: Phase II and Phase III research—interview analysis.

studies discussed previously, suggesting that the interview findings are addressing practices and issues that have been identified across a wide range of studies of behavior in complex organizations spanning decades.

The interview sample used to construct this picture of integration was relatively small. This was conducted as an exploratory effort, so considerable experimentation, refinement, and validation still lies ahead. Nevertheless, based on the balance of evidence obtained so far, a useful (i.e., usable by practicing program managers and systems engineers) operational definition of integration should include these elements:

■ Program objectives, defined by overall rather than localized or discipline-based success factors, are held in common across all disciplines.

■ The program's constituent disciplines understand and commit to work toward meeting those program-level objectives with highest priority.

■ The program's constituent disciplines understand the others' roles and how they contribute to achieving the objectives.

■ The disciplines respect and defer to the others' respective roles, levels of authority, and contributions to achieving the objectives.

■ The management team actively promotes collaboration over competition within the program and with associated stakeholders.

These elements serve as a starting point to orient the reader toward a working definition of how program management and systems engineering disciplines can work together in a more effective and productive way. These elements, or practices if they are applied within a specific context, are guidelines for effective integration. They are consistent with what many would consider to be leading practices. They are not a concluding statement on how to improve integration between program management and systems engineering, although many organizations would see significant improvements if they embraced them in their operations. Rather, they are a waypoint in a journey to refining the integration concept.

The evidence collected thus far suggests that what differentiates the organizations that successfully integrate these disciplines from those that do not reaches well beyond whether they use leading practices or not. The difference is an orientation toward integration that informs the choice of a number of attributes and practices employed, the relationships and attitudes of people from top to bottom, and the skills that are rewarded in an organization. A key question is whether integration results from successfully employing a set of practices or whether it represents an orientation toward how an organization, its functional disciplines, and its people operate, and what sets of capabilities and values it develops. Part II of this book will explore these ideas in much greater detail. In the meantime, this chapter concludes with a synopsis of integration that begins to frame this exploration.

> ## Definition: Integration of Program Management and Systems Engineering
>
> Integration is a reflection of the organization's ability to combine program management and systems engineering practices, tools and techniques, experience, and knowledge in a collaborative and systematic approach in the face of challenges, in order to be more effective in achieving common goals/objectives in complex program environments.

5.5 Summary

Integrating program management and systems engineering functions in organizations can be described in terms of its outcomes—quotes from program managers and systems engineers described what happened in their organizations when integration worked and when it did not. The evidence presented showed that at least intuitively, if not explicitly, the majority of organizations are making at least some attempt to foster integration between their program managers and systems engineers. However, upon closer inspection, only a relatively small proportion of respondents reported that their organizations have fully integrated program management and systems engineering functions. This was confirmed also by the small number of organizations that committed to formal programs, resources, or methods to integrate these functions.

Part of the challenge is having as a starting point a useful, multifaceted understanding of what integration between these disciplines entails. It is more than just having and employing a set of accepted practices or standards. Integration reflects a state of an organization and its operations. As such it is not a simple concept, but rather a multidimensional indication of a number of attributes, activities, and orientations in operation within the organization. One can generate a list of practices associated with integration—many do—and such a list may be temporarily helpful, but perhaps ultimately distracting from the real work in organizations that is demanded by true integration.

One important caveat is that the discussion so far has focused on greater and lesser levels of integration and on its relationship with unproductive tension between program management and systems engineering. While it is important to establish a clear concept of integration, more important still (not least with practitioners) is whether it has a positive impact on program outcomes, including overall performance and benefits delivered. The answer to that question, not surprisingly, is that integration does positively impact program outcomes. More detailed discussion of those impacts will take place in Chapters 6 and 12.

At the conclusion of Part I of this book, the assessment is that the stakes are high—society desperately needs programs to be more successful than they are currently. In the future, the need for the programs that support and deliver these complex socio-technical systems to be successful may have societal impacts. Outcomes associated with the prevailing approaches to integrating these functions suggest that there remain significant opportunities for improvement. There are real reasons why integration is challenging, ranging from the way professionals gain, maintain, and update their skills, to the organizational environments and processes in which those professionals are engaged. The good news is that there are numerous examples of organizations that produce exceptional outcomes by operating in a more integrated fashion. They offer many lessons about how to achieve this level of performance by describing the strategies, policies, and methodologies used to achieve a higher level of integration, and thus better outcomes for the organization and its projects and programs. The following chapters will attempt to convey those lessons.

5.6 Discussion Questions

1. Which of the integration elements discussed in the chapter seem most relevant in your experience? Which are most elusive and why?
2. How would you go about gauging the level of integration between program management and systems engineering in your organization? How does your organization score on integration between these disciplines?
3. Does your organization have a formal and deliberate approach to integrating the program management and systems engineering disciplines? What are the current elements or practices? What new formal practices would you add based on what you have learned from this chapter?
4. Do you believe that true integration between disciplines results from application of leading integrating practices or from an underlying orientation toward integration? Why?
5. What are the organizational implications of the definition of integration provided at the end of the chapter? What elements or functions of the organization must be engaged to increase the level of integration in the organization according to this definition?
6. What benefits or outcomes at the program level might you predict if the program were operating in a fully integrated fashion? If there were poor levels of integration throughout the program instead?

5.7 References

Barnard, C. I. (1968). *The functions of the executive*. Cambridge, MA: Harvard University Press.

CMMI. (2010, November). *CMMI® for development: Improving processes for developing better products and services*, Version 1.3, CMMI Product Team, CMU/SEI-2010-TR-033.

Conforto, E. C., Rossi, M., Rebentisch, E., Oehmen, J., & Pacenza, M. (2013). *Survey report: Improving integration of program management and systems engineering*. Presented at the 23rd INCOSE Annual International Symposium, Philadelphia. Retrieved from www.pmi.org/~/media/PDF/Business-Solutions/Lean-Enablers/PMI-INCOSE-MIT-Integration-Study.ashx

Deal, T. E., & Kennedy, A. A. (1982). *Corporate cultures: The rites and rituals of corporate life*. Boston: Addison-Wesley Publishing Company.

Eisner, H. (2008). *Essentials of project and systems engineering management* (3rd ed.). Hoboken, NJ: John Wiley & Sons.

Fiedler, F. E. (1964). A theory of leadership effectiveness. In L. Berkowitz (Ed.), *Advances in experimental social psychology*. New York: Academic Press.

HarperCollins. (2014). *Collins English dictionary, complete and unabridged*, (12th ed.). New York: HarperCollins Publishers.

Lawrence, P. R., & Lorsch, J. W. (1967). Differentiation and integration in complex organizations. *Administrative Science Quarterly 12*(1), 1–47. doi:10.2307/2391211

Mayo, E. (1933). *The human problems of industrial civilization*. New York: Macmillan.

Schein, E. (1992). *Organizational culture and leadership: A dynamic view*. San Francisco: Jossey-Bass.

Schein, E. (1996). Three cultures of management: The key to organizational learning. *Sloan Management Review, 38*(1), 9–20.

Taylor, F. W. (1917). *The principles of scientific management*. New York: Harper.

Weber, M. (1947). *The theory of social and economic organizations* (A. M. Henderson & T. Parsons, Trans.). New York: Oxford University Press.

Part II

BUILDING CAPABILITIES TO EFFECTIVELY EXECUTE ENGINEERING PROGRAMS

Part II takes a deeper dive into the integration of program management and systems engineering. It starts with the presentation in Chapter 6 of an organizing framework developed through the research underlying this book that resulted in the Integration Framework. The research found that integration includes the elements of processes, practices, tools, organizational environment, and people with integration competencies. The full framework contains elements that provide a roadmap for the content in this part of the book.

It should be noted that the knowledge foundation for this book is not just restricted to the formal research that has been discussed previously. Beginning particularly in Part II, other sources of insights about integration are introduced to provide more detailed examples of practices and methods suitable for implementation. In most cases, these examples are based on published studies. In others cases, they are anecdotal, drawn from practitioners' experience, but consistent with other reported evidence of effective integration practices.

Chapter 7 presents a case study of the development of the F/A-18E/F Super Hornet aircraft, a complex program that was one of the most successful programs in

U.S. military acquisition history. It provides a compelling example of how integration played a defining role in delivering differentiated program and enterprise performance, and illustrates the application of the concepts discussed in the Integration Framework.

The principal elements of the Integration Framework are explained in detail in Chapters 8, 9, and 10. Chapter 8 explains how the formally codified processes, practices, and tools in an organization help to enable integration between program management and systems engineering, and across other functional boundaries. It includes examples of practices, tools, and techniques that provide structure and cadence to work, both episodically and pervasively, and that emphasize integration across the program rather than just high performance within specialized disciplines.

Chapter 9 shows how common roles, organizational structures, and cultural values foster an organizational environment that leads to productive collaboration and sharing in settings where tasks or interactions are atypical or nonroutine. It highlights practices that shape how program participants work and interact with one another, and determine the nature of their relationships.

Chapter 10 explores the need for individuals, including program managers and chief systems engineers, but also other team members, to have the proper skills and background in order to fill the critical roles needed to integrate the various functions and disciplines in a program and contribute to overall program success. This need is met through careful selection of qualified program managers and systems engineers, development programs that expand and reinforce the integration mindset, and the availability of organizational resources that enable effective collaboration in the face of business and technical challenges.

Chapter 11 examines how the focus on integration might evolve over the life of a program. This chapter is intended to provide a program manager or chief systems engineer a time-phased perspective to help frame important decisions about the elements of integration that should be emphasized at given points in the program. A typical program timeline illustrates which integration actions are appropriate at specific program phases.

Part II concludes with Chapter 12 and a discussion of how increased integration between the program management and systems engineering disciplines produces real and diverse benefits in programs. The core elements for measuring integration include rapid and effective decision making, effective collaborative work, and effective information sharing. The specific benefits that result from integration span a broad range of performance indicators beyond traditional project performance measures reflecting the various ways that program performance can be improved through integration between program management and systems engineering. A case study of the program to provide an improved tactical electronic support capability for Anzac class frigates for the Royal Australian Navy illustrates the array of activities and outcomes that define a successful program that relies on integration for improved performance.

6

HOW INTEGRATION
WORKS IN PROGRAMS

6.1 Introduction

Improving the level of integration is a journey that will be unique to each organization. The journey's ultimate goal is to develop and strengthen the organizational and behavioral competences that drive higher performance, stronger team engagement, and results that leave customers delighted. Frameworks can help organizational leaders and change agents evaluate where they are, where they want to be, and possible steps for transitioning from a current to an intended future state. This chapter lays out a framework that defines the key factors impacting effective integration between the program management and systems engineering disciplines, and how those factors link to overall program performance.

The framework presented here highlights how various factors work in concert to produce outcomes in complex behavioral networks. Since integration is a multifaceted concept, this framework explains the core dimensions and observed practices, organizational approaches, and skillsets in use by successful programs with high levels of integration.

This framework emerged from the multiyear research activities described in the book's introduction. The concepts presented here lay out the research findings and establish the basic knowledge foundation for the framework. The discussion includes some explanation of the process by which the framework emerged to better illustrate some of its key dimensions and elements. The following sections in this chapter explain in greater detail this journey and present the Integration Framework. More detailed explanations of the elements of the framework are presented in subsequent chapters.

6.2 The Integration Framework

The integration of program management and systems engineering is defined in this book as:

> a reflection of the organization's ability to combine program management and systems engineering practices, tools and techniques, experience, and knowledge in a collaborative and systematic approach in the face of challenges, in

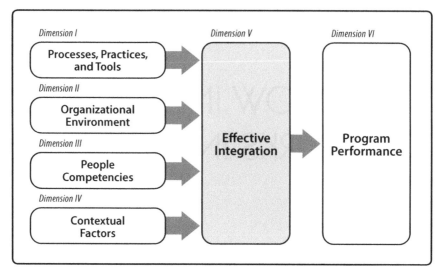

Figure 6-1: The Integration Framework for program management and systems engineering

order to be more effective in achieving common goals/objectives in complex program environments.

The Integration Framework encompasses six main dimensions, shown in Figure 6-1. The center of the framework, figuratively and literally, is "effective integration." On the right side is the program performance dimension. Multiple findings from the research indicated that greater integration leads to improved program performance. This evidence is discussed in detail in Chapter 12.

On the left side of the framework are four dimensions that when combined contribute to greater integration between the program management and systems engineering disciplines. These dimensions are processes, practices, and tools; organizational environment; people competencies; and contextual factors.

In each dimension shown in Figure 6-1 there are several variables and associated elements. The following subsections examine each dimension in more detail, define the dimension, and highlight some of the key insights that emerged during the research on integration.

One objective of this framework is to characterize integration as an organizational and behavioral competence through the elaboration of the multiple integration factors. Evidence from the research suggests that the individual elements, such as processes, practices, and tools from program management and systems engineering areas, are just one piece of a larger puzzle of organizational capabilities.

6.2.1 Dimension I: Processes, Practices, and Tools

The processes, practices, and tools dimension features:

- The use of multiple standards
- The clear definition of roles and responsibilities for the program manager and chief systems engineer, as well as the team members involved in program execution

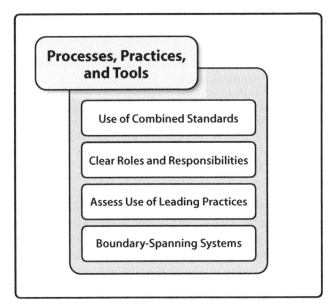

Figure 6-2: Key elements of the processes, practices, and tools dimension of the Integration Framework

- The frequent assessment of the use of standardized leading practices and processes
- The use of systems or processes that bridge the boundaries between disciplines in the program in order to improve communication and information sharing

Figure 6-2 illustrates these key elements of the processes, practices, and tools dimension identified during the research on integration.

Many organizations across a variety of industries recognize the value of program management and systems engineering, whether building a nuclear power plant or developing an IT system for a public transportation company. Often the way the knowledge and practices in these disciplines are assessed is through the discipline's standards and published knowledge base.

The Phase I research found that the use of standards from each domain, respectively, was strongly aligned with the formal role of the practitioner. That is, the systems engineers used systems engineering standards almost exclusively and the program managers used program and project management standards almost exclusively (Conforto, Rossi, Rebentisch, Oehmen, & Pacenza, 2013). The analysis showed that the degree of integration between program management and systems engineering was substantially lower in organizations that were not using standards from both those disciplines (Reiner, 2015). Nearly two-thirds of the respondents from the Phase IV integration survey indicated that their organizations used at least one standard from both the program management and systems engineering domains (Reiner, 2015). The analysis found that those organizations using both standards showed greater integration performance compared with organizations that did not use combined standards. One program manager described his organization's approach this way: "[W]e took the best part of each approach to build our own approach and define methods to be customized to every single program," (Conforto, Rebentisch, & Rossi, 2013).

The use of multiple standards from both disciplines sheds light on a team's ability to create "hybrid" methodologies. In this context, a hybrid methodology can be defined as:

> The combination of principles, practices, techniques and tools from different management approaches to develop a systematic process aimed to fit the management capability to the business context and needs and specific types of programs. The goal is to maximize program performance and product results, and allow the team to balance predictability with flexibility, reduce risks and increase innovation, in order to deliver better results to the business and added value to all stakeholders (translated from Conforto, Barreto, Amaral, & Rebentisch, 2015).

More recently, research on organizational agility showed that hybrid management frameworks are emerging to deal with increasingly diverse sets of program challenges and contexts, and more complex and innovative program environments (Conforto, Rebentisch, & Amaral, 2014). Teams must be able to combine and tailor standards, management approaches, practices, and tools to create hybrid methodologies specifically designed to their program's needs and challenges.

Establishing clearly defined roles and responsibilities for both program managers and chief systems engineers emerged as one of the main factors that contributed to integration (Conforto, Rebentisch, & Rossi, 2013; Rebentisch & Conforto, 2014). Significant overlap between the primary responsibilities of program managers and systems engineers was observed in a few areas (e.g., risk management, life cycle planning, external supplier relations). As discussed in Chapter 5, however, the lack of clearly defined roles and responsibilities between program managers and systems engineers was reported as a primary source of unproductive tension between program management and systems engineering. The Phase I study (Conforto, Rossi et al., 2013) showed that almost half of the organizations had clearly and formally defined program manager job positions, whereas only one-third had formally defined chief systems engineer positions.

Using regular, formal assessments of the program manager's and systems engineer's practices and capabilities is another element that improves integration. More than two-thirds of the "fully integrated" organizations in the Phase I research indicated that they used assessments regularly to ensure integration, ultimately reducing unproductive tension between program management and systems engineering. The same survey showed that six out of ten organizations used the results of the assessments to make process improvements focused on specific areas of competency (Conforto, Rossi et al., 2013). These assessments are associated with a formalized approach to integration, which was also linked to greater levels of integration between the program management and systems engineering disciplines.

The Phase I study (Conforto, Rossi et al., 2013) did not focus in detail on specific processes, practices, and tools used by programs and organizations to improve integration between program managers and systems engineers. However, subsequent interviews with 16 professionals from various industry sectors revealed that processes, practices, and tools were an essential part of their efforts to better integrate those disciplines (Conforto, Rebentisch, & Rossi, 2013; Rebentisch & Conforto, 2014). A wide variety of practices were mentioned—each selected and tailored for the task being performed by the specific organization. These included integrated planning and problem solving strategies and the use of integrated performance measurement systems (i.e., key performance indicators). A common theme in these tools and practices is that they structure program activities in a way that naturally spans boundaries and brings together different perspectives and disciplines during the course of the work of the program. Chapter 8 provides a more wide-ranging discussion and practical examples of program management and systems engineering integration tools, processes, techniques, and methods that help span discipline boundaries in programs.

6.2.2 Dimension II: Organizational Environment

The Phase II and III research (Rebentisch & Conforto, 2014) found clear differences between highly integrated and less-integrated organizations on dimensions associated with the "organizational environment." Organizational environment is a broad concept that encompasses a diverse set of variables. For instance, some describe organizational culture as the way by which organizations indicate to organizational participants what is important for organizational effectiveness (Deal & Kennedy, 1982; Schneider, 1987). It defines what the company rewards, supports, and expects. Integration-oriented organizational characteristics define the set of elements that are relevant to achieving greater degrees of integration. Figure 6-3 summarizes some of the key elements of the organizational environment dimension based on multiple research findings (Becerril, Rebentisch, Chucholowski, Conforto, & Lindemann, 2016;

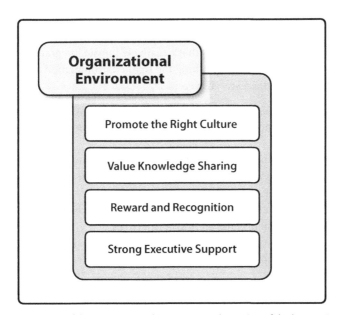

Figure 6-3: Key elements of the organizational environment dimension of the Integration Framework

Conforto, Rebentisch, & Rossi, 2013; Conforto, Rossi et al., 2013; Rebentisch & Conforto, 2014).

One of the elements of the organizational environment dimension is to "promote the right culture" regarding integration. This means developing a culture of trust, openness, and collaboration and shared responsibility between professionals from different areas of the organization. Discussions with program managers and chief systems engineers highlighted the potential for conflicts related to their respective goals and responsibilities. Both may have similar information and be working side by side, but have very different responsibilities and priorities. While the systems engineering priority may be to deliver a system that can be verified against its requirements and validated by the customer, program management is focused on delivering that system within optimized cost and schedule and all program requirements in order to achieve the benefits and results expected.

The Phase II and III research (Rebentisch & Conforto, 2014) identified these elements of a culture that promotes integration: clear and shared goals; a working environment based on trust, respect, and collaboration; empowering both the program manager and the systems engineer with a certain degree of autonomy, but providing strong support for a collaborative decision-making process; and clearly stating that both responsibilities are central to integration and program performance.

A critical thread that runs through these elements is knowledge sharing. It is a primary enabler of trust, collaboration, and shared decision making. It also is necessary if the program manager and chief systems engineer are going to be able to work with a degree of autonomy in their own domains without creating conflicts. Knowledge sharing is the lifeblood of a collaborative, multidisciplinary environment. However, there are a number of challenges to the free flow of knowledge in organizations.

Very often organizations have to deal with issues related to the tendency of teams and people, departments, and business units to focus inward. In potentially every organization, there may be behaviors that negatively impact integration, thereby preventing the organization from establishing the right environment. Among those most commonly identified in the research were:

- Cultural differences between program management and systems engineering. This results from divergent backgrounds and assigned roles and responsibilities in the program.
- Conflicts of interest or hidden agendas, such as departments or groups having diverse priorities that are not clear to every participant in the program, especially the program manager and chief systems engineer.
- Lack of process ownership with autonomy to make decisions from the program management and systems engineering perspectives.
- Lack of trust or respect for each other's discipline or role. Participants not valuing the others' contributions to achieving the best outcome.

It is the responsibility of the organization's leadership to actively promote integration and shape the culture. Reward and recognition as well as strong executive support may be manifest in many ways. For instance, how leaders respond to challenges or unforeseen events in programs can profoundly shape the organizational environment.

Not discouraging or punishing people who raise issues, problems, or risks sends a clear signal that knowledge sharing is highly valued. Integration can be hampered if problems or issues are not properly communicated and addressed. The Phase IV research results showed that the degree of integration correlated with how actively and directly the leaders were involved in developing and promoting collaborative behaviors among program team members (Reiner, 2015).

By identifying, rewarding, and recognizing actions that lead to greater integration, the organization's leaders show that integration is important and relevant for the program's performance and business results. In addition to strong executive support, having a clear strategy for increasing integration will contribute to creating the right environment and the organizational conditions to promote and increase integration.

Promoting the appropriate culture, valuing knowledge sharing, rewarding and recognizing people, and promoting strong executive support are just as necessary as having the right processes, practices, and tools to help improve the degree of integration in the organization. Chapter 9 provides an in-depth discussion and practical examples regarding the elements related to the organizational environment dimension.

6.2.3 Dimension III: People Competencies

According to recent research, talent deficiencies significantly hamper 40% of strategy implementation efforts (PMI, 2014, p. 3). Helping individuals develop their skills and abilities is a complex and continuous task for companies. It requires long-term investment and strong leadership and management support in order to reach outstanding levels that will help organizations create so-called "high-performing" teams. Individual competence is generally recognized as the combination of:

- Knowledge, experience, and information
- Skills, including technical capabilities to perform a certain job activity
- Attitude, which means being able to apply the knowledge and skills to solve a problem or perform a given task

The people competencies dimension focuses on how organizations develop competencies in people so they can participate in and enable the integration of the program management and systems engineering disciplines. People competencies (see Figure 6-4) in this context focus on elements found in the integration research that are relevant to developing integration capabilities in program teams. Individuals, including program management and systems engineering team members, must have the proper skills and background in order to fill the roles; employ the processes, methods, and tools; and co-create the organizational environment needed to integrate the various functions and disciplines in a program and contribute to overall program success.

Experience in various roles relates to one's general understanding of how work is done and what is required for success in each domain. In the context of integration, this does not necessarily imply that program managers must have work experience as a chief systems engineer in order to enable the integration of the two disciplines. In some organizations, a natural career progression is from engineer to program manager through a series of assignments, and indeed some people may function as both

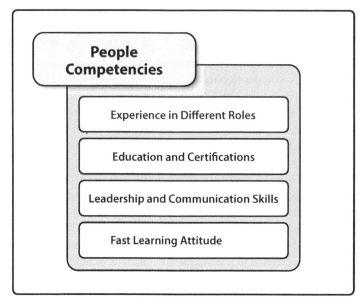

Figure 6-4: Key elements of the people competencies dimension of the Integration Framework

program manager and chief systems engineer or alternate between the two functions. However, it may not be possible in all cases to have one person fill the role of both program manager and chief systems engineer, or even desirable in some technically challenging or complex programs. The Phase IV study found that only one-quarter of the program managers had served as a chief systems engineer previously. In contrast, 71% of the chief systems engineers declared they had served as a program manager at some point (Reiner, 2015). The Phase IV research also showed that greater integration performance correlates positively to the accumulated years of professional experience, with more experience associated with a higher degree of integration (Reiner, 2015). Generally speaking, with greater experience, and perhaps increased exposure to different perspectives, comes improved integration between the disciplines.

Interviews highlighted the need for learning and skill development to enable program managers and chief systems engineers to have at least a minimal understanding of the principles, key concepts, and practices of each field (Rebentisch & Conforto, 2014). Other common themes that emerged from the interviews associated with greater degrees of integration included:

- Opportunities to receive formal education and training to help each discipline understand the other's perspective
- Selecting the core program management team to comprise people from multiple skill and competency backgrounds to increase the likelihood of making better-informed decisions throughout the duration of the program
- Focusing on communication skills improvement so that program managers and systems engineers create a more collaborative and participative working relationship

A program manager working for a manufacturing company in the capital goods and machinery sector illustrated the challenges that, in many cases, must be overcome by skilled leaders. Generally, programs in this organization have approximately 300 professionals on the team, and a typical program lasts for a minimum of one year. It was challenging for the program manager to report progress to executive management. The program manager was responsible for carrying out planning revisions in order to adjust the schedule to the execution and program goals. The systems engineers seemed to know what they had to do and did not appear to care much about the status reporting. The program manager felt that the chief systems engineer did not understand the value of the report, and this behavior was affecting program management activities. In this case, the communication process was not defined, and there was little understanding of each other's role in and contributions to the program. This might be due to a lack of understanding of each other's activities (knowledge contributions), or simply reflect an attitude of discounting the importance of each other's role in the program that led to a breakdown in communications.

The Phase II and III research found individual competencies that can improve integration between program management and systems engineering, including good leadership and communication skills, comprehensive understanding of the main principles, concepts, and processes of each discipline, and a fast learning attitude (Rebentisch & Conforto, 2014). Developing the right set of competencies for the work of the program is key to integration performance and program success; therefore, organizations should consistently promote formal education and ongoing training in both disciplines so participants in each can learn from the other and share their different experiences and knowledge more effectively (Rebentisch & Conforto, 2014). Chapter 10 discusses in greater detail the development of integration competencies in people.

6.2.4 Dimension IV: Contextual Factors

The fourth dimension of the Integration Framework captures contextual factors that may positively or negatively impact the degree of integration in a given program and business context. Some of the elements of contextual factors identified during the integration research include:

- Program characteristics such as the size of the program
- The number of entities involved (e.g., suppliers, partners, clients)
- The team characteristics such as team size, location, and workload
- The organization structure, for example project organization structure, matrix, or functional organization (PMI, 2013b)
- Elements related to stakeholders, such as the degree of alignment between the stakeholders in the program

These elements are summarized in Figure 6-5.

Because there are potentially many factors that influence integration between the program management and systems engineering disciplines, and subsequently impact program performance, identifying them is important to developing and tailoring an appropriate strategy for integration. This should be done throughout the life of the

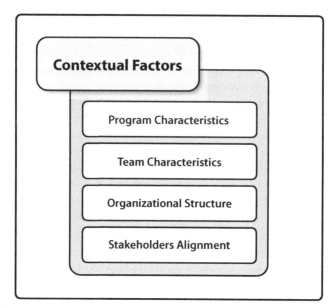

Figure 6-5: Key elements of the contextual factors dimension of the Integration Framework

program, but, more importantly, beginning in the early stages of a new program. Even in the same organization these factors may vary from one program to another.

The research revealed several program characteristics that may be assessed in order to develop a tailored approach to integration for a specific program. For example:

- **Use of emerging technologies.** What are the challenges, unknowns, and knowledge necessary to address the program-specific problems? What disciplines must contribute and how will their knowledge be integrated within the program?
- **Program pace.** How urgently does the program need to be completed and at what pace the benefits delivered? Does the relative degree of urgency require close coordination across discipline or stakeholder boundaries or an adaptation of the program strategy?
- **Program stability.** Do product or client requirements change frequently during the course of the program, or are there unclear and frequent changes in the objectives and goals of the program?
- **Number of stakeholders or entities involved in the program.** Will the complexity of the activities and the volume of technical and management decisions become an important consideration in defining how the relationships between functions are defined?
- **Relevance of the program as a part of the company's portfolio in fulfillment of its strategic plan.** Is this program particularly important within its portfolio, and how might that affect the way the program manager and chief systems engineer approach developing greater degrees of integration?

The Phase IV research found correlations between a number of team characteristics such as program managers, chief systems engineers, and the core team working in close geographical proximity, "positive attitude towards challenges," "shared and common vision of what shall be created in the program," and how quickly the "PM [program manager] receives requested information from the team members," with factors associated with greater integration, such as "efficiency of communication between PM [program manager] and CSE [chief systems engineer]" (Reiner, 2015). This is illustrated by a program manager from a global IT solutions provider for government and defense who observed that, depending on the size of the program, the company executives will assign one program manager and one systems engineer, and they usually work together as "one team." They will be located in the same office to facilitate more frequent interactions to discuss program-related issues, to make more rapid decisions, and, ultimately, positively impact integration.

The importance of team characteristics may vary from one organization to another, and how each characteristic is expressed in formation of the team may influence (positively or negatively) how integrated the disciplines are. Some general team characteristics to consider when tailoring the approach to increasing integration include team size, (co-)location, workload and time allocation to the program, team structure, and degree of leadership involvement in the work of the team.

The vehicle maker Tesla addresses a number of organizational factors in the way it organizes the development of its electric cars. First, the company hires professionals with demonstrated ability to solve complex problems (a people competencies dimension). Then the company organizes these professionals in small and co-located teams (a contextual factors dimension). This improves communication and allows them to make decisions faster. For example, the team in charge of creating the design of the Tesla Model S was formed by the chief designer and a team of three designers sitting next to their teammate engineers. Tesla leadership argues that their "communication allows them to move incredibly fast" (Dyer, Gregersen, & Furr, 2015). Information sharing (i.e., communication) is one of the key elements of effective integration.

The organizational structure, the third element in the contextual factors dimension, may affect the specific approach used to increase integration between program management and systems engineering within a program. The level and types of communication and collaboration between the disciplines, and their counterparts across the organization, may be shaped by the following characteristics:

- The number of entities (e.g., suppliers, partners, clients, other organizations) that are directly involved in the program
- The program dependence on other programs that must be executed simultaneously
- The number of employees allocated to work full time in the program versus the number working part time
- The alignment between the organization's strategic goals and the client requirements for the specific program

Stakeholder alignment is in many ways related to and complementary with organizational structure. It involves coordinating the respective goals and actions of the various program stakeholders so that they constructively produce the program benefits. An example that illustrates this is the National Aeronautics and Space Administration's (NASA, 2011) Mars Science Laboratory, part of the Mars Exploration Program and perhaps best known for its Curiosity Rover component. A program of this size and complexity is impossible to be executed without the involvement and contribution of many institutions. The entire program was structured with multiple partners and suppliers (multiple teams) working in a tightly coordinated process. The Jet Propulsion Laboratory and NASA served as the program management office with many professionals orchestrating multiple projects across different institutions (government and private) to build all of the equipment necessary to accomplish the mission.

These examples illustrate the integration factors that, depending on the program context, may positively or negatively impact the overall level and approach to integration and will affect overall program outcomes. Because there are many aspects that can influence integration between program management and systems engineering, the organization must be able to properly identify and manage the various contextual factors that may influence integration. The contextual factors of integration are discussed and illustrated in examples across multiple chapters in this book including Chapters 11 and 14.

6.2.5 Dimension V: Effective Integration

Effective integration is the core dimension of the framework; it is the "heart" of the model. Integration is industry agnostic and applies to all types of programs, albeit in different forms depending on the context of the program.

In the previous sections, the four dimensions of the Integration Framework, including processes, practices, and tools; organizational environment; people competencies; and contextual factors, were described. The Effective Integration dimension is a result of a combination of these four dimensions. It is important to understand that effective integration comprises three key elements, shown in Figure 6-6: rapid and effective decision making, effective collaborative work, and effective information

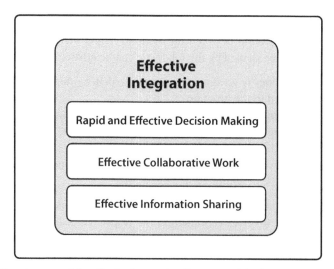

Figure 6-6: Key elements of the effective integration dimension of the Integration Framework

sharing. These three elements are present in varying degrees in every program whether it is small or large, irrespective of the objective (a product, a building, a dam, a bridge, or a spacecraft), and regardless of the industry sector.

The Phase II and III research identified that programs with effective integration have a rapid and effective decision-making process between program management and systems engineering professionals. In this process both program managers and chief systems engineers have the authority and autonomy to execute their respective responsibilities and then produce decisions collaboratively. Rapid and effective decision making also results from a number of other behaviors, such as:

- The involvement of all members of the program execution team, as well as the program manager and chief systems engineer in the decision-making process. This means that all team members are directly engaged and actively participating in this process.
- The program manager takes into account technical goals. Besides management goals (i.e., cost, time, program benefits, business value, etc.), the program manager also considers technical goals as critical to the program (e.g., requirements, specifications) when prioritizing tasks or making decisions.
- The chief systems engineer considers management goals when prioritizing tasks or making decisions.
- Identification and alignment of the final authority to confirm a decision. For instance, as indicated by some who participated in the research, the program manager made most of the final program business decisions, especially those that directly impact schedule and budget. The chief systems engineer was mainly responsible for technical decisions.

Rapid and effective decision making also depends on having clearly defined authority in the program. The lack of a clear definition of authority was the second most cited source of unproductive tension between program managers and chief systems engineers (Conforto, Rossi et al., 2013; Rebentisch & Conforto, 2014). In some organizations only the program manager has the power to make decisions related to the program. Even though the decision may be largely technical, the program manager will still have the final call.

The second key element of effective integration is effective collaborative work. A co-creation attitude and shared accountability characterize a collaborative work environment. Valuing and promoting collaboration over competition was one of the most cited characteristics by professionals who described their programs as well integrated. This means that both program manager and chief systems engineer have a shared set of objectives defined by the success of the overall combined effort. It defines with clarity and understanding each member's role and how they collaboratively contribute in order to achieve a greater result. Finally, it means respecting the value of others' role and contribution to achieving the objectives.

During the Phase II and III research interviews (Rebentisch & Conforto, 2014), a chief systems engineer in an aerospace program noted that he faced a major problem. The program manager was pushing the program to a decision gate, but the team needed more time to detail and complete all the specifications related to a supplier.

Even though the program manager was pushing hard to meet the deadline, the team had agreed that more time was needed to create good specifications. In the end, the program manager understood that it was not a good idea to force a deliverable out and jeopardize quality over schedule, which might result in massive rework and additional costs.

Some of the key factors related to collaborative work that can improve integration performance include:

- Broad interest and involvement of the program manager in technical aspects of the program. The program manager is positively engaged in and committed to resolving technical issues. The same applies to the chief systems engineer who is positively engaged in and committed to resolving program management issues.
- Team members embrace challenges. They collaboratively tackle problems and challenges with enthusiasm and commitment.
- The team members have a shared and common vision of what should be created by the program. They have a shared set of priorities and desired results.

The third element of the integration dimension is effective information sharing. Information sharing is related to the type of communication and exchange of information or data necessary to plan, execute, and successfully deliver a program. According to Conway's Law (Conway, 1968) an organization that designs a system (broadly defined) will produce a design whose structure is a copy of the organization's communication structure. For such an organization, Chase (1974) suggests that facilitating communications is an essential function.

Traditionally, the task of ensuring communications among stakeholders is considered to be a responsibility of the program manager (PMI, 2013a). Information sharing is related to process indicators such as time to retrieve information, access to information when it is needed, information availability to all team members, etc., which, when improved, can lead to greater integration. Based on the Phase IV research (Reiner, 2015), the effective information sharing dimension includes:

- The effectiveness of the communications between the program manager and the chief systems engineer. How effective is the communication between these two roles and between team members?
- Time for acquisition of necessary information for both program management and systems engineering. For example, how long does it typically take to request and receive necessary information about any aspect of the program, whether technical or management related?
- Information transparency. Do all team members have access to all program-related information that they need to perform their jobs successfully?

In summary, the three elements of effective integration, rapid and effective decision making, effective collaborative work, and effective information sharing, are indicators of the state of integration in the program. Each element has its respective set of indicators to be defined in organizations and programs. Chapter 12 provides a more detailed discussion on how integration is measured and its impact on overall program performance.

6.2.6 Dimension VI: Program Performance

An important principle of the Integration Framework is the importance of defining clear goals for integration. What are the key outcomes the organization expects from achieving greater integration? It could be to reduce schedule overruns, improve the quality of budget management, increase client satisfaction, raise technical quality, etc. This dimension of the Integration Framework deals with the performance of the program in terms of tangible and intangible management and technical indicators and outcomes as well as the overall program benefits and results.

In the research on integration, none of the professionals interviewed revealed that they had clearly defined objectives related to integration itself. In other words, these organizations did not have specific goals for integration and did not have defined metrics to measure integration. Many organizations measure success based on schedule, budget, and scope for both projects and programs. Research shows that one of the key challenges in the program management domain is benefits realization. Unlike projects that have defined deliverables whose value is generally linked to customer satisfaction, scope, budget, and time, programs are designed to deliver a broader array of business benefits. Those benefits can range from new capabilities to financial return to opening new markets. But those benefits are often delivered throughout the life of the program, which can last for many years. It is important also to define specific goals relating to the development of integration (i.e., its associated capabilities, and how it is to be measured) and then putting the right processes and measures in place to capture those benefits.

Program performance can be measured using various perspectives. One perspective deals with the performance of the product and the resulting outcome of the program. Measures can vary from the product features to benefits for the users. Another is the program performance according to its management perspective, including company's shareholders, executives, and so on. For example, the program was completed on time, within budget, produced the expected financial return, and delivered the expected tangible and intangible benefits.

Figure 6-7 shows four program performance indicators used to explore the impact of greater integration (Reiner, 2015). The indicators proposed are fairly generic and could be used for a wide range of program types. However, it is recommended that each organization develop its own set of outcome-related performance indicators based on its own objectives, and then from those identify links to integration.

The analysis of the Phase IV research (Reiner, 2015) found a positive correlation between greater levels of integration and better program performance. Of two groups, one with greater levels of integration and another with lesser levels of integration, the group with greater levels of integration also had higher levels of program performance. Chapter 12 describes in detail the key variables related to rapid and effective decision making, collaborative work, and information sharing that will impact program performance and how these elements are correlated with the other dimensions of the Integration Framework.

Figure 6-8 provides a complete overview of the Integration Framework with its six dimensions and all key elements as discussed in this chapter. The following chapters of

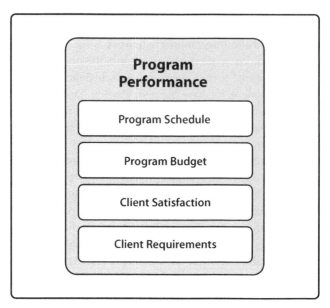

Figure 6-7: Key elements of the program performance dimension of the Integration Framework

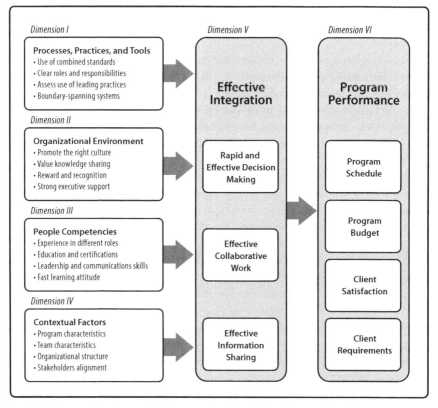

Figure 6-8: The complete Integration Framework with all dimensions and key elements

this book address in detail the core dimensions of this framework. Chapter 8 describes practices, tools, and techniques (Dimension I) related to improved integration. Chapter 9 discusses the organizational environment elements related to improved integration (Dimension II). Chapter 10 describes the people competencies that positively impact integration (Dimension III). The contextual factors (Dimension IV) are discussed across multiple chapters and are supported by multiple cases presented in this book, including the ones in Chapters 7, 12, and 14. Chapter 12 specifically addresses how effective integration (Dimension V) impacts program performance (Dimension VI).

6.3 Summary

The framework presented in this chapter shows the key factors associated with the integration of program management and systems engineering disciplines in programs and organizations based on research conducted over a three-year period. Integration is not simply the combination of standards, practices, tools, and techniques and defining roles and job responsibilities. Instead, it is a broad concept that encompasses multiple dimensions of the organization and the program, and it is grounded in three key elements:

- Rapid and effective decision making
- Effective collaborative work
- Effective information sharing

In order to develop this capability, organizational leaders would be wise to invest in developing people competencies; nurturing the appropriate organizational environment; the adoption of the right practices, tools, and techniques; and the implementation of processes to identify and improve contextual factors that may impact integration and, consequently, program performance.

There are a few actions that might be useful to organizations that are dealing with a variety of programs:

- First and foremost, understand and clearly define integration within a specific organizational context. Integration must be clearly formalized and understood by all participants in the program and the organization.
- Define clear goals for integration. Identify metrics and mechanisms to monitor results from integration and its impact on other areas of the organization. The research indicated that organizations generally do not have clear processes to track and improve integration.
- Consider a framework to properly address integration and its key dimensions to enable greater overall performance.

6.4 Discussion Questions

1. What are the key differences between the Integration Framework and frameworks that describe either program management or systems engineering practices?

2. Why is adopting a standard (or multiple standards) for practices, tools, and techniques valuable for improving integration?
3. Why is it important to define clear goals and objectives for integration?
4. Using the framework to evaluate your own organization, in which dimensions is your organization strongest and weakest?
5. What are the gaps within your organization highlighted by the Integration Framework that you believe, if closed, would help to improve the level of integration between systems engineering and program management?
6. Who are the key stakeholders inside your organization who can provide additional insight to support evaluation of the organizational and behavioral competences that support integration?

6.5 References

Becerril, L., Rebentisch, E., Chucholowski, N., Conforto, E. C., & Lindemann, U. (2016, May 16–19). A simulation-based analysis on the integration of program management and systems engineering. *Proceedings of the International Design Conference,* Dubrovnik, Croatia.

Chase, W. P. (1974). *Management of systems engineering.* Malabar, FL: Krieger Publishing Company.

Conforto, E. C., Barreto, F., Amaral, D., & Rebentisch, E. (2015, August/September). Modelos híbridos unindo complexidade, agilidade e inovação: A próxima tendência do gerenciamento de projetos. *Mundo Project Management.*

Conforto, E. C., Rebentisch, E., Amaral, D. C. (2014). *Project management agility global survey.* Cambridge, MA: Consortium for Engineering Program Excellence, Massachusetts Institute of Technology.

Conforto, E. C., Rebentisch, E., & Rossi, M. (2013). *Case study report: Improving integration of program management and systems engineering.* Cambridge, MA: Consortium for Engineering Program Excellence, Massachusetts Institute of Technology.

Conforto, E. C., Rossi, M., Rebentisch, E., Oehmen, J., & Pacenza, M. (2013). *Survey report: Improving integration of program management and systems engineering.* Presented at the 23rd INCOSE Annual International Symposium, Philadelphia, USA. Retrieved from www.pmi.org/~/media/PDF/Business-Solutions/Lean-Enablers/PMI-INCOSE -MIT-Integration-Study.ashx

Conway, M. (1968, April). How do committees invent? *Datamation.*

Deal, T. E., & Kennedy, A. A. (1982). *Corporate cultures: The rites and rituals of corporate life.* Boston: Addison-Wesley Publishing Company.

Dyer, J., Gregersen, H., & Furr, N. (2015, August 19). Decoding Tesla's secret formula. *Forbes Tech.*

National Aeronautics and Space Administration (NASA). (2011). *NASA's management of the mars science laboratory project.* Retrieved from https://oig.nasa.gov/audits/reports/ FY11/IG-11-019.pdf

Project Management Institute (PMI). (2013a). *The standard for program management* (3rd ed.). Newtown Square, PA: Author.

Project Management Institute (PMI). (2013b). *A guide to the project management body of knowledge* (PMBOK® guide) (5th ed.). Newtown, Square, PA: Author.

Project Management Institute (PMI). (2014). *Rally the talent to win: Transforming strategy into reality*. Retrieved from www.pmi.org/~/media/PDF/Publications/Rally-the-Talent-to-Win.ashx

Rebentisch, E., & Conforto, E. C. (2014, May). *Integration means results: Why systems engineering and program management must align*. PMI Global Congress, EMEA, Dubai, UAE.

Reiner, T. (2015, May). *Determination of factors to measure the effective integration between program management and systems engineering*, Rheinisch-Westfälische Technische Hochschule (RWTH) Aachen Master's thesis.

Schneider, B. (1987). The people make the place. *Personnel Psychology, 40*(3), 437–453. doi: 10.1111/j.1744-6570.1987.tb00609

INTEGRATION IN PRACTICE IN THE F/A-18E/F SUPER HORNET PROGRAM

7.1 Introduction

What does it look like when program managers and systems engineers work together in an integrated fashion? Chapter 6 spelled out the broad elements of integration in an organization. But how do the elements of integration actually work, and how do they work *together* in a program? The case study detailed in this chapter[1] provides an example of a program that was successful, but, more importantly, that success was decisively enabled by employing the principles described in the Integration Framework. This success was achieved in a setting where there were numerous competing demands for attention and resources; where the product requirements were complex and failure could be both punishing and an ever-present possibility; and where multiple specialized interests presented challenges to successful integration.

The F/A-18E/F Super Hornet shown in Figure 7-1 is a twin-engine aircraft designed to fly from Navy aircraft carriers to perform both air-to-air and air-to-ground combat missions. The prime contractor was McDonnell Douglas Corporation (now Boeing Corporation). Northrop (now Northrop Grumman) was the principle subcontractor and built the aft fuselage. General Electric (GE) was responsible for the engines (Bailey, Nash, & Woolsey, 1999, p. 3). The F/A designation represents its dual role as a fighter and an attack aircraft. The E/F is an evolutionary design derived from the F/A-18C/D still in service. The "E" version carries a crew of one while the "F" is a two-seat configuration. As a carrier-based aircraft, it is often the go-to platform for military air operations in regions of the world where limited military base infrastructure might inhibit other aircraft from operating.

Its development provides an example of a program that embodies effective integration. It holds a rarefied position as one of the few complex military programs to complete its development phase ahead of schedule (adherence to timeline) and within budgeted cost (adherence to budget), as shown in Figure 7-2. In addition, this program provided several additional benefits. The aircraft completed its development phase weighing 1,000 pounds under its specification (client requirements

Figure 7-1: The twin-engine aircraft F/A-18E Super Hornet (U.S. Navy, 2006)
Photo by Photographer's Mate 3rd Class Chris Thamann. Public Domain

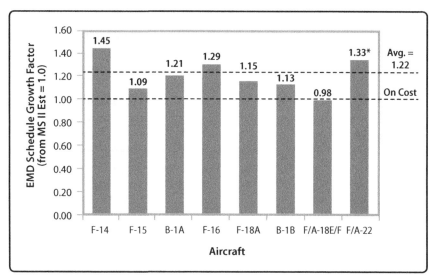

Figure 7-2: F/A-18E/F met its development cost targets, unlike other, similar aircraft development programs
Younossi et al, 2005, p. 10. Reproduced with permission of RAND CORPORATION via Copyright Clearance Center, Inc.

fulfillment) with one-third fewer parts than predecessor aircraft, a heavier payload, longer range, increased reliability, and margin for additional growth in capabilities (White, 1997). Not only is it meeting its program requirements regarding quantity of aircraft delivered, but it is also expanding into new applications that boost the overall production. This is in contrast to the norm in military aircraft development programs where cost escalates to the point that the overall fleet buy is truncated to a fraction of the original specification. Building the full program requirement of aircraft benefits the workforce and supply base by having a stable production program over the space of many years. The overall program benefits to the Navy are even more impressive from the standpoint of significant reduction in the system's total cost of ownership (factoring in operations and maintenance, logistics, and sustainment costs compared with operating the diverse array of aging legacy aircraft that this type replaces). These points make it truly unique among military aircraft programs.

When viewed through the lens of the key dimensions characterizing effective integration, the Super Hornet program represented a shift away from functional stovepipes to embrace rapid and effective decision making, collaborative work, and information sharing. Program management and systems engineering became more integrated in this program. By virtue of the relationship between the government customer and its contractor base, it also presents a more complex integration case because both the government and the contractors each had program management and systems engineering disciplines to be integrated into a large, unified program. Effective integration at the program level included integration across the contractual boundary, often a more challenging integration task than between disciplines within a single organization. Considering all the stakeholders that needed to be integrated to make the program a success, this presented a significant challenge.

The transition away from traditional stovepipe mindsets toward a more integrated approach was initiated by the top levels of leadership within the Navy's Naval Air Systems Command (NAVAIR) and McDonnell Douglas Corporation. This case study traces the history of the program as it made this transition. It illustrates the principles of integration in practice and conveys a sense of what it is like to be in a program where integration is practiced and prioritized. Much of the information about the F/A-18E/F in this chapter draws extensively from two case studies published by the Institute for Defense Analyses: *The F/A-18E/F: An Integrated Product Team (IPT) Case Study* (Bailey, 1998) and *Integrated Product and Process Development Case Study: Development of the F/A-18E/F* (Bailey et al., 1999). Both case studies are used here with permission.

7.2 F/A-18E/F Super Hornet Program Background and the Context of Integration

In mid-1990, after only two years, the U.S. Navy program to develop a new stealthy attack aircraft known as the A-12 was already at least US$1 billion over cost and 18 months behind schedule. In January 1991, the U.S. Secretary of Defense canceled the program. The A-12 was to have replaced the 1960s-era A-6 attack aircraft, which were aging and increasingly vulnerable to new threats. Still stinging from the A-12 cancellation, the Navy chose as a replacement a lower-cost, lower-risk derivative of the F/A-18C/D already operating in the naval air fleet. The objective of the F/A-18E/F program was to develop, test, produce, and deploy an upgraded F/A-18 with increased mission range, increased aircraft carrier recovery payload, additional growth potential, and enhanced survivability. The F/A-18E/F was designed as a multirole fighter to perform the same type of missions and counter the same threats as earlier models of the F/A-18, but with some incremental increase in capability (Younossi, Stem, Lorell, & Lussier, 2005, pp. 2–3).

The F/A-18E/F, or simply "E/F," was immediately critical to naval air planning and the Navy overall. Modernization was essential for both combat effectiveness and operational affordability because the existing fleet of F/A-18C/Ds consisted of aging aircraft with limited options for capability improvement. Moreover, in the wake of the cancellation of the A-12, the U.S. Congress had mandated that the E/F could not exceed the cost of the C/D by more than 25%. The Navy's reputation as an agency capable of effective aircraft procurement was at stake. In hearings on the follow-on aircraft to the A-12 (eventually cancelled as well), Senator John Glenn said, "The Navy's ability to manage such a program is atrocious." Congressional sentiments like this helped focus the Navy's attention on schedule, cost, and risk (Bailey et al., 1999, pp. 3–4).

7.3 Twelve Days of August: A Start on the Integration Journey

In early August, 1991, Captain Craig E. Steidle, the Navy Program Manager for the F/A-18, held a "mini program review" of the proposed concept for the E/F. During the nine months prior to this review, teams from McDonnell Douglas, Northrop, GE, and the Navy had been working to define the configuration and high-level requirements for the E/F. When they came together for the review, it was clear that there was no agreement across teams. In the words of McDonnell Douglas's Integrated Product Team (IPT) Manager:

> Everybody was protecting their own rice bowls. The electronic warfare team wanted the best of the best. The low observables team wanted the most stealthy aircraft possible. The cockpit displays team wanted the very best and so on. The result was a weapon system that was over weight and over cost. Captain Steidle's conclusion during this review was that "We don't have a program here. What we have is a mess."

Larry Lemke was the McDonnell Douglas Vice President and General Manager of the F/A-18 at that time. He and Captain Steidle worked throughout the night outlining what they thought had to be the next steps if there was to be a viable E/F program. As the McDonnell Douglas's IPT Manager described it:

> They decided to bring together people who were knowledgeable in all the many areas needed to define the E/F configuration and high-level requirements.

So they convened a twelve-day meeting in St. Louis which began the following Monday and ended a week later on a Friday. The Navy had 35 to 40 people at that twelve-day meeting. There were also people from MDC, Northrop and General Electric. The idea was that at the end of the twelve days, they would either have a viable, affordable program or there would be no program.

At the beginning of the 12 days, Captain Steidle, along with Mike Sears, McDonnell Douglas's Deputy F/A-18 Program Manager, outlined for everyone the high-level objectives for the E/F. In comparison to the C/D, the E/F had to have:

- More range (fly farther without refueling)
- Improved survivability
- More bring back (weight of stores that could be brought back and landed on a carrier)
- More carriage capability (could carry more bombs to a target)
- More growth capability built in (extra physical space for future growth)

Captain Steidle instructed everyone at the meeting that these were the essential objectives against which tradeoffs would be made. However, because Congress mandated that the E/F could not exceed costs of the C/D by more than 25%, a different approach was called for. In the McDonnell Douglas's IPT Manager's words:

> Before this meeting, the approach was to throw everything on the table and see what it cost. This time, affordability was an issue. Each group was tasked to think about what could be done differently. Given the high-level objectives of the E/F, we were asked to identify what has to be in the aircraft and what wasn't essential. We were told to question the what and the how of everything we did. What could we do to reduce weight and cost without impacting the high-level requirements?

During the 12 days, the larger group broke into teams to address specific areas; the teams would convene at the beginning and end of each day. Otherwise, each team worked its area. Over the 12 days they had to trade off weight, fuel capacity, volume, materials, the size of the radar cross-section, and cost. Operational analysis was going on throughout all of this in order to understand what was being gained at a system level with the changes that the teams were making. It was during this period that the concept for a Navy-contractor Integrated Test Team during Developmental Test & Evaluation emerged. Northrop proposed changes to the bulkhead (the critical interface between the McDonnell Douglas and Northrop sections of the airplane) that resulted in a large weight savings. McDonnell Douglas proposed savings by going with a modest avionics upgrade in which 90% of the avionics were common with the C/D.

At the end of 12 days, the basic air vehicle requirements were in place. In McDonnell Douglas's IPT Manager's words:

> This was a focused effort to define the configuration so we could proceed to the next step. We came out of it with something that was good enough to be costed. And it brought everyone along at the same time (customer and contractor). We came out with a very clear direction. There was not much debate after that about what was in the aircraft. But we still had to guard against requirements creep.

In the fall of 1991, McDonnell Douglas, Northrop, and GE worked with Naval Air Systems Command (NAVAIR) to flesh out the requirements. As the McDonnell Douglas's Integrated Product Team Manager described it:

> We had a "spec jamboree." We broke into the same teams. We took the require-ments and the configuration from the twelve days and used the C/D spec as a starting point. We took that specification apart and re-assembled it to reflect the E/F we had defined. Where there were still disagreements, they were noted, and assigned to teams for resolution. Most of these were closed in the next couple of weeks. With this process, we were able to hammer out the impor-tant details of the E/F specification, includ[ing] input from a wide range of stakeholders, and do it in a very short time.

During these 12 days, the E/F changed from something that was "gold-plated" with specifications and features that were not critical to performance and over cost to something that represented an affordable evolution from the C/D. This was achieved by maintaining a customer focus and making appropriate tradeoffs, and set the stage for success.

7.4 Enabling Integration by Reducing Program Complexity

The technology requirements for the aircraft were deliberately crafted to control tech-nological risk and to constrain cost. In October 1991, the Navy formally requested designation of the E/F as a major modification effort rather than as a new program start. Although the new E/F design entailed major airframe modifications, the Navy intended to incorporate existing C/D avionics and a derivative of the existing engine (Younossi et al., 2005, pp. 22–23). Right from the beginning, the program aimed for an integrated solution, balancing the program management concerns of cost and schedule with systems engineering tradeoffs to reduce risk and complexity. The formal Engi-neering and Manufacturing Development phase of the program began in July 1992 (Younossi et al., 2005, pp. xv–xvi).

The E/F is 4.2 feet longer than the legacy platform, has a 25% larger wing area, and can carry 33% additional internal fuel. The airframe design was largely new with very little commonality with the original design, but aerodynamically similar to the C/D. It incorporated some limited radar cross-section reduction techniques, such as new inlets and attention to door and panel edges. It also had 42% fewer parts than its C/D pre-decessor even though the airframe was approximately 25% larger. By reducing part count, costs from many sources were reduced (Bailey et al., 1999, p. 11). Nevertheless, the E/F's airframe cost grew by 12% during the development program. It was offset by the declines in other cost categories such as System Engineering and Program Manage-ment, System Test and Evaluation through the use of the Navy-contractor Integrated Test Team, and support. The net result was no cost growth overall (Younossi et al., 2005, pp. 33–34).

The E/F used a derivative engine based on the engine core developed for the F412 engine, which had been planned to power the A-12 aircraft. The F414 engine also benefited from its design lineage from the F404, which powers the C/D (Younossi et al., 2005, p. 46).

The E/F avionics for the initial release of the E/F incorporated the suite from the C/D model, with more than 90% of the E/F's electronics in the initial production aircraft common with the C/D (Younossi et al., 2005, p. 40). Some upgrades to the subsequent production aircraft were included as preplanned product improvements from the beginning of the program. Because the avionics system is a federated system, these upgrades could be easily incorporated when available, without any significant effect on the overall weapon system availability (p. 43). One program benefit resulting from the extensive reuse of the avionics from the C/D model was that the E/F program certified the aircraft to employ over two dozen weapons. This meant that the E/F had full combat capability very early in its initial operations, whereas typical aircraft development programs may require years to accumulate that full range of capabilities (p. 31).

The F/A-18 Program Office managed approximately 2,000 full-time equivalent staff at a number of sites. The F/A-18 program was about a US$5 billion a year program, distributed between the operational support of existing aircraft, production of the C/D model, Engineering and Manufacturing Development of the E/F model, and sales to foreign customers (Bailey, 1998, p. 3). The E/F used an existing workshare breakout based on the history of contracts on the F/A-18A/B/C/D development and production. McDonnell Douglas was considered the prime contractor and Northrop was a major subcontractor on the effort. The E/F team of McDonnell Douglas and Northrop had substantial experience on the C/D. Both contractors had experienced design teams in place and drew heavily from existing suppliers and the industrial base (Younossi et al., 2005, p. 24).

The outcome of these design decisions was that the overall complexity of the E/F program was reduced considerably. This reduced the scope of the program and allowed the participants to focus relatively more of their attention on their approaches to working together more effectively and efficiently. This was important because by early 1992, the senior Navy leadership had made it clear that the E/F program would not proceed unless the cost estimates for the development program and for the average unit flyaway costs remained under strict ceilings dictated by likely funding realities (Younossi, 2005, pp. 22–23).

7.5 A Parallel Process in NAVAIR to Improve Integration

While the requirements for the E/F were being developed, NAVAIR was undergoing a major reorganization to integrate the various disciplines required to develop the aircraft. In the early 1990s, NAVAIR was organized around strong functional stovepipes, each reporting within its own organizational structure. In the words of the former Commander of NAVAIR, Vice Admiral Joseph Dyer, "We had strong functional management and weak program management. Each person reported up his or her own functional chain of command. The program manager subcontracted work to each of the functional organizations and was left herding cats." Disagreements between functional organizations were raised up the functional chain to be resolved at the top level rather than at the level at which they surfaced.

Not only was program management relatively weak, but under this organization decision making could not be characterized as rapid and effective. Work proceeded in a serial fashion across functional organizations leading to a great deal of rework. For example, the development of a Request for Proposal, in which the Navy produces a formal, documented request for contractors to bid on a defined set of requirements, would begin with an operational concept produced by one functional stovepipe. It would then move to engineering for a more detailed delineation of requirements. It would then move to the logistics organization. From there it might go to contracting, then finance, and then the legal department. In Dyer's words, "As the activity moved from one functional area to the next, it would be clear that a decision made earlier could not be implemented by the next area. So things were sent back, rework had to be done. This was expensive and caused delay."

Not only was this inefficient with a lot of rework, but the appropriate tradeoffs among functional disciplines were not being made. Dyer described this as "setting out to design a race horse and ending up with a camel. Every organization tried to optimize from their perspective." This was clearly not an example of effective collaboration.

In 1992, the then Commander of NAVAIR commissioned a team of nine people to develop a new concept of operations for acquisition management within NAVAIR. This team recommended that NAVAIR move away from functional stovepipes to a product orientation where all functional areas worked together as a team. This recommendation followed a series of briefings from industrial organizations that had made this transition. These included Hughes, GE, Chrysler, Ford, Boeing, and McDonnell Douglas.

7.6 The E/F Program Pilots a New Way of Working Together

A high-level plan was developed to transition to IPTs. The E/F program was selected to be a prototype for implementing IPTs. In 1994, (then) Captain Joe Dyer, who had been part of the team that wrote the concept of operations, was appointed as the program manager.

One of the early decisions outlined in the concept of operations was to matrix the functional organizations across the IPTs. Rather than serving as functional stovepipes in a sequentially organized workflow, they would now serve as resources of expertise in staffing IPTs. From this high-level vision, there were many details remaining to be worked out.

Dyer's first step in breaking down the functional boundaries was to co-locate the system engineers and the program manager within the same building in Crystal City

(Arlington), Virginia. When looking back to this period, Dyer pointed to the importance of co-location noting that the head of engineering protested by saying "You're going to dilute our engineering resources. You'll have our engineers worrying about contracting and finance." To which Dyer responded, "You're right"—because that was the purpose of the co-location.

One key enabler to effective integration of program management and engineering was the organizational structure that was put into place on both the government and contractor side. During 1994 and 1995, a series of meetings were held to define the IPT structure for the program and to develop the detailed procedures for how the IPTs would work in practice. In a 1996 symposium, Dyer made the following observation:

> When we first started putting together IPTs, all of our functional groups wanted their own IPT—the Test and Evaluation people wanted a Test and Evaluation IPT, the logisticians wanted a Logistics IPT, the contracting officers wanted a Contracting IPT. By the time you got through, this looked just like where you came from. So we applied a test for IPTs—it had to be something the fleet asked for. The fleet never, ever called me up and said "Get me some T&E over here in a hurry" or "Boy, would we like to have some logistics." We focused our IPTs on product and then asked "What does it take to deliver the product?" These are the disciplines that have to come into every IPT (Dyer & Conger, 1996).

The IPT structure corresponded to the product hierarchy, as shown in Figure 7-3.

Figure 7-3 shows the entire Weapon System broken down into product definition, production, business operations, and support. Product definition is further broken down into airframe, propulsion, and so on; each of these is further decomposed.

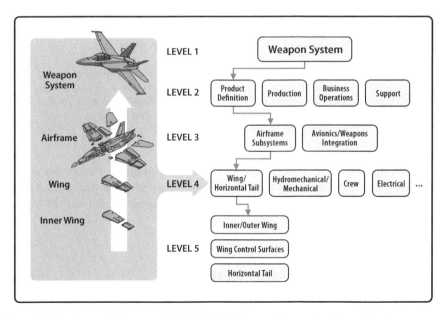

Figure 7-3: Product architecture of the F/A-18E/F Super Hornet is mirrored in the program organization

Adapted from McDonnell Douglas Corporation graphic

The example shows the breakdown for airframe and then for wings/horizontal tail. There are IPT leads at each level down to the lowest level (Level 5) product components. This same structure forms the basis for the work breakdown structure (WBS), the earned value management system (EVMS), and a number of key technical performance measures as described in more detail below. It is worth noting that this structure served as the vehicle for integrating program management concerns (i.e., cost and schedule performance) with systems engineering concerns (i.e., technical performance measures) in a way that provided visibility and accountability over the entire aircraft. The IPT leads on the contractor side had a NAVAIR counterpart on the government side. This alignment of organizational structures facilitated government-contractor communication and joint problem solving.

During 1994 and 1995, a series of meetings were held to define the IPT structure for the F/A-18 program and to develop the detailed procedures for how the IPTs would work in practice. The Deputy Program Manager for the F/A-18 program at the time was Captain Gib Godwin. In Godwin's words:

> There were two meetings that I can only describe as watershed events. The first was in Albuquerque in September 1994. This was a one-and-a-half-day meeting during which we defined the IPT structure. We had about 20 people there—the whole leadership team consisting of the top level (Level 1) IPT leaders plus competency specialists (e.g., engineering, contracting). Then there was a second meeting at Key West in February 1995 that lasted for two days. We brought in people from different functional areas that were not with the F/A-18 program so that they would be objective. We defined in some detail how the IPT/Competency Based Organization would work. There were a lot of issues that had to be addressed such as who would do performance reviews, who signs timecards, and so on.

At this point, there was a lot of resistance. As Godwin notes,

> People said it's too hard to do. It represented a big redistribution of power within the organization away from engineering to more of a balance across functional areas. Engineering had the dollars before. Now the dollars are distributed pretty evenly among the three Level 1 IPTs. I don't want to give anyone the impression that this was easy. It was difficult, frustrating, and gut wrenching.

In looking back to this earlier period, Godwin pointed out that a few key people were energized and worked very hard to bring about the transition. This included key people within the functional organizations as well as the early top-level IPT leaders (Bailey, 1998, p. 5).

7.7 Improved Decision Making

One of the key tenets of the program was to create a culture of rapid and effective decision making. This was accomplished through several mechanisms. The first was the creation of cross-functional IPTs that encompassed multiple perspectives for better decisions, more effective trade-offs, and less rework. A number of people on the program expressed the view that no one person, no matter how smart, can make decisions as well as a team of people with the right skills and attitudes. This highlights the importance of involving team members in the decision process, and facilitating the communication between these members by designing an organizational structure tailored to the program's needs and characteristics.

A second mechanism was through a culture that encouraged early identification of risks. That culture permeated the entire program both on the contractor and the government side. In the words of one of McDonnell Douglas' IPT leads, "Our definition of good management is recognizing problems and asking for help early on. Anybody can define a risk. It's okay to have risks, we just need a risk mitigation plan." He went on to delineate three necessary components for an effective risk management system:

> First, you want to identify potential problems early. Secondly, you've got to have management that doesn't shoot the messenger. It's critical that your customer has the same opinion. You have to have people who don't go ballistic when they have a problem. And third, you've got to have management that will provide help when asked. The person at the top has got to have that attitude. And in asking for help, you have to be able to say what you need.

Several people noted that team members were not punished for bringing bad news, but did get into trouble for holding back information.

A third mechanism was through decision making and problem solving at the lowest possible level of the organization rather than continual escalation of decisions to the highest levels of the organization. This was achieved through clear IPT roles and responsibilities, budget authority, and accountability. In this scenario, it is critical that program managers and systems engineers understand and consider technical as well as management goals and aspects when prioritizing and making decisions.

The responsibilities of the team leaders were documented in the form of IPT charters. There were clear boundaries for what was and was not within their scope of responsibility. They were given authority through control of their own budgets. They also wrote performance appraisals for their team members. In the words of one McDonnell Douglas IPT leads, "Team leaders have to balance cost, quality, and schedule. They have to be good business folks as well as engineers."

7.7.1 The WBS Aligned with the Product

The WBS was aligned with the product breakdown structure, or the structure of the product itself, to provide a common framework for integrating program management concerns with engineering concerns. The organizational structure put into place on the F-18 E/F program corresponds to the product hierarchy shown in Figure 7-3:

- At Level 1 is the F/A-18 Program Manager whose responsibilities include the A/B, C/D, and E/F models. Also at Level 1 is the Deputy Program Manager for the E/F.
- At Level 2, there is the IPT Manager, responsible for the product definition activities. Also at Level 2 are the managers for Production, Support, and Business Operations.

- At Level 3, under the IPT Manager, there are the two major parts of the aircraft for which McDonnell Douglas is responsible: the Airframe subsystems and the Avionics/Weapons Integration.
- Level 4 (under Airframe subsystems) includes five teams: Wing/Horizontal Tail; Forward Fuselage; Hydromechanical/Mechanical; Armament, Crew, Electrical; and Support Equipment.
- Level 5 (under Wing/Horizontal Tail) includes three teams: Inner/Outer Wing; Wing Control Surfaces (leading, trailing edge flaps, and aileron); and Horizontal Tail.

Each of the Tier 5 integrated product teams was allocated a dollar and schedule budget and a technical performance budget (defined as allocations of weight, power, cooling, etc.). This WBS became the integrating framework to balance program management concerns with more systems engineering concerns. Each WBS element was decomposed into multiple work packages that were further decomposed into a detailed set of tasks and associated resources (labor hours and dollars). Resources expended were compared with progress achieved on a weekly basis. The technical performance measures (e.g., current estimated weight, power, and cooling requirements) were updated at the same time. If a technical requirement was not being met (e.g., the weight allocation for the inner wing structure exceeded the threshold allocated) solutions were developed being mindful of the cost and schedule consequences. To continue the example, perhaps a lighter but more expensive material would solve the weight problem or perhaps another team was under-running its weight allowance and could adjust its weight budget to compensate for the overrun in the inner wing. Regardless, decisions could be made considering tradeoffs across all teams and considering cost and schedule impacts. This level of very close monitoring and continual adjustment contributed to the aircraft being developed within cost and schedule, and under weight.

The early structuring of the organization into IPTs brought together a number of functional disciplines to perform the necessary systems engineering tradeoffs that were required to build an affordable aircraft. Assembling these teams early achieved more effective tradeoffs, but required a funding profile that included higher early expenditures than those seen in previous programs—but with smaller expenditures occurring later. The E/F program's ability to deviate from previous funding profiles was a benefit of the Navy program office's close and cooperative involvement.

One benefit from this was the more than 50% reduction in the number of Drawing Change Notices or Engineering Orders per production drawing when comparing E/F's rate to A/B's rate:

- At first flight, the E/F had less than one Drawing Change Notice or Engineering Order per production drawing.
- The E/F's predecessor, the A/B, had well over two changes per drawing at the same point in the program (Bailey et al., 1999, p. 17).

The product and team structure were not static but continually evolving. As the E/F moved from development into production, the product definition teams became smaller while the production teams grew. Both types of teams remained multidisciplinary. The Level 4 lead for the Wing IPT stated:

> The guy who is the team lead for the production of the wing was a member of my Product Definition Team six months ago. Now he has his own team and we sit next to each other in the production building.

7.7.2 Promote Collaborative Work

Another hallmark of the E/F program was effective collaboration. This included collaboration within teams, across teams, and across the boundary between contractor and government. In the words of one government team lead, "We say to people, put your E/F hat on, join the team, and learn all perspectives. I'm a facilitator and a consensus builder. Team leaders are not defending their stovepipe, but working together."

Collaboration between government and contractor personnel can, perhaps, be seen most clearly in the Integrated Test Team (ITT), which carried out the flight testing of the E/F model during the Development Test and Evaluation (DT&E) phase. On most programs, the early DT&E phases are conducted by the contractor with key testing activities witnessed by government personnel. Later in DT&E, the bulk of testing is performed by the government. The ITT was a government-contractor team working together in testing, reporting, and analyzing anomalies and tracking status. As with all the F/A-18 IPTs, there were multiple disciplines on the test team including engineers who were involved in the design of the aircraft and who were available to analyze problems discovered during flight test. The flight tests were performed both by the contractor and by Navy pilots, and the results of the tests were shared across the entire team. One of the advantages of this integrated government-contractor team approach was more cost-effective use of the test aircraft. Under the old way, there were periods during flight testing when the Navy would be running their own tests. This was nonproductive time for the contractor. According to Captain Bob Wirt, Government Flight Test Director, the contractor costs per aircraft were US$50,000 per day. Thus, these nonproductive periods were very costly. "Now every day is a development test with the contractor productive. Because this is a joint government-contractor team, the Navy is analyzing the results both as part of the test team and as a customer."

The ITT went beyond integrating the contractor and Navy test teams and included Navy personnel from the Operational Test and Evaluation (OT&E) Force. Typically, DT&E and OT&E were serial activities and stovepipes of their own. At the completion of DT&E, the program would throw the product "over the wall," so to speak, to the OT&E staff. The stovepipe between DT&E and OT&E was supported by the OT&E community who believed that this helped to maintain their objectivity. This also meant they lacked knowledge of the aircraft and its capabilities. In the words of Dyer "some of us believed that the impartiality of ignorance was overrated." The commander of the OT&E Force for the Navy, Rear Admiral Jack Zeer, believed that having members of the OT&E Force be part of the ITT would be a positive change because they could learn about the aircraft while still maintaining their objectivity and professionalism. Not only did they maintain objectivity, but this proved to be another means of reducing the schedule and cost, and ultimately led to a better aircraft.

When asked how the F/A-18 program had managed to foster real teamwork between government and contractor personnel, Dyer (Dyer & Conger, 1996) responded:

> Leadership matters and personalities matter. Mike Sears, who was the Vice-president for F/A-18 at McDonnell Douglas, and I grew up working together on earlier models of the F/A-18. We had a trust and an openness and a communication with one another that we knew we could build on. We knew that we could flow it down to others and that we would both insist on it. We engendered, empowered, and insisted that we get communication between government and industry and, in those few cases where that didn't work, we rolled heads.

Dyer made it very clear that it is everybody's job to be a team player. As an example, he related the following scenario:

> We had a new government guy join us from another location. He stood up at a meeting and began by saying "The contractor has failed to provide." You could have heard a pin drop, the other members were so quiet. We realized that we hadn't heard that kind of language for a long time. And I told him "What you just said is not acceptable. If the contractor hasn't provided something, it's your problem too. What are you doing about it?"

Dyer concluded the story by adding, "There really is a cultural change required. We're not taught to be team players" (Bailey, 1998, p. 12).

7.7.3 Empowerment of Teams

Empowerment of IPTs permitted decision making to be driven to the lowest possible level. Moreover, resources were allocated to levels consistent with risk assessment authority, responsibility, and the ability of people. The teams were given the authority, responsibility, and resources to manage their product and its risk commensurate with the team's capabilities. The authority of team members was defined and understood by the individual team members. The team accepted responsibility and was held accountable for the results of its efforts. Management practices within the teams and their organizations were team-oriented rather than structurally, functionally, or individually oriented.

The words often heard in reference to the E/F team leaders were "responsibility, authority, and accountability." The team leaders were responsible for delivering the product and for maintaining frequent and open communication with their NAVAIR counterparts. They were given authority through control of their own budgets. They also wrote performance appraisals for their team members. Every team was allocated a budget for dollars, schedule, weight, and other relevant performance parameters such as power and cooling requirements. Accountability was achieved through the weekly reporting of these measures. Cost and schedule performance were tracked through weekly earned value reports down to the Level 5 teams.

The Level 4 leader for the Wing IPT described the leaders' responsibilities this way:

> Team leaders have to balance cost, quality, and schedule. They have to be good business folks as well as engineers. As a Level 4 team leader, I am running my own business. It's necessary to define the business boundary and what I need to run that business. We had casualties among the Level 4 and 5 leads in the early days. IPT leaders have to have a different set of skills (Bailey et al., 1999, pp. 21–22).

One of the key objectives in transitioning to IPTs was to break down barriers across functional areas, doing work concurrently that was previously done in a sequential fashion. A second objective was to surface, address, and solve problems early and at a low level. IPT leaders had a lot of flexibility and autonomy to address issues as long as they operated within clearly-defined boundaries. They were in charge of their own resources.

Dyer made the following point:

> We used to have responsibility for the quality of the product distributed all over the command. Now we say "Mr. Program Manager and Mr. Level 1 IPT Leader, you're responsible for the product." That was the shift that made us. Because all of the sudden, people who used to be adversaries—T&E, logistics—became the folks who are going to save you and keep you from being embarrassed, who are going to keep you from building a product that doesn't work (Bailey, 1998, pp. 12–13).

7.7.3.1 A Team in Action: The Engine Stator Problem

The E/F has two General Electric F414-GE-400 engines. In November 1996 during flight test, a stator or stationary airfoil fractured. The debris from the stator caused significant damage to the downstream compressor stages, leading to a total failure in Stage 6 and a high-pressure stall. The test pilot landed safely and the problem was reported. The engine was shipped back to GE and an investigation was begun to determine the cause of the fracture. Over the weekend, conference calls were held between the program office and GE, and on Sunday the decision was made to halt flight testing.

At this point, it was clear that the problem was related to high-cycle fatigue, but the exact cause was not known. The next step was to dismantle all existing engines in the remaining test aircraft. These engines were inspected in order to determine whether the problem appeared in multiple engines, indicating that the fracturing was a gradual process, or whether the fracture was only in the one engine, suggesting that it was a result of a special combination of conditions that the test aircraft met during this one flight. The former was the case, that is, fracturing was found in more than one engine.

In the words of the E/F Level 2 IPT Leader for Propulsion,

> Under the old way of doing things, GE wouldn't communicate issues until they had a plan to go forward. They felt that problems and their solutions were entirely their responsibility. Now, if there's an issue we're the first to know. This actually works to GE's advantage because we have talented people here

who can help. If there's a problem, we've probably seen it before. Under the old way, things wouldn't have been so open. GE was in favor of bringing in outside people. We brought in experts in high-cycle fatigue from the Air Force's Arnold Engineering Development Center, the Naval Research Laboratory, MIT, Purdue and the Department of Energy.

Two weeks after the problem first surfaced, a meeting was held in which all data were discussed. Fifty separate action items were identified relating to various tests that could be performed to identify the cause of the fracturing. One of the hypotheses was then verified through testing. The problem had been caused by a seemingly minor modification made to the stator for improved efficiency.

The solution was to return to an earlier engine configuration. Four engines were ready for the Initial Sea Trials in January 1997. According to the propulsion Lead:

In just six weeks, we went full cycle from having the problem surface to diagnosing it and to installing new parts. We worked 24 hours a day, seven days a week, right through Christmas. All of us—the Propulsion IPT, the Integrated Test Team, McDonnell Douglas, and GE—had a real sense of working as a team. Under the old way of doing things, this would have taken five or six months (Bailey, 1998, pp. 13–14).

7.7.4 Proactive Identification and Management of Risk

The fact that the E/F was an evolution from the earlier C/D model lowered the risk over an entirely new design. In the Level 2 IPT Manager's words, "We knew that cost, schedule and weight were do-able because we had experience on the C/D." Nevertheless, building an advanced fighter/attack aircraft is a complex undertaking where many things can go wrong (Bailey et al., 1999, p. 23).

McDonnell Douglas created the Systems Engineering and Integration organization to control risks and manage the requirements allocation process. The organization included a Level 2 manager and drew heavily from the lower-level product teams. This team took the requirements defined in the system specification and broke them down for allocation to the product teams. The specification for aircraft weight requirement, for example, would become weight requirements for the wing team, the forward fuselage team, and the vertical tail team. All system requirements, including survivability, reliability, cost, and schedule, were allocated in this way. By the time the program reached Preliminary Design Review, 3,000 specification paragraphs had been allocated to the product teams.

The fact that the E/F evolved from the C/D also lowered the risk of the program from the outset. However, proactive identification and management of risk were still essential to the ultimate success of the program. Proactive identification was accomplished through the overarching management philosophy of recognizing problems early on and asking for help. Weekly reporting was instrumental in this process. Once system requirements were allocated to teams, teams used McDonnell Douglas's formal risk management process to develop risk management plans that identified risks and then analyzed them in terms of their likelihood and consequence (Bailey et al., 1999, pp. 32–33).

7.7.5 Master Information Sharing

A high value was placed on open communication and on quantitative information. Dyer pointed out that "with the A-12, there was the perception that everything was fine one day and a disaster the next. Clearly, the right information was not getting to the right people."

The Navy Level I E/F IPT Co-Leader, made the point that:

> With IPTs, we have much more data. We're weighing things that we never considered before because we have so much more information. This can be frustrating to people. IPTs give you knowledge so that each discipline understands what other disciplines really do. This is important because building aircraft is all about compromise (Bailey, 1998, p. 9).

Along with communication, there was a heavy reliance on detailed quantitative information. One of the applications of this was the creation of a common, central database that was used by both the government and contractor to manage the program. This database contained hundreds of metrics, including financial data. In this way, both sides were working from the "same sheet of music."

As noted earlier, each of the teams, right down to Level 5, had allocations of dollars (which the team controlled), weight, reliability, maintainability, operations and support cost, electrical power, growth volume, and performance. Each team reported these measures on a regular basis (depending on the measure, weekly or monthly). Earned value down to the Level 5 teams was reported weekly. In this way, problems with costs, schedule, or technical performance (e.g., exceeding a team weight allocation) were immediately apparent and with clear accountability for who owned the problem.

Detailed and frequent (weekly) earned value reporting was used throughout the program as a management and a communication tool. According to Dyer:

> Earned value has been the centerpiece of the way we've measured the program. At our Critical Design Review for the E/F, we had the government and the industry IPT leader for each block in the work breakdown structure—air frame, landing gear, brake, brake subassembly—present their cost performance index, their schedule performance index, and their weight margin for the design. And early in the development we set up weekly reporting of these measures throughout the program. So I'm never more than a week away from knowing when I'm in trouble and where I'm in trouble.... It's very hard to find leading indicators in this business but we found that granular earned value provides us, if not with a leading indicator, at least a cycle time to identify problems that we've never had before (Dyer & Conger, 1996).

McDonnell Douglas additionally created HornetWEB, Integrated Management Information Control System, and Modular Six Degrees of Freedom to better manage requirements, planning, resource allocation, execution, and program tracking over the E/F program's life cycle (Bailey et al., 1999, p. 25).

7.7.5.1 HornetWEB

The HornetWEB was a secure information system hosted on McDonnell Douglas's intranet and accessible by McDonnell Douglas, the F/A-18E/F subcontractors, and the

Table 7-1: The HornetWEB system enabled access to data from across the entire program	
HornetWEB Sites	**Examples**
Business Acquisition	Contract documents, specifications, new product development, Navy programs, international programs
Program Management	Configuration management, data management, human resources, program directives, measurement program, metrics
Systems Engineering	CALS/CITIS information, reliability and maintainability, survivability, risk management, supportability assurance, management plan, readiness program
Product Development	IPTs, controls and displays, flight controls, transition
Verification	Flight limitations, operational evaluation preparedness
Production	Quality assurance, supplier management and procurement, training systems, variability reduction
Product Support	Support engineering, publications, technical manual, ILS management team interface, maintenance engineering investigations, supportability assurance readiness program

CALS Continuous Acquisition and Life-Cycle Support
CITIS Contractor Integrated Technical Information Service
ILS Integrated Logistics Support
Bailey et al., 1999

Navy program office. HornetWEB helped to provide all stakeholders with real-time access to technical and management information. It was used to enhance workflow management, system development, action item coordination, and electronic document sharing. As a secure system, the data was protected with adequate firewalls, data integrity, and security safeguarding programs.

Specifically, the HornetWEB supported sharing of data from both a user's perspective as well as an author's perspective. With the aid of a network browser and document viewer, users have access to integrated databases and documents that contain the types of information depicted in Table 7-1.

7.7.5.2 Integrated Management Information Control System

In addition to HornetWEB, there was probably no technology or software that had more impact on the program than the Integrated Management Information Control System (IMICS). Whenever E/F success factors are discussed by either contractor or government managers, IMICS inevitably appears near the top of the list. In the program's first award fee letter from the government, the system was cited as a major strength of the program. The team that created the system received the highest awards at both the company and corporate levels within McDonnell Douglas. Most importantly, the system is widely noted as being critical to the program's open communication and rigorous risk management. These priorities were demanded by the Navy in response to the failure of the A-12 program, and McDonnell Douglas formally promised them from the very start of the E/F program.

To meet these objectives of open communication and rigorous risk management, high-level program officials both inside and outside of McDonnell Douglas had to monitor effectively the program and communicate its progress even while decision authority was being pushed to the lower-level IPTs. This was accomplished by first allocating the requirements as far down as Level 5 teams, as described previously. After allocating the requirements, the teams had to be able to systematically measure their progress against these requirements and report this progress to management. The system had to be constructed so that the measurements were easily understood by a wide range of people no matter what part of the program the reports described.

E/F IPTs created specific metrics for schedule, cost, and risk status, as well as for technical performance. Schedule and cost results were reported weekly while supportability and technical performance parameters—such as reliability, maintainability, weight, and radar cross section—were reported monthly. IMICS provided snapshots in time as well as trend analysis. Separate charts also allowed IPT leaders to request help when a performance parameter was not progressing as planned.

IMICS made this reporting useful to management by pushing information up the organization in a system that was consistent in its presentation, but flexible in the level of detail presented. IMICS took data for all metrics and at all levels and rolled them up at whatever level a manager wished to see them. If interested in weight, for example, managers could see the overall aircraft weight progress and trends. They could then "drill down" to lower levels and see how weight was progressing in the Level 4 wing team, or even in the Level 5 control surfaces team. Additional IMICS measures include cost and schedule performance indices as follows:

- Budgeted cost of work scheduled
- Budgeted cost of work performed
- Actual cost of work performed
- Schedule variance
- Schedule performance index
- Cost variance
- Cost performance index
- Budget at completion (dollars)
- Estimate at completion (dollars)
- To complete performance indices

Managers at McDonnell Douglas and in the government had access to IMICS information at all levels of granularity as it was updated each week. Items falling behind their goals were easily identified and progress against corrective action was easily tracked. When an item demanded upper level attention, Dyer, the government program manager, and Mike Sears, the McDonnell Douglas program manager, could each bring the same data up on their screens as they discussed the problem. In more routine situations, the metrics and the presentation charts provided a ready format for the weekly management meetings held at McDonnell Douglas and for progress reports to officials outside.

Because IMICS organized a large amount of data into usable form, and was widely used and distributed both within and outside the government, it made the progress of the program understandable to a wide array of people. This wide communication, in turn, allowed the teams to effectively identify and address areas that put the program's objectives at risk.

7.7.5.3 Modular Six Degrees of Freedom

McDonnell Douglas used common databases and analysis tools, known collectively as Modular Six Degrees of Freedom (Mod SDF) (Bailey et al., 1999, p. 28), to facilitate the exchange of information across the product and the technical discipline-based

Table 7-2: Mod SDF databases and analysis tools				
	Technology Teams			
Mod SDF	**Aerodynamics**	**Flight Control Flying Qualities**	**Structural Loads and Dynamics**	**Materials and Structural Development**
Databases	Aero Database	Control Laws	Loads Database	Materials Database
Analysis Tools	Mission Performance	Flying Quality Criteria	Design Loads	Design Allowables
	Carrier Suit Performance	Control Laws	Dynamic Environment	Composite Allowables
	Weapon Separation Requirements		Aeroelastic Stability Requirements	Full-Scale Test Requirements

Bailey et al., 1999

technology teams to produce balanced requirements and designs. Table 7-2 contains a list of the Mod SDF databases and tools used by these engineering teams.

In addition to the tools listed in Table 7-2, the technology teams relied heavily on the use of simulations supported by Mod SDF to analyze the requirements, software code, and the integrated subsystems. As in the case of the flight control computer system, simulations were used to conduct several levels of testing to ensure the assembly code and flight hardware were operating correctly.

7.8 Program Delivery

As stated previously the E/F program completed its development phase ahead of schedule and within budgeted cost. Further, the aircraft realized benefits by completing its development phase weighing 1,000 pounds under its specification with one-third fewer parts than its predecessor aircraft, a heavier payload, longer range, and increased reliability (White, 1997). It was also projected to improve reliability or Mean-Flight-Hours-Between-Failure by up to 25%, and "Organizational" Level Scheduled and Unscheduled Maintenance Man Hours/Flight Hour by over 40% compared with the C/D fleet. As shown in Figure 7-4, very few schedule slips occurred in the E/F program, with the exception of the initial operational capability date (Younossi et al., 2005, p. 6).

It is noteworthy that the program completed within budgeted cost, since funding cuts were imposed twice between 1990 and 2002. The 1993 defense authorization bill authorized US$944 million for the E/F program, US$190 million less than requested. The same bill also set several conditions that had to be met before any of the funds could be obligated. Two of these required the Secretary of Defense to certify that management systems were in place to ensure that total Engineering and Manufacturing Development costs would not exceed US$4.88 billion (in 1990 dollars) and that the

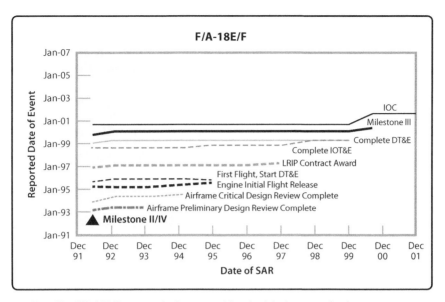

Figure 7-4: The F/A-18E/F program had a very stable schedule during its development
Younossi et al., 2005, p. 8. Reproduced with permission of RAND CORPORATION via Copyright Clearance Center, Inc.

cost of the E/F model would not exceed 123% of the flyaway cost of the C/D model unless the Navy demonstrated that the higher flyaway costs would produce greater warfighting effectiveness (Younossi et al., 2005, p. 65). Funding cuts or instability during a program's development phase typically results in cost overruns later in the program. However, the E/F program was able to absorb those early funding cuts and still complete within its planned budget.

The close integration across the program resulted in benefits in areas such as manufacturing. By creating production processes and hardware designs simultaneously and carefully analyzing the sources of variation in the process, the E/F program was able to reduce production costs and create production processes that reduced defects and rework. For example, concurrent design tradeoffs resulted in E/F wing spars of higher quality and costing 30% less than the C/D wing spars. Numerous iterations and early tradeoffs made while designing the flight control computer system resulted in fewer requirements changes and change memos (Bailey et al., 1999, p. 32).

The completed aircraft have consistently been delivered on or ahead of schedule. In the 1996 Quadrennial Defense Review, the Navy was directed to reduce the total procurement of the E/F from 1,000 to 548 aircraft. The peak annual production was also cut from 60 to 48 aircraft, and the ramp-up to full production was delayed by two years (Cohen, 1997, p. 45; Younossi et al., 2005, p. 68). Despite this significant change to the program plan, demand for the airplane has been strong with 565 Super Hornets delivered by the end of 2015. Benefits to the manufacturer of the strength of the platform include exports to the Royal Australian Air Force and a new application in the EA-18G Growler electronic warfare variant, with 150 aircraft scheduled to be delivered over the life of that program beyond the standard aircraft program.

The aircraft achieved initial operational capability in the U.S. Navy in September 2001, and entered first combat operations a year later in November 2002. It has been involved in combat operations semi-continuously since then. The introduction of the E/F into the fleet reduced the number of aircraft types deployed aboard carriers, bringing significant benefits in operations and maintenance, logistics, training, and equipping.

In June 1996, the E/F Super Hornet program received the first U.S. Department of Defense Acquisition Excellence Award for excellence and superior performance in the engineering and manufacturing development phase of the E/F. In 1999 the E/F program won the prestigious Collier Trophy as a recognition by the aerospace industry of an exceptional aircraft program.

7.9 Integration Practices Observed in the F/A-18E/F Program

The E/F program in its planning and execution demonstrated the application of a remarkable number of attributes from the program management and systems engineering Integration Framework presented in Chapter 6. Table 7-3 summarizes the key insights from the E/F case study organized by the dimensions in the Integration Framework.

7.10 Summary

The F/A-18E/F Super Hornet case study illustrates in some detail a program where integration was a core philosophy, driven by an understanding that the cost of not being integrated was unacceptably high. There was awareness that the traditional ways that teams had worked together in the past would not have met a critical schedule-driven need to provide key strike capabilities to the Navy fleet. What emerged was a program that subordinated the individual functional and organizational identities to the needs of the overall program. The mantra of the program leaders was "the airplane is the boss" and was used to ensure that individuals and teams worked to make the right choices and act as needed to ensure overall success.

This case history not only provides evidence to support the Integration Framework, but also illustrates how the various elements are expressed in an actual program and how they interrelate. The numerous organizations involved in the program were deliberate about their intent to have a more integrated, high-functioning relationship between program management and systems engineering. A number of practices and approaches were employed to encourage increased integration. Senior leadership played a defining role in establishing the vision for greater integration and were willing to expend time, resources, and leadership capital over an extended period of time

Table 7-3: Integration factors evident in the F/A-18E/F case study	
Integration Dimension	**F/A-18E/F**
Integration Processes, Practices, and Tools	■ Clear requirements for the program were established early through a collaborative process involving all program stakeholders. ■ Key technical performance measures defined early and shared across the program. ■ WBS was based on the product architecture to unite management and technical efforts. ■ Common central database (HornetWEB, IMICS) with weekly reporting. ■ WBS linked to EVMS to measure progress against tasks. ■ Mod SDF used as a common analysis environment. ■ Aggressive risk identification and management. ■ Flow-down of various technical- and management-related budgets to the IPTs.
Organizational Environment	■ Leadership at multiple levels advocated and modeled integrated behavior. ■ Strong push by NAVAIR to prioritize integration in program teams. ■ Program/product identity prioritized over functional identity. ■ Use of IPTs to bridge functional groups. ■ Co-location of program management and systems engineering/engineering disciplines. ■ Emphasis on effective communication across functional boundaries. ■ Culture of shared responsibility for outcomes across NAVAIR and McDonnell Douglas.
People Competencies	■ Support at NAVAIR to develop integration competencies. ■ Clear roles and authorities defined. ■ Leadership selection based on experience and ability to foster relationships. ■ Decisions made by capable people at the point where work is performed.
Contextual Factors	■ Urgent aircraft replacement needed after A-12 program cancellation and need to use existing funding. Prior history of arms-length relationships seen as a barrier to effective program execution. ■ The program budget was fixed by multiple stakeholders and there were requirements to stay within budgeted cost. ■ The program was funded as needed to meet its execution requirements and reflect its priority in the Navy acquisition portfolio. ■ Program complexity was reduced by using a derivative product strategy and leveraging existing organizational relationships. ■ Mature technologies were selected to limit overall program scope. ■ Nonessential upgrades were placed on a separate development path for later integration into the system.

to ensure that the entire program participated in enacting that vision. Chapter 10 and Part III of this book examine in greater depth the critical role that leadership plays in advancing integration between these program-critical functions.

7.11 Discussion Questions

1. What were some key similarities between what you read about in the case study and what you experience in your own work? What were some key differences?
2. Which elements of the Integration Framework do you think had the greatest impact on the F/A-18E/F program outcomes? Why?

3. What practice or set of practices would you urge your organization to adopt immediately? What factors from the Integration Framework do you think would be of benefit to your organization if adopted?
4. What principle barriers might you anticipate encountering as you try to replicate some of these practices? How challenging might they be to overcome?
5. Based on what you learned in this chapter, would you consider your current organizational environment to be conducive to the effective integration between program management and systems engineering? Explain. If not, why not?
6. What incentives and motivational factors would you recommend to your own organization in order to better integrate program management and systems engineering?
7. What technique did you think was most effective to ensure that stakeholder concerns were addressed early in the life cycle of the program?

7.12 References

Bailey, E. (1998, April 9). *The F/A-18E/F: An Integrated Product Team (IPT) case study*. Institute for Defense Analyses. IDA NS D-8027.

Bailey, E., Nash, S., & Woolsey, J. (1999, January). *Integrated product and process development case study, Development of the F/A-18E/F*. Institute for Defense Analyses. IDA D-2228.

Cohen, W. S. (1997, May). *Report of the Quadrennial Defense Review*.

Dyer, J., & Conger, C. (1996). *The evolving integrated program team*. Presented at Project Management Institute 1996 Annual Seminars and Symposium, Boston, Massachusetts.

U.S. Navy (2006, April 24). *Photo by photographer's Mate 3rd Class Chris Thamann (RELEASED)*. Retrieved from www.news.navy.mil/view_single.asp?id=33917

White, J. W. (1997). Application of new management concepts to the development of F/A-18 aircraft. *Johns Hopkins APL Technical Digest, 18*(1), 21–32.

Younossi, O., Stem, D., Lorell, M., & Lussier, F. (2005). *Lessons learned from the F/A–22 and F/A–18E/F development programs*. Rand Corporation. Report MG-276. ISBN 0-8330-3749-8.

Endnote

1. Contributed by Elizabeth "Betsy" Clark, SCRAM Principal, President, Software Metrics, Inc.

8

PROGRAM MANAGEMENT AND SYSTEMS ENGINEERING INTEGRATION PROCESSES, PRACTICES, AND TOOLS

8.1 Introduction

All aspects of integration are about individuals and how they coordinate the application of their collective knowledge, expertise, and capabilities to deliver results. Effective integration efforts are accomplished through the application of processes, practices, and tools that help to enable several important abilities:

- Enable communication and common understanding related to the key objectives and activities to accomplish those objectives.
- Provide frameworks for defining specific work activities.
- Establish expectations of each person's contribution.
- Document approaches for coordinating and tracking work efforts.
- Identify critical points where individual and group work efforts must come together.
- Facilitate problem identification and resolution.
- Apply generally accepted approaches that have demonstrated effective results under similar circumstances in the past.
- Support and accelerate the accomplishment of specific work activities.

Some processes, practices, and tools are designed for individual use while others may be structured for group activities. Both uses have appropriate application within complex programs. It is incumbent on the user or users to apply them in a way that facilitates integration across disciplines within a team. If users apply the processes, practices, and tools in ways that focus on their respective functions at the expense of collaboration with other disciplines, then there is likely to be only limited integration. On the other hand, if processes, practices, and tools not only define the work to do but also do it in a way that embeds collaboration, communication, and shared decision making in the tasks, then integration is much more likely.

This chapter uses various examples and also references the F/A-18E/F Super Hornet case study in Chapter 7 to illustrate processes, practices, and tools shown to enable higher levels of integration between program management and systems engineering as well as other disciplines.

No matter which integrating processes, practices, and tools are used, all will likely need to be tailored to the specific program context. This chapter makes the point that processes, practices, and tools should be deliberately designed and implemented in the program as part of efforts to improve integration between the program management and systems engineering disciplines.

The processes, practices, and tools mentioned in this chapter are organized by the timeline of their impact on integration: episodic or pervasive. Episodic integration emerges as the need requires. It is driven by periodicity in that it arises at points along the program timeline and is typically a result of overlay processes governing the program life cycle. Pervasive integration tends to be synchronous with the day-to-day work of the program or its component projects. Here the opportunity for integration runs contiguously.

8.2 Episodic Integration Mechanisms

Episodic integration mechanisms are applied occasionally to certain activities or at specific intervals within a program. These mechanisms are not daily drivers of integration between program management and systems engineering, but rather represent periodic forcing functions that require program managers and chief systems engineers to work together closely to produce successful outcomes.

8.2.1 Program Gate Reviews

Engineering programs often begin with a high-level program concept or idea that represents a strategic opportunity. When executive leadership believes that the concept is worth exploring, the leadership often appoints a sponsor and assigns resources to further develop the concept. Once the concept is fleshed out and specific approaches are identified for realizing the concept, executive leadership conducts a review to determine whether the concept advances to the next phase.

Many organizations require programs and projects to undergo executive-level gate reviews that determine whether they will:

- Receive approval to proceed to the next gate (Go);
- Repeat the review after addressing specific questions or concerns (Recycle); or
- Be terminated (No-Go).

There are several variations of the gate decision process. The majority have some form of the following points (gates), drawn from generic product development programs, where information is presented to a decision-making body for a go/recycle/no-go decision:

■ **Ideation:** A high-level description of the concept with very rough revenue and/or benefits and development cost estimates.

■ **Market rationale/opportunity:** Some type of market research regarding the concept, which may also include a competitive environment analysis.

■ **Business case:** Includes content from previous gate sessions, but is now further defined and scoped along with fairly definitive investment and revenue/benefits expectations.

■ **Develop/build:** This may be broken into several gate decisions where the idea moves to prototype and then toward a full production model.

■ **Test:** The product has moved through a complete validation against original requirements and performance objectives and is ready for production.

■ **Launch:** Full production begins and the product is positioned in the market.

Gate reviews require that all program aspects, such as cost, schedule, performance, risk, requirements, and testing, be presented in their current state of maturity at each individual gate. (Note that the same gate process, albeit with potentially a different decision-making body, will likely be used for each of the component projects as they move from ideation to completion.) These details allow the governance body to evaluate the overall program viability and make appropriate decisions. Gate reviews require that program managers and chief systems engineers work together to prepare the case for the program's advancement to the next gate. Gate reviews are, therefore, one of the few integration mechanisms utilized by most organizations. In higher-performing organizations, the reviews provide a sanctioned vehicle for close collaboration and subject matter expert review that is embraced by the various functions to assess where program performance is in relation to plan. Ideally, the reviews are coupled with the other processes, practices, and tools discussed in this chapter.

The "12 days of August" example from the Super Hornet case discussed in section 7.3 illustrates the benefits of program management and systems engineering working together to prepare to pass successfully through a major gate review. The principal challenge to the program was an undisciplined set of requirements that represented the set of all stakeholders' desires rather than a pragmatic set of the most important attributes of the system. The gate review provided the opportunity to gather all the disciplines together to make the necessary tradeoffs among competing requirements and interests. This resulted in a tight set of requirements that could be evaluated for cost and turned into system specifications for the subsequent phase of the program.

In preparing for gate reviews, the use of systems engineering technical reviews (SETR) may offer a valuable approach for program management and systems engineering integration. SETRs are initiated by the program manager upon being satisfied that the program has met the specific review's entrance criteria and provide program managers with independent assessments of their program's technical health and maturity at key points in the development life cycle. Tailored to reflect the uniqueness of each system, SETRs are used to review and evaluate whether required systems engineering tasks have been satisfactorily completed prior to proceeding to the next stage of development. Led by an independent, experienced technical manager with extensive and deep domain expertise, the SETR team documents its findings and issues a work list containing discrepancies that must be resolved prior to the completion of the review. Each technical assessment culminates in a formal meeting that documents risks and recommendations to program management regarding the continuation of work to the next stage of development. SETRs provide a forum for communication, coordination, and integration across all program disciplines, and thus are most effective when fully integrated into the program plan and aligned with key program milestones and gates.

United Technologies Corporation (UTC) developed a customized version of a gate decision process named Passport, shown in Figure 8-1. The common elements of gate review processes can be observed in Figure 8-1, but the process was tailored to the needs of UTC and integrated into the other elements of its business operating system. This need for tailoring processes and tools is discussed later in Section 8.4, but the point here is that UTC used the concept, adapted to their environment and culture, as a means to further integrate various disciplines across the organization. Roth (2010) points out that at UTC, "The Passport Review Board consists of a management chair and representatives from marketing, finance, engineering, manufacturing, aftermarket, quality and service organizations." (p. 115). While the review board serves an important function in terms of decision making regarding the investment of resources, the real value is the collaboration it encourages across disciplines prior to each gate

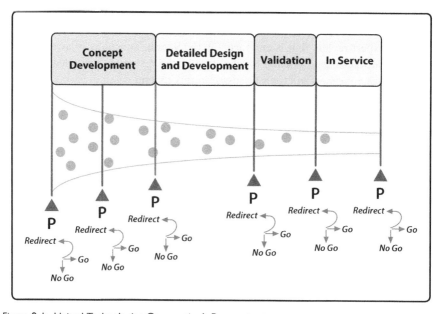

Figure 8-1: United Technologies Corporation's Passport gate process

review process. The outcome is increased likelihood of success for the program based on the cross-discipline work that has gone into the program planning process.

8.2.2 Joint Planning

Lucae, Rebentisch, and Oehmen (2014) point out that concept development and planning for engineering programs combines three critical components, each of which must integrate with the others:

- **The product concept** attempts to define the interrelationships between the value of the program, customer needs, and product requirements associated with the strategic opportunity.
- **The business plan** validates the strategic opportunity by evaluating the product's alignment with business strategy, the market for the product, the level of investment required for development and production, and the return to the organization on its investment.
- **Program organization and processes** outline how the organization will develop and produce the product, including critical program activities, the associated human and other resources, stakeholders who will be engaged, and governance.

In addition, each of the above components identifies potential risks that could impact the program both positively, in terms of new opportunities, and negatively, in terms of threats that could hinder success. Research consistently indicates that effective execution of these planning and scoping activities at the start of a program can improve its overall performance and its ability to deliver the desired business benefits (Oehmen, 2012). Even though collaborative planning is recognized as a critical practice for integration, the active involvement of key stakeholders in the program is often neglected (Conforto, Rebentisch, & Amaral, 2014). The lack of inclusive and coordinated planning has been recognized as one of the most common sources of problems in programs, leading to unproductive tensions across different areas and between team members involved in the product development process (Conforto, Rossi, Rebentisch, Oehmen, & Pacenza, 2013, p. 3).

There are a variety of tools, templates, and software applications that organizations can use to help support scoping and planning activities. For example, organizations may develop their own template for program plans to capture all of the relevant artifacts that need to be in the final program plan such as customer information, procurement needs, program governance, and operation charts (Lucae et al., 2014). But the important point is that the early planning stages of a program provide a rich opportunity to collaborate and integrate disciplines, and this practice increases the likelihood of success while at the same time minimizing unproductive tension later in the program.

There are a number of planning-related practices that help to integrate program management and systems engineering, not only at the start of a program, but also throughout. These include:

- **Program kickoff workshops:** A program kickoff meeting brings together all key stakeholders, including engineers, program managers, and factory teams, in the case of product development programs, at the beginning of the program to gather insight and information from each stakeholder and identify critical dependencies as early as possible before critical decisions and commitments are made. The assembled team may work through a variety of activities to capture the important elements of what will eventually become a detailed program plan, including: action items, due dates, milestones, needed resources, and responsibilities; documentation of the communication needs between functions and program contributors; risks and opportunities; and traceable and vetted assumptions (Lucae, 2014). In the Super Hornet case, the fact that development teams from McDonnell Douglas, Northrop, General Electric, and the Navy could not agree on configuration management and high-level requirements forced a restart of the planning process. The 12-day meeting in St. Louis pushed the program leadership and team to develop a shared view and clear definition of what they were collectively developing. That shared view and clear definition ultimately resulted in a specific program plan and established agreed measurements through the use of work breakdown structure, earned value management system, and technical performance measures for each integrated product team.

- **Model-Based Program Planning:** Various artifacts describing the program, including the product breakdown structure, work breakdown structures, systems engineering and business process models, organization breakdown structure, and cost breakdown structure can be combined into a single model representing the relationships within a program to display its overall structure, relationships, and critical dependencies. The French nuclear firm AREVA in 2014 created such a model to manage the early design phase of a new nuclear power plant to be developed with four partners over a period of 10 years. The model was based on hundreds of tasks and thousands of documents and captured the relationships between the product breakdown structure, work breakdown structures, list of activities of each of the projects, organization breakdown structure, cost breakdown structure, and generic systems engineering processes. The output was an extensive description of the activities, deliverables, detailed log sheets, and project control indicators based on deliverables and their status, gates, or cost. The model was used to analyze the impact of potential changes in specific areas in the program throughout its life, and as a basis for estimating cost and identifying inconsistencies between the organization and the system structure that could render the program too complex to manage.

8.2.3 Dedicated Team Meeting Space

The creation and use of dedicated team meeting space and standup meetings is a proven process in a variety of domains. Toyota helped popularize this concept for managing programs in recent years through its use of the "obeya." This approach has spread across industry sectors and has gained even broader acceptance as "agile" approaches for managing programs and projects has grown.

An obeya provides a dedicated, common space for teams and subteams to meet. The name comes from a Japanese term that translates into English as "big room" or "war room," but refers in traditional practice to a room where a cross-functional team meets to figuratively or literally break down the product completely and investigate changes to it in real time. This allows the team to make rapid trade-off decisions that are acceptable to the multiple perspectives of the team. The traditional use of obeya stimulates the creation of shared awareness of the product system as it exists in reality, rather than only on paper or in a database.

Typically, an obeya has critical artifacts and resources to support the team during the meetings. It is flexible so each team can decide what components and resources are critical for a particular program. On the walls, teams usually affix a summary of the program goals, key milestones, deliverables, and a key performance indicator dashboard containing metrics and graphics with the current state of the program. It is also quite common to have prototypes of the product or parts of the product, drawings of the product, and charts showing the system architecture, risk, issues, actions boards, and so on.

It is quite common to use an obeya for a group of programs, so multiple teams can share and benefit from the same resources. Having one common obeya promotes information dissemination throughout the organization. The obeya can be used for everything from daily standup meetings to steering meetings to executive and customer reviews. Teams and subteams are constantly updating the program content and display so that it always reflects the current state of the program. Obeya use could be either episodic or pervasive, depending on the level of integration in the program. The obeya thus serves as a communications channel for all disciplines involved in the development activities of the program—again, encouraging integration of processes and methods.

Several examples of the dedicated space concept are illustrated in the Super Hornet case. First, the program leadership clearly understood that lack of agreement over configuration and high-level requirements could not be solved through virtual communication or top-down leadership. So the leadership group assembled in St. Louis for 12 days to work in the same space collectively to solve the program's challenges. That process was repeated for developing the structure for the program's IPTs. But also on a day-to-day basis, the IPTs shared space in Crystal City, Virginia to facilitate communication, joint problem-solving and real-time decision-making.

8.2.4 Pulsed Product Integration and Iterative Development

Drawing on concepts from Agile development and the fast prototyping approach, pulsed product integration and iterative development is sometimes described as the "daily build" of product components into more complex components or into complete products. Iterative development comprises the use of short cycles to create and deliver product increments, parts of the product, or other deliverables related to a program. It is time-boxed, which means the length of the short cycles is the same throughout the program. Organizations usually define 2 to 3 weeks for each iteration. Each iteration starts with a planning workshop in which the team will define what has to be accomplished in the next 2 or 3 weeks, clarify the goal and priority(s) for the iteration, and how the team plans to deliver the results. The planning session is generally based on a high-level program plan, which contains the key product components, systems, and subsystems to be developed followed by work packages and groups of activities to be performed. After completing the iteration, the team along with the customer and key stakeholders present and discuss the results. The integration with other components will follow. Iterative development at its core is based on experimentation, rapid feedback, and continuous integration.

A similar approach is set-based design. Set-based design begins by decomposing the product concept into submodules, which then requires the establishment of clear interface parameters that define the connections between the submodules. Once the submodules are defined, the team then begins to establish design variables within the submodule. Each team brings their set of design variables to periodic meetings where the Sets are compared and feasible solutions are identified, trade-offs are negotiated, and agreements about the subsequent areas of focus made. This process repeats through a number of cycles, each removing infeasible or suboptimal designs and increasing the detail of the remaining designs until the best design remains (Genta, 2016). The Naval Sea Systems Command used this approach in 2007 to complete preliminary design and contract design for a replacement Landing Craft Air Cushion transport in less than 12 months. Going from only very high-level requirements, the technical teams were able to explore a large number of options before creating functional requirements documents and ultimately specific requirements for the replacement. The integrated team of program management, systems engineering, and other engineering functions played a central role in this process at periodic meetings by "pruning" the number of options under consideration and steering the analysis toward the best overall solution (Mebane, Carlson, Dowd, Singer, & Buckley, 2011). Systems engineering ensured that the diverse elements came together to produce viable systems, and program management ensured that the viable systems will produce the benefits desired for the program.

8.2.5 Summary of Episodic Integration Mechanisms

Episodic integration provides opportunities for improved integration of systems engineering and program management through processes that generate touch points across the program's life. Gate reviews for advancing the program, and possibly the component projects, is a prime example of the use of episodic opportunities for integration. The gate process must be tailored to the type of initiative since the time between gates could range from weeks to years depending on the scope and complexity of the program. Nevertheless, the value is in solidifying and unifying the program team, including the project and engineering team members, around the solution as it unfolds. Missing this opportunity can lead to unproductive tension and confusion among team members. However, when all of the various disciplines are included in the gate review process, there tends to be a shared ownership of the outcome.

Joint planning at the outset and replanning as the program and its component projects move forward is another one of those episodic integration opportunities. One of the key values of joint planning is the early collaboration that brings together multiple disciplines and, therefore, multiple perspectives for realizing program objectives.

When this opportunity is missed and program planning takes place in isolation, it often leads to rework later and missed opportunities for innovative solutions.

Team meeting space also provides opportunities for higher levels of integration. Regularly scheduled standup meetings along with a central "war room" location provides the opportunity for ensuring everyone on the team and associated with the program work has a single view of the status. Without this ongoing commitment to brief meetings on a scheduled basis, misunderstandings and conflict increase, leading to increased cost, redundant or conflicting work activities, and lower team morale.

Episodic integration requires a high level of intentionality since, by its very nature, it is periodic. Gate reviews, for instance, only happen at a few specified points in the life of a program. Reinforcing the value and importance of integration, and institutionalizing the adopted processes as part of the culture, become critically important to sustaining the integration effort. Integrating activities that occur infrequently are less likely to have a sustained influence on the daily behaviors and interactions of the program team than those that are engrained in the daily work and routines of the program. For this reason, episodic integration mechanisms, while immediately beneficial, may be weaker at producing fundamental changes in how an organization achieves integration between program management and systems engineering than pervasive integration mechanisms.

8.3 Pervasive Integration Mechanisms

There are processes, practices, and tools integral to program design and development. They are continuous in nature and thus are "pervasive." The degree of depth associated with use of pervasive integration mechanisms is reflective of the extent to which executive leaders and program teams view the integrated capability as a strategic or business differentiator. As the saying goes, "leaders demonstrate what they value by what they invest in." Despite the fact that processes, practices, and tools are not as attractive as a new product or high-profile outcome, such as a higher stock value, they are key enablers of everything that executives might consider as high profile and of value to the organization. Developing and sustaining consistency in any of the following areas can lead to such potential benefits as:

- Speed to market
- Improved product quality
- A more collaborative and engaged workforce
- Reduction in wasted funds and efforts

The application of pervasive integration mechanisms can help program teams realize such potential benefits for their organizations.

8.3.1 Standards, Methodologies, and Assessments

Recent studies (Conforto & Rebentisch, 2014; Reiner, 2015) have shown that programs with greater integration and better performance often present common characteristics related to the proper use of standards to build an integrated program development methodology. A methodology is the means by which teams within an organization apply a level of consistent discipline to their activities. A methodology is a documented approach for integrating interacting or interdependent practices, techniques, procedures, and rules to determine how best to plan, develop, control, and deliver a defined objective. A methodology usually incorporates and integrates three important elements:

1. How an organization conducts its business, including its requirements and processes
2. Key aspects of the organization's culture and capabilities as well as the environment, industry sector, and context within which the organization operates
3. Proven, recognized best practices or techniques for accomplishing intended results

Organizations may benefit from having a methodology in many ways. A methodology:

- Represents a repeatable approach that can be used across the organization
- Centralizes required documents, templates, and tools so the organization does not have to constantly reinvent its approach
- Enforces control and discipline by detailing the exact steps to be followed; individuals authorized to make key decisions; key information to be reported and to whom; and other related controls
- Standardizes repeatable processes, which then allows for consistent reporting to organizational decision makers
- Incorporates constant improvement and refinement as the methodology is applied through documentation of lessons learned from its use
- Is tailored to the specific and unique characteristics and capabilities of the organization, and to the specific activities or processes for which the methodology is intended
- Provides a framework for staff training and development so that individuals understand their roles in the activities or processes as well as critical interfaces with other staff, executive leaders, contractors, suppliers, and other stakeholders
- Provide greater assurance that those steps deemed critical by the organization are being completed

A methodology is customized to the unique needs, applications, and activities of a specific organization. A standard, on the other hand, reflects broadly accepted principles of what represents good practice or common guidelines. Standards address what is to be done at a high level without specifying exactly how. Standards also provide a common language that helps to ensure effective communication. The International Organization for Standardization (ISO, 2004) cites the American National Standards Institute's definition:

> A standard is a document, established by consensus and approved by a recognized body, which provides, for common and repeated use, rules, guidelines or characteristics for activities or their results, aimed at the achievement of the optimum degree of order in a given context.

Table 8-1: Key distinctions between standards and methodologies	
Standard	**Methodology**
Developed by the diverse community of individuals engaged in the discipline	Developed by staff within the organization or by consultants hired by the organization
Represents good practice as defined by consensus	Represents expected practice within the organization
Promotes use of common terminology	Promotes use of common terminology
Descriptive—illustrates which work elements may be accomplished	Prescriptive—outlines how the organization requires specific work activities to be accomplished
Applicable to most work efforts across most industries	Customized to the specific organization, its industry, and its requirements so there is a better fit with the organization
Provides general guidance related to approaches and tools	Mandates specific approaches, tools, or rules

For comparative purposes, Table 8-1 highlights some of the key distinctions between a standard and a methodology.

A methodology reflects the specific actions, steps, tools, techniques, and reports the organization determines are required for designated activities. Those actions, steps, tools, techniques, and reports are customized to the specific needs and practices of the individual organization. So in building a methodology, a program team may use content from generic standards and customize that content by explicitly incorporating internal rules, roles, and procedures within those areas where they intend to drive certain behaviors and practices. For example, practitioners may combine some of the processes and methods from PMI's (2013a) *The Standard for Program Management,* INCOSE's (2015) *Systems Engineering Handbook,* or others into its methodology. They then decide which specific practices, techniques, and tools best support the standardized processes and methods. Those specifications are then incorporated as organization-specific requirements into its methodology. A methodology can be structured to scale based on specific factors. For example, business activities with high levels of uncertainty or complexity may follow a more rigorous approach, while more predictive activities may use only certain elements of the methodology that are appropriate for the scope of work (PMI, 2013b; PMI, 2011).

The use of commonly accepted methodologies is especially helpful in cases where an effort involves multiple organizations, as when a program and its systems involve teammates or subcontractors. This approach to developing a methodology can facilitate integration between program managers, chief systems engineers, and project managers across a team and helps them to integrate their work quickly and effectively.

Since a methodology is a living, evolving resource, as organizations change, mature, and evolve, so too does the organization's methodology. As the methodology is implemented, executive leaders and users must evaluate the specific practices and the extent to which the company is adhering to its methodology. Such assessments lead to continuous improvement in the methodology as its user community moves closer to being "best-in-class" performers. Similarly, the methodology must also be continuously adapted and aligned with the organization's other technical, business, and management processes as changes occur.

The Super Hornet case identifies several examples of integrated methodologies and processes. The NAVAIR Commander commissioned a "new concept of operations for acquisition management" that shifted from a stovepipe mentality to an integrated, team-based framework for program management. The integrated product team (IPT) structure that flowed from that new concept of operations had detailed procedures for how the IPTs would work in practice. The IPTs utilized common tools and practices, such as a charter, work breakdown structure, and measures associated with earned value management and technical performance applied across the program. Standardized information systems and tools created vehicles for monitoring performance, facilitating communication, and identifying and managing risks across each of the IPTs.

8.3.2 Integrated Product and Process Development

Integrated product and process development, also known as simultaneous engineering or design-build, uses multidisciplinary teams in design to jointly derive requirements and schedules with equal emphasis on product (i.e., design) and process (i.e., manufacturing) development. This approach uses multifunctional, integrated teams that are preferably co-located. The integrated team includes the primary functions involved in the design process; technical process specialties such as quality, risk management, and safety; business groups such as finance, legal, procurement, and other nontechnical support; and customer or market representatives (or advisors) that will be the "voice of the customer."

There are 10 key tenets associated with IPPD, but these can be collapsed into five principles:

- **Customer Focus:** The primary objective of IPPD is to identify and satisfy the customer's needs better, faster, and cheaper. The customer's needs should determine the nature of the product and its associated processes.
- **Concurrent Development of Products and Processes:** Processes should be developed concurrently with the products they support. It is critical that the processes used to manage, develop, manufacture, verify, test, deploy, operate, support, train people, and eventually dispose of the product be considered during product design and development. Product and process design and performance should be kept in balance to achieve life cycle cost and effectiveness objectives. Early integration of design elements can result in lower costs by requiring fewer costly changes late in the development process.
- **Early and Continuous Life Cycle Planning:** Planning for a product and its processes should begin early in the science and technology phase (especially advanced development) and extend throughout every product's life cycle. Early life cycle planning, which includes customers, functions, and suppliers, lays a solid foundation for the various phases of a product and its processes. Key program activities and events should be defined so that progress toward achievement of cost-effective targets can be tracked, resources can be applied, and the impact of problems, resource constraints, and requirements changes can be better understood and managed.
- **Proactive Identification and Management of Risk:** Critical cost, schedule, and technical parameters related to system characteristics should be identified

from risk analyses and user requirements. Technical and business performance measurement plans, with appropriate metrics, should be developed and compared with best-in-class government and/or industry benchmarks to provide continuing verification of the effectiveness and degree of anticipated and actual achievement of technical and business parameters.

- **Maximize Flexibility for Optimization and Use of Contractor Approaches:** Requests for proposals and contracts should provide maximum flexibility for employment of IPPD principles and use of contractor processes and commercial specifications, standards, and practices. They should also accommodate changes in requirements, and incentivize contractors to challenge requirements and offer alternatives that provide cost-effective solutions.

IPPD teams often use requirements breakdown structures (RBS) and work breakdown structures (WBS) to facilitate their scoping and planning activities, and, again, these are opportunities for integration between and across disciplines. RBS are useful where complex systems dictate significant attention be paid to requirements and when integration is crucial. This exercise engages the customer, systems engineer, program team, and program manager in jointly creating a vision for the requirements at a relatively high level. The RBS helps to visualize the intersection of deliverables and requirements, and naturally feeds into a detailed WBS.

The WBS serves as the key framework for organizing the program and the systems engineering effort as well as for estimating and allocating cost, schedule, and performance requirements. The WBS decomposes both the technical and program management effort in successive levels of detail while describing the totality of both the system under development and the scope of the program. The WBS serves as a key program management/systems engineering integration point. Consequently, it must be thoughtfully designed to reflect the balanced needs of both program managers and systems engineers. It must also be tailored to reflect the unique nature of the system and the management approach.

Integrated product and process development was a primary organizing principle in the F/A-18E/F program and the integration of the various stakeholders that was achieved through this approach drove much of its success. Because it was the primary organizing principle for the program, many of its practices map directly to the IPPD principles discussed in this summary.

8.3.3 Work Design Processes

Work design processes such as configuration management can help to increase communication and collaboration across the program. Configuration management is a process for managing version control of requirements, specifications, and work. It is used to track requirements or specifications and any changes that are made that subsequently produce another version of the requirements or specifications. Formal configuration management includes planning, identification, change control, and audits/reviews. Program managers and chief systems engineers must work together to document a configuration management plan that identifies which configuration items will be tracked, and how changes will be managed to ensure that the proper configuration items are updated and coordinated with other users.

Another work design process is standardized work. Standardized work is one of the key differentiators of the Toyota engineering process. Rigorous design standardization supports platform reusability. This allows Toyota to share critical components, subsystems, and technologies across vehicle platforms, resulting in lower product cost and higher quality. Toyota focuses on harmonizing design standardization, process standardization, and engineering skill-set standardization (Oehmen, 2012). According to the *Encyclopedia of Lean Enablers* (MIT CEPE, 2013), standardized work can help improve the flow of work within a program:

> Once [standard work is] in place, work is ensured to be done in a consistent manner and at a consistent rate thereby making impediments more obvious. [Standard work] can be captured in different forms: in manufacturing production capacity sheets, combination tables, work charts; in engineering checklists, shared components across products, product architecture, manufacturing processes, supply chains, test plans, design strategies, as examples. These forms are then used by engineers and front line supervisors to innovate/design the processes and by operators to make improvements in their own jobs. As [elements of the standard work] are improved, the new [elements] become the baseline for further improvements.

Aircraft engine manufacturer Pratt & Whitney (P&W), a division of United Technologies Corporation, built its reputation on high-quality, high-performance products. Consistently delivering on its brand promise requires that the company have highly integrated teams where system-level team leaders, functional specialists, and subcontractor program managers, who are involved in design, production, and final assembly, have aligned work processes that enable them to effectively coordinate their work. P&W views its integrated teams and continuous improvement of its standardized processes as a competitive advantage. In fact, the company developed and patented a process called Engineering Standard Work, the evolution and application of which was captured in a case study by Roth (2010).

> Most organizations have developed templates for standard work, which require people developing standard work to include the what (task being described), who (person responsible for the work), when (sequence and frequency), the where (at what location), the how (methods to be used in their descriptions), and why (reasons work is performed as it is). Standard work descriptions are kept close to where that work takes place. In manufacturing cells, binders with the relevant standard work descriptions are kept in the work areas. In business process and engineering, there are binders, or computer accessible files with standard work descriptions. The goal is to produce work instructions that are simple and visual.

> A special case of standard work is Pratt & Whitney's development of Engineering Standard Work (ESW). While the concept is similar to what is described above, ESW is based on six elements of engineering work that are documented—workflow maps, tools and methods, design criteria, design standards, lessons learned, and practitioner proficiency assessments—each of which has assigned owners to review and make ESW changes. The detail,

focus, and magnitude of Pratt & Whitney's ESW efforts are noteworthy. The company faced engineering knowledge shortages as mergers and market conditions caused the company to close its military engine operations in Florida and move them to Connecticut in 2000. Many engineers did not make this move, and Pratt & Whitney found that they could not rely on engineers passing experience on as they normally had done. They had to capture and document the knowledge and develop a process focus in engineering, which their ESW efforts addressed.

Difficulties in meeting developing schedules for the Joint Strike Fighter F135 engine caused them to stop all engineering development activities for two months in 2001 to write engineering standard work documentation. From the F135 and GP7000 programs, they created 450 workflow maps, 9,000 activity pages, and 17,000 documents overall for their engineering processes, Pratt & Whitney recovered time lost and executed the F135 program within budget and schedule targets. An assessment in 2002 found that every $1 spent on ESW paid back $4 in cost savings. Engineering change orders decreased by 50% from 2001 to 2002 (and continued to drop in 2003), and for all design-quality escapes, estimated as having cost $46 million, 70% were attributed to ESW execution failures.

The key point for this discussion of work design processes is that work processes may either isolate functional disciplines from one another or integrate those disciplines as illustrated in the examples of Toyota and Pratt & Whitney. The best examples demonstrate that work processes are deliberately designed so that integration is a natural outcome of the work itself. These tailored work processes should be intimately connected with standards, methodologies, and assessments.

8.3.4 Requirements Management

Requirements management is another pervasive mechanism that forces conversation between program managers and chief systems engineers. Effective requirements management practices help program managers and chief systems engineers align their work so that customers receive ideal solutions and desired program benefits, and value is realized for the business.

Requirements management is also one area of potential conflict between program managers and chief systems engineers. The program manager is pressured to keep activities on track and the chief systems engineer is challenged to elicit, document, and validate good requirements for design and development. If the two cannot effectively collaborate with customers and other stakeholders to ensure there are stable requirements, both may share responsibility for program failures associated with cost, schedule, performance, and solutions.

As shown in Figure 8-2, many requirements management activities cascade across each of the domains of portfolio, program, and project management. Requirements often start at the concept or portfolio level as a high-level view associated with investment or business opportunities. The high-level view is captured in an initial business case that is cascaded to a program for further exploration and elaboration. At the program level, the program manager and chief systems engineer build on the high-level view by eliciting, documenting, and validating high-level requirements from customers

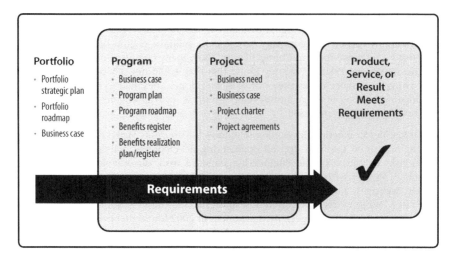

Figure 8-2: Requirements across the portfolio, program, and project domains

Requirements Management: A Practice Guide, Project Management Institute, Inc., 2015. Copyright and all rights reserved. Material from this publication has been reproduced with the permission of PMI.

and other stakeholders. Those high-level requirements help to frame the program roadmap, benefits register, and a more detailed business case. In turn, the program may further cascade elements of the high-level requirements to specific projects for more detailed development. Each level of requirements elaboration ultimately has to deliver the product, service, capability, or result that delivers value from the program. Integrated approaches are mandates to accomplish such an objective.

But requirements management is as much art as it is science. In large-scale engineering programs, there can be thousands of stakeholders, each promoting different aspects of value and often in conflict with other stakeholders' definition of value. Capturing a value proposition reflective of the highest level of value requires a team in which the individuals can apply their own competence, wisdom, and experience, and then negotiate with the team to reach consensus (Roth, 2010). Program managers and chief systems engineers should consider not only traditional requirements, but also needs, context, operations, interpretations, interoperability, and compatibility characteristics. They should also have a good understanding of customer culture (Oppenheim, 2011).

The requirements management approaches utilized may need to be adapted based on the level of requirements stability as reflected in Figure 8-3.

Effective and integrated requirements management was core in the Super Hornet program. The program leadership team developed initial technical requirements to utilize as much relevant existing technology as possible to reduce both the level of complexity and potential risk. Then the integrated product team was empowered to collaborate with other integrated product teams to negotiate tradeoffs and to develop alternate solutions when technical requirements were not being met in terms of cost and schedule performance.

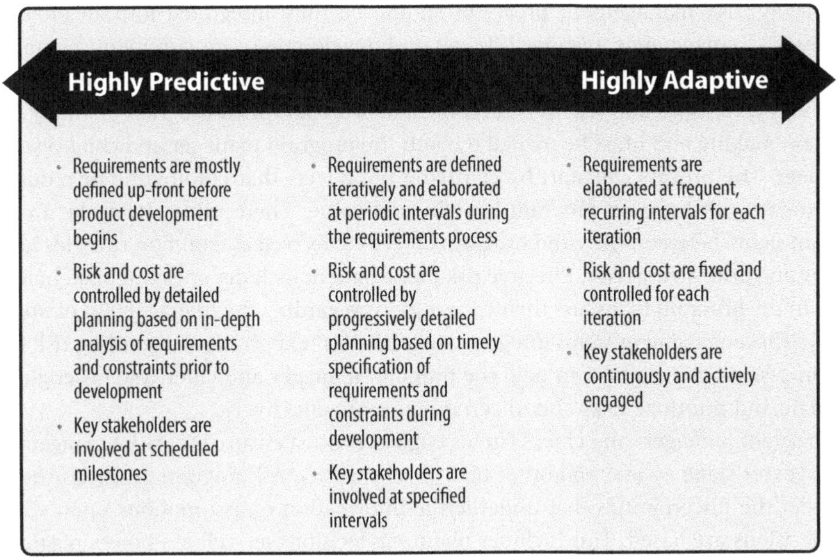

Figure 8-3: Life cycle types and requirements process

Requirements Management: A Practice Guide, Project Management Institute, Inc., 2015. Copyright and all rights reserved. Material from this publication has been reproduced with the permission of PMI.

8.3.5 Risk Management

Every engineering program features some level of uncertainty and risk that must be managed so the program delivers the solutions customers expect within established parameters. Effective risk management must also ensure that the sponsoring organization realizes its desired benefits. That is why risk management practices must be pervasive and integrated at the program level. But it is also important that the program manager and chief systems engineer work together in identifying and managing risks. It is easy to fall into the trap that the program manager focuses on business risk and the chief systems engineer focuses on technical risk, but these risks are often interrelated such that risks in one area may have implications for risk in others. Using risk management as an opportunity for better integration will often result in surfacing risks that, in isolation, may be totally missed.

There is no shortage of guidelines and standards to help practitioners manage risk effectively. Sometimes one guide may conflict with another, but many of the recommended approaches align or fill gaps in the others. While all of the guidelines and standards provide valuable insights, the program manager, chief systems engineer, and program team must tailor the program's risk management approach to its particular needs. Tailoring is essential to ensure that risk management activities support overall program goals rather than simply checking a box that risk management plans and mitigation approaches have been documented. While risk management requires ongoing work effort, effective tailoring and application of risk management approaches can produce positive results.

Ideally, risk management processes should be fully integrated into all program activities—management, technical design and development, procurement, planning, and so on—and at both the program and project levels. The assessment and reduction of uncertainties and risk must become a natural part of all program planning and decision making and must be owned by both the program manager and chief systems engineer. The process can start by clarifying the effects that eliminating or reducing uncertainty can have on program benefits and value. There must always be a clear "line of sight" between risks and program objectives as well as common rules for identifying and prioritizing risks. Effective risk management includes engaging stakeholders early in the program to discuss their expectations regarding the management of uncertainty. This engagement helps integrate stakeholders' expectations regarding risk into the process. Such insights can help the program manager and chief systems engineer evaluate and prioritize risks and uncertainties more effectively.

Program managers and chief systems engineers must ensure that risk management takes center stage at gate and other high-level reviews. All program decisions should consider the uncertainties that underlie the information or assumptions upon which the decisions are based. This includes planning decisions as well as choices regarding technologies, supply chain partners, or requirements. Indicating the level of uncertainty involved in these decisions helps decision makers to qualify the choices and subject them to the appropriate follow-up review.

There is debate as to whether risk management should be performed by a specific individual with core risk management competencies, or whether program teams should include team members with expertise in a range of risk management practices. Rather than an "either/or" proposition, it should be a "both/and" practice. Having a risk management function that embodies specific risk management tools and methods can be beneficial if that function helps program and project teams utilize those practices effectively. However, from the start of the program to its conclusion, execution of risk management activities should be part of the program processes that engage appropriate program personnel, including program managers and chief systems engineers. Such an approach ensures that risk management remains an ongoing part of deliberations and decision-making processes at all levels.

Funding for risk management activities such as identification and quantification should be available so that effective risk management starts at the beginning of the program planning process and continues throughout the program's life. In addition to exploring potential threats associated with program risks, the program manager, chief systems engineer, and program team members should explore the opportunity side of risk management to uncover potential improvements to program performance, deliverables, and solutions.

In the Super Hornet case, risk management was the responsibility of every team member from the start of the program. That responsibility was collectively managed when the program leadership team decided early on to reduce program risk by using as much existing technology as possible. Program leadership also emphasized the importance of early risk identification, but also responsibility for identifying mitigation options. The program team culture engendered transparency by facilitating problem solving and rejecting blaming behaviors when problems surfaced.

8.3.6 Technical Performance Measurement

There are numerous decision-making tools, processes, and methods for use by program managers in collaboration with chief systems engineers, but very few techniques call for integration through technical performance measurement. Such methods are useful for identifying potential risks in an integrated and collaborative approach using various parameters such as technical, cost, and schedule.

Technical performance measurement is an analysis and control technique that is used to:

■ Anticipate the probable performance of a selected technical parameter—generally, the key performance parameters or critical requirements that when not met put the project or program in jeopardy due to lack of benefit achievement over a specific period of time.
■ Record the actual performance observed of the selected parameter.
■ Through comparison of planned versus actual performance, assist the manager in decision making.

While program managers are balancing the program's performance objectives and benefits, chief systems engineers are developing a system to meet the program's performance requirements. The technical performance measures serve as a key program management/systems engineering integration point to ensure program success—both business and technical.

Performance measurement and management derives ultimately from the definition of program benefits. Technical performance measurement should flow from the program's benefits register to all activities and be tied to the overall performance measurement system of the program.

A well-thought-out program of technical performance measures provides an early warning system for review of technical problems and supports assessments of the extent to which operational requirements will be met as well as assessments of the impacts of proposed changes in system performance. Technical performance measures can help identify trade space for the program manager, develop the program's test plan, and provide key inputs into major program decisions.

The effort required to perform technical performance measurement is not insignificant and could be very costly. Consequently, great care must be taken in the selection of the technical parameters chosen to be measured, which are then tailored to the system. First, the parameters should be derived from or at least traceable to key program performance requirements. Second, processes must be in place to track parameters that are of high risk to program and system success. Finally, the program manager and chief systems engineer will likely consider including those parameters which are high cost drivers.

The Super Hornet work breakdown structure provided the integrated framework for the integrated product teams (IPTs) to manage technical performance at both the program level and the IPT level. Each IPT had its own work breakdown structure, technical performance measures, and allocated budgets in specific technical performance measures such as weight. But they also had visibility to the progress of other IPTs through shared reporting and tracking systems. The regular reporting and tracking of technical performance measures allowed the IPTs to identify issues and opportunities for trade-offs with other teams, ultimately reducing technical and program change orders.

8.3.7 Governance

Governance is a structured mechanism through which individuals with oversight responsibility and authority provide guidance and decision making for important organizational activities. Within the program and project domains, an organization's governance structure reinforces an integrated management approach between program management and systems engineering.

PMI's *Governance of Portfolios, Program, and Projects: A Practice Guide* (PMI, 2016) proposes that governance serves the following key functions:

- Oversight
- Control
- Integration
- Decision making

As shown in Figure 8-4, each governance function maintains specific activities for which the governing body is responsible, such as conducting reviews/audits as part of its controlling function or resolving/mediating risks and issues as part of its decision-making function (PMI, 2016).

Because programs can be large endeavors that consume considerable internal and external resources, the integration functions that program governance performs require that program teams, and especially the program managers and chief systems engineers who lead them, collaborate effectively. If the program governance body is strong, its oversight and decision-making functions can challenge a weak team or facilitate the work of a team that has strong collaboration. Weak program governance can fail to address ineffective program leadership, potentially exacerbating the team's weaknesses and making successful program performance that much more challenging. On the other hand, a highly collaborative team could insulate itself against weak governance through effective bottom-up management that pushes the governance body to fulfill critical functions that will enable the program team to fulfill its responsibilities.

Governance processes should be tailored to fit the scope and level of control necessary for the program to function effectively. Program management governance models may vary by organization—whether government or corporate ventures—as well as by size.

Because it was a program sponsored by the U.S. federal government, the Super Hornet program had two levels of governance. The highest level of governance was the U.S. Congress, which established specific parameters that the program had to meet subject to oversight by Congressional committees. Congress also impacted the program's funding through the annual appropriations process. The program level of governance involved the actual program leadership, which was shared between the government (Navy) and its primary contractor (McDonnell Douglas). The second level

Functions Domains	Oversight	Control	Integration	Decision Making
Program Governance Alignment Domain	• Establish governing body • Create program governance charter • Create program governance management plan	• Manage quality reviews and phase gates • Conduct planning for prioritization and funding	• Integrate program strategy • Create integrated roadmap with strategy execution tracks	• Establish decision-making process • Determine program prioritization and funding • Perform go/no-go decisions or components • Reallocate resources
Program Governance Risk Domain	• Create risk management plan • Establish risk escalation process	• Conduct project audits • Manage program internal/external dependencies	• Integrate dependency management	• Resolve and remediate risks/issues
Program Governance Performance Domain	• Create performance management plan • Establish reporting and control processes	• Monitor benefits realization • Monitor program and component health	• Perform integrated performance reporting	• Assess changes to *benefits* realization • Assess changes based on performance and strategic changes
Program Governance Communications Domain	• Create communications management plan	• Communicate roles, responsibilities, and authorities	• Communicate integrated roadmap • Disseminate consolidated program reporting • Disseminate program information and impacts to stakeholders	• Report decisions made with justification

Figure 8-4: Program governance functions and activities

Governance of Portfolios, Programs, and Projects: A Practice Guide, Project Management Institute, Inc., 2016. Copyright and all rights reserved. Material from this publication has been reproduced with the permission of PMI.

of governance was not only accountable to Congress but also provided oversight to ensure that the program achieved its overall mission within established parameters.

The Super Hornet case focused specifically on how program governance functioned to ensure the program met its objectives. The case identified how the governance body ensured the program used a highly integrated team structure and managed a challenging change process. The case pointed out that decision making was pushed to the integrated product teams and that the governance body maintained high levels of engagement throughout the program, including resolving key issues that were beyond the scope of the integrated product teams. The governance bodies regularly monitored key progress measures that reflected high-level management and technical requirements.

8.3.8 Summary of Pervasive Integration Mechanisms

Pervasive integration mechanisms, like those demonstrated throughout the Super Hornet case study, require ongoing collaboration and alignment among program managers, chief systems engineers, and their teams. Tools such as methodologies help teams organize how they will work together and identify key program considerations that must be addressed in planning, development, tracking, and reporting activities throughout the program's life. The methodology may define how the team will work throughout the program to manage requirements, risk, and technical performance.

Requirements management, process and work design, and technical performance management require ongoing engagement within the program team. As customer needs are elaborated and technical solutions for meeting those needs are explored, the team must have consistent methods for documenting, verifying, and tracking those needs, while at the same time exploring alternatives and developing specific solutions.

Ongoing risk management is used to look holistically at all program elements that can impact program performance and is thus a critical point of integration. Risks may surface at any point during a program's life so risk management activities by the full program team must be active.

Program leadership represents the interface between the program team and the executive leaders who are part of the program's governance body—those who make critical decisions affecting the program. Thus, the program manager and chief systems engineer must work together to address the governance body's concerns, provide relevant information to support good decision making and report back to the team to ensure effective communication and alignment with executive direction.

8.4 A Note on Tailoring

As discussed earlier, most standards are not intended to be used as is. The standards provide the "what" of the discipline, but there is a need to then develop a specific methodology covering "the how" using the standards for guidance. Similarly, tools and techniques can be and are useful for developing an organization's methodology, but require adaptation and tailoring to the organization. However, more tailoring is often required even after developing the foundational methodology as all programs are not the same. In recognition of this fact, PMI's *The Standard for Program Management* (PMI, 2013a) and *A Guide to the Project Management Body of Knowledge (PMBOK® Guide)* (2013b) discuss tailoring considerations related to the program and project domains.

The ability to tailor program documentation is essential to success. The majority of program processes, procedures, plans, and other governing documentation are based on industry, organizational, or government templates that are prescribed, so as not to reinvent the wheel or omit critical information and lessons learned. For these templates to capture all pertinent information, they are often written to capture the needs and governance requirements of large, highly resource-intensive programs. When adapting these templates to smaller programs or projects, it is essential to determine the aspects of the template that are not applicable, so as to use wisely the available resources (time, money, and people). A small program may not have the resources to perform with the same degree of rigor as a large-scale program.

Tailoring is not only about content reduction, but includes the addition of value-added content as well. If it is deemed beneficial to add content regarding the needs of a particular program, that content should be added with explanation. A programmatic or technical consensus may be required for the team to agree upon the volume and scope of the content that can be added or removed as part of the tailoring process. Many organizations have tailoring guides describing the tailoring process for specified documentation based on the type and use of the product under development.

A challenge to the addition of content during the tailoring process may come in the form of a review by a functional organization whose focus is compliance-oriented review. Functional organizations that are separate from program execution may tend to be resistant to tailoring attempts as they may lack the perspective and insight available to those who are actively engaged in the work of the program. When presented with this situation, it is essential that program managers and systems engineers engage functional managers. Program success will depend on the collaboration and willingness of all stakeholders including the functional managers. It may well be that the functional managers do not have the background required to comprehend, without a degree of mentoring, how tailoring helps the program to meet its objectives. In this case, both parties will often grow from this interaction creating an organization that is ultimately more efficient. This interaction creates a learning organization with open dialogue.

Tailoring played an important role in the Super Hornet case. While the program unfolded, it was clear that "business-as-usual" structures, processes, and practices would not yield successful outcomes. So the program established a unique framework that tailored each of those elements for the specific characteristics of the program. The integrated product team structure, the procedures that detailed how they worked, and the tools that enabled integrated planning and reporting were all selected and adapted to meet specific program objectives, whether those objectives were performance related or related to enabling an integrated environment. While it took time and effort to establish the program framework, in the end that investment paid off, as evidenced in the strong, integrated team efforts that delivered solid program performance.

In summary, tailoring facilitates customization of reviews, processes, and other decision support information to accommodate the unique nature of a program while still meeting the statutory, regulatory, and other governing requirements for decision making and oversight. Additive tailoring should only be performed when it adds value to the program's outcome. Similarly, reduction tailoring should be done carefully so that it does not remove an important aspect in the process.

8.5 Summary

A number of processes, practices, and tools exist and can be useful additions to the development of complex programs. There are certainly many more than those covered in this chapter. One of the key values of the tools and techniques discussed is the opportunity they provide for integration of systems engineering and program management. While each could prove useful for either discipline, the full value is achieved when used in collaboration rather than in isolation.

Whether episodic or pervasive, these integration processes, practices, and tools serve to:

- Structure the work that each discipline does in the program.
- Provide common norms/rules of behavior that encourage awareness of and collaboration with other disciplines beyond just systems engineering and program management.
- Link tools together so that the information and process flow is seamless, particularly across handoffs and boundaries.
- Provide increased understanding through a common information and performance measurement system.
- Engender joint accountability from program managers and chief systems engineers (and other disciplines) for outcomes that achieve the program's intended benefits.

Finally, every effort should be made to institutionalize the integration of disciplines enabled by the processes, practices, and tools by developing a standard, baseline methodology for the organization. The methodology must be tailored not only to the organization, but also to the unique nature and characteristics of the specific program to which the methodology is applied—and done so thoughtfully and intentionally.

8.6 Discussion Questions

1. How might the processes, practices, and tools presented here be useful to a program with which you are currently involved?
2. What other tools and techniques have you found useful?
3. How might you use one or more of the processes, practices, and tools discussed in your organization as a means by which to encourage greater collaboration between program management and systems engineering?
4. Reflecting on programs you have been involved with in the past, how might your organization have benefited from tailoring?
5. Do you see evidence of integration processes, practices, and tools that are being practiced between program management and systems engineering in your organization? If your answer is "yes," which tools do you find most effective and why?

8.7 References

Conforto, E. C., & Rebentisch, E. (2014). Executive report: *Improving the integration of program management and systems engineering—Case study analysis*. Executive report 3rd phase. Cambridge, MA: Consortium for Engineering Program Excellence, Massachusetts Institute of Technology.

Conforto, E. C., Rebentisch, E., & Amaral, D. C. (2014). *Project management agility global survey*. Cambridge, MA: Consortium for Engineering Program Excellence, Massachusetts Institute of Technology.

Conforto, E. C., Rossi, M., Rebentisch, E., Oehmen, J., & Pacenza, M. (2013). *Survey report: Improving integration of program management and systems engineering*. Presented at the 23rd INCOSE Annual International Symposium, Philadelphia, USA. Retrieved from http://www.pmi.org/~/media/PDF/Business-Solutions/Lean-Enablers/PMI-INCOSE-MIT-Integration-Study.ashx

Genta, J. (2016). *Set-based design and U.S. Navy design and acquisition*. MIT SM Thesis.

International Council on Systems Engineering (INCOSE). (2015). *Systems engineering handbook: A guide for system life cycle processes and activities* (4th ed.). D. Walden, G. Roedler, K. Forsberg, R. Hamelin, T. Shortell (Eds.). Hoboken, NJ: John Wiley & Sons.

International Organization for Standardization (ISO). (2004). *Standardization and related activities: General vocabulary*. Geneva, Switzerland: Author.

Lucae, S. (2014). *Improving the fuzzy front-end of large engineering programs— Interviews with subject matter experts and case studies on front-end practices*. Diploma thesis, Nr. 1392. Retrieved from http://cepe.mit.edu/wp-content/uploads/2014/04/SL_Improving-the-fuzzy-front-end-of-engineering-programs_print.pdf

Lucae, S., Rebentisch, E., & Oehmen, J. (2014). Understanding the front-end of large-scale engineering programs. *Procedia Computer Science, 28*, 653–662. doi:10.1016/j.procs.2014.03.079

Massachusetts Institute of Technology Consortium for Engineering Program Excellence (MIT CEPE). (2013). *The encyclopedia for lean enablers*. Retrieved from http://cepe.mit.edu/encyclopedia_overview/

Mebane, W. L., Carlson, C. M., Dowd, C., Singer, D. J., & Buckley, M. E. (2011). Set-based design and the ship to shore connector. *Naval Engineers Journal, 123*(3), 79–92. doi:10.1111/j.1559-3584.2011.00332.x

Oehmen, J. (Ed.). (2012). *The guide to lean enablers for managing engineering programs, version 1.0*. Cambridge, MA: Joint MIT-PMI-INCOSE Community of Practice on Lean in Program Management. URI: http://hdl.handle.net/1721.1/70495

Oppenheim, B. W. (2011). *Lean for systems engineering with lean enablers for systems engineering*. Hoboken, NJ: John Wiley & Sons.

Project Management Institute (PMI). (2011). *The practice standard for scheduling* (2nd ed.). Newtown Square, PA: Author.

Project Management Institute (PMI). (2013a). *The standard for program management* (3rd ed.). Newtown Square, PA: Author.

Project Management Institute (PMI). (2013b). *A guide to the project management body of knowledge (PMBOK® guide)* (5th ed.). Newtown, Square, PA: Author.

Project Management Institute (PMI). (2015). *Requirements management: A practice guide*. Newtown Square, PA: Author.

Project Management Institute (PMI). (2016). *Governance of portfolios, programs, and projects: A practice guide*. Newtown Square, PA: Author.

Reiner, T. (2015, May). *Determination of factors to measure the effective integration between program management and systems engineering*, Rheinisch-Westfälische Technische Hochschule (RWTH) Aachen Master's thesis.

Roth, G. (2010). *United technologies corporation achieving competitive excellence (ACE) operating system case study*. Cambridge, MA: Lean Advancement Initiative and MIT Sloan School of Management. URI: http://hdl.handle.net/1721.1/81998

Additional Resources

Kleinsmann, M., & Valkenburg, R. (2005). Learning from collaborative new product development projects. *Journal of Workplace Learning*, *17*(3). doi:10.1108/13665620510588671

Markeset T., & Kumar, U. (2003). Integration of RAMS and risk analysis in product design and development work processes: A case study. *Journal of Quality in Maintenance Engineering*, *9*(4). doi:10.1108/13552510310503240

9

THE ORGANIZATIONAL ENVIRONMENT

9.1 Introduction

Organizational structures, behaviors, and norms shape how program participants work and interact with each other and determine the nature of relationships. Much of the confusion encountered in problem solving today results from misconceptions about the nature of change in organizations, social systems, and their environments. Moreover, it has become evident that traditional hierarchical organizational forms, planning methodologies, and response strategies are inadequate for addressing complex problems. This is especially true when applied to emerging conditions having an increased rate of change, increased complexity, and increased uncertainty.

In an effort to understand how to develop better organizational environments for the integration of systems engineering and program management, this chapter analyzes the organizational structural dimensions of the Integration Framework, the environmental elements influencing the programs within the organization including cultural factors, leadership, and team building, and the nature of the participants' relationships.

9.2 Structural Dimensions of Integration

All organizations are developed through an ecosystem of related and unrelated and formal and informal projects, programs, networks, alliances, partnerships, and functional operations. This ecosystem defines the organization's structure. Because organizations are evolving systems, the structures within the organization continue to grow and change as the strategic goals of the organization change. Significant time has been spent on the development of new organizational paradigms that are "characterized by ... decentralized decision-making, greater capacity for tolerance of ambiguity, permeable internal and external boundaries, empowerment of employees, capacity renewal, self-organizing units, and self-integrating coordination mechanisms" (Campagnolo & Camuffo, 2010). In other words, emerging organizational paradigms are aligning with team-based behaviors.

The difficulty of governing these new structural paradigms leads to greater uncertainty and turbulence within the wider organization. In their study of program complexity from a systems engineering perspective, Oehmen, Thuesen, Parraguez Ruiz, and Geraldi (2015) define complex programs as "characterized by feedback loops and unforeseen emergent behavior that can spiral out of control, but are fundamentally still tractable by structure (if costly and time consuming) analysis" (p. 7). The following case studies and research focuses on the transformation of organizations to produce greater integration across functional boundaries such as program management and systems engineering.

The story that best illustrates the power of strong collaborative organizational cultures comes from the world of computer animation. Walter Isaacson's (2011) biography of the computer industry's most imaginative genius, Steve Jobs, describes the business and cultural relationship behind *Toy Story*, the blockbuster film that revolutionized the animated movie genre and helped to advance the organizational relational transformation between Disney and Pixar. When Steve Job's Pixar and Disney began negotiations in the early 1990s, Pixar was a small, financially unstable software company, while Disney was the industry giant. Pixar had no track record, while Disney had the brand and distribution clout. This leverage disparity made the merger negotiations between Disney and Pixar lengthy, tough, and contentious. Disney's Eisner "showed little curiosity about the artistry or technology at the [Pixar] studio. Steve Jobs likewise didn't spend much time trying to learn from Disney's management" (Isaacson, 2011, p. 433). The relationship that resulted from these initial negotiations was that Disney would provide majority financing to Pixar to create three movies, which Disney would own and distribute. Disney also used its position to try to exert control over Pixar's creative process (Catmul, 2014).

Observed from the perspective of organizational relational theory, the initial arrangement between Pixar and Disney was tightly controlled and hierarchical to maintain Disney's dominance, but as the relationship evolved, control became less important and relational norms took hold (Catmul, 2014, pp. 289–292). In particular, after Pixar produced a string of blockbuster films, leaders at Disney apparently came to believe that achieving the full creative potential of Pixar's animation required an intimate understanding of their approach. As a result, a rejuvenated relationship implemented such values as collaboration and trust, creative risk taking, and experimentation, ensuring reinvention as the norm, and a commitment to build the relationship and narrow the cultural barriers (Catmull, 2014).

In spite of an unbroken string of 11 blockbuster films and becoming the leading animation studio in Hollywood, Pixar's executives still expressed concern about how to battle complacency (Catmull, 2008, p. 9). How do you create a culture that regularly identifies and solves new problems to avoid succumbing to inertia? In describing

Pixar's string of blockbuster films, Ed Catmull, co-founder of Pixar Animation studios and President of Pixar and Disney Animation, stated: "[w]hile I'm not foolish enough to predict that we will never have a flop, I don't think our success is largely luck. Rather, I believe our adherence to a set of principles and practices for managing creative talent and risk is responsible" (p. 2). After Pixar's 2006 merger with the Walt Disney Company, a series of steps were taken to make sure the creative vision that was Pixar's hallmark survived the merger of these two leading entertainment giants. Catmull inspired the idea of having teams lead through his "director driven studio" model where storytelling was in the hands of the filmmakers themselves (p. 6). Employees could be assigned to primary and secondary teams depending on their skills and passions. Teams changed dynamically as the needs of the studio changed, without requiring traditional top-down reorganization. As evidenced in this chapter, an organization that develops creative leaders, fosters team building, and merges the technical and the creative cultures will have far greater chances of success than one that exists in a traditional, rules-based, hierarchical structure.

One of the hallmarks of Pixar's collaborative approach to team building was to engage employees across the organization. Catmull and other executives sought feedback from all staff, regardless of their position, regarding company operations as well as its work-in-progress films (Catmull, 2008, p. 6). Hierarchy and status were of less relevance. "Everyone must have the freedom to communicate with anyone. This means recognizing that the decision making hierarchy and communication structure are two different things" (p. 8). The director eventually made the final decisions, but not before everyone had been given a voice in the process. Working together and having the ability to share work in progress with everyone and receive valuable feedback along the way created confidence in the individual, while enhancing the group's creativity and advancing the organization's mission.

Does Pixar's experience apply to the integration between program management and systems engineering? The parallels between Pixar's "director driven studio" model and engineering programs is more direct than might initially be apparent. The director at Pixar is responsible for telling a great story, leading the creative team, and arguably for the overall success of the film. The production manager keeps track of all the details of production and ensures that the film is delivered on time and budget with high technical quality. Both are essential to the ultimate success of the film. There are, of course, other important roles that contribute to a successful film, such as technology directors, finance, and marketing, whose efforts and contributions must be coordinated during the production process. Both director and production manager roles share a number of similarities with both program managers and systems engineers; the mapping of roles between the two domains involves a number of overlaps. But the key point is that Pixar worked hard to create an organizational climate that ensures that every voice is heard and can communicate their perspective, needs, and ideas to the film and that no one individual or group dominates the process. Catmull (2014) remarks that "if any one of those groups 'wins,' we lose" (p. 138).

Creating a Team-Driven Process for Solving Problems

Ed Catmull (2014), in his inspirational story *Creativity, Inc.*, sets the vision and the sources of his inspiration and how Pixar fostered its creative community, and how these ideas were later transitioned to Disney Animation under his leadership. Some of the key principles behind Catmull's successful strategy are:

- "Give a good idea to a mediocre team, and they will screw it up. Give a mediocre idea to a great team, and they will either fix it or come up with something better. If you get the team right, chances are that they'll get the ideas right."
- "It is not the manager's job to prevent risks. It is the manager's job to make it safe to take them."
- "The people ultimately responsible for implementing a plan must be empowered to make decisions when things go wrong, even before getting approval. Finding and fixing problems is everybody's job. Anyone should be able to stop the production line."
- "Don't wait for things to be perfect before you share them with others. Show early and show often. It'll be pretty when we get there, but it won't be pretty along the way. And that's as it should be."

9.2.1 The Shaping of Programs

Pinto and Winch (2016), in their recent analysis of program-shaping research, call for a broader, more inclusive perspective on what it takes to successfully manage projects and programs by reorienting our frame of reference away from the long-accepted execution-based program delivery model with its natural boundaries toward one that embraces a fuller and better understanding of the links between programs and strategy that successful programs require.

In his research on project management, Morris (2000) recognized that project management concentrates too much on tools, techniques, and organizational issues, and not enough on the things that deliver real business benefit. Programs are often created to manage multiple related projects in a cohesive way and to obtain benefits and control not available by managing projects individually (PMI, 2013a). All organizations must possess an effective structure for management that will lead to the longevity and sustainability of the organization to achieve strategic objectives. The components of the organization may not necessarily be interdependent or have related objectives, but the organization must ensure that the strategies of its component parts—stakeholders, programs, teams, operations—align with the organization's overall strategy. Portfolio management serves as a bridge between organizational strategy and program, project, and operations management (PMI, 2013b). In essence, organizations must ensure that the right programs are selected to leverage its competitive advantage and to enhance stakeholder value, and, most importantly, provide input to the potential change of strategic direction for the organization.

Figure 9-1 shows the relationship between the organization's strategy and the organization's program benefits management. The interaction among the various interests

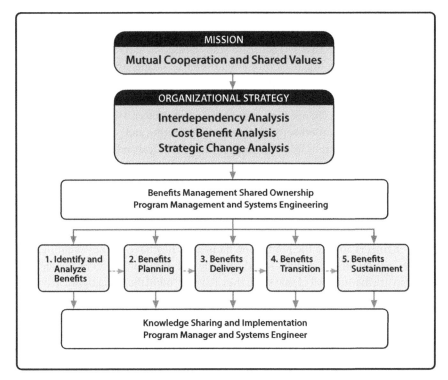

Figure 9-1: Shared ownership of benefits management

Adapted from *The Standard for Program Management*, Project Management Institute, Inc., 2013. Copyright and all rights reserved. Material from this publication has been reproduced with the permission of PMI.

in an organization is not just top-down, but the goals in each component part of the organization influence the others. As defined by *The Standard for Program Management* (PMI, 2013a), the program benefits management domain comprises a number of elements that are central to the successful conduct of programs. The purpose of program benefits management is to focus program stakeholders, including program sponsors, managers, and teams, on the outcomes and benefits to be provided by the various activities conducted during the program's duration (p. 33). Since organizational priorities are driven by the business case, it is important to ensure that program benefits are identified, analyzed, delivered, and transitioned to the operational areas, and are sustained once they are transferred. The sustainment of benefits is not just of concern to the program manager, but also a major deliverable of the systems engineer. INCOSE (2015) describes the business or mission analysis of the systems engineer as "defining the problem domain, identifying major stakeholders, identifying environmental conditions and constraints that bound the solution domain . . . and developing the business requirements and validation criteria" (p. 51). The process of developing business mission requirements aligns with the program manager's goals of identifying and analyzing benefits and opportunities, and ensuring product and program sustainability. Systems engineering and program management should support one another in defining what must be done and gathering the information, personnel, and analysis tools to elaborate the business requirements (PMI, 2013a, p. 55).

As illustrated in the Disney Pixar case study, fostering success in an organization requires a focus on the organization's environmental factors and its efforts to foster collective creativity. There is no approach that works for all organizations, but experience teaches that creating a vision then empowering others is an approach that has worked where episodic change is required to succeed (Kotter, 1996). The relationship that exists in an organization between systems engineering and program management is not significantly different from the sophisticated technical and creative relationship that was critical to Pixar's and Disney's integration.

Merging the technical with the creative is a challenge faced by all program managers and systems engineers. The program manager is like the director. The program manager has to see things through the lens of the audience (the customer) and is, therefore, responsible for the creative part, the art, the "building of the right thing." Systems engineers are like the production manager. They have to know lighting, camera angles, sound, details of each scene, and the like and manage all of the technical people that are manning all of that stuff; they have to "build the thing right." They both must share a vision of what the scene will look like in the end, as the director/program manager has to be able to communicate the vision to the production manager/systems engineer in mutually understood language he or she can understand.

9.3 Organizational Environmental Factors

Organizational environmental factors, everything outside the program's boundary, may consist of corporate, environmental, and governmental variables that constrain the ability of a program to achieve its goals. Some of the influences from outside the program are internal to a larger organization, and some come from completely external sources. Organizational factors outside of the program influence the selection, design, funding, and management of the program (PMI, 2013a, p. 30). External environmental factors may include the market and overall economic conditions, political climate, resources, health and safety, cultural diversity, technology, legislation and regulations, and quality and risk.

Understanding environmental factors is critical to the program team's success. For example, if program objectives are not aligned with organizational strategic goals, the program will likely be bogged down in internal organizational friction. External stakeholder support is also essential to program success. Customers and end-users are part of the program team, and without their continuous feedback, it is unlikely that the program will produce "the right thing." Smart program managers will always assess the competitive and regulatory environment. Without competitive awareness and regulatory alignment, program success is impossible.

Three organizational environment factors—culture, leadership, and interdisciplinary teams—can be employed to encourage or discourage the team behaviors shown to be key to integration and program success.

9.3.1 Culture

Bringing together diverse cultures is a responsibility of all organizations. Culture is typically defined as the collective values, philosophy, and practices of the organization's members. Culture can also have many meanings within an organization such as the business culture, the corporate culture, the peer culture, the team culture, the country culture, and the creative culture. Catmull (2008) described Pixar's success as being built on merging two very different cultures—the technical and the creative (p. 3). "At Pixar, when the technology is strong, it inspires the artists. And when the artists are strong, they challenge the technology" (p. 3). The result is that they appreciate one another's talents and their common goals. The development and fostering of mutual understanding of strengths and weaknesses for program managers and systems engineers creates an understanding of individual goals that can be valuable in moving the program forward.

Many models of organizational culture exist. Some models suggest descriptions of cultural factors (for instance Hofstede, 1994; Schein, 2004) and others classify culture types. Table 9-1 contrasts Hofstede's cultural factor classification with Disney Pixar's cultural environment.

Best, Smit, and de Faber (2013) researched interventions and their relationship to organizational culture and program management. Their findings corroborate evidence from existing research that organizational culture is the most important factor influencing program culture. Loo (2002) studied factors that may act as barriers for best practices and highlighted organizational culture as such a possible barrier. In Loo's study, cultural barriers included the need to manage the changing culture of the organization, pressures for innovation, the mild distrust between executives and staff, and too much focus on the bottom line (pp. 95–96).

Superior program management is attained when the organizational culture is based on effective trust, communication, cooperation, and teamwork (Kadefors, 2004; Kerzner, 2013, p. 45). Disney Pixar's key principles as described by Catmull (2014), are

Table 9-1: Mapping of Disney Pixar cultural attributes to Hofstede's cultural factors

Cultural Factors	Description	Disney Pixar
Power distance between management and teams	High Power—Top-down control Low Power—Implies greater equality and empowerment	Low Power Distance—Focus on autonomy and power of teams
Individualism vs. Collectivism	The degree to which individuals are integrated into groups	Focus on how a team is performing, not on the talents of the individuals within it
Uncertainty avoidance	Tolerance for ambiguity versus predictability	Acceptance of differing thoughts/ideas
Long- versus short-term orientation	Focuses on the extent to which the group invests for the future ■ Short term: Traditions are honored ■ Long term: Views adaptation and circumstantial, pragmatic problem solving as a necessity	Long-Term Orientation: Values continuous change, cooperative iteration, and reinvention as the norm

Adapted from Hofstede, 1994

essentially a list of trust-building behaviors: empower people, let them make mistakes, cooperatively iterate to perfection, and use relationships not rules to encourage behavior. Without the willingness of team members to actually share knowledge, the team is not able to integrate the skills and experiences from different disciplines (Reiner, 2015, p. 41).

The impact of culture on an organization is demonstrated in Siemens's research and development (R&D) activities in India reported in a case study by Thomke and Nimgade (2001). The report illustrates the logic of global development strategies and the operational challenges of managing globally distributed program teams. Issues presented by this approach included task division, work process control, incentives, and culture.

The Siemens case study evaluated the management of global R&D networks in a changing industry as well as probing the role and significance of cultural issues across countries on three different continents—the United States, Germany, and India. In the early 1990s, Siemens corporation made a strategic decision to outsource its R&D development to India. Central to the case is the tension that arises between the three different development sites as some large and significant programs ran into reliability and scheduling problems. Siemens's leaders were faced with a choice: either maintain more control at headquarters in Munich by continuing to bring decision making back to Germany whenever there were major problems, or grant more autonomy to the regional R&D centers in India. Recognizing the importance of their strategic commitment to Bangalore, in the end, more decision-making and project management responsibility was given to the R&D centers in India.

From the program manager's perspective, many issues surfaced and lessons were learned in this case, including the importance of developing a clear strategic plan, centralized control and management of resources, establishment of a plan to deal with local governments, managing virtual teams and cultural differences, allocation of responsibility for research and development, standardized procedures and flexible processes, centralized decision making, reduction of operation costs, established training programs, and planning and managing political, economic, and legal risk (Thomke & Nimgade, 2001). This case echoes the lessons from other case studies, including Disney Pixar: the importance of letting the creativity develop from the bottom up where the expertise lies (in this case in software development in India), rather than assuming that all the knowledge and legitimacy resides at the top.

9.3.2 Leadership

While leadership is discussed as a "people competency" in Chapter 10, it is worthwhile to note here that individual leadership skills are essential to creating integrated, team-based organizations. Reviewing Catmull's list of key principles, it becomes clear that the set of behaviors that can only be collectively described as "leadership" are needed to implement those practices. His second principle, "It is not the manager's job to prevent risks. It is the manager's job to make it safe to take them," is an example of this leadership. The leader takes ownership of risks that go sideways, protects the individuals who take them, and uses the failure as a learning experience.

In any program, the opposing ambitions of managers and their teams can become unhealthy. It is a leader's responsibility to see this and guide it, not exploit it (Catmull, 2014). When one considers that complex programs require the ability to achieve integration across disciplines, influence multiple governance structures, energize numerous stakeholders, empower program teams, and create the vision for innovation, the need for transformative leadership skills becomes more apparent (Greiman, 2013, p. 393). To foster integration and teamwork, top management must be involved in promoting and supporting team behaviors and creating an environment that encourages team building and trust building at all levels of the organization.

The current reality of the program is a constantly changing phenomenon. A leader must be able to improvise in order to cope with the dynamic environment. Put simply, improvisation is coming up with solutions to address emerging challenges quickly to continue to create value without disrupting the overall cadence or flow of the program. Improvisation has been broadly defined as the practice of reacting and of making and creating. Improvisation is linked with aspects of time and, particularly, pressure to achieve against a demanding or compressed timetable, which is a typical attribute of most large-scale infrastructure initiatives (Leybourne, 2008). Programs that are surrounded with uncertainty and complexity need to explore new ways of delivery outside of the hierarchical, structured approach of most program management regimes. Improvisation as a developing theory of program management is not universally adopted by the professional bodies; however, it fits within the program tailoring approach.

Large-scale programs by their very nature encounter a great deal of complexity and uncertainty requiring creative, innovative, and customized approaches to management and leadership. Boston's Big Dig was defined by uncertainty due to the extensive unknown subsurface conditions, the potential for catastrophic loss due to high-risk inner-city tunneling, and the complex stakeholder and socio-technical environment requiring agility and an improvisational approach. Like project and program management, "[t]rue systems engineering requires the ability to work with uncertainties and assumptions—not just determinate inputs—and to handle the distinct tradeoffs that different sets of assumptions generate (INCOSE, 2012, p. 7). Organizational leaders must understand the value and implications of an improvisational approach to integrating systems engineering and program management, and how decision making and responsibility will be allocated in these newer more complex team environments that are less rules-based and more focused on collective creativity.

9.3.3 Interdisciplinary Teams to Solve Large Problems

Interdisciplinary teams lie at the heart of systems engineering and program management integration, yet very little research focuses on the structure, role, and how teams are integrated. Importantly, team dynamics, human behavior, leadership, and the like are all recognized in *The Standard for Program Management* (PMI, 2013a) as being critical to program success, but the Standard would be huge if it had to include everything that was related to effective program management. To solve large problems in science, environment, medicine, and societal development, funding agencies in the United States,

Europe, and Asia have sponsored a wide range of interdisciplinary, cross-university research programs. Examples are the European Large Hadron Collider to investigate particle physics, the multinational Antarctic Drilling program to investigate climate change, and the information sciences. A vision for these programs is to create innovation that is greater than the sum of the parts.

Team building has been defined as "the process of taking a collection of individuals with different needs, backgrounds, and expertise, and transferring them into an integrated, effective work unit" (Cleland & Ireland, 2002). As defined previously in Chapter 5, integration is a reflection of the organization's ability to combine program management and systems engineering practices, tools and techniques, experience, and knowledge in a collaborative and systematic approach in the face of different challenges to be more effective in achieving common goals/objectives in complex program environments.

Considerable research has focused on how organizations combine their expertise through the development of teams (Grant, 1996; Nordhaug & Gronhaug, 1994). Teams collaborate in different ways and for different purposes. The emergence of fields such as computational biology and artificial intelligence suggests a positive relationship between integration, team performance, and innovation.

Catmull highlights the importance of team work in describing the gestation of *Toy Story 2* and the main character's dilemma to stay or to go his way: "Talented storytellers had found a way to make viewers care, and the evolution of this storyline make[s] it abundantly clear to me that '[g]etting the right people and the right chemistry is more important than getting the right idea'" (Catmull, 2014).

9.3.4 Key Observations on Organizational Environment

Based on the above discussion, a number of insights emerged with respect to shaping an organization environment supportive of integration. Of particular note:

- Adjust organizational boundaries to avoid silo thinking and parochial interests.
- Ensure that the strategies of the organization's component parts—stakeholders, programs, teams, operations—align with the organization's overall strategy.
- Take into account the systemic structures, cultural factors, and the relationship of the organization with its external stakeholders.
- Use relationships, not rules, to encourage behavior.
- Focus on how teams perform and not just on the individuals within the teams.
- Team members must be willing and incentivized to share knowledge and integrate the skills and experiences from different disciplines.

9.4 The Challenges of Integration in Large-Scale Programs: Systems Failure

There are many challenges to integration discussed in the program management and systems engineering literature that focus on organizational factors such as organizational structure, governance, complexity, uncertainty, and technical difficulties.

Organizational leaders are concerned that their organizations possess an effective structure for management that will lead to the longevity and success of the organization. Each of the following case studies discusses the relationship between program management and systems engineering responsibilities, how cultural and environmental factors influence program outcomes, and what needs to change within the organization to improve the chances for success.

9.4.1 The Hubble Space Telescope Program

When U.S. National Aeronautics and Space Administration (NASA) launched the Hubble Space Telescope (HST) in 1990, astronomers boasted that Hubble would probe the universe to a degree unparalleled by earthbound observatories and the images it would capture would be of unrivaled quality. The Hubble program fulfilled some of these claims, but the first picture—a severely blurred image of a star cluster in the Carina constellation—fell far short of the crystal representation everyone expected and a difficult truth became strikingly evident: the telescope was flawed (NASA, 2011). HST was eventually repaired through a servicing mission from the space shuttle, exceeded its original performance specifications by 50%, and became one of the longest and most successful science missions in the process.

Too often program estimates are approved without understanding the real implications of a flawed cost-control process. The official mishap investigation board reported that throughout its duration, the HST program experienced cost and schedule issues of "crisis proportions." These pressures, inevitably, were imparted to contractors. Possibly believing that surfacing issues with potential to further increase costs or delay schedules could instigate contention, contractors began reporting only the risks they thought were real (NASA, 2011, p. 3). According to NASA's official Optical Systems Failure Report (NASA, 1990), the most unfortunate aspect of the optical system failure was that the data revealing these errors were available from time to time in the fabrication process, but were not recognized and fully investigated at the time (pp. iv–v). Reviews were inadequate, both internally and externally, and the engineers and scientists who were qualified to analyze the test data did not do so in sufficient detail (p. v).

The HST program failure is attributed primarily to the fact that program management maintained an isolated focus on cost and schedule to meet the bottom line. The important lesson here is that when program managers and systems engineers are working together to solve problems, there is a greater likelihood that the systems engineer will have a better understanding of the technology, and the program manager will have a better understanding of the budget constraints. Once they are "speaking the same language," they can better convince the sponsors why changes are needed to accommodate the challenges that evolve from technological complexity and shifting stakeholder expectations.

9.4.2 The Heathrow Terminal 5 Program

Terminal 5 at London Heathrow airport is an example of a program delivered on time and budget with all the physical and electronic infrastructures built according to specifications. This alone is a remarkable feat in the world of large-scale infrastructure programs where being late and over budget is the rule rather than the exception. Nevertheless, on opening day, due to imperfect commissioning, failure of integration, and an untrained workforce, the systems immediately collapsed with missing baggage everywhere and hundreds of flights canceled (Davies, Gaan, & Douglas, 2009b). The outcome contradicted the extensive planning and the awareness of the risks involved in newly constructed airports. A joint British Airport Authority (BAA) and British Airways team worked over three years to ensure that systems, people, and processes would be prepared for the opening. The "start-finish" team worked during six months of systems testing and operational trials prior to opening, including 72 trial openings, each involving 2,500 people, to prepare workers, processes, systems, and facilities for the public opening at 4:00 am on March 27, 2008. (Davies, Dodgson, & Gaan, 2009a). Moreover, BAA's T5 delivery strategy was informed by a systematic benchmarking study undertaken between 2000 and 2002 of every major UK construction program over £1 billion undertaken in the past 10 years and every international airport opened over the previous 15 years (Davies et al., 2009b, p. 114). BAA's research specifically identified poor systems delivery and integration during the final stage of program execution as a major reason why international airports failed to open on time (p. 115). So what went wrong? In the Heathrow Terminal 5 case the Chief Facilities Manager, Catherine Tann, summed up the integration problem this way:

> When I started I thought it was all about systems, but as we get to the end of the project, I've learnt actually it's all about discipline and trying to get different people from different suppliers, the T5 Programme, BA and other parts of BAA to work together to solve the inevitable problems (Doherty, 2008, p. 155).

The key lesson learned from the Heathrow Terminal 5 case is that integrative programs are essential in developing strategies for maintaining sustainability over the long term. Despite the extensive preparation, testing, and benchmarking, there was a disconnect between the program teams, including systems engineering and the operations teams. Program sustainability requires an organizational environment that promotes integration to maintain operability, services, and benefits of the program not just during the life of the program, but the life of the program's assets as well.

9.5 Characteristics of Successful Program Integration

9.5.1 The Systems Perspective

Despite numerous failures, the literature also describes successful programs resulting from good systems governance and integration such as the Øresund Bridge linking Denmark and Sweden (INCOSE, 2015, pp. 40–42), the NASA MARS Pathfinder program (Nicholas & Steyn, 2008), and the I-15 Reconstruction Program in Salt Lake City (FHWA, 2011). Governance, and its related organizational structure, is an important environmental factor for achieving success. It requires that individuals with oversight responsibility and authority provide guidance and decision making for programs and projects. Miller and Lessard (2001) in their study of 60 large civil engineering programs describe the organizational structure of these programs, the shaping of a program, the program's institutional framework, and the capacity of self-regulation and governance. The up-front effort involved in shaping the program so it can survive turbulence improves the chances of success, but this requires leadership and systems thinking. Müller (2009) discusses governance at the program and organizational level linking program and strategic management. As noted by Locatelli, Mancini, and Romano (2014), for programs delivered in complex environments, the governance needs to be transformed from a corporate/program perspective to a "systems perspective." As the authors describe, system governance increases the likelihood of program success.

The most beneficial time for developing a "systems perspective" occurs during the up-front planning or earliest stages of the program planning (IEEE, 2005; Miller & Hobbs, 2005). For example, in the recent planning of the California High Speed Rail, the government has addressed the importance of a statutory oversight authority and a legislatively mandated risk management plan. Closely related to systems governance is "systems thinking"—a method developed to understand how systems influence one another within the whole. Systems thinking is what distinguishes systems engineering from other types of engineering, and is the underlying skill required to perform systems engineering (Beasley & Partridge, 2011). Due to the degree of the impact in the above examples, program leaders and sponsors must focus on resolution through greater integration between the technical experts and the program managers to increase the likelihood for success.

9.5.2 Incentives as a Tactic for Systems Integration

Incentives must align with key business success opportunities in order to ensure integration of systems engineering and program management. Incentives are usually defined in terms of financial incentives, including rewards for early delivery and penalties for late delivery (INCOSE, 2015, p. 144). However, incentives have also been highlighted in terms of leadership and value propositions (p. 9). The questions are whether incentives are likely to produce better products, cause people to work harder, or get work done in a safer way. Incentives should never be based on speed alone, unless there are disincentives or penalties for being late. Ironically, program leaders often do not consider the downside and disincentives for poor performance, and instead focus on rewards for being ahead of schedule or under budget. Incentives play an important role in integration because they create opportunities for developing a more cooperative relationship between the various disciplines involved in a program and to strengthen the cultural divisions among the parties. As an example, if the systems engineers and program managers are both rewarded for meeting performance standards, there will be a shared commitment to meet these requirements. On the other hand, if program managers are rewarded for speed without a corresponding recognition for systems engineers, schedule will take the lead and engineers are faced with producing a product faster and sometimes cheaper, but not necessarily a better product, or one that complies fully with performance requirements. To resolve this disconnect, incentive planning should be part of the program's strategy from inception. The incentives should include policy and contractual obligations that foster positive, cooperative outcomes and encourage integration of systems engineering and program management goals and objectives.

9.5.3 The Impact of Change Practices on Successful Outcomes in Program Organizations

In a connected, complex, and turbulent environment, organizations that are prepared to change their products, processes, and delivery at a rapid pace likely will be the most successful. The responsibility for leading change has increasingly fallen upon the program manager (Crawford, Aitken, & Hassner-Nahmias, 2014; Turner, 1996). A recent study suggests that program management professionals are embracing change implementation practices, and that these practices can have a major impact on program success and outcomes (Crawford et al., 2014). The introduction of *Managing Change in Organizations: A Practice Guide* by PMI (2013c) emphasizes the need for leveraging change management inherent in the standards for portfolio, program, and project management. The *2012 Pulse of the Profession® In-Depth Report: Organizational Agility* (PMI, 2012) concluded that organizations achieving higher-than-average success rates from their portfolio of programs and projects have not only increased their use of standardized program practices, but have adopted rigorous change management to better adapt to shifting market conditions.

A recent survey of 148 program practitioners investigated some contemporary issues surrounding the overlap between program management and change management, and links with strategic change (Leybourne & Greiman, 2015). There is evidence that involving program and change managers to influence and inform decisions about strategic direction at the organizational level is beneficial, especially as they are the managers who are more instrumental in ensuring effective implementation and execution of change initiatives. Findings also suggest that not only are program managers building a "wider business awareness" related to the way change impacts organizations generally, but also that program and change managers are acting more strategically to deal with emerging issues from within and outside of the organization (Leybourne & Greiman, 2015). Unfortunately, it is apparent that there is insufficient knowledge of the differences in the skill sets of program and change managers. This is an area where further study would benefit the academic and practitioner communities, and assist in the understanding of the systems engineer and program manager's role in change management.

9.6 The International Space Station: A Model in Systems Integration

The International Space Station (ISS) is perhaps the most famous of all systems engineering programs known for its convergence of science, technology, and human innovation. It demonstrates new technologies and makes available research break-throughs not possible on Earth. The space station has been continuously occupied since November 2000 and during that time more than 200 people from 15 countries have visited the space station (Stockman, Boyle, & Bacon, 2010). This program crosses cultural barriers and raises many issues relevant to an organizational environment that values and promotes integration of systems engineers and program managers including organizational integration, knowledge sharing, leadership, and team trust.

In relation to the major cost and schedule issues, the systems engineering challenge on the ISS was equally monumental. NASA had to quickly learn how to adapt its system engineering approaches to include an awareness of those of the international partnership (Stockman, et al., 2010).

NASA has its own challenges maintaining centers each with its own systems engineering differences and approaches. These challenges include enabling integration of discipline-oriented design tools into systems models that capture performance behaviors, integration of multiorganizational products, and identifying advanced technology requirements. NASA had to learn how to operate as a "managing partner" to accommodate its international partners, including different perspectives on approaches, designs, and operational risk and safety. A major effort was involved in developing the partnership agreements, allocating costs and usage rights, and determining operational control. Under the new ISS partnership, NASA leadership was concerned about maintaining schedule and cost on the ISS program because failures would not be tolerated by the U.S. Congress. Initial program strategy was for no international partner to be on the critical path, which would allow NASA more control to reduce risk. As it turned out, however, the Russians ended up providing the first two major modules that were at the front of the critical path. NASA was the first international partner among equals, with each board chaired by the NASA representative. In cases where consensus could not be reached, the NASA representative technically had the right to make a decision for the board; however, this right was rarely used in practice.

NASA business leaders and engineers had to solve many major systems engineering challenges. It had to figure out how to coordinate and integrate all of the international partners and their highly integrated modules. While it was not easy, they eventually worked out a process that addressed the concerns of multiple countries with differing cultural and engineering approaches to major program development and execution. NASA's lessons learned report issued the following recommendations for NASA systems engineers (Stockman, et al., 2010):

- "Systems engineering involves communications, critical to international partnerships, so before worrying about technical interfaces, make sure the integrated product teams and communication bandwidth between partners are optimal. This fundamentally includes face-to-face meetings, so regular international travel is a large and essential part of the systems engineering cost" (p. 87).
- "In an International Space Station like project where so many different countries and companies contribute hardware and software, the interfaces must be extremely simple" (p. 87).

■ "Maintaining a high level of competent and experienced personnel over a two decade long program requires strategic level planning and execution of workforce planning" (p. 87).

All of the above required not only integrated teams, but an integrated organizational structure, as shown in Figure 9-2. Boeing plays a critical role on this team as the lead systems engineer for the program. Boeing provides the experience to co-lead with NASA the Integrated Product Teams (IPTs) executing the systems engineering management that is a major challenge on this program because of the multipartner integration. It is a challenging role since Boeing could not officially negotiate with other countries and often had to provide the technical lead while NASA provided official signature on detailed international agreements known as Protocols. Currently, the overall program team is managed through an ISS Control Board Structure (Figure 9-2). The ISS team uses top-level control boards and panels to manage the ISS hardware and software configuration along with operational products. At the very top of the process is the Space Station Control Board (SSCB) that manages the multilateral control of the configuration. A NASA Space Station Program Control Board exercises control over the several layers of more detailed ISS subsystem control boards associated with the

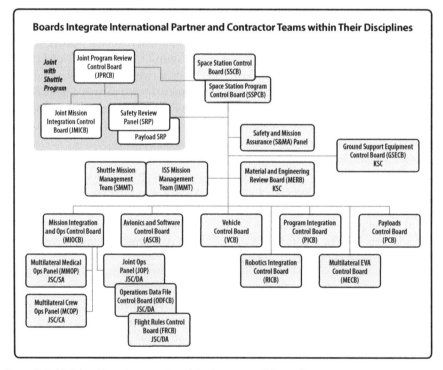

Figure 9-2: High-level board integration of the International Space Station program
Stockman et al., 2010, p. 19

U.S. elements. This process was also integrated with the Space Shuttle control boards. Each partner utilizes a similar control mechanism for their elements.

Coordinating the inclusion of the international partners whose system engineering approaches differed significantly was a major challenge of the ISS program. The problem was summed up well in a 1969 speech by Robert Frosch prior to the ISS and prior to becoming NASA Administrator:

> I believe that the fundamental difficulty is that we have all become so entranced with technique that we think entirely in terms of procedures, systems, milestone charts ... reliability systems, configuration management, maintainability groups and other minor paper tools of the "system engineer" and manager. We have forgotten that someone must be in control and must exercise personal management, knowledge and understanding to create a system.... Systems, even very large systems, are not developed by the tools of systems engineering, but only by engineers using tools (NASA, 2010).

The lesson here is that whether you are a systems engineer or a program manager you cannot rely on tools to understand how program performance and organizational value is measured and controlled, but instead must rely on leadership skills that encourage an environment of inclusivity, collective creativity, shared ownership, and large scale transformation.

9.7 Summary

Creating an organizational environment that narrows the cultural divide, fosters team building, develops respect for each-others' views and opinions, and builds trust between executive management and program teams is central to developing a community where collective creativity can evolve. Involving program managers and systems engineers at the organizational level to influence and inform decisions about strategic direction is beneficial, especially as they are the managers who are more instrumental in ensuring effective implementation and execution of change initiatives. Moreover, as noted in the NASA Hubble Space Telescope program, leaders must possess "soft skills" to enhance team building and better identify managerial shortcomings before they result in broken team interfaces and technical mistakes.

The key learnings from this chapter for building a sustainable framework for integration include the importance of developing relationship competencies in participants throughout the program, creating a shared set of objectives, clear roles, respecting the value of the others' role and contribution, and valuing and promoting "collaboration" over competition. However, these factors will only be relevant if the organization is able to develop people competencies as well. This chapter has shown that if one creates an organizational environment for successful integration and effective implementation of change, successful outcomes are more likely because one will have integrated divided cultures and added value to the organization.

9.8 Discussion Questions

1. Name some of the key organizational factors discussed in the Disney Pixar case study that would help facilitate the integration of systems engineering and program management within your organization.
2. Why is the relationship among organizational strategy and program management important in developing integration among systems engineers and program managers?
3. What is meant by program culture and how can a divided culture be better integrated?
4. What leadership qualities are required at the organizational level to facilitate integration?
5. Why is change management important to the integration of systems engineering and program management?
6. Why is interdisciplinary team building at the heart of integration and how can an organization create an environment where team building is the central focus of the organization's strategy?

9.9 References

Beasley, R., & Partridge, R. (2011, June 20–23). *The three T's of systems engineering: trading, tailoring, and thinking.* Paper presented at the 21st Annual Symposium of the International Council on Systems Engineering (INCOSE), Denver, CO. doi:10.1002/j.2334-5837.2011.tb01290.x

Best, A., Smit, J., & de Faber, L. (2013). Interventions and their relation to organizational culture and project management. *Procedia: Social and Behavioral Sciences, 74,* 329–338. doi:10.1016/j.sbspro.2013.03.019

Campagnolo, D., & Camuffo, A. (2010). The concept of modularity in management studies: A literature review. *International Journal of Management Reviews, 12*(3), 259–283. doi:10.1111/j.1468-2370.2009.00260.x

Catmull, E. (2008). How Pixar fosters collective creativity. *Harvard Business Review.* Retrieved from https://hbr.org/2008/09/how-pixar-fosters-collective-creativity

Catmull, E. (2014). *Creativity, Inc.: Overcoming the unseen forces that stand in the way of true inspiration.* New York: Random House.

Cleland, D. I., & Ireland, L. R. (2002). *Project management: Strategic design and implementation* (4th ed., pp. 517–524). New York: McGraw-Hill.

Crawford, L., Aitken, A., Hassner-Nahmias, A. (2014). *Project management and organizational change.* Newtown Square, PA: Project Management Institute.

Davies, A., Dodgson, M., & Gaan, D. (2009a). *From iconic design to lost luggage: Innovation at Heathrow Terminal 5.* Working Paper No. 10-09. Danish Research Unit for Industrial Dynamics.

Davies, A., Gann, D., & Douglas, T. (2009b). Innovation in megaprojects: Systems integration at London Heathrow Terminal 5. *California Management Review, 51*(2), 101–125. doi:10.2307/41166482

Doherty, S. (2008). *Heathrow's Terminal 5: History in the making*, London: Wiley-Blackwell.

Federal Highway Administration (FHWA). (2011). *Lessons learned: Summary of lessons learned from recent major projects*. Washington, D.C., US: Office of Innovative Program Delivery (IPD), Department of Transportation. Retrieved from www.fhwa.dot.gov/ipd/project_delivery/lessons_learned/lessons_learned.aspx

Grant, R. M. (1996). Prospering in dynamically-competitive environments: Organizational capability as knowledge integration. *Organizational Science*, 7(4), 375–387. doi:10.1287/orsc.7.4.375

Greiman, V. (2013). *Megaproject management: Lessons on risk and project management from the Big Dig*. Hoboken, NJ: John Wiley & Sons.

Hofstede, G. (1994). *Cultures and organizations: Software of the mind*. New York: McGraw-Hill.

IEEE. (2005). *Application and management of the systems engineering process*, (5th ed.). New York: Author.

International Council on Systems Engineering (INCOSE). (2012). *Pathways to influence: The emerging role of the systems engineer in an increasingly complex world*, A Report on the 2012 INCOSE International Symposium Executive Summit, San Diego, CA: Author.

International Council on Systems Engineering (INCOSE). (2015). *Systems engineering handbook: A guide for system life cycle processes and activities* (4th ed.). D. Walden, G. Roedler, K. Forsberg, R. Hamelin, T. Shortell (Eds.). Hoboken, NJ: John Wiley & Sons.

Isaacson, W. (2011). *Steve Jobs*. New York: Simon & Schuster.

Kadefors, A. (2004). Trust in project relationships: Inside the black box. *International Journal of Project Management*, 22(3), 175–182. doi:10.1016/S0263-7863(03)00031-0

Kerzner, H. R. (2013). *Project management case studies* (4th ed.). Hoboken, NJ: John Wiley & Sons.

Kotter, J. (1996, July 16–19). *Leading change*. Cambridge, MA: Harvard Business Review Press.

Leybourne, S. (2008). Improvisation and Agile project management: A merging of two ideals? *PMI Research Conference*, Warsaw, Poland.

Leybourne, S., & Greiman, V. (2015, June 22–24). Change management and the changing project: Expectations, opinions and themes. Published in the *Proceedings of the IRNOP Conference*, London.

Locatelli, G., Mancini, M., & Romano, E. (2014). Systems engineering to improve the governance in complex project environments. *International Journal of Project Management*, 32(8), 1395–1410. doi:10.1016/j.ijproman.2013.10.007

Loo, R. (2002). Working towards best practices in project management: A Canadian study. *International Journal of Project Management* 20(2), 93–98. doi:10.1016/S0263-7863(00)00042-9

Miller, R., & Hobbs, B. (2005). Governance regimes for large complex projects. *Project Management Journal* 36(3), 42–50.

Miller, R., & Lessard, D. (2001). *The strategic management of large engineering projects: Shaping risks, institutions and governance*. Cambridge, MA: MIT Press.

Morris, P. W. G. (2000). Researching the unanswered questions of project management. In Slevin, D. P., Cleland, D. J., Pinto, J. K. (Eds.), *Project management research at the turn of the millennium: Proceedings of PMI Research Conference 2000* (pp. 87–102). Newtown Square, PA: Project Management Institute.

Müller, R. (2009). *Project governance*. Aldershot, UK: Gower Publishing.

National Aeronautics and Space Administration (NASA). (1990, November). *The Hubble space telescope optical systems failure report*. U.S. Government.

National Aeronautics and Space Administration (NASA). (2010). From the Archive: Robert Frosch on Systems Engineering, *Academy of Program/Project and Engineering Leadership (APPEL) News*. Retrieved from http://appel.nasa.gov/2010/02/21/aa_1-5_f_frosch-html/

National Aeronautics and Space Administration (NASA). (2011). System failure case studies. *Communication Aberration, 5*(7), 1–4. Retrieved from https://nsc.nasa.gov/SFCS/SystemFailureCaseStudyFile/Download/517

Nicholas, J. M., & Steyn, H. (2008). *Project management for business, engineering, and technology*, (3rd. ed.). Burlington, MA, USA: Butterworth-Heinemann.

Nordhaug, O., & Gronhaug, K. (1994). Competences as resources in firms. *International Journal of Human Resource Management. 5*(1), 89–106. doi:10.1080/09585199400000005

Oehmen, J., Thuesen, C., Parraguez Ruiz, P., & Joana Geraldi (2015). *Complexity management for projects, programmes, and portfolios: An engineering systems perspective*. Retrieved from www.pmi.org/~/media/PDF/learning/project-complexity/complexity-management-engineering-systems.ashx

Pinto, J. K., & Winch, G. (2016). The unsettling of "settled science": The past and future of the management of projects. *International Journal of Project Management 34*(2), 237–245. doi:10.1016/j.ijproman.2015.07.011

Project Management Institute (PMI). (2012). *Pulse of the Profession®: In-depth report: Organizational agility*. Newtown Square, PA: Project Management Institute.

Project Management Institute (PMI). (2013a). *The standard for program management* (3rd ed.). Newtown Square, PA: Author.

Project Management Institute (PMI). (2013b). *The standard for portfolio management* (3rd ed.). Newtown Square, PA: Author.

Project Management Institute (PMI). (2013c). *Managing change in organizations: A practice guide*. Newtown Square, PA: Author.

Reiner, T. (2015, May). *Determination of factors to measure the effective integration between program management and systems engineering*, Rheinisch-Westfälische Technische Hochschule (RWTH) Aachen Master's thesis.

Schein, E. H. (2004). *Organizational culture and leadership*. San Francisco, CA: Jossey-Bass.

Stockman, B., Boyle, J., & Bacon, J. (2010). *International Space Station systems engineering case study*. Air Force Center for Systems Engineering. Retrieved from www.nasa.gov/externalflash/iss-lessons-learned/docs/design_ISS_SE_Case_Study.pdf

Thomke, S., & Nimgade, A. (2001, October 16). Siemens AG: Global development strategy (A). *Harvard Business Review*. Retrieved from https://hbr.org/product/siemens-ag-global-development-strategy-a/602061-PDF-ENG

Turner, J. R. (1996). Project management: A profession based on knowledge or faith? Editorial. *International Journal of Project Management. 17*(6), 329–330. doi:10.1016/S0263-7863(99)00020-4

Additional Resources

Bone, M., Cloutier, R. L., Gill, E., & Verma, D. (2009). *A case study: Application of the systems engineering modeling in the early phases of a complex space system project*. 7th Annual Conference on Systems Engineering Research. Retrieved from http://www.lr.tudelft.nl/fileadmin/Faculteit/LR/Organisatie/Afdelingen_en_Leerstoelen/Afdeling_SpE/Space_Systems_Eng./Publications/2009/doc/A_case_study_S09-56.pdf

National Aeronautics and Space Administration (NASA). (2013). *NASA procedural requirements. NASA systems engineering processes and requirements*. Washington, D.C., NASA, Office of the Chief Engineer. NPR 7123.1B.

10

DEVELOPING INTEGRATION COMPETENCIES IN PEOPLE

10.1 Introduction

While the previous chapters addressed Dimensions I and II of the Integration Framework: processes, procedures, tools, and the organizational environment, this chapter delves into Dimension III, the people competencies, and explores the issues of leadership, followership, attitudes, and team learning with the goal of the organization's success and its value proposition at the forefront. The chapter provides background on the NASA Space Shuttle programs and the JSOC's Tactical Intelligence Fusion for Fires (TUFF) program, and the relevance of these cases to the development of project and program competencies. The research shows that "the sources of unproductive tension are more likely to be the result of organization and people factors" than any other factors (Rebentisch & Conforto, 2014, p. 40). Finally, three practical models—Crew Resource Management, Control Theory, and Decision Theory—are presented as guidance for practitioners to improve team competencies to navigate complexity effectively.

10.1.1 Background/Case Study

On September 12, 1962, U.S. President John F. Kennedy issued a now-famous challenge to the United States. He said, "We choose to go to the moon in this decade and do the other things not because they are easy, but because they are hard, because that goal will serve to organize and measure the best of our energies and skills" (Kennedy, 1962). Kennedy's speech provided a sense of purpose that inspired a generation of scientists, engineers, managers, and leaders.

In a lesser-known portion of the same speech, Kennedy noted that "the growth of our science and education will be enriched by new knowledge of our universe and environment, by new techniques of learning...by new tools and computers for industry, medicine, the home as well as school" (Kennedy, 1962). One of the many new tools invented, or at least matured, during the 1960s space program was the discipline of systems engineering. In 1963, in response to slipping schedules, NASA named George Mueller to the position of Associate Administrator of the Office of Manned Space Flight (OMSF). Under Mueller, OMSF was reorganized into:

> a managerial nervous system... [where managers and engineers] who were used to operating in the confines of their own silos were required to communicate daily with their functional counterparts at other field centers and on other teams... [and] there was an almost iron-like discipline of organizational communication (McChrystal, Collins, Silverman, & Fussell, 2015, p. 100).

According to General Stanley McChrystal, "What Mueller instituted was known as 'systems engineering'... [an] approach, contrary to reductionism, [that] believes that one cannot understand a part of a system without having at least a rudimentary understanding of the whole" (p. 101). In the mid-2000s, McChrystal used NASA's systems engineering managerial concepts to transform the Joint Special Operations Command into a "Team of Teams" (McChrystal et al., 2015).

Most managers aren't fortunate enough to have a George Mueller or a Stan McChrystal on their teams or leading their organizations, nor do they have access to the billions of dollars that were poured into the Apollo Program or the "Surge" in Iraq. Typically, most managers deal with the day-to-day problems of constrained budgets, somewhat dysfunctional organizations, and real people. Thus, begins the true story of the TUFF program.

TUFF is a multiple-intelligence process that integrates electronic support target location, identification, and imagery into a fused intelligence data product that supports the military's targeting and firing processes. In other words, TUFF supports the *Find-Fix-Finish* "Kill Chain" process by *finding* and identifying the target with electronic support, *fixing* the target with imagery (a drone-based camera), and *finishing* the target by providing a fused intelligence product to decision makers who apply effects (e.g., bombs) on the target. The contractor produces electronic support equipment, and also serves as the lead systems integrator for TUFF. This case study describes the evolution of one project under the TUFF program umbrella, TUFF for Small Unmanned Aerial System (TUFF-SUAS).

The customer's goal was to develop the TUFF capability on a widely deployed SUAS, aka drone. The end-user concept of operations, use-cases, and physical systems were defined during an analysis of alternatives phase, which captured the operational-level requirements. The project planning team, which consisted of the portfolio manager, program manager, and systems engineer, embarked on a requirements decomposition effort to develop a systems-level requirements document.

The portfolio manager who oversaw the TUFF program also managed the contractor's larger software architecture called Linebacker. The portfolio manager's vision was to extend Linebacker to include the TUFF use case. The program team, which now included specialty engineers from both the software and systems integration divisions of the contractor, embarked on a design phase to decompose the systems-level requirements and create a detailed system specification. This is where the program ran into problems.

During the system specification process, it became clear from the systems engineer's perspective that Linebacker capabilities did not trace to TUFF's originating requirements. It also became clear that, from the program manager's perspective, extending Linebacker to address TUFF requirements was beyond the scope of the program. These realizations caused tension between the portfolio manager and program manager because, from the portfolio manager's perspective, TUFF no longer aligned with either his vision or his portfolio. In the end customer requirements prevailed because the program manager was able to show traceability, or lack thereof, between Linebacker capabilities and TUFF requirements. When the team conducted a preliminary design review with the external stakeholders (customers and end-users), the extended project team, consisting of both internal and external stakeholders, agreed that utilizing legacy electronic support capabilities instead of extending Linebacker was an achievable goal given cost and schedule constraints.

Because TUFF no longer fit within the portfolio manager's portfolio, it was moved to a different, more aligned portfolio. Also, since the Linebacker software was no longer required, the lead systems engineering role transferred from the software development team to the systems integration team. TUFF's new lead systems engineer had experience as a project manager; was well versed in external systems integration, hardware/software development and integration, and test and evaluation; and had extensive industry experience working with end users. The program manager had an operational background and a master's degree in systems engineering and so had a deep understanding of and respect for the systems engineering role. Systems engineers are not glorified specialty engineers; systems engineering requires unique skills and a particular mindset, systems thinking, which will be explored in-depth. This mutual understanding enabled the program manager and systems engineer to "speak the same language." It should be noted that, in the contractor's organization structure, the systems engineer also serves as the project manager.

Based on the new direction received at the preliminary design review and the new alignment strategy, the program manager and systems engineer rewrote the system requirements document, which was quickly approved by all stakeholders (internal and external) during the following quarterly Program Management Review. The program manager and systems engineer were speaking the same language as one another as well as the same language as the customer. This mutual understanding flowed down to the specialty engineering team who developed the system specification document that was implemented flawlessly over the following year. Through mutual understanding, iterative processes, and good communication, the project team and external stakeholders had a shared awareness of both the problem and the solution at every stage of the project. The team delivered an advanced prototype in a hands-on demonstration environment. The project was below budget, ahead of schedule, and exceeded customer expectations.

Since the TUFF-SUAS delivery in August 2015, the contractor has received follow-on funding to support the system's deployment. The contractor has also received funding to develop TUFF capabilities on two additional SUAS systems. In the time since TUFF-SUAS inception, the Linebacker capabilities have been extended such that they are now compatible with TUFF requirements to be designed into current and future TUFF instances. Through excellent program management and systems engineering integration, TUFF expanded the contractor's business both horizontally and vertically and became an important source of new customer acquisition.

The success of TUFF-SUAS would not have been possible without the organizational environment discussed in the previous chapter. The flat, team-based organizational structure and collaborative culture facilitated seamless portfolio realignment when the tension between Linebacker and TUFF became apparent. Moreover, the contractor's hiring practices produced a broad pool of multidisciplinary talent that enabled the right set of people to come together as a team. The program manager believed in the program, worked through the initial adversities, and had an innate appreciation for the role and value of systems engineering. The systems engineer had a systems thinking mindset to view the problem as a whole, the leadership skills to manage a diverse technical team, and the technical prowess to manage the overall project execution. These competencies and others will be explored and developed in this chapter.

The balance of this chapter focuses on the building of competencies by responding to the following questions:

- What are the individual competencies that program managers and systems engineers should have to lead a program to successful outcomes?
- How does an organization identify and develop these competencies?
- How do organizations integrate the skill sets into effective teaming relationships on a consistent, repeatable basis?

10.2 Identifying Integration Competencies

The Phase I research identified the individual competencies that program managers and chief systems engineers thought were important to their roles. As shown in Figure 10-1, program managers identified communication skills, leadership skills, and stakeholder management as the most important competencies, while chief systems engineers said that systems thinking, requirements management, and conflict resolution were most critical to their job. These skills are also highlighted in the TUFF case study. For instance, the program manager clearly demonstrated leadership and stakeholder management skills by driving the program forward despite the obstacles and challenges, while the chief systems engineer took a holistic view of the problems and demonstrated technical leadership and systems thinking.

10.2.1 Leadership

What is effective leadership? This question has been answered in multiple ways across institutions and cultures. Leadership has been described as both an art and a science, depending on personal, global, and cultural contexts (Nahavandi, 2012). Müller and Turner's (2010) comprehensive research on project leadership examines the leadership competency profiles of successful project managers across project environments using

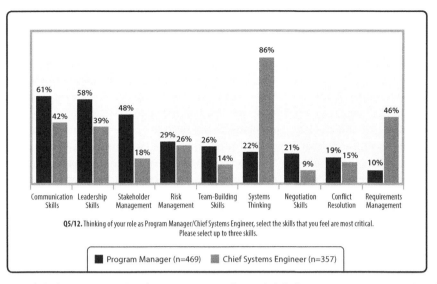

Figure 10-1: Survey results identifying perceptions of critical skills for program managers and chief systems engineers
Conforto, Rossi, Rebentisch, Oehmen, & Pacenza, 2013, p. 20.

the 15 dimensions of leadership competency (Dulewicz & Higgs, 2005). Müller and Turner (2010) considered 400 responses to a leadership development questionnaire to profile the intellectual, managerial, and emotional competencies (IQ, MQ, and EQ, respectively) of project managers of successful projects (pp. 440–441), which identified one IQ subdimension, critical thinking, and three EQ subdimensions, influence, motivation, and conscientiousness, in successful managers across all types of projects (p. 440), as highlighted in Table 10-1.

Successful leadership competencies were also addressed in a Gallup (2015) report, *The State of the American Manager: Analytics and Advice for Leaders*. The report identified five dimensions that collectively describe a "talented" manager and contribute to employee engagement: *motivator, assertiveness, accountability, relationships, and decision*

Table 10-1: Successful leadership competencies	
Leadership Dimension	**Definition**
Critical Thinking	The leader gathers relevant information from a wide range of sources, probes the facts, identifies advantages and disadvantages, makes sound judgments and decisions, and develops awareness of the impact of any assumptions made.
Influence	The leader can persuade others to change a viewpoint based on the understanding of their position and the recognition of the need to listen to this perspective and provide a rationale for change.
Motivation	The leader has the drive and energy to achieve clear results and make an impact.
Conscientiousness	The leader displays clear commitment to a course of action in the face of challenges and matches "words with deeds" in encouraging others to support the chosen direction.

Müller & Turner, 2010, pp. 447. Reprinted from *International Journal of Project Management, 28*(5), Müller, R., & Turner, R., Leadership competency profiles of successful project managers, pp. 437–448, 2010, with permission from Elsevier.

making (p. 15). These dimensions align with the competencies identified by Müller and Turner and, as a whole, they can be viewed as a definition for the quality of *leadership* that was identified by program managers as a critical skill. For example, the EQ competency *conscientiousness* captures the talent dimensions of *assertiveness* and *relationships*.

From these definitions, one can see that the other program manager critical skills, communication and stakeholder management, are embedded in and are aspects of the leadership competencies and dimensions. The Phase II and III research found from the perception of some chief system engineers the need for program managers to have adequate technical knowledge of their programs and a background in systems engineering so that they could "speak the same language" (Conforto & Rebentisch, 2014, p. 17). While specialty engineering experience is not required for program management effectiveness, domain expertise and the ability to relate to and empathize with team members must be a program manager prequalification and core competency. With complex programs, chief systems engineers also need to recognize and appreciate the program manager's responsibilities and pressures, and consider the implications that their technical decisions will have on the program manager's objectives of controlling cost, meeting schedule, and delivering benefits.

Empathy and ethical behavior are reflected in the EQ quality *conscientiousness* and *talent dimension relationships*. Empathy and ethical behavior result in trust-based relationships that are crucial to team effectiveness. This idea is reflected in various codes of ethics and professional conduct (IEEE, n.d.; INCOSE, n.d.; PMI, n.d.). From a program management perspective, ethical considerations impact every aspect of a program's operations and are a critical component of the successful completion of most programs. Since the success of a program depends upon high ethical standards, it must be considered a core competency in all project and program frameworks (PMI, 2007). Ethical behavior by program managers, systems engineers, and individual contributors is foundational to trust, and effective team-based organizations are founded upon it. Teams do not work without trust. Finally, intercultural communications and relations as well as an ability to understand and appreciate cultural differences and work habits should be considered as important factors in knowing how to lead.

10.2.2 Systems Thinking

In the Phase I research, systems engineers identified systems thinking as their most important skill (Conforto et al., 2013b). System thinking, like leadership, is a broad concept. According to INCOSE (2015, p. 19), Peter Senge identified systems thinking as a key discipline with his book *The Fifth Discipline* and developed the language and graphical representation structures needed to communicate systems engineering concepts. Senge (2006) writes, "Systems thinking is a discipline for seeing wholes." Specifically, systems thinking is needed to resolve dynamic complexity, which exists in "situations where cause and effect are subtle, and where the effects over time of interventions are not obvious" (p. 71). It is a framework for seeing interrelationships rather than things, for seeing patterns of change rather that static 'snapshots'" (p. 68). Senge goes on to say, "[t]oday, systems thinking is needed more than ever because we are becoming overwhelmed by complexity" (p. 69). Systems thinkers' attitudes are critical also to program managers particularly for decision making, for risks management, and program management.

Even though systems thinking definitions diverge, there is consensus on the primary mechanisms that enable or obstruct systems thinking development. In a field study focused on the U.S. aerospace sector, the mechanisms that were determined to enhance systems thinking included:

- Experiential learning (on the job learning)
- Individual characteristics such as open-mindedness and curiosity, risk-taking, and humility
- A supportive environment in which to develop systems thinking

According to the research, a supportive environment would include systems training in coordination with work environment, management of schedule and cost constraints to develop systems thinking, jobs and opportunities to see the system view, and clear communication on how the strength of systems thinking is assessed (Davidz, 2006, pp. 194–195).

INCOSE (2015) notes that Barry Richmond developed simulation languages to model systems thinking behaviors and also postulated eight thinking tracks that, combined, constitute systems thinking. For example, "10,000-meter" thinking is a high-level skill that allows one to see the "the 'big picture,'" but relinquish the opportunity to make fine discriminations" (Richmond, 2010, p. 3). Similarly, "system-as-cause" and "dynamic" thinking are also "'filtering skills' that help to 'filter' our nonessential elements of reality when constructing mental models" (p. 3). Constructing mental models is one-half of the activity that Richmond defines as "thinking;" the other half is simulating them (p. 2). The mental exercise of constructing mental models requires the three aforementioned thinking skills as well as "operational" and "closed-loop" thinking, both of which are needed to communicate the stock-and-flow language of systems thinking (p. 7). Simulating the behavior of mental models requires "scientific," "empathic," and "generic" thinking (p. 7–8). Generic thinking is reflected in Senge's eight "systems archetypes," which are "patterns of structure that recur again and again" in systems across domains (Senge, 2006, p. 93). By studying the system archetypes, their associated dynamics, and leverage points, practitioners can identify the structure of complex systems and apply effective interventions (i.e., make good decisions).

The system archetypes are essentially heuristics for understanding complex system constructs. Maani and Majaraj (2001) indicate that "heuristic competence is highly analogous with the notions of systemic thinking types." In Section 10.4.3 below, a systems thinking heuristic for decision making is proposed—Boyd's OODA Loop. The decision-management process, along with risk management, will be shown in Section 10.3.1.3 to be a high-leverage integration activity for resolving unproductive tension and releasing creative energy in program teams.

10.3 Developing Integration Competencies

Organizations are increasingly defining more of their activities as projects and programs. It is important to recognize that while the Phase I research focused on program managers, the research on project management often refers to "project" in the global sense where it encompasses the entire field of project management including program and portfolio management. The demand for project managers and the interest in project management competencies is increasing (Bredillet, Tywoniak, & Dwivedula, 2015; Crawford, 2007). This evolution in theory and practice has placed the project manager and his or her competencies at the center of a project's and, therefore, an organization's success. However, the project management research mainly addresses individual competencies held by project managers rather than organizational competencies (Bredillet et al., 2015; Crawford, 2005; Medina & Medina, 2014; Morris, Crawford, Hodgson, Shepherd, & Thomas, 2006; Stevenson & Starkweather, 2010). As a result, the project manager is seen as a "hero" who carries on his or her shoulders the heavy load of responsibility for a project's success or failure (Loufrani-Fedida & Missionier, 2015). The "hero" attitude is also highlighted in the research findings shown in Figure 10-1, where both program managers and systems engineers rated team building skills as low on their list of important skills.

Leaders in every organization must have the ability to create a vision, a sense of purpose, and a tension that unleashes creative energy (productive tension). In contrast to the research trends and commonly held beliefs, rare is the singular leader, lone genius, or "heroic" project manager. As Joshua Wolf Shenk (2014) discusses in his book *Powers of Two*, "the pair is the primary creative unit." Like the fictional Sherlock Holmes and Dr. Watson, the program manager and systems engineer comprise that creative unit. Research supports this conclusion. One thinks of larger-than-life characters like Steve Jobs and Bill Gates as having single-handedly built both the technology and their companies and one views these highly publicized and overdramatized individuals as the embodiments of success and their actions the models for how to be successful. The less-dramatic truth, though, is that these men and other successful men and women like them did not act alone, but built teams.

Scholars of project management have defined successful projects as those in which the "people side" has been well managed (Morris & Pinto, 2007, p. 17). Recent research reflects that the domain of people factors impacting integration of the systems engineering and program management roles comprises experience, education, and professional development through on-the-job training (Reiner, 2015). For complex environments, the literature suggests that program managers deploy highly experienced systems engineers in order to set up an effective and efficient systems engineering capability in their projects (Ansorge, 2004). The relation of experience of team members on the performance of projects and programs is considered as a field of interest of ongoing research (Kovacic, Filzmoser, & Denk, 2014). The work experience of program managers and systems engineers is expected to be highly relevant for integration and its effects on program performance (Reiner, 2015, p. 45).

The Phase II and III research found that unproductive tension can be overcome by viewing integration as a "team competency and by implementing proven integration practices such as the following" (Rebentisch & Conforto, 2014, p. 37):

■ Develop an integrated career path for program managers and systems engineers.
■ Promote formal education and training in both disciplines so they can learn from each other.
■ Recognize the value of multidisciplinary teams—multiple competencies and skills.
■ Create and communicate an overarching vision of the program—its challenges and goals.
■ Overcome personal assumptions, listen carefully, and consider one another's experience and knowledge.

Having established the importance of effective, integrated teams, the question becomes "How does one develop the integration competencies that create effective teams?" The following discussion will cover the integrated career path, education and training, and multidisciplinary team practices. Vision, communication, and empathy are considered to be skills that fall under the leadership competency.

10.3.1 Integrated Career Path

Fighter pilots and U.S. football teams have truly integrated career paths. Fighter pilots never fly by themselves. They are always part of a formation or package of supporting and supported aircraft that are interdependent—bombers are covered by fighters who are covered by electronic attack who are covered by fighters and also support the bombers. Quarterbacks always need receivers to throw to, and would get tackled without a good offensive line. The offense is supported by the defense whose role is to prevent the other team from scoring. Programs, though, don't have such obvious interdependencies. It is often left to the personality of the program manager, the program's leader, to drive team-oriented behaviors (teamwork) (Senge, 2006, p. 93). These observations are in line with Gallup (2015) findings that show that only 30% of U.S. workers report that they are engaged, and that low engagement costs the U.S. economy $319 billion to $398 billion annually (p. 8). The Phase I research found four conditions in successful organizations that create program management and systems engineering integration and team-oriented behaviors:

■ Use standards from both domains.
■ Formalize the definition of integration.
■ Share responsibilities in key areas.
■ Develop integrated engineering program assessments.

10.3.1.1 Use Standards from both Domains

The Phase I research found that program managers and chief systems engineers tend to use standards from their own domains exclusively. The research also found that a relatively high number of professionals do not use standards at all, especially in engineering firms. Figure 4-7 in Chapter 4 shows the distribution of respondents with respect to standards that they use. In the previous section on individual competencies, it was taken as a given that professionals would possess and maintain competency in their field. The research data show that this assumption may not hold in many cases. Moreover, these data show that most professionals have little to no knowledge of or appreciation for the competencies of their team members. In contrast, fighter pilots know exactly what their wingmen will do and quarterbacks know exactly what their receivers will do in dynamic situations. They know one another's jobs and they trust one another.

Given the importance of planning and managing the technical aspects of programs, an effective chief systems engineer will have a strong foundation in program management as well as depth in their own domain. The chief systems engineer's role ranges from developing and defending the basis of budgets, planning and monitoring technical activities, identifying and mitigating technical risk, and engaging stakeholders to becoming an integral part of the program's management team. Similarly, program managers must have sufficient technical depth to effectively communicate with systems engineers and the rest of the technical team.

In order to integrate the program management and systems engineering roles, organizations desiring a high level of integration and team-oriented behaviors should consider cross-training program managers and systems engineers to provide an appreciation for and familiarization with the other professional's job.

10.3.1.2 Formalize the Definition of Integration

Successful organizations have been shown to formalize what integration means for them. These definitions of integration vary widely, and this book is an attempt to provide a unified definition by proposing leading practices for integration.

One way to view formalizing integration is from the perspective of roles and responsibilities. The Phase I research investigated this aspect by asking professionals which job responsibilities fell under the respective roles of program management, systems engineering, or both. From this dataset, the researchers concluded that professionals believed that program managers generally have responsibility for overall program results and for the goals and objectives of the program. They also thought that chief systems engineers were primarily responsible for technical requirements and systems definition. These roles and responsibilities are consistent with previous discussions and with other research. The majority of professionals identified program/project risk as an area of shared responsibility (Conforto et al., 2013b, p. 10).

Other formalized approaches to integration involve the application of methodologies and other processes and tools, as explored in Chapter 8. Ideally, defined and documented roles for program managers and chief systems engineers would be aligned with and contribute to those other elements of the integration framework. Perhaps most importantly, a formal approach to integration would be part of the way the organization operates, and as such would enjoy top-down support from the organization's leaders.

10.3.1.3 Shared Responsibilities: Creative Tension

According to INCOSE's (2015) *Systems Engineering Handbook*, "Systems engineers and project managers bring unique skills and experiences to the program on which they work . . . [and] there is a 'shared space' where systems engineers and project managers have to collaborate to drive the team's performance and success" (p. 104). That "shared space" is the technical management process, which includes planning, assessment and control, decision management, risk management, configuration management, information management, measurement, and quality assurance (p. 104). Risk and the risk management process are simultaneously a shared responsibility and an opportunity to productively resolve the natural tension between the two roles (Conforto, Rebentisch, & Rossi, 2013a, p. 20). Program managers and systems engineers, by the nature of their roles and responsibilities, view risk differently. These different perspectives cause tension, which can be resolved either productively or unproductively (Conforto et al., 2013b, p. 5).

In his seminal work, *The Fifth Discipline*, Peter Senge (2006) describes creative tension as the gap between the current "as-is" reality and an individual or organization's "to-be" vision (p. 140). That gap, if addressed and managed productively, is the source of creative energy. A formalized risk management process could provide a forum for program management and systems engineering integration and the release of creative tension. The *Systems Engineering Handbook* (INCOSE, 2015, pp. 114–122) provides a thorough overview of the risk management process, and risk was discussed in Chapter 8.

Not highlighted in the research is the shared responsibility of decision management. According to INCOSE (2015), "it can be argued that all SE [systems engineering] activities should be conducted within the context of supporting good decision making" (pp. 110–111). The *Systems Engineering Handbook* (pp. 121–122) also outlines opportunity management as analogous to risk management, but considers potential positive outcomes instead of, or in addition to, negative ones. INCOSE (p. 110) also refers to opportunities as "decision situations."

Together the decision management and risk management processes are the essence of program management in all three dimensions of cost, schedule, and performance. Whereas decision management is focused on opportunities, risk management forces the program team to take a disciplined "trust-but-verify" outlook toward those opportunities. The two processes synergistically create tension and provide an opportunity for integration through team-based decision and risk management processes.

10.3.1.4 Develop Integrated Engineering Program Assessments

The decision and risk management processes provide high-leverage opportunities for regular management reviews and assessments. The *PMBOK® Guide* (PMI, 2013a) Risk Management Knowledge Processes, the *Practice Standard for Project Risk Management* (PMI, 2009), *The Standard for Program Management* (PMI, 2013b), and INCOSE's (2015) *Systems Engineering Handbook* contain similar standards with regard to risk management and provide an excellent opportunity for integration of the system engineer's and program manager's risk management responsibilities.

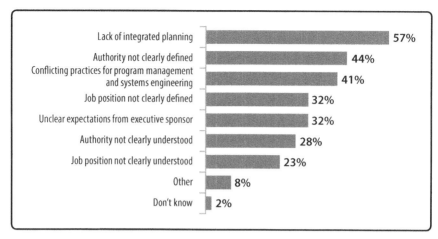

Figure 10-2: Sources of unproductive tension
Conforto et al., 2013, p. 3.

The Phase I research found that the lack of an integrated planning process, as shown in Figure 10-2, was the largest source of unproductive tension according to practitioners, which provides another high-leverage integration opportunity. Note that Figure 10-2 also shows that most sources of unproductive tension are role/responsibility issues and standard practice issues as addressed above.

Integrated planning is an opportunity to build team-based behaviors, overcome unproductive tension, and release creative energy. So why do managers, teams, and organizations not do more integrated planning? Experience reflects an answer that is simple and pragmatic: program planning is an indirect cost that, for project-based organizations, cannot be charged directly to a contract task and must be deducted from corporate profit. In project-based organizations, the bid-and-proposal process is led by the business development (sales) team, which captures business with very little input from the technical program teams. The program team is engaged once direct charges to a contract line item are established, well after the scope of work has been defined. This cost-driven environment not only undermines "buy-in" or commitment from the technical contributors, but, as will be seen in the upcoming discussion on crew resource management, eliminates an opportunity for training and developing the team competencies discussed thus far.

10.3.1.5 Control over Program/Project Launch and Planning

As identified in *The Guide to Lean Enablers for Managing Engineering Programs* (Oehmen, 2012), integrated planning can be inhibited when the program team is pushed to start development prematurely. The Future Combat System example in Chapter 2 revealed that leaders within the U.S. Department of Defense pushed the start of development of that very complex system before technical requirements and components had been validated through systems engineering (Pernin et al., 2012). The U.S. Government Accountability Office cited the rushed development and limited use of systems engineering as contributing factors to the program's failure (GAO, 2007).

Finding that "Redesigning major projects while they're being delivered is a major cause of delay and costs overrunning" (UK Cabinet Office, 2015), the United Kingdom's Major Projects Authority instituted a comprehensive review and assessment process. The Authority's process requires rigorous front-end planning on all projects and programs over a specific financial threshold before funds can be released to start development. The level of rigor ensures that planning activities are both comprehensive and integrated. Then at key points throughout the project or program, detailed performance assessments and evaluations are required before additional funds are released. Between its founding in 2011 and 2015, the Authority had conducted more than 200 assessments on active programs and projects. The outcomes of those reviews shifted many programs and projects from being at risk of failure to improved performance (UK Cabinet Office, 2015).

10.3.2 Education and Training

Unfortunately, most research is focused on project management rather than program management. However, because of the relationship between projects and programs, project management research is cited here and in other chapters in support of competencies required for program managers. It is generally accepted that there is a causal link between project manager competence and project success (Morris & Pinto, 2007). In addition to any area-specific skills and general management proficiencies required for the project, effective project management requires that the project manager possess three areas of competence: (1) knowledge of project management, (2) performance as a project manager, and (3) the project manager's personal effectiveness, which encompasses attitudes, core personality characteristics, and leadership (PMI, 2013a, p. 17). PMI in its *Project Manager Competency Development Framework* (PMI, 2007) identified five performance competencies for project managers—initiating, planning, executing, monitoring and controlling, and closing a project; and six personal competencies for project managers—professionalism, communicating, leading, managing, cognitive ability, and effectiveness.

Researchers have noted a move from project management research that focuses on process to research that focuses on people (Cooke-Davies, 2002; Leybourne, 2007, p. 189). Organizations are increasingly looking for project managers able to deal with "soft" issues related to people and relationships who not only manage projects but also drive value (Gerush, 2009).

Research has shown that systems engineering involves applying multiple disciplines to the system development process (INCOSE, 2010; Keating et al., 2003). Systems engineering has also been described as a managerial and technical methodology developed in the last 60 years to improve the governance (and hence the performance) of projects designed and delivered in complex environments (Locatelli, Mancini, & Romano, 2014, p. 1407). To achieve these results, governance must be transformed from the project and pure "project management" to a more holistic system view of "system management" (p. 1407). This requires technical discipline to ensure a rigorous execution of the development process and management discipline that organizes the technical effort throughout the system life cycle. This all requires leadership skills that include a high degree of emotional intelligence that enable the best leaders to maximize their own and their followers' performance (Goleman, 1998). Goleman in his defining work on emotional intelligence described it in terms of the following five skills: self-awareness, self-regulation, motivation, empathy, and social skill. Other researchers have confirmed that the presence of emotional intelligence not only distinguishes outstanding leaders, but can also be linked to strong performance (Barry & du Plessis, 2007; McClelland 1998; Mem, Elahi, Bhatti, & Khalid, 2006).

INCOSE (2012), in its report *Pathways to Influence: The Emerging Role of the Systems Engineer in an Increasingly Complex World*, included the "ability to influence" as a significant skill of the systems engineer, with success measured by management's answer to the question: "Can I put my systems engineer in front of the chief executives of my organization?" (p. 2). This requires the development of a broad set of management and leadership skills in addition to technical competency. Similar to project and program managers, the ability to influence includes the development of soft skills, an understanding of the human elements of the systems, and the organizational systems that develop them, and an ability to translate systems thinking into language and nomenclature that makes sense to these top-level leaders (p. 5). Keys and Case (1990) suggest that one powerful method for developing a base of influence is to first establish a reputation as an expert in the project domain that is being undertaken. A project manager who lacks the necessary technical skill or competency cannot command the ability to use influence as a mechanism to secure the support of other important stakeholders or be perceived as a true "leader" of the project team (Mangenau & Pinto, 2007).

10.3.3 Developing Multidisciplinary Teams

The high-level roles of program managers and systems engineers, their overlapping responsibilities, and the idea of utilizing integration best practices for overcoming unproductive tension and unlocking creative energy were discussed in Section 10.3.1.3 above. But what if the program manager and chief systems engineer were the same person? Would that not immediately relieve unproductive tension? Conforto and Rebentisch (2014, p. 9) found that in some organizations, the program manager and chief systems engineer were the same person.

Loufrani-Fedida and Missionier (2015) in their recent study of critical competencies from a multilevel approach in four project-based organizations (IBM, Hewlett-Packard, Arkopharma, and Tenex) recommended that both practitioners and current academic researchers stop looking for the perfect, "ideal" project manager who would possess all of the necessary critical competencies for projects. Instead, managers should consider sharing responsibility between the individual and organizational competencies and not expect a project manager to possess all the required competencies. This research supports the previous discussion on the fallacy of the lone creative genius or dramatic heroic figure, which was debunked by Shenk (2014) in *Powers of Two*. The research also further supports the overall theme of this chapter that creative tension is a necessity for world-class program execution.

10.3.3.1 NASA Challenger Case Study

The NASA Challenger case study highlights the conflicts in roles and the ethical crisis that can arise when a key member of the engineering team also functions as the program manager (Boisjoly, 2006). On February 25, 1986, during the Roger's Commission Hearings on the Space Shuttle Challenger disaster, testimony from one of Morton-Thiokol's (MTIs) chief engineers, Roger Boisjoly, revealed that one of the key participants in the go/no-go decision on the evening before the flight, MTI's Vice President of Engineering, Mr. Robert Lund, was asked to take off his engineering hat and put on his management hat. Mr. Lund's perspective as a program manager resulted ultimately in a different decision than he had made as an engineer (Rogers Commission, 1986, p. 1420). During the hearings, Mr. Lund divulged his reason for changing his mind:

CHAIRMAN ROGERS: "How do you explain the fact that you seemed to change your mind when you changed your hat?" (p. 1456)

MR. LUND: "I guess we have got to go back a little further in the conversations than that. We have dealt with [NASA's] Marshall [Space Flight Center] for a long time and have always been in the position of defending our position to make sure that we were ready to fly, and I guess I didn't realize until after that meeting and after several days that we had absolutely changed our position from what we had been before. But that evening I guess I had never had those kinds of things come from the people at Marshall that we had to prove to them that we weren't ready. . . . And so we got ourselves in the thought process that we were trying to find some way to prove to them it wouldn't work, and we were unable to do that. We couldn't prove absolutely that that motor wouldn't work." (pp. 1456–1457)

CHAIRMAN ROGERS: "In other words, you honestly believed that you had a duty to prove that it would not work?" (p. 1456)

MR. LUND: "Well, that is kind of the mode we got ourselves into that evening. It seems like we have always been in the opposite mode. I should have detected that, but I did not, but the roles kind of switched." (p. 1457)

Boisjoly (Rogers Commission, 1986) stated:

> From this point on management formulated the points to base their decision on. There was never one comment in favor, as I have said, of launching by any engineer or other non-management person in the room before or after the caucus. I was not even asked to participate in giving any input to the final decision charts.

Essentially, "NASA placed MTI in the position of proving that it was not safe to fly, instead of proving that it was safe to fly" (Boisjoly, 2006). These statements show

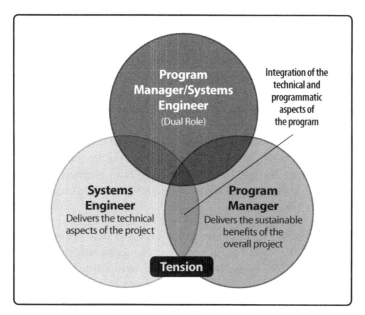

Figure 10-3: Systems engineer and program manager roles overlap and create potential for unproductive tension

a decision process that is out of balance with a complementary risk management process and a disruption of the natural tension between the program management and systems engineering. In the years since the Presidential Commission made its report on the Space Shuttle Challenger accident, NASA has prosecuted an intensive, across-the-board effort dedicated to returning to safe, reliable space flight. This recovery activity has three key aspects: the technical engineering changes being selected and implemented; the new procedures, safeguards, and internal communication processes that have been put in place; and the changes in personnel, organizations, and attitudes that have come about including that astronauts be encouraged to make the transition into management positions.

Importantly, the NASA Challenger case study highlights the seriousness of decision making where assuming one role, in this case the role of the program manager, had a devastating impact on the final outcome because of the differing approaches to decision making as a program manager versus a systems engineer. Though integration of the program management and systems engineering roles has benefits, it is important to recognize that responsibility for final decision making must be clearly allocated based on a strategically planned governance system that focuses on the delivery of sustainable benefits, in this case a successful space mission. As shown in Figure 10-3, it is also important to recognize that the natural tension between the program management and systems engineering responsibilities is beneficial to decision making and risk management when integration practices are followed and the tension is treated productively.

A few key takeaways from the NASA case study include:

- The respective roles of the systems engineer and the program manager must be clearly defined and allocated based on experience and competency.

- Dual roles for systems engineers and program managers must be understood in the context of the organization's decision-making process.
- Integration best practices can be a useful tool for overcoming unproductive tension and unlocking creative energy.
- The systems engineers' ability to influence must be balanced against their responsibility and authority.

10.4 Managing Integration Competencies

As shown in the case studies in this chapter, competency is an underlying characteristic of program management and systems engineering, and includes a set of skills, attributes, and knowledge that results in effective performance. Competencies must be measurable and are required for successful individual, team, and organizational performance. They reflect an organization's values, culture, and business strategies. All organizations must have competency models that describe successful performance for organizations, programs, and a particular role or position. Three examples of competency models for integration described below have proven successful in the training of highly successful teams.

10.4.1 Crew Resource Management as a Model for Integration

A proven model for integrating a set of highly trained individuals into a high-performance team is the aviation industry's Crew Resource Management (CRM) program. The need for CRM and the story of its evolution are germane to integration and competency because, paradoxically, as aircraft technology got better and more reliable, the accident rate increased and air travel grew less safe. Accident investigations concluded that the increased complexity of the modern aircraft system was beyond the capacity for a single person to manage, and that the hierarchical crew structure was ineffective for handling such complexity. Similarly, in the ever-increasing complexity of the information age, hierarchical management structures are also ineffective.

CRM was developed in the 1980s in response to an increasing number of major aircraft accidents attributable to "human error." Two deadly crashes of U.S. airliners in the 1970s in particular spawned the birth of CRM.

- Eastern Airlines Flight 401 flew into the ground (controlled flight into terrain) December 29, 1972. Crew members were preoccupied with a burnt-out landing light and did not notice that the autopilot altitude control function had been turned off. The crew thought they were on "altitude hold," but the airplane was in a slow descent. Since it was 11:30 pm over the Florida Everglades, they had no visual indication that they were descending. The accident was completely attributed to "human error."
- United Airlines Flight 173 crashed December 28, 1978 near Portland, Oregon, due to fuel starvation. The crew was also preoccupied with a landing gear malfunction. Despite repeated reminders by the flight engineer about the fuel state, the captain continued to troubleshoot the landing gear problem.

The investigation of Flight 173 by the National Transportation Safety Board (NTSB) resulted in a recommendation (Priority Action) to:

> Issue an operations bulletin to all air carrier operations inspectors directing them to urge their assigned operators to ensure that their flight crews are indoctrinated in principles of flight deck resource management, with particular emphasis on the merits of participative management for captains and assertiveness training for other cockpit crewmembers (CRM, 2015).

In 1981, United Airlines began training its crews in CRM; the rest of the commercial industry as well as the Department of Defense aviation community followed. Today, myriad CRM training programs exist. The major air carriers have their own, internal CRM programs, while smaller carriers receive CRM training as a contracted service. Regardless of the source, CRM training is required by the FAA for commercial air carriers and is described in FAA (2004) Advisory Circular (AC) 120-51E, *Crew Resource Management Training*. Since CRM was implemented, potential disasters have turned into stories of heroism.

Two properties of CRM are notable and germane to program management/systems engineering integration. First, "CRM training focuses on situational awareness, communications skills, teamwork, task allocation, and decision making within a comprehensive framework of standard operating procedures (SOP)" (FAA, 2004, p. 1). This notion of a standards-based framework is reflected in the Phase I research (Conforto et al., 2013b), which found that the use of industry standards (e.g., PMI *PMBOK® Guide*, INCOSE *SEBoK*) was highly correlated with organizations that reported high levels of integration and low levels of unproductive tension (p. 14). A key finding from the research was that to improve integration, organizations should use standards from both areas, but be "flexible" and adapt them when necessary (p. 15). Having a set of comprehensive standards, then, is a prerequisite to team-based learning.

The second notable property from CRM is that, "CRM training is based on awareness that a high degree of technical proficiency is essential to safe and efficient operations. Demonstrated mastery of CRM concepts cannot overcome a lack of proficiency. Similarly, high technical proficiency cannot guarantee safe operations in the absence of effective crew coordination" (FAA, 2004, p. 5). A related finding in the Phase II and III research was that "The PM [program manager] usually does not have a technical background," which results in poor communications between the program manager and systems engineer and the rest of the technical team. A key takeaway from the research is that, for complex programs, familiarity with systems engineering is essential so that the program manager and systems engineer speak the "same language" (Conforto & Rebentisch, 2014, p. 17). In considering a program management/systems engineering training program, it is worthwhile to consider the essential properties of the FAA's CRM implementation policies. FAA Advisory Circular AC 120-51E (2004) notes under the basic concepts of CRM that "while there are various useful methods in use in CRM training today, certain essentials are universal" (p. 6). CRM training should focus on:

- A training program centered on clear, comprehensive standard operating procedures

- The functioning of crewmembers as teams, not as a collection of technically competent individuals
- Instruction of crewmembers on how to behave in ways that foster crew effectiveness
- Development of opportunities for crewmembers to practice the skills necessary to be effective team leaders and team members
- Exercises that include all crewmembers functioning in the same roles that they normally perform in-flight
- Effective team behaviors during normal, routine operations

CRM is all well and good for discrete situations like an airplane flight, but what about the day-to-day grind of projects and programs? Projects and programs can benefit from discrete "phases" by using control theory and agile approaches.

10.4.2 Control Theory

Driving a car looks like a continuous operation that takes very little thought. However, to the controls engineer who builds the steering and stability system in cars, it is not. Driving a car, in fact, is a continuous series of very small and fast but discreet inputs by the driver that keep the car moving in the right direction at the correct speed. Perceptual control theory (PCT) suggests that purposeful behavior is the "ability of organisms to produce pre-selected results in a disturbance-prone world" (Marken, 2010). When applied to teams, PCT is a three-step process where, once focused on a goal, the team:

1. Talks about the goal daily to keep it at the forefront of team members' minds
2. Reviews performance regularly to ensure information is shared
3. Recognizes the value contribution of individual team members

The leadership core of the team must spend time and pay personal attention to each individual. This third step is the individual nurturing that a leader must be able to do so that people care (Forssell, 2014, p. 61–62).

10.4.3 Decision Theory and the OODA Loop

Business decision models abound and decision theory is an important subject in understanding organizational competencies. A useful heuristic for decision making is John Boyd's OODA Loop (Boyd, 1976). John Boyd was an American fighter pilot who, when analyzing American success in air-to-air combat during the Korean War despite inferior equipment, found that it was the superior decision-making ability of the U.S. pilots that won the day. Boyd found that the decision making boiled down to a continuous cycle of Observing, Orienting, Deciding, and Acting (OODA) and that the outcome of a competitive engagement, be it fighter combat or business, was dependent upon whose OODA loop was faster and more accurate. Two concepts are important: accuracy and speed.

As was shown in the discussion on creative tension, creative energy is derived from the gap between current reality and a compelling vision. For the ensuing effort to be productive and successful, both current reality and the vision itself must be clearly defined. One of the great examples of bridging the gap between vision and reality to improve the quality of life of people comes from the developing world. In 2012 The World Bank established the Global Partnership for Social Accountability (GPSA) with the purpose of bridging the gap between what citizens expect and what governments do. The GPSA works with civil society, governments, and the private sector to help solve challenges through strategic social accountability mechanisms. The GPSA highlights the benefits of constructive engagement in which citizens and civil society organizations can engage with policymakers and service providers, generate information, and align incentives to bring about greater accountability and responsiveness to citizens' needs. The GPSA supports 23 projects, through grants and capacity building in countries ranging from Bangladesh to Ghana to Paraguay. In addition, an extensive knowledge and learning agenda allows GPSA grantees and other partners to enhance the implementation of social accountability interventions (World Bank, 2015). The key takeaway is the significance of using creative energy to align strategic goals through partnership and teaming efforts that provide benefits for all.

One must clearly observe current reality and orient to that reality before deciding and acting on a course of action. In today's complex environment, current reality is a constantly changing phenomenon so today's leader must be able to improvise. Improvisation as a competency was discussed in more detail in Chapter 9, but is recognized here as an important methodology critical to understanding competencies in integration as well (Jaafari, 2003; Leybourne, 2007; Snider & Nissen, 2003).

10.5 Summary

The overarching theme of this chapter is that tension is not only a given, but is also a necessity for achieving goals and realizing visions. The concept of creative tension as a catalyst for releasing creative energy has been discussed at length. When not managed properly, though, tension can be unproductive and, as in the case of the Challenger, have catastrophic results. By applying integration practices to the program manager/systems engineer teaming relationship, tension can be a creative force toward world-class results. The program management/systems engineering team can and should be viewed as a creative duality as described in *The Powers of Two* (Shenk, 2014).

The Apollo and Space Shuttle programs were the archetypes of complexity in the Industrial Age of the twentieth century. In the twenty-first-century Information Age, everything is complex. Organizations and business must master this complexity in order to survive. Blockbuster Video and MySpace were household names at the turn of the twenty-first century. By the end of the first decade, they didn't exist. Countless other examples can be found. PMI's (2014) *Pulse of the Profession*® report emphasizes the need for organizational leaders to take action to become high performers in the twenty-first century. Leadership and systems thinking are competencies that must be developed and managed for organizations to be successful. Proven tools and techniques were presented that, if adopted, would foster the multidisciplinary teams needed to deal effectively with complexity in any domain. Working together, the systems engineer and the program manager can establish better strategies and solutions in the programs in which they are involved, and thus in the greater world.

10.6 Discussion Questions

1. What are some leadership skills needed for creating and communicating an overarching vision of the program, its challenges, and goals?
2. What is a source of creative energy in your organization and how can it be used to release creative tension?
3. What is systems thinking and how can it be used to better integrate the roles of the systems engineer and the program manager?
4. What are the important lessons learned from the success of the TUFF case study in terms of systems engineering and program management integration?
5. What was the conflict discussed in the NASA Challenger Case Study and how would you structure your programs to prevent this problem from happening?
6. Describe three "shared spaces" where systems engineers and program managers can collaborate and drive programs forward.
7. Why does the project management research mainly address individual competencies held by project managers rather than organizational competencies? Why are organizational competencies important in developing successful programs?

10.7 References

Ansorge, W. R. (2004). Systems engineering: A benefit or ballast in astronomical infrastructure projects? *Modeling and Systems Engineering for Astronomy, 11.* doi:10.1117/12.550926

Barry, M.-L., & du Plessis, Y. (2007). Emotional intelligence: crucial human resource management ability for engineering project managers in the 21st century. *AFRICON 2007, 1–7.* IEEE. doi: 10.1109/AFRCON.2007.4401530

Boisjoly, R. M. (2006). *Ethical decisions: Morton Thiokol and the space shuttle Challenger disaster.* Retrieved from onlineethics.org/Topics/ProfPractice/PPEssays/thiokolshuttle/shuttle_telecon.aspx

Boyd, J. R. (1976). *Destruction and creation.* Retrieved from www.goalsys.com/books/documents/DESTRUCTION_AND_CREATION.pdf

Bredillet, C., Tywoniak, S., & Dwivedula, R. (2015). What is a good project manager? An Aristotelian perspective. *International Journal of Project Management, 33*(2), 254–266. doi:10.1016/j.ijproman.2014.04.001

Conforto, E., Rebentisch, E., & Rossi, M. (2013a). *Case study report: Improving integration of program management and systems engineering.* Cambridge, MA: Consortium for Engineering Program Excellence, Massachusetts Institute of Technology.

Conforto, E. C., Rebentisch, E., & Rossi, M. (2013b, October 27–29). *Improving integration of program management and systems engineering.* Presented at PMI Global Congress North America, New Orleans, Louisiana, USA.

Conforto, E. C., Rossi, M., Rebentisch, E., Oehmen, J., & Pacenza, M. (2013). *Survey report: Improving integration of program management and systems engineering.* Presented at the 23rd INCOSE Annual International Symposium, Philadelphia, USA. Retrieved from http://www.pmi.org/~/media/PDF/Business-Solutions/Lean-Enablers/PMI-INCOSE-MIT-Integration-Study.ashx

Conforto, E. C., & Rebentisch, E. (2014). *Executive report: Improving the integration of program management and systems engineering—Case study analysis.* Executive report 3rd phase. Cambridge, MA: Consortium for Engineering Program Excellence, Massachusetts Institute of Technology.

Cooke-Davies, T. J. (2002). The "real" success factors on projects. *International Journal of Project Management, 20*(3), 185–190. doi:10.1016/S0263-7863(01)00067-9

Crawford, L. W. (2005). Senior management perceptions of project management competence. *International Journal of Project Management, 23*(1), 7–16. doi:10.1016/j.ijproman.2004.06.005

Crawford, L. W. (2007). Developing the project management competence of individuals. In J. R. Turner (Ed.), *Gower Handbook of Project Management* (4th ed., pp. 678–694). Aldershot, UK: Gower Publishing.

Crew Resource Management (CRM). (2015). (Class II, Priority Action) (X-79-17). Retrieved from Wikipedia, https://en.wikipedia.org/wiki/Crew_resource_management).

Davidz, H. L. (2006, February). *Enabling systems thinking to the development of senior systems engineers,* PhD Thesis, Massachusetts Institute of Technology.

Dulewicz, V., & Higgs, M. J. (2005). Assessing leadership styles and organizational context. *Journal of Managerial Psychology, 20*(2), 105–123. doi: http://dx.doi.org/10.1108/02683940510579759

Federal Aviation Administration (FAA). (2004). Crew resource management training (CRMT). *Advisory Circular (AC) 120-51E.* Washington, D.C.: Author.

Forssell, D. (2014). *Perceptual control theory: Science and applications: A book of readings.* Hayward, CA: Living Control Systems.

Gallup, Inc. (2015). *State of the American manager: Analytics and advice for leaders.* Retrieved from www.gallup.com/services/182216/state-american-manager-report.aspx

Gerush, M. (2009). *Define, hire, and develop your next-generation project managers.* Cambridge, MA: Forrester Research Inc.

Goleman, D. (1998, November-December). What makes a leader? *Harvard Business Review, 76*(6), 93–104.

Government Accountability Office (GAO). (2007). *Defense acquisitions: Role of lead systems integrator on future combat systems program poses oversight challenges.* Retrieved from www.gao.gov/new.items/d07380.pdf

International Council on Systems Engineering (INCOSE). (n.d.). *INCOSE Code of Ethics.* Retrieved from www.incose.org/about/leadershiporganization/codeofethics

International Council on Systems Engineering (INCOSE). (2010). *Systems engineering competencies framework 2010-0205.* San Diego, CA: Author.

International Council on Systems Engineering (INCOSE). (2012). *Pathways to influence: The emerging role of the systems engineer in an increasingly complex world*, A Report on the 2012 INCOSE International Symposium Executive Summit, San Diego, CA: Author.

International Council on Systems Engineering (INCOSE). (2015). *Systems engineering handbook: A guide for system life cycle processes and activities* (4th ed.). D. Walden, G. Roedler, K. Forsberg, R. Hamelin, T. Shortell (Eds.). Hoboken, NJ: John Wiley & Sons.

IEEE. (n.d.). *Section 7.8 IEEE Code of Ethics*. IEEE Policies, Section 7—Professional Activities, Part A. Retrieved from www.ieee.org/about/corporate/governance/p7-8.html

Jaafari, A. (2003). Project management in the age of complexity and change. *Project Management Journal, 34*(4), 47–57.

Keating, C., Rogers, R., Unal, R., Dryer, D., Sousa-Poza, A., Safford, R., Peterson, W., & Rabadi, G. (2003). System of systems engineering. *Engineering Management Journal, 15*(3), 36–45. doi:10.1080/10429247.2003.11415214

Kennedy, J. F. (1962). *Text of President John Kennedy's Rice Stadium Moon Speech*. Retrieved from http://er.jsc.nasa.gov/seh/ricetalk.htm

Keys, B., & Case, T. (1990). How to become an influential manager. *Academy of Management Executive. 4*(4), 38–51.

Kovacic, I., Filzmoser, M., & Denk, F. (2014). Interdisciplinary design: Influence of team structure on project success. *Selected papers from the 27th IPMA (International Project Management Association), World Congress, Dubrovnik, Croatia, 2013, 119*(0), 549–556. doi:10.1016/j.sbspro.2014.03.061

Leybourne, S. A. (2007). The changing bias of project management research: A consideration of the literatures and an application of extant theory. *Project Management Journal, 38*(1), 61–73.

Locatelli, G., Mancini, M., & Romano, E. (2014). Systems engineering to improve the governance in complex project environments. *International Journal of Project Management, 32*(8), 1395–1410. doi:10.1016/j.ijproman.2013.10.007

Loufrani-Fedida, S., & Missionier, S. (2015). The project manager cannot be a hero anymore! Understanding critical competencies in project-based organizations from a multilevel approach. *International Journal of Project Management, 33*(6), 1220–1235. doi:10.1016/j.ijproman.2015.02.010

Maani, K. E., & Maharaj, V. (2001). *Systemic thinking and complex problem solving: A theory building empirical study*. University of Auckland. Auckland, New Zealand. Retrieved from www.systemdynamics.org/conferences/2001/papers/Maani_1.pdf

Mangenau, J. M., & Pinto, J. K. (2007). Power, influence, and negotiation in project management. In P. W. G. Morris and J. K. Pinto (Eds.), *The Wiley Guide to Project Organization and Project Management Competencies*. Hoboken, NJ: John Wiley & Sons.

Marken, R. S. (2010). Perceptual control theory. In *Corsini Encyclopedia of Psychology*, Hoboken: John Wiley & Sons. Retrieved from http://onlinelibrary.wiley.com/doi/10.1002/9780470479216.corpsy0656/abstract

McChrystal, S., Collins, T., Silverman, D., & Fussell, C. (2015). *Team of teams*. New York: Penguin Random House, LLC.

McClelland, D. C. (1998). *Assessing competencies: Use of behavioral interviews to assess competencies associated with executive success.* Boston: McBer & Company.

Medina, R., & Medina, A. (2014). The project manager and the organization's long-term competence goal. *International Journal of Project Management, 32*(8), 1459–1470. doi:10.1016/j.ijproman.2014.02.011

Mem, S. N., Elahi, M., Bhatti, Z. A., & Khalid, U. (2006). Role of emotional intelligence in virtual project management. *IEEE International Conference on Management of Innovation and Technology, 2,* 642–646. doi:10.1109/ICMIT.2006.262298

Morris, P., & Pinto, J. K. (Eds.). (2007). *The Wiley guide to project organization and project management competencies.* Hoboken, NJ: John Wiley & Sons.

Morris, P. W. G., Crawford, L., Hodgson, D., Shepherd, M. M., & Thomas, J., (2006). Exploring the role of formal bodies of knowledge in defining a profession: the case of project management. *International Journal of Project Management, 24*(8) 710–721. doi:10.1016/j.ijproman.2006.09.012

Müller, R., & Turner, R. (2010). Leadership competency profiles of successful project managers. *International Journal of Project Management, 28*(5), 437–448. doi:10.1016/j.ijproman.2009.09.003

Nahavandi, A. (2012). *The art and science of leadership* (6th ed.). Upper Saddle River, NJ: Prentice Hall.

Oehmen, J. (Ed.). (2012). *The guide to lean enablers for managing engineering programs, version 1.0.* Cambridge, MA: Joint MIT-PMI-INCOSE Community of Practice on Lean in Program Management. URI: http://hdl.handle.net/1721.1/70495

Pernin, C. G., Axelband, E., Drezner, J. A., Dille, B. B., Gordon IV, J., Held, B. J., . . . Sollinger, J. M. (2012). *Lessons from the Army's future combat systems program.* Rand Corporation. Retrieved from www.rand.org/content/dam/rand/pubs/monographs/2012/RAND_MG1206.pdf

Project Management Institute (PMI). (n.d.). *Code of ethics and professional conduct.* Newtown Square, PA: Author. Retrieved from www.pmi.org/~/media/PDF/Ethics/ap_pmicodeofethics.ashx

Project Management Institute (PMI). (2007). *Project manager competency development framework* (2nd ed.). Newtown Square, PA: Author.

Project Management Institute (PMI). (2009). *Practice standard for project risk management.* Newtown Square, PA: Author.

Project Management Institute (PMI). (2013a). *A guide to the project management body of knowledge (PMBOK® guide)* (5th ed.). Newtown, Square, PA: Author.

Project Management Institute (PMI). (2013b). *The standard for program management* (3rd ed.) Newtown, Square, PA: Author.

Project Management Institute (PMI). (2014). *Pulse of the Profession®: Navigating complexity.* Newtown Square, PA: Author.

Rebentisch, E., & Conforto, E. C. (2014, May). *Integration means results: Why systems engineering and program management must align.* Presented at PMI Global Congress, EMEA, Dubai, UAE.

Reiner, T. (2015, May). *Determination of factors to measure the effective integration between program management and systems engineering,* Rheinisch-Westfälische Technische Hochschule (RWTH) Aachen Master's thesis.

Richmond, B. (2010). The thinking in systems thinking: Eight critical skills. *The Systems Thinker, 21*(3) 2–9.

Rogers Commission (1986, June 6). *Report of the Presidential Commission on the Space Shuttle Challenger Accident,* Volume 4 Index, Hearings of the Presidential Commission on the Space Shuttle Challenger Accident, Testimony of Robert Lund, Vice President, Engineering, Thiokol; Roger Boisjoly, Seal Task Force, Thiokol, Joe Kilminster, Vice President, Shuttle Project, February 25, 1986 Session, pp. 1420–1463. Retrieved from http://history.nasa.gov/rogersrep/v4index.htm

Senge, P. M. (2006). *The fifth discipline: The art and practice of the learning organization.* New York: Doubleday.

Shenk, J. W. (2014). *The powers of two: Finding the essence of innovation in creative pairs.* New York: Houghton Mifflin Harcourt.

Snider, K. F., & Nissen, M. E. (2003). Beyond the body of knowledge: A knowledge-flow approach to project management theory and practice. *Project Management Journal, 34*(2), 4–12.

Stevenson, D. H., & Starkweather, J. A. (2010). PM critical competency index: IT execs prefer soft skills. *International Journal of Project Management, 28*(7), 663–671. doi:10.1016/j.ijproman.2009.11.008

United Kingdom Cabinet Office. (2015). *Major projects authority annual report 2014–15.* Retrieved from www.gov.uk/government/uploads/system/uploads/attachment_data/file/438333/Major_Projects_Authority_Annual_Report_2015.pdf

The World Bank. (2015, August 11). *GPSA: Bridging the gap between what citizens expect and what governments do.* The International Bank for Reconstruction and Development and the International Development Agency. Retrieved from www.worldbank.org/en/news/feature/2015/08/11/gpsa-bridging-the-gap-between-what-citizens-expect-and-what-governments-do

Additional Resources

Alexander, I. F., & Beus-Dukic, L. (2009). *Discovering requirements: How to specify products and services.* Hoboken, NJ: John Wiley & Sons.

Browning, T. R., & Eppinger, S. D. (2000). *Modelling the impact of process architecture on cost and schedule risk in product development,* Working Paper Number 4050, revised April 2000. Massachusetts Institute of Technology Sloan School of Management. http://hdl.handle.net/1721.1/2739

Daniel-Allegro, B., & Smith, G. R. (2016). *Exploring the branches of the systems landscape.* les éditions Allegro Brigitte D.

Kossiakoff, A., & Sweet, W. N. (2003). *Systems engineering principles and practice.* Hoboken, NJ: Wiley Interscience.

Melvin J. W., & Suh, N. P. (2002). *Beyond the hierarchy: System-wide rearrangement as a tool to eliminate iteration.* International Conference on Axiomatic Design. Retrieved from http://web.mit.edu/pccs/pub/2002/melvin-axiomaticdesign-1.pdf

National Aeronautics and Space Administration (NASA). (2007). *Systems engineering handbook.* Washington, D.C.: Author.

National Aeronautics and Space Administration (NASA). (2008). *Procedural handbook for NASA program and project management of problems, non-conformances, and anomalies,* NASA-HDBK-8939.18. Washington, D.C.: Author.

Smith, R. P., & Eppinger, S. D. (1997). Identifying controlling features of engineering design iteration. *Management Science 43*(3), 276–293. doi:10.1287/mnsc.43.3.276

Thunnissen, D. P. (2005). *Propagating and mitigating uncertainty in the design of complex multidisciplinary systems.* PhD thesis. California Institute of Technology, Pasadena, CA.

von Bertalanffy, L. (1968). *General system theory foundations, development, applications.* New York: George Braziller.

11

INTEGRATION THROUGHOUT THE PROGRAM LIFE CYCLE

11.1 Introduction

This chapter introduces the life cycles of program management and systems engineering and the impact each has on the delivery of benefits and sustainable outcomes. Case studies from various business and industry sectors illustrate how the integration focus evolves from one stage of the program to another. Different integration principles and actions will be emphasized during the evolution of a program. The program's life spans from the development of the strategic intent of the program through the delivery of sustainable benefits. Research illustrates that integration throughout the life of a program influences the ultimate success. To understand the importance of life cycle management, this chapter focuses on the distinguishing characteristics of the program management and systems engineering life cycles, the activities that occur during each cycle, the optimal behaviors, and how the convergence of these life cycles might better enhance outcomes of programs in the future.

11.2 Integration and the Generic Life Cycle

Meredith and Mantel (2011) point out, "Like organic entities, programs have life cycles. From a slow beginning they progress to a buildup of size, then peak, begin a decline, and finally must be terminated. Also, like other organic entities, they often resist termination." Research on large-scale global programs highlights the significance of the interconnected network of businesses, organizations, and government entities participating in the program across the life of the program (Meredith & Mantel, 2011; Miller & Lessard, 2001; Morris & Hough, 1987). The program network is a temporary structure that includes distinct stages and changing stakeholders and governance structures.

Programs provide the important linkage between the sponsoring organization's strategic goals and the individual projects and other work that are the specific means for achieving them (PMI, 2013a, p. 19).

Integration has been referred to as an up-front, strategy-driven activity and also as an essential element of commissioning commonly referred to in program management as the program delivery stage. A 2007 study of outcomes of integration as a program management concept in industrial programs concluded that by coordinating the end dimension of integration with common rules and a customer-centric approach, the program is adding value to the commissioning process as it thus reveals the purpose of it, and in that way limits its diversity (Kirsilä, Hellström, & Wikström, 2007). Greater integration between program management and system engineering reduces unproductive tension, a cause of program delays, cost increases, and, sometimes, even program failure. The reduction of tension is important as programs proceed.

The duration of programs can vary widely depending on the strategies, policies, and goals of the organization. Some programs can last 30–40 years, such as oil and gas concessions, or as short as a year or less for research and development of software or other technology products. Programs typically consist of four stages:

1. Concept
2. Development
3. Production
4. Utilization

Figure 11-1 shows the generic life cycle stages for a variety of projects and programs from standards organizations to commercial and government organizations. Although these stages differ in detail, they all have a similar sequential format that emphasizes the core activities of concept, development, production, and utilization. Typical decision gates are presented in the bottom line of Figure 11-1. Research reveals that individual program components may not follow this sequence, but may be started and then stopped, improved, reformed, adjusted, or reauthorized and restarted. It is also possible that individual program components can be found to not contribute to the overall strategy or goals of the organization or the program and be abandoned completely. As indicated, large public programs conducted by the U.S. Department of Defense, Department of Energy, and National Aeronautics and Space Administration typically have long lifespans that require longer upfront setup and planning, involve numerous stakeholders, and dictate early finance and acquisition decisions. Software and technology companies, on the other hand, tend to focus more on customer interface and product requirements development in the early stages.

Large-scale public programs are often years in the planning due to the dynamic characteristics of public policy making and constantly changing stakeholder expectations (Greiman, 2013, pp. 12–24). For example, Boston's Central Artery/Tunnel (aka the Big Dig) program was planned over a long period of time, from the initial approval of the cost estimate in 1975 until it was substantially completed in 2007. During this time, it transitioned through eight state governors and numerous changes in rules and regulations regarding the financing and management of the program.

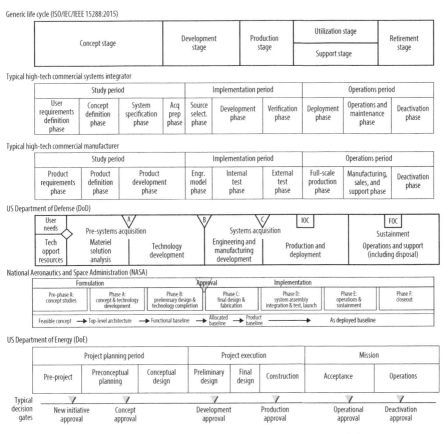

Figure 11-1: Generic life cycle systems engineering stages, their purposes, and decision gate options

11.3 Life Cycle Stages for Systems Engineering

From a systems engineering perspective, INCOSE (2015) notes:

> A system "progresses" through a common set of life cycle stages where it is conceived, developed, produced, utilized, supported, and retired. Life cycles for systems engineering vary according to the nature, purpose, use and prevailing circumstances of the system. Each stage has a distinct purpose and contribution to the whole life cycle and is conserved when planning and executing the system life cycle. The stages thus provide organizations with a framework within which organization management has high-level visibility and control of program and technical processes" (p. 27).

Table 11-1 depicts the broad systems engineering life cycle stages, their purposes, and decision gate options. Life cycle stages for systems engineering overlap the life

Table 11-1: Systems engineering life cycle stages

Life Cycle Stages	Purpose	Decision Gates
Concept	Refine, identify, and define stakeholders' needs Explore feasible concepts Propose viable solutions	Decision options: ■ Proceed with next stage ■ Proceed and respond to action items ■ Continue this stage ■ Return to preceding stage ■ Reform and adjust project activity ■ Put a hold on project activity ■ Terminate project
Development	Refine system requirements Create solution description Build system Verify and validate system	
Production	Produce systems Inspect and verify	
Utilization	Operate system to satisfy users' needs	
Support	Provide sustained system capability	
Retirement	Store, archive, or dispose of the system	

INCOSE, 2015, p. 28

cycle stages for program management in the early stage of concept definition. But they diverge in the execution stages of development and production when systems engineering focuses on the technical details of design, verification, and validation, and the program manager focuses on the overall program performance and delivery of benefits, including high-level finance and budgetary requirements. Some stages may overlap in time such as the utilization and support stages. The program execution process includes activities related to four stages of the systems engineering life cycle: development, production, utilization, and support.

11.4 Program Management Life Cycle Characteristics

The Standard for Program Management (PMI, 2013a) describes the three overarching phases that programs move through as the program life cycle: Program Definition, Program Benefits Delivery, and Program Closure. These phases include subphases and a number of supporting activities, as shown in Table 11-2. While the phases and subphases are defined in the standard, the related activities vary depending on the needs of the program.

Table 11-2 lists a few of the activities present in most programs.

In programs with a high number of projects and other related work, there is a cyclic process in the Program Benefits Delivery phase where projects are initiated at various points within the phase. Initiation of some components of the program may occur very late in the life of the program, while closure has already been achieved on other components of the program. For example, if a city is building a large, inner-city infrastructure with multiple projects that include roads, bridges, tunnels, interchanges, housing, and utility systems, the bridge project may be completed months or years before the tunnel project begins. The various activities of planning large public programs include:

■ The formation and structure of the owner/sponsors coalition
■ The engagement of stakeholders and the local community

Table 11-2: The program management life cycle phases and activities		
Program Management Life Cycle Phases	**Program Management Life Cycle Subphases**	**Program Life Cycle Activities**
Program Definition	Program Formulation	Formulate vision and goals
		Identify benefits
		Engage stakeholders
		Develop scenarios establish benchmarks
		Employ experts
	Program Preparation	Conduct cost/benefits analysis
		Develop business case
		Identify activities to be integrated
Program Benefits Delivery	Component Planning and Authorization	Develop feasibility studies
		Develop delivery methodology
		Review enterprise environmental factors
		Conduct Phase-Gate review
	Component Oversight and Integration	Form cross functional teams
		Integrate program organization—people, processes, and systems
		Integrate change control processes
		Integrate project activities, (i.e., procurement, scope, risk, quality, budgets, schedule, delivery, etc.)
	Component Transition and Closure	Conduct component planning and authorization
		Conduct oversight and integration
		Complete component transition and closure
		Integrate program, customer, and operational functions and teams
Program Closure	Program Transition	Plan for the operational, financial, and behavioral changes necessary by program recipients to continue monitoring performance
		Implement the required change efforts
		Monitor the performance of the product, service, capability, or results from a reliability and availability-for-use perspective
		Provide on-demand support and respond to customer inputs
		Develop business cases and the potential initiation of new programs to respond to operational issues, political, social, and economic changes, cultural shifts, or logistical issues
	Program Closeout	Conduct program financial closure
		Transition benefits
		Compile and disseminate lessons learned
		Ensure continued benefits sustainability

Based on PMI, 2013a

■ The public dialogue and review of the alternative concepts of the program
■ The development of the regulatory, environmental, and governance framework
■ Changes in the political environment, financing, and governmental approvals

Each of the above activities involve collaboration and integration between the systems engineer and the program manager. The delivery of large-scale programs requires a focus not only on the long up-front planning process, but also on the long-term operations and finance, "particularly since initial design and initial choice of technology commit the owner of the facility (public or private) to the resultant cost of mainte-nance and operations for three to five decades" (Miller, 1997). Program life cycles are generally considered iterative or adaptive rather than predictive. In an adaptive or iter-ative life cycle the product is developed over multiple iterations and detailed scope is defined for each iteration only as the iteration begins (PMI, 2013b, p. 38).

There are also notable differences in the life cycle content of programs across indus-tries and products. A research and development process is going to have a very different look than a large infrastructure or space program. For example, in one study of the life cycle of research and development in the life sciences industry, there were impor-tant differences among the venture capitalists in how they viewed the process itself and the behaviors they emphasized during the course of product development (Unger, Greiman, & Leybourne, 2010). In some companies there was more emphasis on cre-ative interventions such as visits, calls, and other meetings and use of external sources of information such as market consultants with all parties and their full organizations and staff. The goals of the intervention included:

■ Creating valid data by fostering reality testing and awareness of each other's biases
■ Building a consensus where possible among and within firms in the syndicate about future strategy and management
■ Building psychological capacity and commitment within one's own venture capital firm to break with syndicate perspective when consensus was not reached on a new round of decisions (Unger et al., 2010)

As described by one venture capitalist, "it is not difficult to produce valid data, the hard part is what you do with it" (Unger et al., 2010). Though almost all of the compa-nies in the study used project and program management methodologies to coordinate complex processes, unpredictable performance, and changing conditions, during the long 5–7 year hold time for the investment the project or program required use of more iterative processes and soft skills making it hard to predict milestones and future risks and probabilities, thus causing disruption to the traditional cost-benefit life cycle analysis (Unger et al., 2010).

11.4.1 Broken Life Cycles and Benefits Management

The Heathrow Terminal 5 and NASA's Miniature Seeker Technology Integration cases highlighted in this chapter are typical examples of a broken life cycle where inte-gration of the systems engineering and program management disciplines might have prevented disconnects between the various stages and thus reached stakeholder expec-tations a lot sooner in the process. The Phase I research found that while respondents use systems engineering and project management standards in parallel, almost none use systems engineering standards in parallel with program management standards (Conforto, Rebentisch, & Rossi, 2013).

The balance of this chapter focuses on areas for integration of the organization, people, processes, and systems used by program managers and systems engineers to fulfill their responsibilities and ensure the realization of benefits. As discussed in earlier chapters, program managers often have different roles, responsibilities, and governance structures within an organization than do systems engineers. While systems engineers focus on building the technological ingredients for the program, the program manager is concerned about the high-level interfaces between the projects they coordinate and the ultimate delivery of benefits. The management of benefits is by far the most important role of the program manager and it is integral to every aspect of the program manager's responsibilities.

To evaluate the program's progress, the program governance team employs phases, milestones, and decision gates to assess the evolution of a system as its component projects complete their respective life cycles. The activities performed seek to achieve program goals and serve to control and manage the sequence and transitions between each component project. Programs differ from systems engineering in that the focus is on the delivery of the program benefits rather than just the performance of the underlying projects. In program management, the term benefit is often used to describe a concept similar to that of value. Benefits in program management are typically defined as the achievement of explicit objectives and change that is specified and approved by customer stakeholders. Thiry (2010) explains, "[t]he full collaboration between the business managers and the program manager is essential for successful benefits realization since one of the main reasons for using program management is to integrate the horizontal strategic decision management process."

However, one must not overlook the important role of the systems engineer in supporting the benefits delivery phase through better integration with program management from program conception to benefits sustainment. Ironically, if a program delivers what it promised, the fact that the program is over budget or late is not determinative of the ultimate success of the program (Greiman, 2015). Recognizing that programs differ widely in their organizational structure, so also do the stages and decision gates chosen for a particular program and its components.

11.4.2 Heathrow Terminal 5 Case Study: A Failure in Systems Integration

An important example of integration in program delivery that is often overlooked is the integration of the program team with operations. One can build the perfect program on schedule, within budget, and poised to deliver intended benefits; however, if one fails to integrate the program with the operating organization, the program can ultimately be deemed a failure when the benefits are not fully realized. As an example, Heathrow Terminal 5 (T5) was a program that was on schedule and on budget from the time construction began, defying all the trends of previous similar initiatives in the United Kingdom (Davies, Gann, & Douglas, 2009). T5 was seen as the first step in the regeneration of London's main airport in preparation for the 2012 Olympics. However, on the day the terminal opened, what was to be a grand celebration instead turned into a disaster due to baggage delays, temporary suspension of check-in, and the cancellation of 68 flights. This failure has been attributed to, among other things, a lack of systems integration and coordination between the program and the operating organization—each operating as separate systems. Once the program management team working on T5 thought they surmounted the considerable issues related to building such a vast and technologically sophisticated terminal, they suffered from technological hubris and forgot about the people issues related to the successful functioning of any large technical system (Brady & Davies, 2010).

What really failed in the T5 case was Integrated Project Delivery (IPD). The concept of IPD as defined by the American Institute of Architects (AIA), is a delivery approach that integrates people, systems, business structures, and practices into a process that collaboratively harnesses the talents and insights of all participants to optimize results, increase value to the owner, reduce waste, and maximize efficiency through all phases of design, fabrication, and construction (AIA, 2007). If there is little integration between the program and operations the final outcome is almost certain to fail. Ironically, T5 was a model in systems integration in many ways, yet the outcome was a failure due to the discontinuity in one of the most important areas of integration—program delivery. Integration is important in all aspects of a program because it fosters collaboration, and collaboration fosters knowledge and trust—key elements of program success. In every program there is a need to integrate the processes and systems required to deliver the program benefits with those involved in the operations of the program's end result (Davies et al., 2009). Recognizing the complexity of the delivery process in T5, the CEO in his testimony before the House of Commons stated:

> [W]ith the benefit of hindsight we might have adopted a more humble position, given the track record, (of other airport opening disasters) and it was unfortunate that we created an expectation of perfection in what was an extremely complicated programme (Matthews, 2008).

The systems engineering and program management life cycles share much in common, including the recognition that programs must align with the strategy of the organization, engage business stakeholders, and transition program results into operations in order to deliver benefits. This requires recognizing and implementing the elements of organizational change management as part of the program management throughout the program. The link between the program life cycle and organizational change has been recognized by PMI (2013a). *Managing Change in Organizations* (PMI, 2013c, p. 67) provides evidence that program management includes organizational change management and is a cyclic process that requires continual reevaluation in order to achieve its objectives. Change can be internal, external, planned, or emergent throughout a program's life and requires a capability to deal with situations that are both ambiguous and uncertain (p. 67).

Key Takeaways from the T5 case include:

- Systems engineering is the emerging paradigm in complex environments to transfer the governance from program-based to system-based governance and thereby increase the chance of holistic success (Locatelli, Mancini, & Romano, 2014).
- Integration between systems engineering, the program management team, and the operations team should take place during the earliest stage of the program and continue throughout the program.
- Integrated delivery is an approach that integrates people, systems, business structures, and practices into a process that fosters collaboration and trust.

- Systems integration is a form of governance that can surface problems and solve them long before they spiral out of control.
- The systems engineer and the program manager have overlapping roles that benefit from shared responsibility and collaboration.

11.5 Large-Scale Infrastructure Programs

Large-scale infrastructure programs (LIPs), including rail, transportation, highways, tunneling, energy, wastewater treatment, and gas and oil extraction and distribution, have unique structural and delivery methodologies that can differ significantly from the traditional prototype developed in the aerospace, defense, and telecommunications industries. Since these programs are heavily financed and governed by public authorities, the design and engineering of these programs are subject to stringent standards and codes. For example, all federally funded projects and programs in the United States are subject to procurement processes that may include a low bid or design-bid-build delivery approach, and be characterized by low change allowance. These programs are also subject to complex interfaces, extensive oversight, progressive design development, and constantly evolving stakeholder interests and influences. For example, in the recent planning of the California High Speed Rail, the government addressed the importance of a statutory oversight authority and a legislatively mandated risk management plan. The program costs include all aspects of managing, designing, and building the proposed high-speed rail system. This includes construction of the high-speed train system (track, stations, buildings, bridges, tunnels, power systems, signaling, etc.), right-of-way, environmental studies and mitigation, design, value engineering, management, rolling stock (trains), testing, commissioning, operations, and all work required to provide a completely operational system ready for revenue service. Due to these unique design characteristics and the size of undertaking, the California High-Speed Train Project (CHSTP) has been divided into eight regional sections to allow for more effective program management. Large-scale programs typically are broken into separate smaller contracts known as work packages (i.e., projects and operational activities) and consist of various stages of completion. Typically, construction commences before design is complete creating greater complexities and interface challenges.

Consistency across the network is crucial in the design of system-wide elements. This includes elements such as the traction power and distribution systems and train control systems. Design criteria and standards are required to guide the preliminary engineering, final design, construction, maintenance, and operational approaches. The lifespan of LIPs tends to be much longer, sometimes as long as 20 to 30 years. LIPs also require considerable community consultation, extensive stakeholder engagement, and large-scale policymaking. They have repetitive and recurring life cycles, draw public scrutiny, require innovative procurement processes, consist of technological complexity, and produce socioeconomic impacts (Greiman, 2013, pp. 12–24).

INCOSE's (2012) *Guide for the Application of Systems Engineering in Large Infrastructure Projects* provides a detailed overview of the unique framework and processes involved in the structure and management of these large-scale infrastructure initiatives. For example, since LIPs are a part of an infrastructure system (e.g., rail systems, electricity distribution network, and highway system) the interrelationships between systems engineering, program management, and asset management are key factors for successful implementation (p. 37). When setting up a LIP, it is necessary to make sure these three fundamental disciplines work together to produce successful outcomes.

There are various models and delivery approaches that can be used on large-scale programs to improve the relationship between the program owners, sponsors, contractors, designers, regulators, and the local communities in which the programs are developed. These delivery models include public-private partnerships, the design-build model to deliver a component project in which the design and construction services are contracted by a single entity, and the design-bid-build model used to separate the procurement of the designers from the procurement of the contractors.

11.5.1 Large-Scale Infrastructure Life Cycle Models

As discussed above, program activities are repetitive and recurring throughout the program. Programs require regular adjustment and realignment, preventing a sequential or linear process. As discussed in Chapter 8, organizations use iterative approaches to manage the overarching factors in large organizations that impact a step-by-step process. With the increase in uncertainty, which evolves from many factors including changes in requirements, technology, stakeholder expectations, organizational design, the law or regulatory environment, and organizational changes in policy or philosophy, there is a need to review and adjust frequently. Most large-scale programs have an extensive process of performance review at several levels prior to the acceptance and payment of any contract as one iterative mechanism. This includes overall technical compliance with scope and schedule specifications, start-up, testing, and test data approval activities. Failure to comply could result in withholding of payments, denial of incentive pay, or termination of the contract (Greiman, 2013, p. 29).

The life cycle of one large-scale public infrastructure program is shown in Figure 11-2 and is very similar to the INCOSE (2015) generic life cycle shown in Figure 11-1. The upfront planning phase can often take decades, as illustrated by many large, civil engineering programs. Project management research as far back as the 1970s shows that the ability to influence the outcome of a project is the greatest and costs are least in the earliest phases (Paulson, 1976). Other research reflects the same dynamic for programs in that the front end of programs are very long—seven years on average—and often very expensive, representing up to 33% of the total budget (Miller & Hobbs, 2006).

Figure 11-2 highlights the cyclical nature of the Boston Big Dig program life cycle, but it does not show the impact of the fast-track methodology where construction would begin on a component project before the entire program design had been completed. For example, construction may have started on the tunnel walls before the final design of the electrical and ventilation systems was completed. Sometimes, this can result in delays and additional costs where the construction methods must be changed

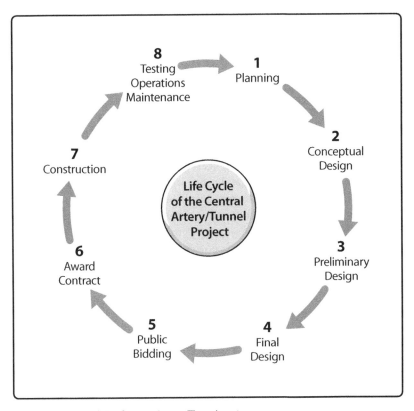

Figure 11-2: Life cycle of the Central Artery/Tunnel project

in order to accommodate a new design. This can also require substantial rework, thus eliminating any benefits the fast-track methodology may have intended. There are other important disruptions to the program life cycle discussed in the case examples in this chapter and the literature, including unexpected events, catastrophic losses, changing stakeholder expectations, discontinuity between program phases, political risk, and economic collapses.

11.6 Life Cycle Integration

In complex programs, program managers and systems engineers need to work closely together, especially in defining the systems life cycle and planning key decision gates to meet their specific needs. Systems engineers may be guided by the *Systems Engineering Handbook* INCOSE (2015), while program managers may be guided by *The Standard for Program Management* (PMI, 2013a). Though program management has overall accountability for the delivery of benefits, systems engineering has accountability for the technical and systems elements of the program (Langley, Robitaille, & Thomas, 2011).

The exact role of the program manager and the systems engineer may vary from organization to organization. Moreover, sometimes the systems engineer also serves as the program manager creating conflicts that cannot always be reconciled, and may lead to serious catastrophic loss (NASA, 1986). Systems engineering tasks are usually concentrated at the beginning of the life cycle, but both commercial and government organizations recognize the need for systems engineering throughout the systems life-span, often to modify or change a system, product, or service after it enters production or is placed in operation. Subsequently, systems engineering is an important part of all life cycle stages (INCOSE, 2015, p. 25).

Program managers and systems engineers are both concerned with management issues such as planning, assessment and control, meeting requirements, leading, and managing risk. In the case of program managers, the program attributes to be managed include program benefits, plans, milestones, finance, resources, infrastructure, and quality assurance. Program managers work to ensure that the overall program structure and program management processes enable the program and its component teams to successfully complete their work and to integrate the components' deliverables into the program's end products, infrastructure, results, and benefits. Systems engineering attributes include responsibilities such as requirements allocation and flow-down, system architecture, structure of and interactions among technical teams, specialty engineering, integration, verification, and validation. The exact allocation of the systems engineering and program management duties depend on many factors, such as customer and stakeholder interactions, organizational structure of the parent organization, and relationships with affiliate contractors and subcontractors. On large-scale infrastructure programs, partnerships between the engineers, contractors, and owner are used to improve schedule adherence, quality, safety, and program performance, as well as to reduce costs, claims, disputes, and litigation (Greiman, 2010).

11.6.1 Generic Model for Integration of the Program Management and Systems Engineering Life Cycle

While there are many important distinctions that must be considered to understand the similarities and differences of program management and systems engineering life cycles, gaining a complete understanding of these factors is more than can be covered in this chapter, or even this book. Nevertheless, Table 11-3 is used to show areas where integration may be possible and, more importantly, where integration may make a contribution to the ultimate success of the program. Table 11-3 illustrates a generic model of the integration of the program management and systems engineering life cycles. The unshaded boxes represent the stages in the program management life cycle, while the shaded boxes represent the stages in the systems engineering life cycle. Column 1 of the table shows the generic life cycles for both program management and systems engineering. Column 2 summarizes the general purpose and activities for each of the stages, and column 3 shows some of the applicable processes and procedures now used in both disciplines. This model is not to suggest that it is the ideal approach to integration, but instead to create awareness and encourage deeper research into the areas for integration of systems engineering and program management concepts, standards, processes, and practices in programs.

Table 11-3: Generic program management and systems engineering life cycle integration		
Program Life Cycle Activities	Purpose/Activities	Processes and Procedures
Concept and Setup	Program setup; benefits and business case analysis	PMI (2013a) 1.1–1.7, 2.1–2.5, 3.1–3.3, 4.1–4.4.2, 7.1
	Preliminary concept Concept selection	INCOSE (2015) 2.1–2.11, 3.1–3.6, 4.1–4.3
Definition and Planning	Identify organizational structures and activities to be integrated	PMI (2013a) 4.3, 5.1–5.3, 6.1–6.6, 7.1.1, 8.3.1–8.3.5
	Refine stakeholders' needs; Define requirements for production, training, and support	INCOSE (2015) 4.4–4.8, 5.1–5.3
Requirements and Specifications Development	Integration of components (cost, schedule, risk, safety, quality assurance, testing, validation)	PMI (2013a) 8.1–8.9
	System analysis is performed Specify, analyze, and design system Planning and execution of activities	INCOSE (2015) 5.4–5.8, 6.1–6.2, 7.1–7.6
Controls, Inspection, and Verification	Control risk, safety, quality assurance, testing, and verification	PMI (2013a) 8.5, 8.7, 6.6.4
	Produce systems; Inspect and verify	INCOSE (2015) 4.9–4.12, 8.1–8.6
Benefits Delivery and Transition to Operations; Lean Systems Engineering; Interoperability Analysis	Monitor performance of benefits	PMI (2013a) 4.3, 7.1.2, 7.1.4
	Operate system to satisfy users' needs	INCOSE (2015) 9.1–9.9, 10.1–10.7
Sustainability, Reliability, and Resilience	Ensure continued sustainability of benefits	PMI (2013a) 4.4–4.5, 8.3.6
	Provide sustained system capability	INCOSE (2015) 10.8–10.14
Closure, Archive, and Benefits Sustainment	Ensure benefits sustainment and document lessons learned	PMI (2013a) 7.1.3, 8.3.6, 8.3.7
	Store, archive, or dispose of the system	INCOSE (2015) 4.13–4.14

Program sponsors need to understand the evolutionary nature of programs and recognize that many large-scale infrastructure programs, and the plans, projects, and other related work they spawn, will often need to evolve in response to changing contextual influences that exert themselves over the often lengthy life of a program (Omega Centre, 2012).

11.6.2 Opportunities for Integration Across the Program Life Cycle

Emerging research in systems engineering is focused on the broader practice as an integrated system at the strategic level of the organization. As described in this chapter, program management and systems engineering behaviors often operate in separate silos due to separate life cycles, standards, missions, goals, influences, cultures, and perspectives. The goal of program management and systems engineering integration in the broader context is to understand the system as a whole from the initial concept and setup of a program to program closure and systems retirement. Recent literature in program management focuses on the need for benefits sustainment management well

Table 11-4: Optimizing the benefits of integration			
Program Management and Systems Engineering Integrated Life Cycle	Program Management Behaviors	Systems Engineering Behaviors	Optimal Behaviors
Concept and Setup	Defines the purpose and goals of the program and secures authorization from the program sponsors	Identifies stakeholders' needs and explores ideas and technologies	Sees the whole system, understands the interrelationships of the systems engineering and program management components and patterns of change
Definition and Planning	Identifies program benefits, processes, and integrative actions crucial to program completion	Refines system requirements, identifies alternatives, and creates solution description	Proactive behavior induction by integration of sustainability in business strategic management
Requirements and Specification Development	Develops specifications to track, review, and regulate progress to meet performance objectives	Identifies the technical requirements and recognizes uncertainty	Sees the technical requirements and programmatic benefits as one system
Controls, Inspection and Verification	Verifies benefit sustainment	Verifies technical sustainment and customer satisfaction	Applies complex systems principles to verify benefit sustainment
Benefits Delivery and Transition to Operations	Coordinates transition to operations with sponsoring organization and stakeholders	Operates system to satisfy customer needs and expectations	Sees benefits holistically and the connection between delivery and operations
Sustainability and Support	Provides sustained system support and ensures benefits sustainability	Provides sustained system capability	Integrates sustained benefits support with system capability
Closure, Archive, Retirement, Benefits Sustainment	Program procurement and financial closure, benefits transition, and product lifetime sustainment	Focus is on the storage, archive, or retirement of the system	Incorporates continuance of benefits sustainment throughout the program life cycle

beyond program closure and transfer to operations. The optimal behaviors in Table 11-4 are identified to emphasize the importance of integration of systems engineering and program management to enhance the likelihood of optimal behavior at every stage of an integrated systems engineering and program management life cycle.

Though the systems engineers will be imbedded in the technical details of the customers' needs while the program manager will be focused on the interdependencies among the projects within the program, an integrated approach creates greater awareness in the development of optimal behaviors.

11.6.3 Whole System Optimization: The MSTI Case

Optimizing the whole system and not suboptimizing is a concept popularized in recent years by the late W. E. Deming (1982). The importance of "whole system optimization" in the integration of the systems engineering and program management is best illustrated by NASA's Miniature Seeker Technology Integration (MSTI) program.

MSTI went into orbit on November 21, 1992. The spacecraft was the first of its kind—a rapid development spacecraft designed and launched in one year. Phillips Laboratories, NASA's Jet Propulsion Laboratory (JPL), and Spectrum Astro, the partners in the endeavor, knew they had met the faster, better, cheaper criteria they had committed to at the onset of the program (Grenville & Kleiner, 2011, p. 1). Five years later, the MSTI team reflected on the long-lasting effects and some of the changes, both subtle and monumental, that came about in each of their organizations as a result of MSTI. The MSTI experience changed JPL's culture, as well as its approach to spacecraft development and missions' management. Prior to the MSTI experience, JPL was unfamiliar with life cycle budgeting. Working closely with the program management team members enabled JPL to understand the ability to evaluate cost over the entire life cycle rather than just at a particular stage of the program. The level of role sharing also was part of the team's success. Although each of the participating organizations focused on their expertise once they had determined their areas of responsibility, they each had a shared responsibility in every function. The following lists a few of the observable results.

- Faster procurement developed into an approach JPL now calls "Fast Track Procurement."
- Hardware acquisition teams are used often in JPL programs.
- The Hardware-in-the-Loop test bed was the precursor to JPL's new Flight System Test Bed that employs much of the same philosophy to simulate test integration used on MSTI (Grenville & Kleiner, 2011).
- Team members moved up quickly in JPL due to the increased responsibility and authority they were given on the MSTI program.

A few examples of the processes that indicate an integration mindset include:

- The schedule was maintained only at a high level in the program management office, and the costs were managed using a cost reporting technique for "cost to completion." Rather than report on past spending, the Responsible Engineering Authorities (REAs) were expected to continually evaluate their ability to complete their tasks within projected costs.
- Faster procurement was achieved using the Hardware Acquisition Team, where a technical team member was matched with a procurement representative for each design function. This pair wrote the specifications together and initiated the purchase requisitions.
- From the organizational perspective, increased responsibility and accountability were given to each team member. Individuals took ownership of their work and the decision process was streamlined. The team made more "good" decisions, rather than optimal decisions.
- The team was co-located, and daily meetings were used to assign tasks and keep the team focused on the launch.
- The standard Problem Failure Report (PFR) was streamlined and electronic reports provided snapshots of the resolved and outstanding PFRs. The report helped REAs

stay on top of potential problem areas. REAs were responsible for looking forward on the program's horizon and notifying the team of any potential problem areas.

The first satellite in the MSTI series, MSTI-1, was launched on November 21, 1992. The spacecraft weighed 150 kg and was built for US$19 million in less than 12 months. Over 200,000 photographs were returned from the spacecraft. From a program management standpoint, all mission objectives were met.

Key takeaways from the MSTI case include:

- Optimize the whole system and not just parts of the system.
- Co-locate teams and hold daily meetings to stay focused on the key issues and hold teleconferences when co-location is not possible.
- Increase responsibility to team members.
- Develop reporting systems that show all failures and resolutions.
- Enhance communication channels both vertically and horizontally within the organization.
- Engage stakeholders at every step of the process to ensure expectations are met.

11.7 Leadership Styles for the Big Dig's Five Stages of Program Management

Because leadership styles can evolve throughout the program depending upon the program's goals, requirements, stakeholder expectations, and changes in governance, it was essential to recognize the different styles of leadership necessary to the various program phases of the Big Dig. Table 11-5 illustrates the various approaches to leadership used on Boston's Big Dig program throughout its life cycle and how knowledge was gained and shared among the program's numerous stakeholders. These leadership styles are not unique to the Big Dig, and can be applied on any program requiring adaptation to the changing needs of the program environment as well as the evolution of the sponsoring organization.

11.7.1 Insights on Leadership Competency

Program managers should develop a competency framework at the inception of the program to identify the various stages and the leadership competencies needed for each stage. Chapter 10 focused on leadership competencies and how to develop these competencies. In addition, there are many resources that provide guidance on developing a leadership competency framework throughout the program (INCOSE, 2015, pp. 21–24; PMI, 2007; PMI, 2015). Though it may be difficult to find a systems engineer and program manager that possess all of these characteristics, it is important to understand the various leadership skills that will be needed throughout the life of the program to guide, inspire, and motivate all stakeholders to manage and overcome issues to achieve program objectives effectively.

Table 11-5: Leadership for the Big Dig's five stages of program management			
Stage	Focus	Style	Gains Knowledge By
Conceptual	Innovative ideas Realistic options Strategies Limitations/constraints Relationship/partnership building	Visionary Inspirational Inclusive	Research Historical data Expert advice Public participation
Start-up	Program structure Governance Alliances Goals Plan Contracts	Strategic Organizational Enabling Negotiating Democratic	Stakeholder feedback Public involvement Brainstorming Consensus building
Implementation	Team building Managing change Getting results	Empowering Facilitating Coaching Energizing Mediating Achieving	Listening Questioning Problem solving Engaging
Monitoring and Control	Assessing progress Enforcing contracts Auditing Resolving disputes	Directive Bureaucratic Interventionist	Investigating Root-cause analysis Lessons learned Resolutions
Closing	Deliverables Product verification Lessons learned Administrative closeout	Transformative Critical analysis	Team evaluations Owner/sponsor input Assessment of achievements Benefit analysis

Greiman, 2013, p. 399. Jointly copyrighted by John Wiley & Sons, and Project Management Institute, Inc. All rights reserved. Reproduced with the permission of John Wiley & Sons, and Project Management Institute, Inc.

11.8 Summary

The life cycle of program management and systems engineering share common characteristics and goals and provide an opportunity for integration that could provide significant benefits to an organization in terms of improving quality, schedule, cost, and long-term investment returns and stakeholder benefit. Integration of the program and systems engineering disciplines should be considered at all stages of the program; but, most importantly, at the inception of the program when the approach to program management is being developed, and also during the transition from the program to operations, when integration will help to ensure a successful delivery of benefits and long-term sustainability.

11.9 Discussion Questions

1. How can the strategic planning phase of programs be used to integrate the disciplines of systems engineering and program management?

2. How are investment appraisal tools such as cost-benefit analysis used to shape investment decision outcomes rather than merely providing objective criteria for selection between alternatives?

3. What is the relationship between integration and change management? How can integration be used to bring about change throughout the program life cycle?

4. How can the benefits of program management and systems engineering integration be optimized throughout the program life cycle?

5. What are the leadership qualities needed to oversee the integration of systems engineering and program management throughout the life cycle?

6. What is meant by discontinuity during the program life cycle and how can it be prevented?

11.10 References

American Institute of Architects (AIA). (2007). *Integrated project delivery: A guide*. Retrieved from www.aia.org/aiaucmp/groups/aia/documents/pdf/aiab083423.pdf

Brady, T., & Davies, A. (2010). From hero to hubris: Reconsidering the project management of Heathrow's Terminal 5. *International Journal of Project Management, 28*(2), 151–157. doi:10.1016/j.ijproman.2009.11.011

Conforto, E., Rebentisch, E., & Rossi, M. (2013, October 27–29). *Case study report: Improving integration of program management and systems engineering*. Presented at PMI Global Congress North America, New Orleans, Louisiana.

Davies, A., Gann, D., & Douglas, T. (2009). Innovation in megaprojects: systems integration at London Heathrow Terminal 5. *California Management Review, 51*(2), 101–125. doi:10.2307/41166482

Deming, W. E. (1982). *Out of the crisis*. Cambridge, MA: MIT Press.

Greiman, V. A. (2010). *The Big Dig: Learning from a mega project, Academy Sharing Knowledge*. The NASA Source of Project Management and Engineering Excellence, APPEL, 47–52.

Greiman, V. A. (2013). *Megaproject management: Lessons on risk and project management from the Big Dig*, Hoboken, NJ: John Wiley & Sons.

Greiman, V. A. (2015). Evaluating megaprojects: What constitutes success. *Rethinking infrastructure: Voices from the Global Infrastructure Initiative*, Vol. 2. London: McKinsey & Company.

Grenville, D., & Kleiner, B. M. (2011). *M.S.T.I., Optimizing the whole system*. Retrieved from www.nasa.gov/pdf/293212main_58529main_msti_casestudy_042604.pdf

International Council on Systems Engineering (INCOSE). (2012). *Guide for the application of systems engineering in large infrastructure projects*, INCOSE Infrastructure Working Group (Eds.). San Diego, CA: International Council on Systems Engineering.

International Council on Systems Engineering (INCOSE). (2015). *Systems engineering handbook: A guide for system life cycle processes and activities* (4th ed.). D. Walden, G. Roedler, K. Forsberg, R. Hamelin, T. Shortell (Eds.). Hoboken, NJ: John Wiley & Sons.

Kirsilä, J., Hellström, M., & Wikström, K. (2007). Integration as a project management concept: A study of the commissioning process in industrial deliveries. *International Journal of Project Management, 25*(7), 714–721. doi:10.1016/j.ijproman.2007.02.005

Langley, M., Robitaille, S., & Thomas, J. (2011). Towards a new mindset: Bridging the gap between program management and systems engineering, *INCOSE Insight, 14*(3), 4–5.

Locatelli, G., Mancini, M., & Romano, E. (2014). Systems engineering to improve the governance in complex project environments. *International Journal of Project Management, 32*(8), 1395–1410. doi:10.1016/j.ijproman.2013.10.007

Matthews, C. (2008). *Testimony of BAA's CEO in Parliament.* House of Commons Transport Committee, London.

Meredith, J. R., & Mantel, S. J. (2011). *Project management: A managerial approach,* (8th ed.). Hoboken, NJ: John Wiley & Sons.

Miller, J. B. (1997). *America's emerging public/private infrastructures strategy: The end of privatization.* Cambridge, MA: Massachusetts Institute of Technology Press.

Miller, R., & Hobbs, B. (2006). Managing risks and uncertainty in major projects in the new global environment, pp. 9–11. *Global Project Management Handbook.*

Miller, R., & Lessard, D. (2001). *The strategic management of large engineering projects: Shaping risks, institutions and governance.* Cambridge, MA: MIT Press.

Morris, P. W. G., & Hough, G. H. (1987). *The anatomy of major projects: A study of the reality of project management.* Hoboken, NJ: John Wiley & Sons.

National Aeronautics and Space Administration (NASA). (1986). *Rogers Commission June 6, 1986 Report of the Presidential Commission on the Space Shuttle Challenger Accident, Chapter V: The Contributing Cause of the Accident.* Washington, DC: National Aeronautics and Space Administration.

Omega Centre (2012, December). *Megaprojects executive summary: Lessons for decision-makers: An analysis of selected international large-scale transport infrastructure projects.* London: Bartlett School of Planning, University College London.

Paulson, B. (1976, April). Designing to reduce construction costs. *ASCE Journal of the Construction Division, Journal of Construction Engineering and Management.* From a paper presented at ASCE Conference, pp. 587–592. San Diego, CA.

Project Management Institute (PMI). (2007). *Project manager competency development framework* (2nd ed.). Newtown Square, PA: Author.

Project Management Institute (PMI). (2013a). *The standard for program management* (3rd ed.). Newtown Square, PA: Author.

Project Management Institute (PMI). (2013b). *A guide to the project management body of knowledge (PMBOK® Guide)* (5th ed.). Newtown Square, PA: Author.

Project Management Institute (PMI). (2013c). *Managing change in organizations: A practice guide.* Newtown Square, PA: Author.

Project Management Institute (PMI). (2015). *Pulse of the Profession® In-depth report: Capturing the value of project management through organizational agility.* Retrieved from www.pmi.org/~/media/PDF/learning/translations/2015/capture-value-organizational-agility.ashx

Thiry, M. (2010). *Program management.* Surrey, UK: Gower Publishing.

Unger, B., Greiman, V. A., & Leybourne, S. A. (2010). A study of postinvestment monitoring practices in life science venture capital firms, *Journal of Transnational Management Development*, *15*(1), 3–25. doi:10.1080/15475770903583377

Additional Resources

Dasher, G. T. (2003). The interface between systems engineering and program management, *Engineering Management Journal 15*(3), 11–14. doi:10.1080/10429247.2003.11415210

Faulconbridge, I., & Ryan, M. (2011). *Managing complex technical projects: A systems engineering approach*. Norwood, MA: Artech House.

Marquet, L. D. (2013). *Turn the ship around! A true story of turning followers into leaders*. New York: Penguin Group.

THE IMPACT OF EFFECTIVE INTEGRATION ON PROGRAM PERFORMANCE

12.1 Introduction

The multiple research phases described in this book (Becerril, Rebentisch, Chucholowski, Conforto, & Lindemann, 2016; Conforto, Rebentisch, & Rossi, 2013; Conforto, Rossi, Rebentisch, Oehmen, & Pacenza, 2013; Rebentisch & Conforto, 2014; Reiner, 2015) found consistent evidence of the positive impact and contribution of greater integration to program performance. Program performance is vital to most organizations since it directly impacts the organization's ability to generate business value. It spans multiple dimensions and metrics from technical performance to program benefits. The evidence supports the claim that organizations should embrace integration as a catalyst for improving program performance.

Program performance is a broad concept and there is a vast body of literature regarding the type and use of metrics to monitor and control performance. Organizations typically develop their own set of metrics according to the organization's specific business characteristics (e.g., industry sector, type of product, program environment). Organizations would also benefit from developing a means to track and improve integration and to measure how integration is contributing to improving the outcomes and results of a given program. In this chapter the main focus is on how effective integration (and its three main elements) impacts program performance. The first step is to understand program performance itself.

12.2 Program Performance

Programs are a mechanism for implementing the core strategy of an organization to maximize value and benefits to the business, clients, stakeholders, and society. They are executed through a temporary organization within the enterprise and consist of multiple related projects organized and executed in such a way as to maximize resource utilization and gains (Oehmen, Rebentisch, & Kinscher, 2011, p. 9). As such, tracking and validating program benefits delivery can be a complicated undertaking.

Successfully completing and delivering results through programs depends on a combination of factors. A diverse set of performance metrics ensures that multiple aspects of program performance are being covered properly (e.g., technical performance, management, business). A systematic view of program performance is most likely to provide a more complete picture of the real progress of the program as well as the outcomes and expected business results.

In any given program there are key elements related to governance and performance that must be well understood, defined, and controlled. For instance, effective program governance includes the alignment of the program goals with the strategic vision and the definition of how program performance is monitored and the outcomes achieved. According to *The Standard for Program Management* (PMI, 2013a), program performance is delivered through five key performance domains: program strategy alignment, benefits management, stakeholder engagement, governance, and program life cycle. In programs, "success is measured by the degree to which the program satisfies the needs and benefits for which it was undertaken" (p. 8). In other words, it should properly meet all expectations for those dimensions. Measuring the performance of a program will require a systematic approach, commitment, collaboration, and shared responsibilities between program managers and chief systems engineers.

Some program benefits are "tangible," quantifiable, and easy to identify, such as financial benefits or the release of a new product. Others are intangible and difficult to measure in detail, such as the impact of a new product on customer satisfaction (PMI, 2013a). In general, successful programs meet several goals related to both types of benefits, and success can be measured by the degree to which the program satisfies the needs and benefits for which it was undertaken (p. 7). Some program benefits are defined by the organization executing the program (e.g., increased market presence, improved financial performance, reduced production costs), and others may be designed by the program's client (e.g., new product platform, new revenue streams, increased operation capability) (p. 33).

A comprehensive program performance management approach will include key metrics from both the management and technical perspective. These metrics should be designed to ensure program benefits delivery, as illustrated in Figure 12-1. Program benefits can be defined as the foundational program management performance domain that describes how the program's planned and intended benefits will be achieved (PMI, 2013a, p. 149). This includes all technical and management plans, processes, activities, and metrics associated with benefits achievement (p. 149).

Program performance management includes the expected results to be realized by the program and how the benefits will be achieved (PMI, 2013a). At the bottom of Figure 12-1 are both the management and technical program performance metrics that encompass the set of measures used to monitor, evaluate, and improve the efficiency, effectiveness, and results of a program (p. 167). The technical metrics illustrate the performance and behavior of the system (or product) during its development. However, it is important to measure and track technical performance metrics that will ensure

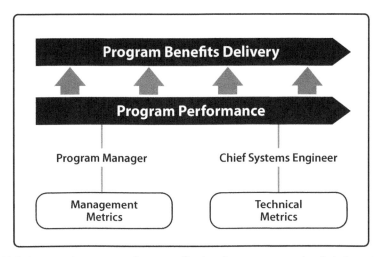

Figure 12-1: Integrated program performance: Combined management and technical metrics

the results and outcomes of the system when it is launched, and the proper alignment with the system's requirements.

The systems engineering measurement process helps define the types of information needed to support program management decisions and implement systems engineering leading practices to improve performance (INCOSE, 2015, p. 130). There are a number of technical measures to consider when designing a performance measurement system for programs that involve complex technical products. Based on work done by Roedler, Rhodes, Schimmoller, and Jones (2007) these measures may be described as:

■ **Measures of Effectiveness,** which account for the measures used to monitor the achievement of the mission or operational objectives of the system, or how well the solution achieves its intended purpose

■ **Measures of Performance,** which describe physical and functional characteristics or attributes related to the system operation considering operational environment conditions

■ **Technical Performance Measures,** which account for attributes or characteristics of a system element according to the defined requirements or goals

There are a number of generic frameworks for developing technical performance metrics and measures to address a variety of programs and industry needs. Figure 12-2 illustrates some examples of management and technical metrics commonly used in programs. It also highlights some of the key steps to develop a systematic process to plan and monitor program benefits delivery (PMI, 2013a).

Program managers and chief systems engineers working in a more integrated environment should also consider other factors that might influence program benefits realization as well as program performance. The Integration Framework suggests that greater integration performance will significantly contribute to improved program

Program Benefits Delivery

- Create a list of planned benefits
- Map benefits to each program component (project or subprograms)

- Describe how each benefit should be measured
- Derive key performance indicators and thresholds for evaluating results

- Define target dates and milestones for benefit achievement
- Define group or organization responsible for delivering each benefit

Program Performance

Management Metrics

- General scope changes and deviation
- General schedule deviation and forecasts
- General budget deviation, forecasts, and program operational costs
- General management risks and budget impact
- Overall client satisfaction
- Level of stakeholder engagement
- Earned Value Analysis (cost, time, and value)

Technical Metrics

- Requirements trends
- System definition change and backlog trend
- Interface trends
- Requirements validation trends
- Requirements verification trends
- Work product approval trends
- Review action closure trends
- Risk exposure trends
- Risk handling trends
- Technology maturity trends
- Systems engineering staffing and skills trends
- Process compliance trends

Figure 12-2: Examples of management and technical metrics
PMI, 2013a, & 2013b; Rhodes, Valerdi, & Roedler, 2009; Roedler et al., 2007.

performance and, therefore, this dimension should be included in and aligned with program metrics and measurement.

This chapter focuses on the relationship between integration and common program performance metrics. Program performance is important for both the program management and systems engineering disciplines. There are generally accepted practices and tools; therefore, it is not the core focus of this chapter to explain how to develop a program performance management system or set of metrics. Nonetheless, it is important that the organization develop a comprehensive understanding of both areas, including practices, tools, and techniques to define, implement, and track performance measures, leading to better decisions and ensuring program results and benefits realization.

12.3 Measuring Integration in Programs

12.3.1 Why Measuring Integration Matters

Increasing levels of integration helps teams deliver better program results. Integration is composed of three main factors: rapid and effective decision making, effective

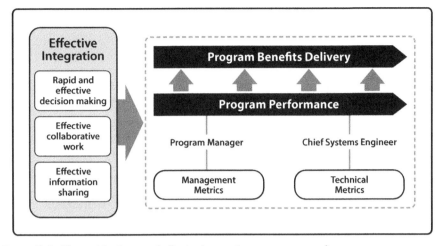

Figure 12-3: The positive impact of effective integration on program performance

collaborative work, and effective information sharing. Organizations should, there-fore, develop processes and dedicate resources to identify, develop, and monitor these factors to assess whether these behaviors are present in programs. Figure 12-3 illus-trates the relationship between effective integration and a broad overview of program performance.

Despite its importance, measuring and monitoring integration performance is not a common practice. None of the professionals interviewed during the Phase II & III inte-gration research (Conforto, Rebentisch, & Rossi, 2013; Rebentisch & Conforto, 2014) indicated they had well-defined and systematic processes to measure the effectiveness of the integration between program management and systems engineering.

12.3.2 The Key Elements to Measure Integration

How should integration be measured? The first step is to develop a clear understanding of what constitutes integration (see Chapters 5 and 6), a composite list of the integra-tion elements, and some performance indicators for these elements. The indicators described in this section are summarized in Figure 12-4, and will be explained in more detail in the following sections. They are introduced here to provide an overview and develop an awareness of ways to assess whether these elements of integration are present in the program. This then sets the stage for improvement efforts to increase the degree of integration in the organization, which is covered in greater depth in Part III.

12.3.2.1 Rapid and Effective Decision Making

Decision making is a multistage and complex process. In general, a decision process involves choices from a set of alternatives and constraints, producing results that are associated with those choices, which could either mean a gain or a loss, or a positive or a negative outcome (Bellman & Zadeh, 1970, p. 147). Better program decisions are made when there are empowered program managers and chief systems engineers who

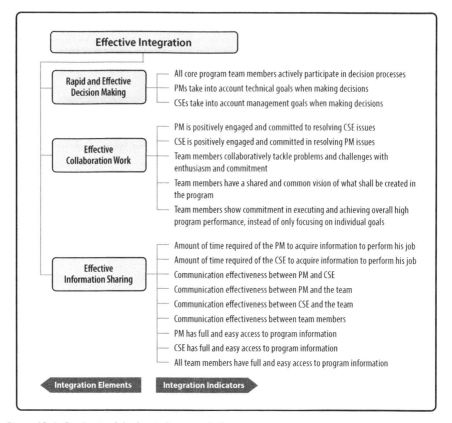

Figure 12-4: Synthesis of the key indicators of effective integration
PM   Program Manager
CSE   Chief Systems Engineer

share a common vision of the program goals and expectations. Program managers and chief systems engineers must develop a clear and shared decision-making approach to deal with changes, problems, risks, and opportunities during the course of a program.

Decisions must be made in the right timeframe and lead to the expected outcomes. This is the case for all types of programs, regardless of the industry sector or business environment. For example, the decision to select a supplier to develop a critical part of the product must be completed in a timeframe that allows for the involvement of the supplier in the initial design process in order to avoid rework, additional costs, and schedule delays.

For every program, there are indicators of how decisions are made that can be periodically assessed to evaluate how the decision-making process overall aligns with principles of integration. The following indicators of an integrated decision-making process are adapted from indicators used in the Phase IV research (Reiner, 2015):

- All core program team members actively participate in program decision processes.
- Program managers take into account technical goals (e.g., requirements, specifications) when prioritizing tasks or making decisions.

■ Chief systems engineers take into account management goals (e.g., time, cost, business value) when prioritizing or making decisions.

12.3.2.2 Effective Collaborative Work

The organization's leadership, along with the program managers and chief systems engineers, should strive to create a collaborative, trustful work environment that is focused on working together to achieve clearly defined goals. Team members should work collaboratively and proactively to solve problems as quickly as possible. The program manager and chief systems engineer should nurture and develop a mutual understanding of both technical and management issues. This is a fundamental element of their program leadership, and addressing this may require considerable attention from them as it runs counter to the prevailing culture of specialization and competition in many organizations.

The Phase IV research identified a number of attributes of collaborative work from a broad range of sources. These were used to collect data and assess the impact of collaboration on integration as well as program performance. The following indicators of collaborative work in the program are adapted from indicators used in the Phase IV research (Reiner, 2015):

■ The program manager is positively engaged and committed to resolving technical issues.
■ The chief systems engineer is positively engaged and committed to resolving program management issues.
■ Team members collaboratively tackle problems and challenges with enthusiasm and commitment.
■ Team members share a common vision (set of priorities, benefits, and results of the program) of what will be created by the program.
■ The team members show commitment in executing and achieving overall high program performance instead of just focusing on their own individual performance and results.

12.3.2.3 Effective Information Sharing

Having an effective information sharing process is the third element of integration in programs. Collecting, analyzing, and communicating relevant information is a challenge in many organizations. Tremendous amounts of data, knowledge, and experience are generated, and perhaps not properly documented in a way that benefits other team members. In addition, poor communication may hinder the development of effective information sharing. Effective information sharing begins with program managers and chief systems engineers, but ultimately must enable all team members to have access to information they need to perform their tasks. These behaviors should be assessed and jointly managed by the program manager and chief systems engineer.

The Phase IV research focused on activities that significantly contributed to improving information sharing capabilities in programs. The following indicators of effective information sharing in the program are adapted from indicators used in the Phase IV research (Reiner, 2015):

- The amount of time required of the program manager to request and receive necessary information from team members or the organization
- The amount of time required of the chief systems engineer to request and receive necessary information from team members or the organization
- The effectiveness of communications between program manager and the chief systems engineer
- The effectiveness of communications between the program manager and team members
- The effectiveness of communications between the chief systems engineer and team members
- The effectiveness of communications among program team members
- The program manager has full and easy access to all program-related information needed to perform the job successfully.
- The chief systems engineer has full and easy access to all program-related information needed to perform the job successfully.
- All team members have full and easy access to all program-related information needed to perform their tasks successfully.

The 17 indicators described in the preceding sections were used to develop an "integration index" that served as a single indicator of the overall degree of integration for a program (Reiner, 2015). This index was used in the analysis to identify and compare programs with greater and lesser degrees of integration, respectively. It proved to be a reliable measure of integration and was employed across all the analyses (p. 63). The following section discusses the results of the analysis, indicating that greater integration does indeed coincide with superior program performance. Section 12.5 presents a case study that highlights practical examples of how integration and its key elements contributed to improved program performance.

12.4 Integration as a Catalyst for Program Performance

12.4.1 Greater Integration Leads to Improved Program Performance

To understand how increased integration impacts program performance, a survey was conducted with 157 professionals (program managers and chief systems engineers) from a diverse set of companies around the globe operating in some 18 different industry sectors (Reiner, 2015). Each participant completed a questionnaire covering the concept of integration and its key elements and indicators, along with other aspects of the program such as contextual and organizational characteristics and performance.

The integration index was used to identify two main groups: programs with greater integration (n=90) and programs with lesser integration (n=67). These two groups were used in the analysis to understand how integration related to program performance. The performance outcomes used included:

- **Program schedule:** The overall program results were obtained within the expected timeline.
- **Program budget:** The overall program results were obtained within the expected budget.
- **Client requirements:** The final product of the program met the client's overall requirements.
- **Client satisfaction:** The overall client satisfaction with the program results met or exceeded expectations.

The results of this analysis, presented in Figure 12-5, shows the comparison between the groups with greater and lesser degrees of integration in programs along with their associated program performance outcomes.

The group of programs with greater integration is significantly more likely than programs with lesser integration to have better performance in schedule and budget performance, as well as client requirements and satisfaction.

A more in-depth investigation was performed at the level of individual indicators to identify potential relationships between integration practices and program performance metrics (program schedule, program budget, client requirements, and client satisfaction). This was done by exploring correlations between the 17 integration

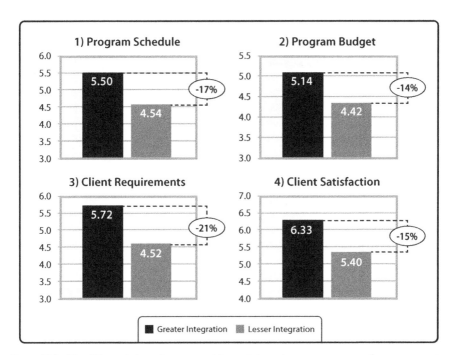

Figure 12-5: The differentiation of greater and lesser integration on program performance; greater integration (n=90), lesser integration (n=67)

Reiner, 2015. Courtesy of Thomas Reiner, RWTH Aachen University.

Table 12-1: Integration elements with the highest correlation coefficients with program performance metrics					
Integration Factors	Integration Variables	Program Schedule	Program Budget	Client Requirements	Client Satisfaction
Rapid and Effective Decision Making	Involvement of all members of the core program team in the decision-making process	✓	✓	✓	✓
Effective Collaborative Work	Team members collaboratively tackle problems and challenges with enthusiasm and commitment	✓		✓	✓
	Team members have a shared and common vision (set of priorities, benefits, and results of the program) of what shall be created in the program	✓		✓	✓
	The team members show commitment in executing and achieving overall high program performance, instead of just being focused on their own individual performance and results	✓		✓	✓
Effective Information Sharing	The efficiency of communications between the chief systems engineer and the team members	✓	✓	✓	✓
	The efficiency of communications between the program manager and team members	✓	✓	✓	✓
	All team members have access to all program-related information that they need to perform their tasks successfully	✓	✓	✓	✓

variables and the four program performance variables. The findings indicating strong and significant correlations are presented in (Table 12-1).

12.4.2 The Impact of Integration Behavior on Program Performance

Although these results are consistent and aligned with the idea that there are positive results from greater integration in programs, it does not provide much intuition for the sensitivity of program performance to integration, nor a clear picture of how integration works during program execution. To further develop insight about how integration impacts program performance, System Dynamics Modeling techniques were used to create a simulation model of a generic program to investigate how the different elements of integration between program management and systems engineering influences program execution (Becerril et al., 2016).

System Dynamics Modeling is a simulation technique used to analyze complex and dynamic systems that have multiple relationships between the system elements (endogenous and exogenous) and that display feedback between the different elements in the system. It is a fairly well-established technique and is based on information feedback systems and decision-making processes (Browning, Fricke, & Negele, 2006; Forrester, 1961; Sage & Rouse, 2009). These models are useful to explore and understand correlations and potential causal relationships in component parts of programs and projects (e.g., between phases, schedule and budget, workflow, and rework) (Ford, 2009). System Dynamics Modeling has been applied in large programs to assess decisions and evaluate their impact on outcomes (Becerril, et al., 2016; Sterman, 1992, 2000).

Becerril et al. (2016) focused on two main areas: (a) how integration regulates the exchange of information among projects in a given program by affecting the communication and collaboration capabilities of the organization; and (b) how integration influences the resource allocation process by regulating how the program manager and the chief systems engineer make decisions together. The model developed was based on a well-documented model of a project (a model of a program would add unnecessary complexity to this analysis) with tasks to complete, handoffs between phases, delays in task completion, imperfect quality and rework and the like, and added elements from the Integration Framework and research. The data identifying relationships between elements of the Integration Framework and performance in programs collected by Reiner (2015) were used to construct the model and calibrate it. Though this simulation analysis is based on a project model, it is seen as a reasonable abstraction of a program organization. To be consistent with the conventions used in this book, the term "program" will be used when describing the model and its outcomes.

One aspect of program performance explored by the simulation was schedule deviation relative to the initially planned completion deadline for the program. Figure 12-6

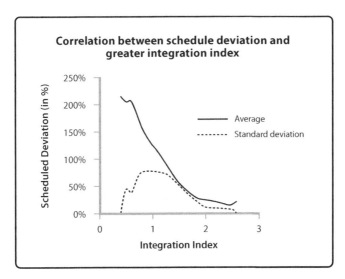

Figure 12-6: Integration index versus schedule deviation
Becerril et al., 2016. © Lucia Becerril. Used by permission.

shows the schedule deviation (in percent) relative to the degree of integration, which in this simulation can vary between 0 and 3, with 3 indicating the highest level of integration.

The results clearly indicate that under the parameters considered in this simulation, the schedule deviation tends to be low when the program manager and chief systems engineer functions are more highly integrated. The standard deviation or variation in the average schedule performance also declines with greater integration between program management and systems engineering (Becerril et al., 2016). The initial, very low standard deviation reflects the simulated program reworking every task until it is completed—every task consumes as many resources as required to complete when there is low integration, but the price to the program is high in terms of schedule delay. In reality, most of the programs that have those very high schedule deviations would probably be canceled or significantly restructured. In broad terms, the model indicates that as the primary elements of integration—rapid and effective decision making, effective collaborative work, and effective information sharing—increase, the amount of time needed to complete the program is reduced substantially, and program execution becomes more predictable.

Additional simulations were carried out using different parameters, with results consistent with the evidence that programs with greater integration will have higher performance. In one analysis, high external schedule pressure to complete the program on time was applied to the simulated program to understand whether higher levels of integration offered any benefit to program performance. The result of the analysis is shown in Figure 12-7. This pressure might be interpreted as constraints levied during the program definition phase by stakeholders to complete the program ahead of schedule (Becerril et al., 2016). In this test, the base case had an initial specified duration of 32 weeks, compared with 25.6 and 19.2 weeks required of the high-pressure and

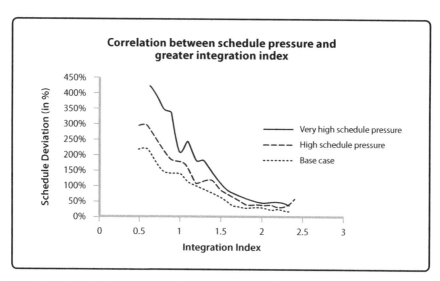

Figure 12-7: Integration index versus schedule pressure and schedule deviation
Becerril et al., 2016. © Lucia Becerril. Used by permission.

very-high-pressure schedule cases, respectively. The results are consistent with those of the overall simulation presented in Figure 12-6. Even as schedule pressure to complete the program increases beyond the baseline, more highly integrated programs tend to have lower schedule deviation and approach the efficiency of the baseline case.

This analysis also highlights that even some degree of integration can bring a substantial improvement to outcomes. As shown in Figure 12-7, the curve displaying the relationship between integration and schedule deviation initially declines fairly rapidly. That implies that programs with even a moderate degree of integration may achieve significant benefits from integration compared with programs having lesser levels of integration (Becerril et al., 2016).

The analysis of the Phase IV survey data showed that variables related to communication efficiency and the quality of information exchange showed positive correlations with better program performance. This suggests that a minimum level of quality of information sharing is necessary to maintain the information flow at a level that positively impacts program outcomes. That is one aspect of the reinforcing loop that characterizes how errors within the information result in errors in the work being done, which in turn leads to additional errors, ultimately resulting in poor program performance (Becerril et al., 2016).

In summary, the research evidence, analysis, and conclusions have shown that increasing levels of integration can have a significant beneficial impact on program performance. The primary behaviors in a program by which this is accomplished are rapid and effective decision making, effective collaborative work, and effective information sharing.

12.5 Case Study: Electronic Support Upgrade for the Royal Australian Navy's Anzac Class Frigate

How do these performance improvements from integration play out in a program? The following case study[1] examines a recent program, highlighting some of the key elements of the Integration Framework and the overall contribution of greater integration to program performance and benefits delivered. It considers the interconnected results of a project that was undertaken as part of a major program within the Australian Department of Defense. The term "project" was adopted in describing this effort to be consistent with the terminology used by the Australian Department of Defence.

12.5.1 Introduction to the Case Study

The Schedule Compliance Risk Assessment Methodology (SCRAM) was developed by the Australian Department of Defence's Capability Acquisition and Sustainment Group (CASG), which is responsible for purchasing and maintaining military equipment and supplies for defense. SCRAM entails a minimally disruptive, independent review of complex projects and programs experiencing schedule slippage in order to identify root causes, recommend remedial actions, and forecast future milestone dates.

SCRAM teams integrate systems engineering and project and program management expertise. The reviews identify risks and issues regardless of their source (i.e., customer, contractor, or elsewhere) and provide rapid turnaround in no more than two weeks from start to presentation of the results. To date, more than 30 different CASG projects within Australia, the United States, and the United Kingdom have undergone SCRAM reviews with several being reviewed multiple times at their own request. Application domains include aerospace, maritime, communications, aircrew training, satellite ground stations, and command and control.

After reviewing a number of projects, the opportunity arose to study a project that was an outstanding success, delivering ahead of schedule, within cost, and with minimal defects found in its first-of-class testing. Rather than look for risks and issues, this SCRAM review focused on identifying the contributors to achieving exceptional outcomes. What emerged was a project that clearly demonstrated effective integration between project management and systems engineering. From the beginning of the project, the foundation was set for effective and ongoing collaboration, continual information sharing, and empowered rapid decision making combined with an unwavering focus on delivering an effective capability to the customer, in this case the Royal Australian Navy.

This case study chronicles events as they unfolded and then summarizes the three key measures of effective integration as they were manifest on this project.

12.5.2 Project Background

The purpose of the project, referred to within CASG as SEA 1448 Phase 4A, was to provide the Anzac class frigates with an improved tactical Electronic Support (ES) capability by replacing the existing ES system. This is one of the Royal Australian Navy's highest-priority projects and has operated under a directive from the Chief of Navy to field the capability as rapidly as possible.

The Anzac class is a Navy frigate first commissioned in 1996 (Figure 12-8). A total of 10 ships were built in Australia, eight for the Australian Navy and two for New Zealand. They are well suited to security, patrol, and military operations in littoral (coastal) areas. Since 2002, they have completed multiple deployments in the Middle East.

ES systems gather information through passive analysis of electromagnetic radiations in order to detect and distinguish between friendly and adversary emissions, and provide warning if an attack appears imminent. In combination with radar systems, ES can identify the source of electromagnetic radiations and assist in determining their direction, distance, and trajectory. ES is one component of a larger domain referred to as Electronic Warfare (EW), the scope of which is beyond this case study.

Maritime EW is a technically complex area. A great deal of electromagnetic "noise" must be sorted through to identify friendly and adversary electronic emissions. A Systems Program Office (SPO) was set up within the CASG to manage all acquisition and sustainment of maritime electronic warfare projects across all classes of ships in the Royal Australian Navy. This function formerly resided within the individual SPOs responsible for a specific class of ship (e.g., submarine, destroyer, frigate). In forming the Maritime Electronic Warfare Systems Program Office (MEWSPO), there was an

Figure 12-8: HMAS Warramunga: The first Anzac ship to receive the full ES system upgrade
Source: Image courtesy of the Australian Department of Defence. Used with permission.

acknowledgment of the technical complexity inherent in this area and the need for a specialized focus in the acquisition and support of maritime EW systems.

As noted above, the purpose of the SEA 1448 Phase 4A project was to upgrade the Electronic Support (ES) capability on the Anzac class ships. To save on costs in the use and sustainment of the Anzac ES system, the decision was made to acquire a common ES system on selected ship classes across the Navy. This approach was intended to save costs in training users and in system sustainment in terms of product maintenance and support. The team of contractors selected to provide the common ES system consisted of the following:

- Exelis in the United States, now part of Harris Corporation, served as the ES hardware prime contractor and provided a wideband receiver and antennas.
- Australian company Jenkins Engineering Defence Systems, or JEDS, provided a low-band radio frequency receiver and system assembly in Australia prior to installation on the ships.
- Australian company Ultra Electronics provided a narrow-band RF receiver.
- United States company Southwest Research Institute, or SwRI, provided antennas and the antenna mast.

There are three additional contractors whose activity or systems were required to integrate with the ES system, namely:

- BAE Systems-Australia or BAES-A, responsible for installing the ES system on the Anzac ships
- Australian company CEA Technologies, the Anzac class phased-array radar Original Equipment Manufacturer
- Saab Australia, responsible for the Combat Management System

These seven companies had to work together to produce a seamless, fully integrated suite of systems. The MEWSPO SEA 1448 Phase 4A project office managed the overall systems integration and worked closely with the Anzac System Program Office, which was responsible for scheduling and coordinating ship maintenance and upgrades.

12.5.3 Setting the Stage for Effective Program Management and Systems Engineering Integration: Precontract Risk Reduction Workshops

At the time this effort began in early 2011, the Exelis team of contractors had been selected to provide the common ES system solution. There was a two-year risk reduction period between this selection and government approval for funding acquisition of the ES system for the Anzac class of ships.

The Anzac ES project was fortunate to have highly experienced people in key management roles. The project director, Dan Keleher, had an extensive background in managing maritime projects and is a professional engineer. Gary Crawford, the engineering manager for the project, was an experienced maritime electronic warfare systems engineer and former Royal Australian Navy officer and EW operator. Crawford, therefore, combined technical expertise with operational experience, giving him an in-depth understanding of issues, risks, and tradeoffs that are important to the operational performance of ES systems.

In mid-2011, the project received early funding to undertake face-to-face risk-reduction workshops over a 12-month period prior to the award of the full contract. These workshops brought together representatives from all the involved contractor organizations to identify the technical risks to the project and to develop strategies to address those risks, working together as one team. In addition to the contractors directly involved in implementing the solution (Exelis, JEDS, Ultra Electronics and SwRI), Keleher funded Saab and CEA to participate in these workshops since their systems had to integrate seamlessly with the ES system. BAES-Australia was included as well. These workshops had the added benefit of maintaining the continuity of the expertise needed for the project across both the pre- and post-contract award periods.

In early 2013, the project received full funding to acquire and install ES systems onto the eight Anzac ships and in an on-shore laboratory facility containing the full suite of hardware and software for operator training and systems troubleshooting without having to take up time on an actual ship. As noted earlier, the ES upgrade for the Anzac ships is afforded a high priority by the Chief of Navy. In Keleher's words, "All along we kept focusing on how we could get the capability onboard more quickly without sacrificing quality or safety." The entire team, government and contractors, stepped up to the challenge. JEDS, for example, doubled its production capacity by setting up a second production facility.

One constraint in implementing major upgrades to ships is that the upgrades are limited to a window of time when each ship is taken out of the water. During these periods, a number of parallel activities occur, including simultaneous system upgrades as well as repairs and maintenance to the ship's hull and systems. Access holes are created in the ship's hull to allow equipment and materials to be brought onboard; in addition, spaces behind bulkheads, under decks and deck heads (ceilings) are removed to provide access to electrical, water, and other systems.

As the project team looked for ways to accelerate the work, a strategy was adopted to preinstall system components into the Anzac ships before the ES system was fully developed and delivered. This consideration included the cabling, the mast, foundations for equipment racks, and a new multifunction console. This approach saved having to reopen ships' spaces at a later time and was made possible by the risk reduction and early systems design activities undertaken earlier. Parameters such as the number and length of cables were known. The initial installation is referred to as "fitted for but not with" the ES system. By taking advantage of the period that the ships were in refit, the remaining system components could be installed when they became available without requiring the ships to be taken out of operation.

As the "fitted for but not with" activity proceeded, it became clear that the completion of maintenance and other work being performed on the ships outside of the ES upgrade project was falling behind schedule. The ship that was planned for installation of the first complete ES system (i.e., first of class) was almost six months behind its delivery schedule. In order to field the capability as quickly as possible, the project switched the installation of the first system to another ship that would be returning to the water sooner. The project had this flexibility because of the "fit for but not with" strategy that had been implemented on other ships. In March 2015, the first ES system for the Anzac ships completed its integration and factory acceptance test at Exelis in the United States and was transported to Australia. Its installation on the Anzac class ship HMAS Warramunga was completed ahead of schedule in the third quarter of 2015. Perhaps even more impressive, minimal defects were found during the initial operation of that system during the ship's sea trials.

The outcome-focused attitude of the project is well summarized in the words of one of the team members interviewed:

> We knew that the Chief of Navy wanted this capability as quickly as possible. When we ran into problems, such as the first ship slipping schedule, we didn't say "tough, it's not our fault. We can't install the system." Rather, we asked "what can we do instead?" And we did it.

The following sections discuss how the ES project demonstrated the three key measures of effective integration.

12.5.4 Promoting Collaborative Work

The risk-reduction workshops set the groundwork early on in the project for mutual respect and direct communications between the government and contractors and among the various contractors. In the words of one of the contractors interviewed:

> On this project, we were empowered to talk to each other directly with no communication bottlenecks. All the players participated in the workshops. We were drawing boxes on a white board and talking about how to integrate them without getting too much into the weeds. The software guys would get together to discuss software interface issues. Dan sat back and let it happen because he could see it was a healthy thing. We'd all get back together at the end of the day and kept an ongoing risk log.

The two government program offices involved, MEWSPO and the Anzac SPO, worked constructively and collaboratively with each other, facilitated by a Project Implementation Plan that clearly defined the roles and responsibilities of each of the SPOs.

12.5.5 Effective Information Sharing

Information sharing among contractors was essential in order to field a capability requiring seamless integration between the phased-array radar, the ES system, and the Combat Management System. A major purpose of the early risk reduction workshops was to gather all contractors together face to face to share information about system interfaces and to address jointly issues and risks. Throughout the project, direct communications among all participants was encouraged.

In addition to the workshops and direct communications, information was shared via computer simulations of each of the interfacing systems provided by the system developers. One of the enduring lessons from systems and software engineering is the value of finding problems early. These computer simulations allowed any interfacing component or system to be tested against the simulated interfaces early in its development. This process resulted in a relatively smooth integration and test of the actual systems and allowed the "fitted for but not with" strategy cited earlier to be adopted.

12.5.6 Rapid and Effective Decision Making

Rapid and effective decision making was demonstrated by the project team's ability to adapt to changing circumstances, all while maintaining a laser-like focus on delivering the capability as early as possible. The change in ship sounds like a simple matter; however, at the time that decision was made by the project team, there was a fair amount of activity geared toward the original ship that was to be first in class as well as associated contractual overhead (including payment milestones). The team stepped up to the challenge of a change in ships and delivered the system several months ahead of schedule.

12.5.7 Outcome: Delivery of Capability to the Navy ahead of Schedule, within Budget, and with Minimal Defects in Sea Trials

It is important to mention that a major contributor to the positive outcome of the SEA 1448 Phase 4A was the strong, consistent, and tireless leadership provided by both Keleher and Crawford. Typical comments include the following:

> Dan Keleher understands that his role is to set expectations and let us do our work. He encourages an outcome attitude. He listens to us and doesn't just tell us what we should do. Throughout the entire project, Dan has worked with us rather than against us. There have been times we've called him at 11:00 at night.... Gary Crawford has an amazing amount of experience and competency. He's very hard working but also relaxed. When he walks in, everyone calms down. We can always talk to Gary or to Dan about anything.

On June 6, 2016, the ES capability installed on the Anzac class was approved for initial operations by the Chief of Navy after completing a successful series of sea trials and operational testing.

12.6 Summary

Integration between program management and systems engineering has not been a specific area of focus for most organizations, but its impact on program performance suggests that it should be. Indeed, it should be systematically defined, measured, and improved as part of the practice of program management. Programs can benefit in many ways from greater integration, including schedule and budget compliance, and meeting client satisfaction and requirements.

One of the first steps in managing integration between these two disciplines is to define a set of variables and a systematic approach to assess their integration within the program. The elements associated with each integration factor discussed in Section 12.3.2 is a good starting point. Contextual variables that are specific to each type of program and industry sector will help to tailor the measurement approach to its specific application. Under a variety of conditions integration may manifest itself differently. This will shape the specific management practices and techniques to be monitored for integration behaviors. The following points may help organizations to be purposeful in improving integration that leads to better program performance:

- **Understand integration.** The first step to measuring integration between program management and systems engineering properly is to develop a clear understanding of the meaning of integration for the team and the organization. The general definition of integration in Chapter 6, along with the three key elements shown in Figure 12-3, is an initial reference point.
- **Develop an approach to assess and improve integration.** Measuring integration between program management and systems engineering can be a complicated task due to its various elements. Defining formal processes, tools, techniques, and metrics is important if this is to be part of a deliberate change program to improve integration. The integration improvement initiative should be linked with the overall program benefits achievement approach to demonstrate both quantitative and qualitative evidence of the value of greater integration for programs and business results.
- **Integration may have different levels of intensity and may impact programs in a wide range of ways.** Consider other dimensions and variables as drivers of integration between program management and systems engineering in a particular context, including program type, industry sector, and organizational environment and culture, as part of tailoring the approach to assessing and improving integration.
- **Treat integration as a competence.** Integration between program management and systems engineering involves attitudes and skills supported by a carefully designed set of tools, management practices, and organizational factors.

This broad perspective should be considered to develop successively higher levels of integration of these two disciplines in programs.

- **Integration requires strong leadership from both a management and a technical perspective.** Particularly within complex programs, program managers benefit significantly from having some technical background or experience. Chief systems engineers and program managers should recognize and appreciate their respective individual responsibilities and pressures, and consider the implications that their management and technical decisions will have on the overall program objectives and results.

12.7 Discussion Questions

1. What steps would you take to improve the awareness of the importance of integration between program management and systems engineering to program performance in your organization?
2. How has integration impacted performance in your organization (based on a program on which you have worked in the past)? In which specific areas of program performance was it relevant for the program manager or the chief systems engineer?
3. Which of the integration elements discussed in Section 12.3.2 and Figure 12-3 were demonstrated in a program on which you worked in the past? Which of these variables had the greatest impact on program performance?
4. Based on the elements of integration (Section 12.3.2, Figure 12-3), can you identify additional variables that might be relevant to measure these elements in your organization or program context?
5. In the Anzac case study, can you identify or infer the presence of additional variables from the integration dimension that were not discussed in more detail?

12.8 References

Becerril, L., Rebentisch, E., Chucholowski, N., Conforto, E. C., & Lindemann, U. (2016, May 16–19). A simulation-based analysis on the integration of program management and systems engineering. *Proceedings of the International Design Conference*, Dubrovnik, Croatia.

Bellman, R. E., & Zadeh, L. A. (1970). Decision-making in a fuzzy environment. *Management Science, 17*(4), B-141–B164. doi:10.1287/mnsc.17.4.B141

Browning, T. R., Fricke, E., & Negele, H. (2006). Key concepts in modeling product development processes. *Systems Engineering, 9*(2), 104–128. doi:10.1002/sys.20047

Conforto, E., Rebentisch, E., & Rossi, M. (2013, October 27–29). *Case study report: Improving integration of program management and systems engineering.* Presented at PMI Global Congress North America, New Orleans, Louisiana.

Conforto, E. C., Rossi, M., Rebentisch, E., Oehmen, J., & Pacenza, M. (2013). *Survey report: Improving integration of program management and systems engineering.* Presented at the 23rd INCOSE Annual International Symposium, Philadelphia. Retrieved from http://www.pmi.org/~/media/PDF/Business-Solutions/Lean-Enablers/PMI-INCOSE-MIT-Integration-Study.ashx

Ford, D. N. (2009). *System dynamics for large complex projects*, Cambridge, MA: Massachusetts Institute of Technology.

Forrester, J. W. (1961). *Industrial dynamics*. Cambridge, MA: MIT Press.

International Council on Systems Engineering (INCOSE). (2015). *Systems engineering handbook: A guide for system life cycle processes and activities* (4th ed.). D. Walden, G. Roedler, K. Forsberg, R. Hamelin, T. Shortell (Eds.). Hoboken, NJ: John Wiley & Sons.

Oehmen, J., Rebentisch, E., & Kinscher, K. (2011, December). *Program management for large scale engineering programs*. LAI Whitepaper Series "Lean Product Development for Practitioners." MIT, Cambridge, MA. Retrieved from http://18.7.29.232/handle/1721.1/79839

Project Management Institute (PMI). (2013a). *The standard for program management* (3rd ed.). Newtown Square, PA: Author.

Project Management Institute (PMI). (2013b). *A guide to the project management body of knowledge (PMBOK® guide)* (5th ed.). Newtown Square, PA: Author.

Rebentisch, E., & Conforto, E. C. (2014, May). *Integration means results: Why systems engineering and program management must align*. PMI Global Congress, EMEA, Dubai, UAE.

Reiner, T. (2015, May). *Determination of factors to measure the effective integration between program management and systems engineering*, Rheinisch-Westfälische Technische Hochschule (RWTH) Aachen Master's thesis.

Rhodes, D. H., Valerdi, R., & Roedler, G. J. (2009). Systems engineering leading indicators for assessing program and technical effectiveness. *Systems Engineering, 12*(1), 21–35. doi:10.1002/sys.20105

Roedler, G., Rhodes, D. H., Schimmoller, H., & Jones, C. (Eds.). (2007). *Systems engineering leading indicators guide* (INCOSE-TP-2005-001-03). Version 2. Cambridge, MA: Massachusetts Institute of Technology. Retrieved from www.psmsc.com/downloads/other/seli-guide-rev2-01292010-industry.pdf

Sage, A. P., & Rouse, W. B. (2009). *Handbook of systems engineering and management*. Hoboken, NJ: John Wiley & Sons.

Sterman, J. D. (1992). *System dynamics modeling for project management*. Cambridge, MA: Massachusetts Institute of Technology.

Sterman, J. D. (2000). *Business dynamics: Systems thinking and modeling for a complex world*. Boston, MA: Irwin/McGraw-Hill.

Endnote

1. Contributed by Elizabeth "Betsy" Clark, SCRAM Principal, President, Software Metrics, Inc.; Adrian Pitman, SCRAM Principal, Director Acquisition Engineering Improvement Capability Acquisition and Sustainment Group, Department of Defence, Australian; and Angela Tuffley, Director, RedBay Consulting Pty Ltd., Adjunct Senior Lecturer, Griffith University, Australia.

Part III

DEVELOPING INTEGRATION COMPETENCIES IN YOUR ORGANIZATION

Having demonstrated the benefits of integrating the program management and systems engineering disciplines in a program, the challenge for many organizations will be what to do next. Part III focuses on this challenge with an exploration of how to bring about effective change in complex organizations. The focus is specifically on the integration of program management and systems engineering disciplines, but the principles of change discussed in this part can be generalized to other areas.

Chapter 13 begins with an overview of what is required to produce sustained change in complex organizations. These organizations will require a systematic, concerted, and deliberate effort to adopt and master these principles of integration. The principles presented here will help organizations to better understand the scope of activities and level of effort involved in developing their integration competencies.

Chapter 14 illustrates these principles of change with case study examples from organizations that have demonstrated performance improvement through the integration of their technical and management disciplines. Their examples illustrate the elements and workings of a deliberate approach to and system of change in real and often complex organizational settings.

Chapter 15 concludes this part by offering practical advice to those who wish to establish a change program to improve the integration of program management and systems engineering in their organization. This includes how to kick off the initiative, the principal roles, and how to sustain and maintain the new state developed through the change efforts.

13

INTEGRATION MEANS CHANGE

13.1 Introduction: The Case for Change

Chapter 12 illustrated how effective integration between program management and systems engineering disciplines produces value for the organization, not only in traditional measures of program performance like requirements fulfilment and client satisfaction, but additional tangible benefits that include a more reliable performance with fewer deadline overruns. These changes foster long-term competitive agility and advantage. When an organization is able to achieve effective program management and systems engineering integration, the benefits are concrete. Integration of disciplines and functions within an organization where it has not previously existed is, however, a transformative change for the organization.

In a dynamic global economy, organizations that are resistant to change often lose ground to those that embrace it. As Jack Welch is reported to have said, "If the rate of change on the outside exceeds the rate of change on the inside, the end is near" (Allison, 2014). If your competitors are transforming at a rate that is greater than yours and are reaping the resulting performance benefits, then adopting new ways of managing work becomes an organizational imperative.

An organization, and particularly an organization that employs systems engineers, program managers, project managers, and sophisticated technical experts, is a complex, interdependent network of resources, processes, and technologies that create value for the organization and its beneficiaries (clients, customer, receivers) through the work they produce. A change program must, therefore, take into account the multiple dimensions of the organization, including stakeholder needs and values, the organizational structure and culture, and the interconnectivity of functions within. Organizational transformation modifies an organization while it is in action and moves it from its current state to an envisioned future—a process that requires a significant change in approach, mindset, the adoption of a holistic view of how the program will work, and a comprehensive plan for execution.

Integration will require change and change is difficult. Most organizations will require concerted and deliberate effort to effectively implement and manage the change to realize benefits. As Roth and DiBella (2015) point out, "Unfortunately,

Support from the top	If behaviors within the organization are to change, accountability needs to begin with the executive sponsor and executive leadership. Establishing a crystal-clear change agenda sets the foundation for a successful project. Executive leaders also need to support continuing improvement efforts aimed at ensuring that the desired changes become deeply embedded in the culture and actions of staff.
Utilize change-sustaining approaches	At the close of a project and throughout the life cycle of a program, efforts to sustain important changes should be built into transition plans and/or the next phase of the life cycle.
Shift paradigms when needed	Shifting mindsets from how business is done now to how it will be done in the future may take minutes or decades. Thus, organizations may need to plan for continuous efforts to communicate the benefits of change to help individuals continue to adjust to a new reality.
Talk and communicate	Change sustainment requires ongoing dialogue and communication so that individuals understand why certain actions, processes, and behaviors are expected of them.
Assimilate and integrate	Utilize change agents for change sustainment.
Invest in planning for sustained results	Through practice and iterations of change, the investment in change will be realized as true project ROI is attained. As additional capacities become available and the organization becomes accustomed to adapting to change, that experience yields a well of resources that can be converted into sustaining prior gains, investment in innovation, and new capacities, product and service lines. This leads to competitive market advantage, building further capacity for additional iterations of change and innovation.
Negotiate results with a portfolio approach	Assess readiness for change before implementing strategies and then adapt to new conditions as warranted.

Figure 13-1: The model for sustainable change

Model for Sustainable Change, Project Management Institute, Inc., 2015. Copyright and all rights reserved. Material from this publication has been reproduced with the permission of PMI.

discrete change efforts fail because they do not take into consideration the broad set of factors that affect organizations in today's dynamic, interconnected world." Transformational change, such as the integration of program management and systems engineering, is not trivial—it requires real work.

Further, sustaining change over time requires ongoing effort to reinforce and support the new way of working together. Harrington, Voehl, and Voehl (2015) proposed a model for taking an intentional approach to change that has sustainment of the change in view from the outset. This model, shown in Figure 13-1, uses the acronym SUSTAIN to draw attention to the central elements that must be included in the preparation and execution of change. As Harrington et al. (2015) point out, the model "is not intended to represent a series of actions, or a step-wise approach. Rather, the intent is that all elements of the model receive ongoing attention and, in fact, the elements are highly interrelated" (p. 5).

13.2 The Need to Be Thoughtful about Change

Why are some organizations more effective at change than others? Why do some achieve or exceed their strategic goals, while others who may be working just as hard or harder consistently flounder, missing deadlines, and exceeding cost targets? Many organizations have extensive change initiatives but often fail to achieve their objectives or are unable to sustain the change. Research has found that a holistic systems approach is required to achieve lasting, effective change (Nightingale & Srinivasan, 2011).

Many organizations can be thought of as complex systems. They exist in a highly dynamic environment, have to satisfy the needs of a diverse set of stakeholders, and are often large and geographically distributed. Such organizations are often termed enterprises.

An enterprise is a complex, integrated, interdependent system of people, processes, and technologies that creates value as determined by its key stakeholders (customers, suppliers, employees, etc.). A change program must, therefore, take into account the multiple dimensions of the enterprise, including its various stakeholder needs and values, the culture of the organization, and the interconnectivities of different functions of the enterprise such as design, manufacturing, and the supply base.

Implementing change in a complex system requires *systems thinking*—a fundamental concept for systems engineers. Systems thinking involves understanding that a system exists within a wider context or environment, and that a system is made up of parts that interact with each other and the wider context. Systems thinkers consider an issue fully, resist the urge to come to a quick conclusion, and consider both short- and long-term consequences (INCOSE, 2015).

Many who seek to implement change in an organization rush into implementation before first laying the groundwork for success. The upfront effort to consider how the organization will respond to the change and how best to nurture the change has significant payoffs.

Organizations are often driven by schedule and cost constraints and a "fire-fighting" mentality that results in the launch of initiatives without first completing the necessary upfront planning and considering the follow-through that will be needed to sustain the change long term. Successful and sustained change in complex organizations requires a system of change that works hand-in-glove with the organization's objectives, business systems, leadership, culture, and daily operations.

13.2.1 Stumbling Blocks to Change

Unfortunately, many enterprise transformation efforts are not successful. Combe (2014a) notes, "Change is difficult, individually and organizationally. Individually, humans seek stability, and research has shown that even when they accept and internalize the value of change, they frequently fail to change" (p. 8). The reason for failure often can be traced to some form of resistance to the change. Resistance to change is typically thought of in terms of individuals not supporting the change—either passively or actively. While individuals are one source, resistance can be defined as anything—people or systems—that pushes against the change. Force-field analysis, the central concept in Lewin's (1947) early work on change, is a better way of thinking about change resistance. In force-field analysis, forces pushing for the change and forces pushing against the change are identified and analyzed. When the forces pushing for the change exceed the forces pushing against the change, then, and only then, will change happen in any sustainable way. Therefore, it is useful to be aware of common sources of resistance so that their force is minimized or eliminated.

Table 13-1: Types of enterprise transformation failures	
Failure Types	**Results From...**
Only in my backyard	Undertaking only local projects, with no consideration for their impact across the enterprise
Activity	Feeling the need to "do something" and measuring/valuing activity rather than progress
Low-hanging fruit	Focusing efforts on whatever is the easiest problem to address
Pet project	Working on whatever a leader or leaders want, whether it is the right thing or addresses root issues
New leadership	Heading down the path set by a new leader with no regard for where the organization is/has been going
Leaders who don't lead	Delegating all transformation work to underlings, with leaders taking no part in the efforts
Hire transformers	Bringing in outsiders to develop and implement transformation, who leave behind no plan
Flavor-of-the-month	Undertaking transformation efforts that shift from one methodology to another, again and again

Nightingale & Srinivasan, 2011, p. 30. Reproduced with permission of American Management Association via Copyright Clearance Center.

Nightingale and Srinivasan (2011) identified eight common failures of transformational change exhibited in Table 13-1. One key element common to all of these failures is the absence of taking a systems approach to change, which results in some form of resistance. Taking a closer look at a few examples from the list illustrates how these types of failures might emerge as a source of failure in integration efforts.

The first failure type listed, "only in my backyard," refers to when one part of the organization makes changes to improve its operation without giving due consideration to the rest of the enterprise. This can refer to a situation where the integration between systems engineering and program management is initiated without consideration for other disciplines that will be affected such as finance or supply chain. Of course, changes in an engineering design can have major implications on the manufacturability or cost of the product. In the case of a major U.S. defense manufacturer:

> [T]he engineering function had decided to downsize significantly the number of its engineers working with the process engineers in manufacturing. Why? The engineering leaders saw no value-added from an engineering perspective. Only after the decision had been translated into action did anyone recognize the critical downstream implications in terms of delays in production and associated cost overruns (Nightingale & Srinivasan, 2011, pp. 30–31).

This is illustrative of a lack of systems thinking that can lead to failure in implementing changes intended to improve program performance.

The "low-hanging fruit" failure type represents those change efforts that focus only on the "easy" problems, and not necessarily the ones that will have the biggest strategic impact. For example, it may be easier to integrate the program management and systems engineering disciplines in certain small programs that are isolated from the rest of the enterprise. However, the impact and performance benefits may likewise be small and isolated. This does not mean that grassroots efforts should be discouraged. Action-oriented approaches that capture local knowledge and energy to make change happen can be leveraged in demonstrating the potential for success, establishing strategic urgency for change, and bringing stakeholders on board to implement enterprise transformation. Eventually, however, efforts to change the organization will have to become widespread, particularly in the primary programs and business lines, if they are to have a systemic and sustained impact on performance. The change must become part of the organization's "DNA."

The "new leadership" failure type often results from a lack of continuity of prior efforts and strategic plans. This failure type is commonly cited in military organizations where leaders are on short rotation schedules. New leaders may want to "make their mark" on the organization and initiate sweeping changes. Rather than build on the efforts of the previous leader, the new leader may take the organization in a new direction without due consideration for the stakeholders vested in the prior strategic plan for the organization. For example, a company selling mice for medical research was undergoing a transformation from a product-based organization to a services-based organization that offered animal housing services and provided mice with specific traits to pharmaceutical customers to help accelerate their time to market of new drugs. However, this company was sold to another organization that did not support the strategy shift to services. This stalled the transformation of the company for about a decade until the company's management was able to retake the reins and complete the transformation, after which services dominated the company's offerings and the mouse product line declined to only a quarter of the company's revenues. (Srivastava, 2012, pp. 11–13). Frequently changing initiatives without a strong tie to overarching strategy leads to change fatigue for all involved.

Ogburn (1957) captured the danger of implementing change activity for the sake of doing something in his reflection on experiences in the armed forces during World War II. He observed:

> We trained hard, but it seemed that every time we were beginning to form up into teams we would be reorganized. Presumably the plans for our employment were being changed. I was to learn later in life that, perhaps because we are so good at organizing, we tend as a nation to meet any new situation by reorganizing; and a wonderful method it can be for creating the illusion of progress while producing confusion, inefficiency, and demoralization (pp. 32–33).

Two cautions are captured in this observation. First, constant change does not support long-term, sustainable change. Second, simply changing the organizational structure fails to evaluate the organization from a systems perspective; often the root cause of an issue is in a different part of the organization from where the consequences are seen. Using a framework for change planning can help to ensure the issues have been considered fully and a comprehensive plan for change developed.

13.3 Frameworks and Models for Change

There are many approaches to and frameworks for managing change. One well-known approach is Kotter's (1996) eight-step process for leading change. However, change in complex organizations often requires more than the rote following of a model. A more systematic approach, along with the requisite capabilities, is required due to the system interdependencies (Roth & DiBella, 2015). This section is not prescriptive of a particular change management model; instead, this section introduces two change frameworks and highlights common elements useful for thinking through and planning for organizational change.

The first is the Change Life Cycle Framework (PMI, 2013a), shown in Figure 13-2. The second is the Enterprise Transformation Roadmap (LAI, 2012) shown in Figure 13-3. The two example change frameworks provide leadership with a decision aid for consideration of cultural, organizational, and change management considerations in the strategic analysis and transformation of the enterprise. The development of frameworks like these is motivated by the fact that most transformation efforts fail in that they are often not sustainable or do not achieve the desired strategic objectives. The frameworks serve as a guide for enterprise leaders as they consider strategic, cultural, and operational changes.

Both frameworks can be grouped into three phases, with each taking a slightly different but complementary focus, as shown in Table 13-2.

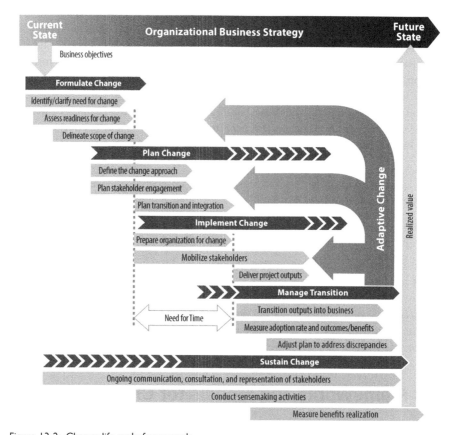

Figure 13-2: Change life cycle framework

Managing Change in Organizations: A Practice Guide, Project Management Institute, Inc., 2013. Copyright and all rights reserved. Material from this publication has been reproduced with the permission of PMI.

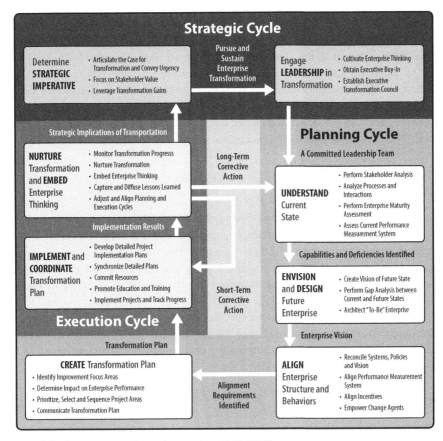

Figure 13-3: Enterprise transformation roadmap (LAI, 2012)

LAI enterprise self-assessment tool (LESAT) version 2.0: Facilitator's guide. Massachusetts Institute of Technology, 2012. Copyright and all rights reserved. Material from this publication has been reproduced with the permission of MIT.

Table 13-2: Three phases of the transformational change frameworks and the primary focus of each

	Change Life Cycle Framework	Enterprise Transformation Roadmap	Primary Objective
Strategic Phase	Formulate Change	Determine Strategic Imperative Engage Leadership in Transformation	The business case for transformation is made along with the engagement of stakeholders
Planning Phase	Plan Change	Understand Current State Envision and Design Future Enterprise Align Enterprise Structure and Behaviors Create Transformation Plan	Analyze and define the current and future state, along with a transformation plan to achieve the future vision
Execution Phase	Implement Change Manage Transition Sustain Change	Implement and Coordinate Transformation Plan Nurture Transformation and Embed Enterprise Thinking	Put the plan into practice and monitor results

Based on PMI, 2013a; LAI, 2012.

13.3.1 Strategic Phase

The change process begins with the establishment of the driving business reason for change. This is shown in the "Identify/clarify need for change" arrow in Figure 13-2, and "Articulate the case for transformation and convey urgency" box in Figure 13-3. This first strategic step can help leaders avoid many of the transformation failure modes described above; therefore, the Strategic Phase begins with identifying the strategic imperative for change and, at a high level, stating the strategic objective of the change. This is about developing the high-level business case and answering the questions:

- Why do we need to do this?
- What is the business value we are trying to achieve?
- What if we do not integrate?

Leadership is engaged by further developing the business case in business terms, not program management or systems engineering terms. A lack of executive support leads to minimal value realization. Executive buy-in is not just about obtaining resources for the work, but it is the enabling activity that will effect cultural and process change. There must be unified support at the executive level with an active sponsor as a link between the leadership and the work undertaken.

The Change Life Cycle Framework specifically calls out conducting an assessment of the organization's readiness for change. This is an important step, discussed in more detail later in this chapter, in that attempting change that impacts or is impacted by organizational culture can quickly derail the change process and lead to failure.

13.3.2 Planning Phase

Both frameworks emphasize the need to understand the current state, envision the future state, and plan the approach/roadmap to change. The planning phase is entered with a committed leadership team cultivated during the strategic phase. The planning phase begins with a grounded understanding of the current state. Lack of understanding regarding the pretransformation situation can cause conflict with existing processes and result in overlooking interdependencies.

Defining the future state is about developing a clear picture of where the enterprise will end up. It is not about figuring out the details of how to get there, but the blueprint for what the results will look like. The "to-be" is compared with the "as-is" to identify where changes are needed. This leads to or informs the sequence of integration activities such that the impact on current productivity is minimized. Engaging key stakeholders early helps to ensure everyone is working toward the same objective, and helps with investment and mindshare in the final outcome—leading to organizational success. Identifying stakeholders emerges from the stakeholder mapping process as discussed in the sidebar Stakeholder Identification and Analysis.

Now that the future enterprise is defined, there is a need to define the new structures and behaviors necessary to implement. The design undergoes further elaboration and is tested for acceptance and adoption as the integration moves forward.

The planning process creates a transformational program plan. This plan must have elements related to each of the inputs in the Integration Framework: processes, practices, and tools; organizational environment people competencies; and contextual factors. In addition, a benefits roadmap would be one of the outputs of this activity as part of the complete integration transformation program plan.

13.3.3 Execution Phase

With the integration transformation plan defined, execution can begin. It starts with implementing and coordinating the transformation change plan for integration. Program plans by nature should be agile. The plan serves as a baseline for activities, but ultimately it should be responsive to adjustments along the way. Again, using a benefits roadmap allows for testing at the defined milestones to determine if desired progress is being made and whether or not adjustments (process or time) are needed to ensure ultimate success.

A good program plan includes setting up plans for fully imbedding the change in the organization. This means defining anticipated transitioning activity along with metrics to measure success and assigning accountability for results over the long term. This is a central component of programs that results in sustainment of benefits over the longer term (Thiry, 2015).

Both frameworks for change emphasize the cyclical nature of change. The Enterprise Transformation Roadmap shows that each step is part of a cycle. Additionally, the arrows in the middle of the circle show short- and long-term corrective actions. This reflects the importance of consistently evaluating that the enterprise is achieving its goal and being adaptive about the change process. The Change Life Cycle Framework also indicates that change is iterative through the use of the "Adaptive Change" arrows. The constant evaluation that the change is attaining the desired benefits, or "realized value," is shown in arrows at the bottom of Figure 13-2. An enterprise-wide transformation can take years. Therefore, these short-term corrective actions or adaptive techniques are important to ensure the transformation continues to be aligned with the enterprise's changing ecosystem and climate (Combe, 2014a).

Stakeholder Identification and Analysis

The measurement of organizational success in the past was limited to the satisfaction and creation of wealth for the shareholder, termed "shareholder value analysis." Over time, "the process of identifying stakeholders has grown more complicated as enterprises recognized the need to consider stakeholders beyond just the shareholder" (Srivastava, 2014). One of the first and most cited authors in the field of "stakeholder analysis" is Edward Freeman (1984), who defined his research in terms of firms who "affect or are affected by the achievement of the organization's objectives" and who "benefit from or are harmed by and whose rights are violated or respected by, corporate actions."

One must identify the stakeholders before beginning to engage them in the formulation and rollout of the change. It is often tempting to conduct the stakeholder analysis using the organizational structure map. The organization structure, however, does not represent the political and relational aspects of organizational interaction. A better approach is to construct a stakeholder map beginning with the

(*continued*)

recipients of value from the enterprise, and then depict the relationships influencing and affecting the recipient. As Miller and Oliver (2015) noted, "This approach . . . shifts thinking away from understanding the formal, hierarchical organizational structures in which a program or project is taking place to understanding the informal, political flows of an organization where change really takes place (e.g., change network relationships)" (p. 6).

It is easy to miss an individual stakeholder or group of stakeholders when developing the list of stakeholders. Feng, Crawley, de Weck, Lessard, and Cameron (2012) described the importance of identifying all stakeholders and noted that "missing a key stakeholder could jeopardize the chance for the focal organization to successfully achieve its objectives in the long run." However, engaging all of the stakeholders may become unrealistic as the number of stakeholders increases. Therefore, one may need to determine a method of grouping stakeholders by type, influence, or some other identifiable characteristic. But care must be taken not to group arbitrarily or too quickly and thus risk missing a key influencer. All stakeholders exert some level of influence, but clearly some are more influential or powerful than others.

Clarkson (1995) realized that different stakeholders' needs should be weighted in some respect to the influence they wield; all stakeholders matter but not all stakeholders are equal. A method of categorizing stakeholders based on their power, legitimacy, and urgency called "stakeholder salience" was developed by Mitchell, Agle, and Wood (1997). Murman et al. (2002) built upon the concept of stakeholder value in the development of the Value Creation Framework. A closed loop process is part of this framework, which includes identification, proposition, and delivery. Recent stakeholder analysis literature speaks to the increasing complexity of identifying enterprise stakeholders and prioritizing their needs and value delivery; indirect relationships and interactions among stakeholders on a network-level are now being viewed as necessary to incorporate in stakeholder analysis (Feng et al., 2012).

The stakeholder map that results from the stakeholder identification becomes the basis for further stakeholder analysis where the needs and type of communication and interaction are detailed. One should be careful to not confine the stakeholder analysis to only internal stakeholders, but identify and characterize stakeholders external to the enterprise as well. External stakeholders often exert as much, and possibly more, influence on the systems engineering and program management integration effort than many internal stakeholders. A good stakeholder map will include all key stakeholders, taking a systems thinking approach to the entire sphere of influence and power. If the list of stakeholders becomes unwieldy, stakeholders can be prioritized by consideration of stakeholder saliency. This involves consideration of a stakeholder's power, legitimacy, and urgency with respect to the enterprise (Srivastava, 2012).

A widely used paradigm for process change is the plan-do-check-act approach, also known as the Shewhart Cycle (INCOSE, 2015, p. 138). The *PMBOK® Guide* (PMI, 2013b) notes that the plan-do-check-act approach is useful as the basis for continuous improvement as part of the quality management Knowledge Area of projects. As the two frameworks indicate, the basic concept is that one plans the change, measures outcomes along the way, and then adjusts plans and activities in response to progress made against the plan.

Whether one uses one of these or selects another framework or model, the important thing to keep in mind is that the framework and model should be tailored to the type of change and the organizational culture and context within which that change is planned. In no case should a framework or model be used without adaptation to the unique characteristics of the change in view and the cultural environment of the organization. Leaders of the change effort may find the information in the Sidebar, Characteristics of a Change Agent, useful.

Characteristics of a Change Agent

An engaged change agent is a key contributor to successful change. Research conducted by McKinney, Arnold, and Sheard (2015) identified numerous characteristics of an effective change agent. They summarize their findings in three dimensions:

- Philosophy: The attitude of a change agent such as persistence and handling of challenges
- Knowledge: The facts and insights about how the organization works, which is constantly changing
- Skills: The ability to translate knowledge into action

One of the key skills is systems thinking. For example, knowledge of an effective change agent includes:

- What stakeholders care about (so you can connect with their passions)
- Who the key stakeholders are
- Effect of recent and current changes on the efforts
- The political, economic, and social context in which an organizational change effort takes place
- Understanding current operations and systems
- Insight into what effects and consequences the different alternatives may have

McKinney, Arnold, and Sheard (2015) provide tips for success in facilitating change, broken down by the origination of the change (i.e., bottom-up, top-down, or middle-out). This work also discusses indications of when to push for change, taking into account enterprise maturity for transformation.

13.4 Readiness Assessment

As discussed briefly above and highlighted in Figure 13-4, assessing an enterprise's readiness for change is an important part of the strategy phase in a transformational change effort. Certain characteristics of an organization can indicate a priori the chances of success of a transformation. Understanding the current state of an enterprise before a change includes not only the status of the program management and systems engineering organizations, but also elements that indicate the enterprise's willingness to change to support integrated program management and systems engineering disciplines. An assessment can help in identifying enterprise strengths and weaknesses, and guide the transformation. "By gaining insights on current performance, past trends, and desired future performance, decision-makers will be better equipped to design a transformation plan that meets the needs of the organization and will offer the most long-term benefits" (LAI, 2012, p. 12). It is important to understand that what is being assessed is cultural readiness, commitment readiness of key stakeholders and resources, and the capability of the organization to be able to expend resources to implement and sustain the change (Combe, 2014b). This is critical to predicting the potential realizable value from implementing the change.

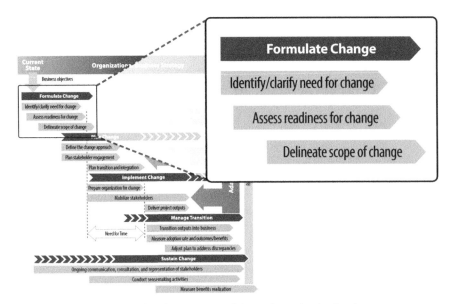

Figure 13-4: Assess readiness for change as part of the up-front planning for change
PMI, 2013a.

As with the change frameworks, this chapter does not prescribe an assessment tool, but does reference industry tools to illustrate the key concepts. For example, the Baldridge Performance Excellence Program presents awards each year that recognize organizations that have demonstrated performance excellence. The assessment criteria for this award may be useful in enterprise assessment, and these criteria cover categories from leadership to process management. Another informative tool for developing a readiness assessment is the Capability Maturity Model Integration (CMMI). The maturity model assesses for four different areas of focus: development, services, acquisition, and people. Although initially created for software development processes, the assessment has also been applied to systems engineering processes and organization business processes. Another assessment framework is the LAI Enterprise Self-Assessment Tool (LESAT) (LAI, 2012). The first version, LESAT 1.0, was developed by MIT's Lean Advancement Initiative in joint collaboration with INCOSE, industry, government, and the United Kingdom Lean Aerospace Initiative. LESAT 2.0 focuses on the capabilities of an enterprise to transform into a high performing enterprise and sustain the transformation. All of these tools provide a framework to assess the current state of the organization against a standard in order to identify areas for improvement, but it is equally important to assess how ready the organization is for change.

As Combe (2014b) points out regarding an organization's readiness to change, "Change readiness takes into account a compilation of multiple viewpoints to assess not only whether various audiences feel confident in making the change, but also to establish root causes of discomfort" (p. 6). Regardless of the assessment method or tool, assessing the enterprise's readiness for change is an important step in achieving success. Combe (2014b) recommends keeping in mind that "Change readiness takes a critical look at the organization's resolve, fit and capacity to successfully deliver the benefits of a proposed program or project, and initiates appropriate actions to bring a current state of readiness to one of confidence in long-term success of the program/project outcomes" (p. 6). And long-term value is the intent behind the integration of systems engineering and program management.

13.5 The Road Ahead and How to Prepare for It

In order to effect transformational change, top leadership within the organization must be fully "on board" to support and champion the effort as noted in the Harrington et al. (2015) SUSTAIN model and Kotter's (1996) change model. This is an important aspect of any change program. Employees and other leaders within the organization will be quick to detect a lack of senior leadership support or engagement, and will respond with their own, mirrored lack of engagement, and in some cases active resistance. Without committed and sustained leadership support, the likely result is that the organization will ultimately revert to the old way of doing things. With senior leadership committed to and personally engaged in achieving the benefits the change will bring about, others within the organization will be inspired to do what it takes to see the change through so that it succeeds and continues to produce value for the organization well into the future.

13.6 Summary

Research indicates that companies that adopt formal approaches to integrating program management and systems engineering roles are likely to achieve more complete integration of those disciplines (Conforto, Rossi, Rebentisch, Oehmen, & Pacenza, 2013). Transformation of an integrated enterprise is critical for maintaining competitiveness in a dynamic economy. Integration, however, requires change. For the change to be successful, a systems approach to implementing change is required. But change programs are notorious for failing to achieve their objectives. Being alert to common sources of change failure can help to avoid these common pitfalls.

Transformational change also requires a holistic approach that effectively integrates the specification and analysis of the current state, the articulation of a future state, and the actual execution of the transformation to achieve the specified future-state vision. This is not achievable without a leadership team that remains committed and engaged to the change effort, understands the need to implement a system of performance metrics, ensures a flow of information across the enterprise including suppliers and customers, and sponsors a system of organizational learning that promotes sharing and collaboration across the program managers and systems engineers. Successful change is incumbent upon understanding and incorporating stakeholder value propositions, both what they want and what they contribute to the enterprise. Enabling a successful transformation requires focus on doing the right thing before doing it right. Lastly it includes understanding both internal and external interdependencies.

The vignettes presented in the next chapter illustrate the scale and scope of such significant change initiatives. They present transformational change programs performed in some of the largest and most successful organizations in the world. In these examples, the importance of careful planning and the sustained engagement of senior leaders cannot be overstated. Additionally, the reader will no doubt notice that each of these initiatives describe efforts that span months and in some cases years, and impact nearly every aspect of the organization. Most importantly, these efforts are not merely activities that "tinker" at the fringes of the organization. Rather, the changes described illuminate strategic efforts designed to permanently alter the way the entire organization operates and performs. This point should not be taken lightly. Whether the change initiative is planned for a large, complex multinational enterprise, a small business, a nonprofit, or a public initiative, the integration program will have an impact up, down, and across the organization—and to deliver and sustain the targeted benefits and improvements, will modify the way the organization performs its work now and in the future.

IBM (2008) reported findings from its survey of CEOs regarding strategy implementation. The top challenges to success included:

- Changing mindsets and attitudes (58%)
- Corporate culture (49%)
- Underestimation of complexity (33%)

This fact may give pause to all who are considering performing such a task. To help soften this challenge and give guidance to leaders about to embark on transformational journeys for their organizations, Chapter 15 provides guidance designed to lay the groundwork for the mission ahead.

13.7 Discussion Questions

1. What are examples of transformation initiatives or changes that your enterprise has already experienced? Were these successful? Why or why not?
2. Why is taking a systems approach to transformation more likely to succeed?
3. Describe a program in which you were involved and how you went about identifying key stakeholders and gaining their commitment to change. What lessons did you learn in the process?
4. What techniques have you found useful for mapping internal and external interdependencies?
5. Can you identify effective change agents in your program management organization? What about in your systems engineering organization?
6. Identify a change transformation case in your program and reflect on who resisted and why they resisted. In your view, did the program manager or chief systems engineer attempt to function as a change agent?

13.8 References

Allison, S. (2014, February 10). The responsive organization: Coping with new technology and disruption. *Forbes*. Retrieved from www.forbes.com/sites/scottallison/2014/02/10/the-responsive-organization-how-to-cope-with-technology-and-disruption/

Clarkson, M. (1995). A stakeholder framework for analyzing and evaluating corporate social performance. *Academy of Management Review, 20*(1), 92–117. doi:10.5465/AMR.1995.9503271994

Combe, M. (2014a). *Change agility: Readiness for strategy implementation.* Retrieved from www.pmi.org/~/media/PDF/learning/change-agility-readiness-for-strategy-implementation.ashx

Combe, M. (2014b). *Change readiness: Focusing change management where it counts.* Retrieved from www.pmi.org/learning/~/media/PDF/Knowledge%20Center/Focusing-Change-Management-Where-it-Counts.ashx

Conforto, E. C., Rossi, M., Rebentisch, E., Oehmen, J., & Pacenza, M. (2013). *Survey report: Improving integration of program management and systems engineering.* Presented at the 23rd INCOSE Annual International Symposium, Philadelphia, USA. Retrieved from www.pmi.org/~/media/PDF/Business-Solutions/Lean-Enablers/PMI-INCOSE-MIT-Integration-Study.ashx

Feng, W., Crawley, E. F., de Weck, O. L., Lessard, D. R., & Cameron, B. G. (2012, October). *Understanding the impacts of indirect stakeholder relationships: Stakeholder value network analysis and its application to large engineering projects.* In Strategic Management Society SMS Annual Conference.

Freeman, R. E. (1984). *Strategic management: A stakeholder approach.* Boston, MA: Pitman.

Harrington, H. J., Voehl, F., & Voehl, C. F. (2015). *Model for sustainable change.* Retrieved from www.pmi.org/~/media/PDF/learning/Model_for_Sustainable_Change.ashx

IBM. (2008). *Making change work: Continuing the enterprise of the future conversation.* Armonk, NY: IBM Corporation. Retrieved from www-935.ibm.com/services/us/gbs/bus/pdf/gbe03100-usen-03- making-change-work.pdf

International Council on Systems Engineering (INCOSE). (2015). *Systems engineering handbook: A guide for system life cycle processes and activities* (4th ed.). D. Walden, G. Roedler, K. Forsberg, R. Hamelin, T. Shortell (Eds.). Hoboken, NJ: John Wiley & Sons.

Kotter, J. (1996). *Leading change.* Cambridge, MA: Harvard Business School Press.

Lean Advancement Initiative (LAI). (2012). *LAI enterprise self-assessment tool (LESAT) version 2.0: Facilitator's guide.* Retrieved from https://dspace.mit.edu/bitstream/handle/1721.1/84694/PRD_LESAT_2_Facilitators_Guide_Feb2012.pdf?sequence=1

Lewin, K. (1947). *Frontiers in group dynamics: Concept, method and reality in social science; social equilibria and social change.* Retrieved from http://hum.sagepub.com/content/1/1/5

McKinney, D., Arnold, E., & Sheard, S. (2015). Change agency for systems engineers. *INCOSE International Symposium. 25*(1), 1209–1231. doi:10.1002/j.2334-5837.2015.00125.x

Miller, D., & Oliver, M. (2015). *Engaging stakeholders for project success.* Retrieved from www.pmi.org/~/media/PDF/learning/engaging-stakeholders-project-success.ashx

Mitchell, R. K., Agle, B. R., & Wood, D. J. (1997). Toward a theory of stakeholder identification and salience: Defining the principle of who and what really counts. *Academy of Management Review, 22*(4), 853–886. doi: 10.5465/AMR.1997.9711022105

Murman, E., Allen, T., Bozdogan, K., Cutcher-Gershenfeld, J., McManus, H., Nightingale, D.... Widnall, S. (2002). *Lean enterprise value: Insights from MIT's lean aerospace initiative.* London, England: Palgrave Macmillan.

Nightingale, D. J., & Srinivasan, J. (2011). *Beyond the lean enterprise: Achieving and sustaining successful enterprise transformation.* New York: AMACOM Press.

Ogburn, C., Jr. (1957). Merrill's marauders: The truth about an incredible adventure. *Harper's Magazine, 214*(1280). Retrieved from https://archive.org/stream/harpersmagazine214alde#page/n39/mode/2up

Project Management Institute (PMI). (2013a). *Managing change in organizations: A practice guide.* Newtown Square, PA: Author.

Project Management Institute (PMI). (2013b). *A guide to the project management body of knowledge (PMBOK® Guide)* (5th ed.). Newtown Square, PA: Author.

Roth, G. L., & DiBella, A. J. (2015). *Systemic change management: The five capabilities for improving enterprises.* London, England: Palgrave Macmillan.

Srivastava, T. (2012). *Lean effectiveness model for products and services: Servicing existing systems in aerospace and technology.* Retrieved from http://dspace.mit.edu/handle/1721.1/79532

Srivastava, T. (2014). *Investigation of the applicability of the MIT enterprise architecting framework to a multi-tiered enterprise: Defense health agency case.* Cambridge, MA: MIT Sociotechnical Systems Research Center.

Thiry, M. (2015). *Program management* (2nd ed.). Surrey, England: Gower Publishing Limited.

Additional Resources

Crawford, L., & Hassner-Nahmias, A. (2010). Competencies for managing change. *International Journal of Project Management, 28*(4), 405–412. doi:10.1016/j.ijproman.2010.01.015

Donaldson, T., & Preston, L. E. (1995). The stakeholder theory of the corporation: Concepts, evidence, and implications. *The Academy of Management Review, 20*(1), 65–91. doi:10.5465/AMR.1995.9503271992

Grossi, I. (2003). *Stakeholder analysis in the context of the lean enterprise.* Master's Thesis, Engineering Systems Division & Sloan School of Management, Massachusetts Institute of Technology, Cambridge, MA. Retrieved from http://hdl.handle.net/1721.1/34797

Kosandal, P., & Farris, J. (2004). *The strategic role of the kaizen event in driving and sustaining organizational change.* In Proceedings of the 2004 American Society for Engineering Management Conference, Alexandria, VA, 517–526.

Matty, D. M. (2011). *Stakeholder salience influence on bureaucratic program enterprise value creation.* Retrieved from http://hdl.handle.net/1721.1/81054

Nightingale, D. (2009, June 15–17). *Principles of enterprise systems.* Presented at Second International Symposium on Engineering Systems MIT, Cambridge, MA. Retrieved from https://esd.mit.edu/symp09/submitted-papers/nightingale-paper.pdf

Piepenbrock, T. (2009). *Toward a theory of the evolution of business ecosystems: Enterprise architectures, competitive dynamics, firm performance & industrial co-evolution.* Retrieved from http://dspace.mit.edu/handle/1721.1/57976

Rouse, W. B. (1998). *Don't jump to solutions: Thirteen delusions that undermine strategic thinking.* San Francisco: Jossey-Bass Publishers.

Senge, P. M. (2006). *The fifth discipline: The art and practice of the learning organization.* New York: Doubleday.

14

SUCCESSFUL CHANGE PROGRAMS THAT IMPROVED INTEGRATION

14.1 Introduction

This chapter presents five short case studies, or vignettes, describing change efforts to develop or strengthen integration capabilities in engineering programs and organizations. The vignettes were chosen to illustrate the diversity of integration challenges that an organization might face, and each highlights the application of different facets of the integration principles discussed previously. They also illustrate different approaches taken to create the changes needed to increase the level of integration between program management and systems engineering or related technical disciplines. As such, this chapter not only illustrates the elements of the Integration Framework presented in Part II, but also provides examples of ways to implement them.

The efforts described in the vignettes take place at both project and program levels. This illustrates the multiscale nature of organizational change. Individual change projects with discrete outcome objectives may be part of an overall program with a larger set of benefits to the organization and its stakeholders defined. When a formal change effort is undertaken within a program, it can in some ways be considered a second program within or parallel to the program, with benefits delivered to the program and to the larger organization. The manager of these change programs may either be a dedicated change program manager (to be discussed in more depth in Chapter 15), a manager within the program, or a business leader in the larger organization. The vignettes that follow will discuss change activities within specific projects or programs to deliver products or services, but within the context of a program to produce sustained change across projects and programs in the larger enterprise.

The first vignette describes some of the earliest efforts to integrate program management and systems engineering. It shows how through a number of different actions Lockheed Missiles & Space Company was able to increase the success rate of the highly classified Corona Satellite Program from 50% to 80% in 18 months, and subsequently to 97% three years later. These improvements resulted from a significant revision of the program management processes by integrating systems engineering into them.

The second vignette illustrates the pioneering use of certification programs to better integrate project and program management with systems engineering by the U.S. government in the Central Intelligence Agency, the Federal Acquisition Institute, and the Department of Veteran Affairs. In many instances, professionals in those agencies were exposed to systems engineering, and the integration of program management and systems engineering for the first time through the certification process.

The third vignette focuses on software development, particularly the integration and collaboration between software engineers and program managers, at Nationwide Mutual Insurance Company. Nationwide discovered that some teams were performing exceptionally well using Agile development practices, but others using the same practices failed. They discovered that the key success criteria were alignment and "co-transformation" of the program management organization along with the "front line" IT development organization.

The fourth vignette describes a highly successful transformation activity undertaken by BMW's Engineering Division. In order to meet ambitious strategic objectives, engineering productivity needed to grow by 30%. A change program management office orchestrated the transformation process from the leadership level, with a three-pronged approach to effect change on the operational level. The focus of the efforts was to increase collaboration across all boundaries, which resulted in a significant change in the way development programs were managed.

The fifth vignette illustrates integration mechanisms that were employed during the Boston Big Dig program. It delivered the world's most complex inner city and highway program, taking on a number of "World's First" technical challenges. A number of mechanisms required to manage a program of such complexity had at its core the need for greater integration between program management and systems engineering functions. The establishment of these mechanisms was the principal driver for integration in the program.

Together, the diversity of experiences and approaches displayed in these vignettes help to illustrate the point that there is unlikely to be a "one-size-fits-all approach" to change, as each organizational and engineering challenge is different. They also demonstrate that this kind of change in processes, practices, and mindsets comes from active and sustained effort by the organization and its leaders.

14.2 Redefining What Is Possible: The Marriage of Systems Engineering and Program Management at Lockheed Missiles & Space Company

In 1957, the Discoverer Satellite Program (Corona was the classified name) was started at Lockheed Missiles & Space Company (LMSC). This program involved a set of new technologies, including the development of a satellite that could carry photographic equipment and that would provide images of then Soviet activities. The goal was to achieve surveillance capabilities equivalent to, and even broader than, those for which the U2 spy plane had been counted on until it and its pilot had been shot down over Russia. This information was considered critical to U.S. defense posture and to the ability to negotiate any military and political accommodations with the Soviet Union. It became an Eisenhower administration major thrust with both capabilities and schedule as key motivations. Responsibility was assigned to the Defense Advanced Research Projects Agency. This case study[1] describes the development of an integrated program management approach at LMSC in the years when the systems engineering discipline was still in its early stages.

LMSC Space Systems Division was chosen for this highly classified developmental effort, which was soon accelerated in 1958 after the launch of Sputnik by Russia. The first attempt to launch this system in a proof-of-flight fashion blew up on the launch pad. The next 12 of these all had disastrous outcomes until finally, on August 12, 1960 after a single day in orbit, Discoverer 13 yielded a capsule recovered with exposed film. Imaging had been provided from a 24-inch camera and film transported into a recovery capsule. This success generated high expectations that this would provide the overhead reconnaissance needed then and for the future. Indeed, Corona provided major knowledge of Soviet and Chinese military activities until 1972, when, after having achieved a near 100% success rate with up to five-foot ground resolution, successor space systems with more advanced technology took over.

But by 1961 it was still a high-risk proposition with the goal of achieving 20-foot ground resolution imagery, obtainable only through low orbit flight circuiting the Earth every 90 minutes. Because of need and failure rates, launches occurred every two-to-four weeks with orbital time of up to four days and capsule retrieval through snaring a parachuted recovery vehicle containing a film cassette. This difficult exercise was accomplished over the Pacific Ocean using a lanyard deployed from the rear of an aircraft based in Hawaii. Extensive training for this remarkable operation by the U.S. Air Force was required. The whole operation involved many elements for potential failure, from the launch of the Discoverer Agena satellite on Thor Delta rockets, originally intended for ballistic missiles, to stability and control of the spacecraft once separated from the launch vehicle. Added to this were the multifaceted elements of spacecraft performance, that of the camera system and the retrieval of the film, and, finally, the separation and recovery of the "bucket" following secure commands to an onboard computer. In fact, out of the first 30 missions through 1961, only 12 were considered successes.

A success rate of only 50% for the system became almost acceptable, although the Air Force and other agencies involved in the program were dismayed at the losses, recognizing the importance of the photography as well as the costs of the system. Explaining failures and the corrective action necessary after each failure involved highly sophisticated analysis on the part of Lockheed and the two associates, ITek for the camera and General Electric for the capsule, but each failure was analyzed thoroughly, with the cause of that failure addressed. Unfortunately, the sources seemed to be random.

Following one failure at a critical time of government need, the Undersecretary of the Air Force came to Lockheed in order to hear an explanation of the latest failure and how Lockheed was going to achieve a higher success rate. After listening to the briefing, he said pointedly:

> Lockheed, you people do an incredible job of failure analysis, but you don't seem to do an equivalent job for success. This is a very complex system we're dealing with and this is a systems issue. Now who is your chief systems engineer?

LMSC Space Systems Division staff unfortunately was not familiar with the term and tried to answer with a variety of identifications within the engineering organization. After all, the existing classic matrix organization followed closely the successful project engineer technical leadership approach of the aircraft divisions. This clearly did not satisfy the undersecretary and he left with some very uncomfortable comments and suggested that Lockheed send its key engineering management to review what he called "systems engineering" with General Shriever's Ballistic Missile Division of the Air Force, which had been developing a process of analysis and design at a systems level with Dr. Simon Ramo and personnel of the new Ramo Woolridge organization.

Following shortly thereafter, a chief systems engineer, reporting directly to the program manager, was appointed with the task of understanding the entire Discoverer program, all elements as they interacted with every aspect of the system, their individual failure modes, and, more importantly, each element's interfaces internally and externally, identifying their implications to success or failure. This integrated systems approach started with requirements and their understanding, including a definition of the means by which they could be verified as fulfilled, establishing a complete, five-tiered architecture for the system, then evaluating an entire set of electrical and electronic circuits as well as structural/mechanical elements, all through integrated schematics. Failure analysis was conducted via these "tools," evaluating each node within the schematics for their potential for failure and necessary preventive measures. Even more important was the recognition that their interfaces involved at least two nodes beyond the point being analyzed—a significant basis for identifying root sources of failure plus corrective as well as fault tolerant actions. The significance of this effort was evident through an improvement from 50% success rate to 80% in just 18 months and then, within three years, to 97% success.

The addition of the chief systems engineer to the program organization also changed the relationship of the program manager from being a strong coordinator to becoming director of all disciplines making up the program, including technical cognizance and authority over those from associate and subcontractor organizations, as well as responsibility for integrated schedules and related controls. This required vigorous and insistent customer support, and a transformation of its Special Projects team to provide leadership and responsiveness for the critical aspects of engineering and management partnered in many ways with Lockheed's program office.

This activity, of course, involved additional and selective manpower, modification of resource allocation, together with budget and schedule adjustments—a major change of mentality within the program management organization. The end result involved not only engineering implementation that included redesign for hardware and software, but also extensive verification and tests requiring facility and communication installations in the factory and at the launch site, all coordinated and, in most cases, directed by the program manager.

This approach soon became the prototype for all programs within the Space Systems Division, as well as becoming a requirement in Air Force program procurement. It also generated a restructuring of the program management organization, establishing the chief systems engineer as the lead technical individual. The chief systems engineer position included a staff responsible for establishing requirements and specifications; defining all interfaces; chairing, performing, or certifying all failure analysis and changes; and assuring that manufacturing, testing, and deployment activities satisfied requirements. With the position's supporting personnel, plus a program controls manager responsible for schedule and budget, program leadership became an effective triumvirate: Program and project administrative structures consisted of program manager (typically with an assistant), chief systems engineer, and controls governing effective program management. This did not obviate the roles of the functional elements (i.e., engineering design, change control, and reliability), usually part of the chief systems engineer group, manufacturing assembly, and test, and so on, plus contract and subcontract relations, procurement, and others generally in the purview of the program manager's Controls organization.

To further emphasize the program management primacy that developed, some programs were able to organize fully using a program organization structure, with engineering, assembly and test, and, in several cases, subcontractors, directly reporting to the program manager. While this became the norm for program startup and major program continuum, it became evident that with as many programs as were underway, there was a hoarding of talent by the largest well-established programs. The imbalance clearly required sharing that talent and experience, requiring the partial reestablishment of the matrix approach, but with the continued managing role of the program manager and his directly reporting chief systems engineer and Controls organizations. In addition, the move, promotion, and salary review of any individual from a program-organized group such as design engineering, test and assembly, and procurement, required the mutual agreement of the program manager and the central organization head. Sorting out these issues took nearly five years, with interchanges of key leadership personnel, compromises reflected in the reference to startups, and transition to central organization involvement as projects matured.

As noted, Discoverer program results signaled the future approach for all programs, including the proposal phases of medium- to large-size projects. The history of all programs became true success stories. For example, the even more complex successor to Discoverer for overhead reconnaissance, named Hexagon, had its initial vehicle scheduled for 30 days in orbit, but achieved 56 and had no failures in 13 subsequent missions.

The arrangement became so related to program success that the progression from chief systems engineer to program manager became the norm for the LMSC Space Systems Division organization to the point that several presidents of that division came through such a chain of assignments. Thus, much as becoming the project engineer was the goal of aspiring engineers in the aircraft world, the goal of the ambitious engineer at Lockheed Space Systems was to be a chief systems engineer on programs, not in the staff position unfortunately prescribed by many other companies, but as the chief technical officer.

14.2.1 Discussion

The new systems engineering function in the Discoverer program introduced not only more thorough root cause analysis of failures to solve the immediate challenge of high failure rates, but also a more proactive system-level understanding and integration of the program on the technical level. It created the thorough engineering underpinnings, from high-quality requirements verification procedures to a five-tiered system architecture, for executing a successful program. It also resulted in better organizational integration. The new role of chief systems engineer did not compete with the program manager, but enabled that role to grow from a mere "strong coordinator" to a true director of all disciplines. Systems engineering provided the "layer" necessary to connect the highly complex engineering reality with the requirements of running a large program. The program manager was thus able to understand and influence technical issues, including those at the subcontractor level. This created a logical career progression from chief systems engineer to program manager to, in several cases, division presidents.

The actions taken in this example to increase integration included:

- Integrating planning and resource allocation for engineering efforts into the program manager's responsibilities
- Restructuring roles of managers and functional leads in the program and in the division
- Developing policies to manage staffing to ensure an appropriate and equitable balance of the right technical people across programs
- Developing leadership transition paths from chief systems engineer through program manager and above
- Adapting to challenges by testing new integration approaches over time to see what works
- Pilot testing new ideas on one program, and then diffusing best practices to others

14.3 Using Certification to Foster Integration in U.S. Government Agency Acquisition Programs

In the early 2000s, a number of U.S. government agencies created and implemented project and program management certification programs for managers of technically complex system development efforts. Eventually these efforts were combined and administered centrally through the U.S. Federal Acquisition Institute. During the roll-out of this certification process, it became apparent that the process of certification was an effective way to bring about change in these organizations, in addition to raising the competency of the workforce, as shown in this case study.[2]

"We don't need this" was a lament that was heard frequently while the U.S. Central Intelligence Agency (CIA) was creating and implementing its project management certification. It was heard again during the creation and implementation of the first government-wide project management certification for civilian federal employees, and, most recently, when the U.S. Department of Veterans Affairs created and implemented its version of the federal project management certification. Specifically, the lament involved systems engineering. It stemmed from project managers as well as others who were involved with projects with relatively limited scope and relatively low complexity. The cry emerged from federal government employees who were advancing their project management knowledge and skills; these people were being exposed to the integration of project management and systems engineering for the first time.

The CIA was an early adopter of project management. The earliest forms were home grown. Later forms benefited from the influences of industry thought leaders including Kevin Forsberg and Hal Mooz who coauthored the popular groundbreaking book *Visualizing Project Management* (Forsberg, Mooz, & Cotterman, 1996). These later forms were based on a detailed multistep cycle that fully integrated project management and systems engineering, and served the needs of CIA's experienced engineers responsible for the larger and more complex projects. Those less experienced who were working on the limited scope and low complexity projects did their best to adopt the fully integrated project management and systems engineering life cycle, but they quickly became frustrated. Their frustration grew, not because of a lack of dedication or effort, but because of limitations in experience, knowledge, and skills. The hundreds of activities, products, and control gates associated with this integrated life cycle were not seen so much as an aid that could be tailored down to serve the needs of their projects, but as a bewildering and burdensome prescription to be followed indiscriminately.

Senior officials at the CIA, who understood the benefits of well-managed projects large and small and who understood that all projects were systems, launched the creation and implementation of the CIA-wide Project and Program Management Certification. The head of the project management office led that effort during the early to mid-2000s. He was to extend the integration of project management and systems engineering to all types of CIA projects and project managers, and to implement this in a manner that helped thousands overcome their perceived frustrations and burdens. The approach he selected involved establishing a CIA-wide certification compatible with *A Guide to the Project Management Body of Knowledge* (PMI, 2013) as well as *Systems Engineering Handbook* (INCOSE, 2015) in their then-current versions. This approach involved creating a knowledge and skill-based certification that helped the employees understand not just the "how" and "when" associated with the life cycle elements, but also the "why." Equipped with an understanding about why the life cycle element existed and what purpose it served allowed employees to make intelligent decisions about the value to their particular project and to tailor it appropriately.

The approach also involved developing a tiered certification system, dividing the certification into four levels; all levels included some aspects of systems engineering, with the third level focusing almost entirely on it. In this way, over a period of five years, CIA employees increasingly appreciated the relevance of systems engineering in their projects; indeed, 89% of them reported that it was applicable to their jobs, a full 30 percentage points higher than they reported prior to the certification program.

During the late 2000s, the Federal Acquisition Institute developed and implemented the Federal Acquisition Certification for Program and Project Managers (FAC-P/PM). That certification was created to extend the integration of project management and systems engineering from the U.S. Department of Defense (DoD) to all civilian federal employees, especially those involved with limited scope and lower complexity projects. The approach called for creating a competency-based program and included structuring the program in three levels; some systems engineering was included in all levels. The competencies that underpinned this program were developed based on surveys of subject matter experts at many of the federal agencies. These surveys, which were based on DoD Directive 5000 ("The Defense Acquisition System"), identified how often and how important particular project management and systems engineering activities were. The competencies resulting from these surveys were mandated by the Office of Federal Procurement Policy in 2007.

A government-wide study, conducted in 2011 to get a glimpse into the early stages of implementation of this program, found that progress was furthest along in agencies where positive project management and training attitudes already existed, and most hampered in agencies that had little history of supporting project management or training. Since then, more agencies have made progress thanks in no small part to the certification training available to their employees that was provided by the Federal Acquisition Institute at no cost.

The Department of Veterans Affairs (VA) was one of the agencies that was out in front with the implementation of FAC-P/PM discussed above. In 2008 the VA formed an Acquisition Academy to address the growing acquisition workforce challenges they were facing; a program management school was created within that academy that tailored the FAC-P/PM to the VA mission and workforce. It too integrated project management and systems engineering into a competency-based program, was targeted at those involved with the smaller and less complex projects, and was structured in three levels with some systems engineering at each level. Post-training metrics indicated that students returned to their jobs able to successfully complete projects they otherwise would have struggled with or failed.

During one systems engineering for project managers workshop, participants reacted to an exercise that may have been representative of those "we don't need this" laments so frequently expressed during the previous decade. The reactions came from managers of relatively limited scope and complexity projects as each of them individually worked to complete a quick-paced timed exercise. The exercise was structured with many levels where progression to the next and more difficult level required the demonstration of increasing amounts of systems thinking. Since students were aware of each other's rate of progression through the levels, an informal atmosphere of competition evolved. During the first few levels, many of the students were openly vocal with their frustrations and laments about how silly and useless the exercise was. As the exercise progressed and the students became more experienced with systems thinking, many of the laments died down. At the end of the exercise, all but one of the students declared that they liked the exercise and understood the value of systems thinking in project management. That one student exception stated that he did not understand the purpose of the exercise.

14.3.1 Discussion

While the majority of those who received the certification training were project managers, the training was also applicable to program managers. The implementation of these certifications was part of a program to enhance the skillsets of the acquisition workforce and to increase their ability to integrate program management and systems engineering across a range of program and project types. As part of a change program, it was important to address the initial (semiautomatic) rejection of the certification content, particularly by managers involved in smaller and less-complex projects who felt they did not need the formality of systems engineering practices. Essential to success was that the certification was based on a tailored and well-researched competence-based model (the "What"), it was a multi-tiered certification system (3–5 levels) that gradually increased the participant's appreciation of the issues and problems that the certification addressed (the "Why"), before providing the tools and methods to deal with them (the "How"). While based on detailed processes and methods, the certification emphasized the development of the ability to tailor the approach to the needs of a particular project, including appropriate process simplifications (the "When").

The experience showed that organizations that run small projects professionally will also run big projects professionally. It also illustrated the need to develop competences step by step, to enable the participants to appreciate the need for certain processes and methods before they are introduced. This example also illustrates how successful changes achieved in one area can be replicated and evolved into new areas through a change program to enable success across a breadth of organizations.

The actions taken in this example to increase integration included:

- Create integrated certification for program managers that drew on both program management and systems engineering standards to raise program manager awareness of systems engineering.
- Provide training to program and project managers on a widespread basis, regardless of the size of their programs or projects.
- Provide a multi-tiered certification system to help increase the depth of understanding about the integration issues between program management and systems engineering.
- Capture successful practices and insights and disseminate them across multiple locations.

14.4 Integrating Software Engineering and Program Management at Nationwide

Nationwide Mutual Insurance Company is one of the largest and most diversified financial services companies in the United States. The company provides products such as retirement planning, auto and home insurance, farm owner insurance, and commercial lines insurance to end consumers and intermediaries. Revenues exceeded US$25 billion in 2015 and the company is forecasting strong continued growth in the years to come. Information technology (IT) plays a vital role in the company's strategy and in delivering its *On Your Side* customer service and protection. As such, Nationwide spends more than US$1 billion on IT on an annual basis and employs thousands of IT employees. This case study[3] demonstrates how Nationwide achieved greater integration through a middle-out change program in its IT organization.

The company spends a significant portion of this budget on software projects, including new development, enhancements of existing systems, purchasing software packages, and integration of systems of acquired companies. Projects range from small (<$50K) to very large (>$50M) and everything in between. Prior to 2009, the delivery of these projects was done in traditional fashion using primarily "waterfall" development with teams created for specific project deliveries led by a project or program manager. The emphasis was on a strict development life cycle and phases, tight controls, and extensive planning. While the company had a good track record of finishing projects, they were often late in delivery and quality levels were less than desired.

At the same time, a few projects or teams within IT were having tremendous success delivering on-time solutions with high quality levels—levels virtually unheard of within the company hallways. These groups were using a software development philosophy known as Agile to produce the results. The core characteristics of Nationwide's Agile teams at the time were short, rapid cycles of work, business involvement throughout the development process, team collaboration and self-direction, visual management, reflection, and an emphasis on software engineering excellence. These teams also stayed together from project to project. Teams were not formed for projects; rather, projects came to the teams. But not all teams using this philosophy were delivering great results and the process seemed to particularly alienate program managers.

Nationwide's IT leaders quickly recognized that the results of the successful teams needed to be replicated throughout the organization to achieve quality and delivery goals. A few successful Agile teams were great to have, but not all that impactful on an over US$1 billion organization. Successful teams were characterized by a disciplined system of rules and a high degree of collaboration between program managers and software engineers. Those teams experiencing less success were characterized by a lack of process discipline and an attitude of exclusion. In particular, they relegated program and project management to the periphery of the development life cycle. This created two primary problems. First, in Nationwide's complex environment of thousands of software applications, no team can isolate itself. Changes to one system inevitably impact another, and isolated teams with no view into other activities can cause tremendous problems by not understanding the dependencies. Second, the teams were unable to effectively communicate with a diverse set of business customers—they lacked the savvy and knowledge of how and when to involve business customers beyond setting the scope of the project and periodic check-ins.

The question became then, how to scale the practices and processes of the successful teams across the company? The answer to this question was provided by studying the successful teams themselves, and in a pivot from thinking about Agile in a development silo, to thinking about Agile and program management together. Nationwide stumbled onto this connection without knowing it at first. In looking at successful teams, they were always characterized by an interested and supporting management system. Whereas the unsuccessful teams had contentious relationships with management—especially program management—at best, the successful teams had managers that had essentially adopted the same philosophies as the teams and applied them to the work of management. This led to the hypothesis that it was not that the frontline staff was unable to transform at scale to this new Agile way of delivering software, but rather that without a parallel management transformation, the results were doomed. In other words, to transform the software development system, managers had to change not only the way they viewed the work done by the development teams, but also their own way of working.

Nowhere was this more prevalent than in program management. To that point in time, Nationwide's program managers were focused on control and risk mitigation—meaning, detailed planning activities and resource allocations were fine-tuned and then applied to the staffing and control of the teams' work. The program managers acted at an arm's length distance from the teams, preferring to focus on the big picture of delivery and continually refining their plans and putting in countermeasures if the plan went off track. Weekly or monthly status reports were the norm, along with formalized and bureaucratic processes for any changes to the plan. The program plan was king, and any variance from the plan on the part of the project was looked upon as a problem to be solved by the project manager. The company used metrics such as schedule adherence, resource utilization, and change rate (change = bad) to evaluate teams. Red status was viewed in a negative light and program managers were incentivized to get the project to green as fast as possible, using any means available. The primary role of the manager when a project went off track was to get it back on track. But often the real question that needed answered was, "Was the project ever on the right track from the start?"

Contrast the goals of traditional IT program management with that of Agile software development: deliver planned results versus deliver desired results. This insight at Nationwide was strongly driven by the adoption within senior IT executives of a "growth" versus a "fixed" mindset, inspired by Carol Dweck's (2006) book *Mindset: The New Psychology of Success*. Traditional program management focuses on planning, change controls, and periodic status reporting. Agile software development focuses on discovery, short learning cycles, visual management, and daily huddles. These two perspectives are set up to be in conflict with each other. To correct these differences, the company undertook a transformation in how software was developed, and the roles and expectations of all those involved in the process. A new organization was created, the Application Development Center (ADC), with a focus on technical excellence and process discipline.

The ADC built upon the successes of the original Agile teams, while incorporating the supporting roles, including the program manager, directly into the model. Standardized role definitions and behaviors, referred to as "standard work" were defined for everyone. Accountability and reinforcement systems were put in place. A point to note though is that all of these things were put in place to create a system that learns and adapts, continuously improving process and practices.

For program managers, this meant changes to their daily interactions with the teams. First, an acknowledgment was made that not everything can be planned, and in fact, some things should not be planned. Nationwide's project plans were implying a level of precision that belied the ability to accurately schedule the unknown. Software development, similar to product development, can have standard processes to get to an answer, but cannot have standardized answers, which is what many of the program managers were trying to do in their planning. When the inevitable problem happened, instead of looking at it as an opportunity to learn, program management looked at it as a nuisance to be corrected at all costs. The standard work of program managers included new rules on how to interact with the ADC teams. This included participation in daily "huddle meetings" (a 15-minute meeting relying on visual management boards, focusing on progress, problems needing help, and creating transparency and accountability), usage of the visual management boards for real-time status updates, acting as an escalation point for the teams, and coordinating dependencies through a visual representation in the team work areas.

New metrics were put in place to drive the right behaviors. Scrapped were metrics such as change rate and resource utilization in favor of team productivity and customer happiness. All metrics for the programs were displayed visually to create an environment of transparency and accountability. If the team was not meeting its goals, then everyone needed to know about it and be involved in finding a solution. The program manager became a coach of sorts for the team. The new primary role of the program manager evolved to provide the guardrails and goals, while not micromanaging every part of the solution.

The results of the transformation were incredible. In the period 2009–2015, critical defects released into production decreased by 50% per year, every year, on average. Employee engagement (as measured through Gallup's Q12 process) increased every year as well. Productivity levels also increased, with over 75% of releases above industry benchmarks. More important for long-term sustainability were the underlying cultural changes that occurred. All members of the teams are aligned toward a common purpose in delivering great solutions for customers. The program management and technical staff are no longer adversarial and instead work together to solve problems, eliminating a culture of distrust and blame. Nationwide created a culture of collaboration and integration between program management and software engineering staff that continues to provide tremendous value for all stakeholders.

14.4.1 Discussion

The changes described in this case involved both programs and projects, but the overall effort to improve integration was implemented through a change program that worked with the programs and projects. The resource base for the change program relied on an existing Lean Six Sigma infrastructure in the company with a cadre of change agents/facilitators to help with training and implementation.

Nationwide discovered that many established program management practices often hindered success with Agile projects because they tried to enforce traditional control and risk management practices that were incompatible with the Agile approach. Traditional primary success metrics were schedule adherence, resource utilization, and (low) change rates, because change was seen as something bad. A new mindset had to be developed: focus management attention on "desired results" rather than "planned results." A new entity called the Application Development Center became the organization that helped to instill this new mindset throughout both the software engineering as well as the program management community, and focused both on technical excellence as well as process discipline. Program managers changed their team interactions from weekly or monthly "status reports" to daily interactions, focusing on meaningful rolling planning activities at a useful and realistic level of detail. The performance measurement system was changed to evaluate team productivity and customer happiness, and performance tracking was done in a transparent and openly visual way. This resulted in significant improvements across the board, including continuous significant reduction of critical defects, increase in employee engagement, very high productivity levels, and a pervasive culture that focused on delivering great solutions for customers.

The actions taken in this example to increase integration included:

- Change program to improve program management integration with developers, leveraging existing change agents and infrastructure to roll out change initiatives across the company.
- Track down the root cause of inconsistent execution of Agile across the organization: a lack of process discipline and an attitude of exclusion between program and project management and the software developers.
- Redefine the program management orientation to better align with the Agile development approach.
- Create the Application Development Center with a focus on technical excellence and process discipline.
- Create standard work for managers explaining how they should interact with the development teams, including reporting and priorities.
- Develop a new set of performance metrics for program managers to track development progress.

14.5 Managing Change in Engineering Program Organizations: Boosting Productivity in BMW's Engineering Department

14.5.1 Introduction

This case study[4] describes a change program that unfolded over the period from 2007 to 2012. It was managed by a program management office and involved a large number of individual projects to bring about the overall vision of the BMW Group and the BMW engineering division contribution to achieving that vision. The integration of the many projects, most of them technical, resulted in a more integrated program management and engineering environment.

14.5.2 BMW Company Background

The BMW Group is one of the most successful car and motorcycle manufacturers in the world. BMW, MINI, and Rolls-Royce are three of the strongest premium brands in the automobile industry. BMW is regarded as one of the world's most reputable companies, setting records for reputation excellence with consumers. BMW reported the best sales volume performance ever achieved in the company's history in 2011, with all-time sales records for each of its BMW, MINI, and Rolls-Royce Motor Cars brands (1.7 million in 2011, up 21% from 2006.)

Despite these significant achievements, BMW Group is relatively small compared with the big global auto manufacturers. Its financial performance, brand value, reputation, and technology base would make it an attractive acquisition target. In 2007 the company laid out a strategy for the future called Number ONE that identified actions needed to continue to grow and remain a strong and independent auto manufacturer.

14.5.3 The Challenge for the Engineering Organization

Klaus Draeger became a member of the Operating Board of BMW with responsibilities for research and development in November 2006. He faced a tremendous challenge: not only was the Engineering Division (the "E-Division") already stretched to the limit, but mid- and long-term corporate strategy called for yet another push to grow the number of offered models while at the same time maintaining a stable engineering workforce. The goal that emerged was to increase the efficiency within the Engineering Division by one-third, which was interpreted as increase the number of development projects by one-third, reduce the development lead time by one-third, improve product quality by one-third, and do all of this using the same budget and staffing by the year 2012.

At the same time, engineering was to remain on the front line of BMW strategy, with a goal of stabilizing engineering spending at 5–5.5% of total revenues. An aggressive innovation strategy combined the evolutionary development of combustion engines with "revolutionary" development of alternative hybrid and fully electric drive trains; increased the standardization of the product architecture, commonality, and modularity of systems to realize cost efficiency; and supported the long-term growth strategy with an increasing size of the product portfolio (see Figure 14-1).

14.5.4 Engineering Change and Integration Program

The Engineering Division responded with the E^3 Program, an integrated change management program that had five major aspects (see Figure 14-2).

14.5.4.1 BMW Corporate and Division Strategy

The E^3 Program was put into place to transform the engineering organization to a state where it would be able to support the very ambitious corporate strategy including an expansion of the model range, increase of vehicle quality, and reduction of engineering

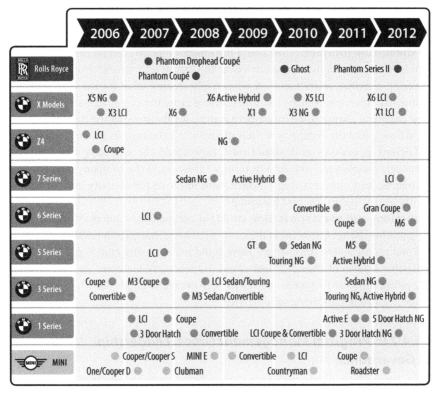

Figure 14-1: One of the challenges facing the E-Division at BMW: An expanding range of vehicles
Source: BMW June 2012 investor presentation.

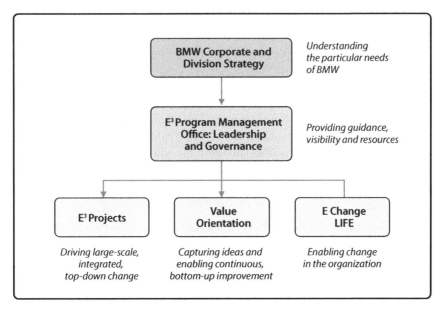

Figure 14-2: The five elements of BMW's engineering transformation program

cost per vehicle, with a stable number of employees. The transformation activities addressed three top-level challenges, expressed in the name "E^3":

- **Exhilarating products.** How could the engineering division be closer to the customer's needs and more responsive to the customer's needs? How could engineering activities better focus on what really creates value for the customer; and ultimately increase customer satisfaction and grow the customer base? How could the company change some fundamental attitudes about "what the customer wants" and how could the company technically deliver it through its product?
- **Efficient processes and structures.** How could the company develop better products, in less time, and for less money? How could the company develop more products, and more exciting products, and improve productivity and innovation without driving up cost and lead time?
- **Emotions and team spirit.** How could the company develop openness and willingness for change? How could the company assure that employees take ownership of and responsibility for change? How could the company enable managers to be effective leaders of change? How could the company maintain an attractive and inspiring work environment, as well as keep everyone employed while at the same time drastically improving productivity?

14.5.4.2 E^3 Program Management Office: Leadership and Governance

At the top level, an integrated leadership team starting with the head of the E-Division provided the necessary guidance, visibility, and resources to the E^3 program. The leadership team was involved in the definition of the program objectives, its execution, and its supervision. It included the entire top-level management team of the E-Division, which was a key factor in assuring that the transformation program focused on achieving an overall optimal solution across the functional domains in engineering. Each manager was empowered and held accountable for the results in their areas of responsibility.

Two internal departments in particular played vital roles in the E^3 change efforts and were coordinated through the Program Management Office (PMO): Engineering Strategy Department (part of the E-Division) and Change Management Consulting Department (part of the human resources division). Within BMW, the various strategy and process development groups associated with the different departments within the engineering division also played a major role in supporting the E^3 program and were aligned through the PMO.

About 20 people were involved in central PMO activities (though not all full time):

- Six full-time staff in the PMO, which represented about 80% of the staffing from the strategy department, with other participants from Controlling and Internal Communications
- Two support staff for benchmarking activities supporting E^3

- Three leading and developing bottom-up improvement activities
- Others providing consulting support for specific E^3 projects

14.5.4.3 E^3 Projects

Benchmarking studies by the strategy group showed that other German premium car manufacturers held a structural advantage over BMW as they were part of larger corporations and benefited from "engineering economies of scale" through platform architectures. If BMW was to remain independent, it would have to dramatically increase its engineering efficiency. Many of the things that would have to be improved included engineering processes, product design and product life cycle management, and the way in which engineering projects were managed. In short, the changes addressed activities that spanned the entire E-Division and, consequently, would constitute strategic initiatives in the division.

In deciding how to approach these strategic initiatives, there were two fundamental options: have executives define projects and tell the management what to do or empower the management to identify and solve challenges themselves. A combination of both approaches was chosen. Initially, to be able to rapidly address the biggest challenges, the E-Circle convened and by May 2007 had identified the top 25 challenges; later these became the first E^3 projects. While the large-scale projects started up, it was clear that many of them would not yield tangible results for a year or more. The question arose: How could the entire engineering organization be involved in the improvement effort? After several scouting and benchmarking activities, both within and outside the company, the *Wertschöpfungsorientierung* or "Value Orientation" (WO) bottom-up improvement initiative was started based on Lean management philosophy.

A centralized, top-down process was used to drive large-scale changes in the organization. This consisted of a top-level steering committee led by the head of the E-Division that developed and prioritized projects to drive significant change into the engineering organization. Those projects typically averaged 2–3 years in duration, but could be shorter or longer depending on the project objectives. The projects involved 20–500 people. Examples included projects to increase standardization of product architecture, increase parts commonality between products without compromising customer-facing individuality, and virtualization of the expensive and lengthy prototyping process.

One of the strong enabling points of the E^3 projects was an effective governance structure. Direct oversight by a small executive board allowed E^3 project managers direct access to the top management level. At the same time, the project managers were supported by a network of strategy and process development groups. This created several important enablers for rapid and effective action:

- A high level of motivation for project members—being assigned to an E^3 project was seen as a sign of high reputation or status in the E-Division
- Close alignment of the projects with the overall strategic goals
- Access to the necessary funding

- Access to the right people
- Effectively removing obstacles in the organization
- Fast decision times

14.5.4.4 Value Orientation

A decentralized and distributed bottom-up approach was used to enable employees to drive local, small-scale improvements. Those activities were centered on a Lean product development framework emphasizing in particular efficiency improvements (i.e., productivity improvements and cost reductions). It provided a framework for defining and executing relatively small-scale improvement projects as well as providing a project governance and monitoring system and a structured way to engage colleagues from other organizational units.

Practically speaking, the majority of the E-Division personnel would not directly contribute to E^3 projects, but they would need to play a significant role in achieving the strategic targets. This was enabled through the bottom-up initiative.

Lean principles served as a foundation for this approach. Engaging the improvement and problem-solving abilities of the entire E-Division workforce was necessary in order to meet the group strategy targets. BMW already had experience with applying Lean principles and practices in its production operations in its WPS (BMW value creation-oriented or Lean production system). Engineering Strategy Department consultants benchmarked Lean approaches starting with WPS, but also read books and articles, investigated other companies, and worked with university academics to understand how Lean was being applied in product development. After studying what others were doing, BMW decided to create its own program to drive transformation from the "engineering shop floor." WO was developed as "the implementation of E^3 at the local level" or "E^3 for everyone." The core of the WO framework was a focus on value, with a number of other widely accepted Lean principles added that were adapted specifically to the product development setting.

Employees formally identified challenges and improvement opportunities and presented those ideas to their superiors. They applied for resources and support from their own teams, and also from other teams, to execute them. To facilitate the work, the improvement activities were structured around the Lean philosophy. Employees were also provided with a defined toolbox of methods that they could use in their projects. A group of WO experts was created who received two, 3-day trainings in Lean methods. Their task was to support complex WO projects with their expertise.

14.5.4.5 E Change LIFE

E Change LIFE was a dedicated change program initiated and supported by both the head of the E-Division as well as the BMW board member responsible for human resources. Its aim was to involve all 8,000 members of the engineering division in the change process, starting with nearly all managers, to create openness and willingness for change as well as establish a feedback culture. In essence, it was meant to transform the work mindset of all the members of the E-Division, hence the use of LIFE in the title. It consisted of several modules, discussing the imperatives for change, the corporate strategy and how it relates to the engineering strategy, as well as mechanisms to engage in the change. It contained various mechanisms for feedback among managers and employees. The day-and-a-half workshops were set up in such a way that they provided opportunities for all employees of the engineering division to interact with colleagues from other departments within engineering.

The workshops were led by upper and middle managers rather than trainers or consultants and were followed up by 2-hour workshops about six months later. The workshops took place in a casual atmosphere. Toward the end of each workshop, an executive would join the workshop and enter into a dialogue with the participants, discuss the business principles, and reflect with them on how to live and operationalize them.

14.5.5 Results

These measures contributed to significant improvements in productivity and helped BMW achieve its targets. From 2006 to 2011, total revenue grew by 40%, 21% more vehicles were delivered, the vehicle quality increased by 32%, and the model range was expanded significantly by 30%. At the same time, the number of car models and derivatives in the pipeline increased by 53% and the workload by 35%, while the engineering cost per derivative and workload decreased by 38% and 31%, respectively. The overall lead time decreased by 14%, even though the development process of key models became more complex after the introduction of product architectures, platform design, and front-loading of the development of product lines. Moreover, partway through the changes the global economic downturn negatively impacted the auto industry. Based on the improvements that had already taken place, BMW managed to remain profitable and did not cut its workforce as many other automakers did. It emerged from the downturn stronger and more competitive than many rivals, with a rapid return to normal profitability.

One interesting aspect of the efficiency improvement activities is the overall cost reduction that could be achieved. Figure 14-3 summarizes the cost reductions that the top-down E^3 projects and bottom-up WO projects contributed to the organization. Each year, the budget of the E-Division was re-baselined, subtracting reported cost improvements from the next year's budget. That meant that, for example, the cost savings achieved in 2009 were realized within a budget that had already been reduced by the cost savings achieved the previous year. Figure 14-3 illustrates how top-down and bottom-up improvement initiatives complemented one another over the life cycle of the transformation.

A new car development program demonstrated the overall impact of these changes, and particularly the integration that resulted from the tools, processes, mindsets, and climate that emerged from the diverse array of different change efforts underway in the E-Division. One of the early E^3 projects focused on the validation of vehicle concepts with minimal or no physical prototypes. The solution presumably lay in using computer-based design or virtual tools to eliminate, where justified and useful, physical prototypes. BMW had used virtual tools in design for as long as 10 years before this new mandate arrived. While many of the tools were already available, it was not a

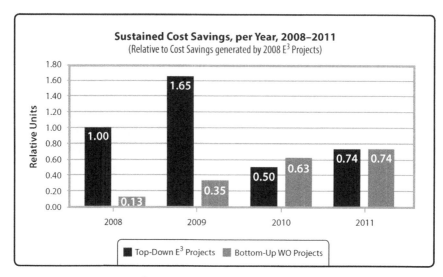

Figure 14-3: Savings from the E^3 program realized over a four-year period

straightforward transition to use them in a way that dramatically reduced development time. Suppliers who previously only supplied hardware or software were now asked to provide simulation and modeling results. Other departments, like procurement, had to become part of the effort because of these new working relationships, but few people initially had a complete picture of the entire process.

More fundamentally, the mindset of engineers and project managers on how to use these tools to do their work had to change. They needed to be deliberate about using the tools to reduce costs and development cycles and to think fundamentally about the cost structure in validation activities. After two years of effort on the E^3 virtual prototyping project, the 6-series 4-door coupe project was launched as a pilot for this approach. Its development was completed two years later. In its development it used no prototypes and was validated completely with virtual design and test methods. Not only was the program successful in the market, but the quality was virtually perfect.

While the E^3 project created the capability to do this, it was up to the program manager to execute it. Models were used across all program functions, tracking parts for instance, but the overall approach was driven by the need to finish the program in two years. Because of this successful example, other program managers began following suit and the lessons learned were captured and spread to other programs.

14.5.6 Discussion

Top-down, large-scale transformation projects tackled central themes, such as department-wide approaches to engineering architecture or virtual prototyping. Bottom-up initiatives provided processes and methods for enhancing value creation. An outreach program articulated the need for transformation as well as highlighted the opportunities for participation to each member of the organization. Top-down projects yielded significant savings and productivity improvements quickly, but exploited the most immediately impactful projects early on. The bottom-up approach consistently "ramped up" productivity improvements over the years to eventually achieve a comparable level of savings to the top-down projects and, importantly, targeted the transformation toward a more collaborative culture in the E-division.

The actions taken in this example to increase integration included:

- Senior leaders provided the vision and resources for the change and were personally involved in supporting it.
- The company and division strategy were communicated to all employees in special meetings and used to define the change projects.
- A PMO managed the change program and provided resources to enable local leaders and employees to implement the change. An internal professional change management group with change agents, toolsets, and a model for change assisted the PMO.
- Projects included both top-down and bottom-up change initiatives to engage the entire workforce.
- The scope of changes addressed product, processes, tools, communication, leadership, and culture.

14.6 Delivering the World's Most Complex Inner-City Infrastructure Program: Boston's Big Dig

14.6.1 Project Overview

Boston's Central Artery/Tunnel (CA/T) program, commonly known as the Big Dig, was the largest, most complex, and technically challenging highway initiative in U.S. history and included unprecedented planning and engineering. Larger than the Panama Canal, the Hoover Dam, and the Alaska Pipeline initiatives, it was built through the heart of one of the nation's oldest cities. The Big Dig has been depicted as one of the great achievements of the twenty-first century despite its numerous technical and operational challenges (Tobin, 2001). Its list of engineering firsts includes the deepest underwater connection and the largest slurry wall application in North America, unprecedented ground freezing and tunnel jacking, extensive deep-soil mixing to stabilize Boston's soils, the world's widest cable stayed bridge, a complex fiber-optic cable system, and the largest tunnel ventilation system in the world. This case study[5] describes the introduction of many new practices that resulted in greater integration during a massive and complex program.

Almost 30 years in the making, the front-end planning phase began in the 1970s, the first shovels went in the ground in the early 1990s, and the project was substantially completed in 2007. The program was complicated by the fact that it was staged as a fast-track program, where initiation was beginning on some projects while closure had been achieved on other parts of the program.

The Big Dig, like most large-scale infrastructure programs, grew from a vision of a small group of people who saw a city in need of revitalization. The program had numerous challenges, including working in one of the most congested urban areas in the country, and coordinating more than 132 major work projects, 54 major design packages, thousands of subcontractors, more than 9,000 processes and procedures, and organizing more than 5,000 workers during its peak years of construction. The Big Dig was not always on schedule and budget; however, it did eventually deliver one of the most complex, inner-city tunneling efforts in the world.

The Big Dig program included many individual projects, some of which were very large. The change mechanisms used to create greater integration between the program management and systems engineering functions in this massive and complex entity are applicable in programs of all sizes.

14.6.2 Organizational Structure

The Big Dig was a project-based organization that had a complex governance structure that unfolded over a long period of time and was delivered within a complex stakeholder environment. The program had two major sponsors: the federal Department of Transportation (DOT) and the Commonwealth of Massachusetts through the Massachusetts Highway Department (MHD) and the Massachusetts Turnpike Authority (MTA). In 2009 the MHD and the MTA were merged under a new mega-transportation agency, the Massachusetts Department of Transportation (MassDOT). The sponsors acted as the clients of the private-sector management consultant: the joint venture of Bechtel Parsons Brinckerhoff (B/PB). Bechtel, the Reston, Virginia–based construction and engineering company, has managed an impressive list of programs, including the Washington, D.C. Metro, the Hoover Dam, and the Channel Tunnel. The New York–based firm Parsons Brinckerhoff, also a world leader in transportation infrastructure initiatives, including the New York City subway system, the Taiwan high-speed rail, and the Woodrow Wilson Bridge, had collaborated in joint ventures with Bechtel many times. The two firms' combined expertise in planning, engineering, project controls, and construction management providing the full range of skills necessary to manage large and complex public works initiatives. Since many of the decisions were delegated to the project teams, the two firms played a significant role in the oversight of the workers and in daily decision making requiring full integration of project teams across the organization both horizontally and vertically. Though the overall responsibility for the Big Dig remained with the government sponsors and owners, B/PB was responsible for managing daily operations, including the integrated design and construction program, the integrated scope, schedule, cost and budget, and the program benefits delivery.

Though systems engineering is typically used in the aerospace and defense industries, it is increasingly being used in the civil engineering sector to make complex programs more manageable. Systems engineering was used at the Big Dig to integrate the various components of the 135 major projects in the program and provide a holistic view to the complex engineering systems and requirements. The head of engineering management served both as deputy program manager for the Big Dig organization as well as manager of engineering. This dual role enabled a more comprehensive approach to the problems of integrating large systems involving critical infrastructure and unique design development. The Engineering Management Department consisted of an integrated team of systems integrators and engineers including the Area Managers, the Systems Integration Manager, the Geo Technical Manager, the Chief Structural Engineer, the Urban Design Manager, the Chief Bridge Engineer, the M&E Systems Manager, the Environmental Manager, and the Director of Systems Commissioning, all of whom reported directly to the Deputy Program Manager for Engineering. One of the important roles of systems engineering was analysis of the safety failure modes for all critical infrastructure projects.

Due to the innovative technology, the enormous level of uncertainty, and the potential for catastrophic loss, comprehensive risk management and quality assurance was established and integrated into the program at all levels in a tightly controlled environment. Further, integration was provided by an extensive process of performance review at several levels prior to the acceptance and payment of any contract. This included overall technical compliance with scope and schedule specifications, start-up, testing and test data, and approval activities (Greiman, 2013, p. 136).

Systems integration was essential to ensure that the designers, engineers, management consultants, contractors, and each project owner worked closely together to ensure a collaborative environment and shared mission of quality excellence. A system review process was developed to evaluate compliance to the contract, establish requirements, procedures, and practices, including the review of content, effectiveness of the work product and identity of deficient areas, and opportunities for improvement. Systems engineering included the management of electrical power distribution, integrated project control systems, environmental analysis, traffic surveillance and controls, corrosion control, seismic exposure evaluation, transit of hazardous cargo, geotechnical instrumentation, and the immersed tube tunnel ventilation system.

14.6.3 An Integrated Project Organization

One approach used to cope with the changing needs of the program was to change the project structure from a traditional management model where each project employer operated as a distinct entity to an integrated project organization (IPO)—in essence a program management office. From the inception of the program, engineering management, construction, and program management were integrated at all levels of the IPO. Although the personnel were not formally integrated until 2001, the program processes, procedures, and specifications mandated integration among the engineers, contractors, and project managers. The transition to an IPO at the Big Dig occurred almost seven years after inception of the program during the first year of peak construction, when integration was desperately needed.

Importantly, the integration of B/PB into the MTA program staff required the revision of many processes, which were incorporated in changes to the Resident Engineers Manual (CA/T, 2001). Though integration of teams, sponsors, and management consultants has been widely supported in the literature as an important governance tool, and was recognized as a credible solution at the Big Dig, it has also been criticized on some programs for compromising the independence of the government as a watchdog

(Richards, 2003). Ideally, integrated project organizations should be formed at the early planning phase and then evaluated and monitored for independence and effectiveness throughout the duration of the program.

14.6.4 Integrated Project Teams

Extensive environmental feasibility studies, risk assessments, and other documentation were completed prior to initiation and continued to evolve throughout the program's long life. As noted by the National Academy of Engineering Board on Infrastructure and the Constructed Environment (2003), few infrastructure initiatives have utilized as many innovative tools to control risk and cost as the Big Dig. For example, team members had a shared and common vision of the goals and objectives of the program. The specifications required the project managers to take technical goals into account when prioritizing their tasks or making decisions and, conversely, the systems engineer was required to take management goals into account when prioritizing their tasks or making decisions. Incentives on the Big Dig were based on a shared commitment to achieve high program performance instead of individual performance. As examples of this shared commitment, rewards were given to the team rather than individuals for innovation in various programs including:

- Safety and health risk management (SHARE)
- Contractor quality innovation (Contractor Quality Awards)
- The value engineering and improved construction means and methods program (VECP)

14.6.5 Partnering

One of the most important initiatives for problem solving, conflict resolution, and the reduction of tension on the Big Dig was through the partnering process. The concept of "partnering" was first utilized by DuPont Engineering on a large-scale construction project in the mid-1980s, and the U.S. Army Corps of Engineers was the first public agency to use partnering in its construction projects. Partnering is now widely used by numerous government and construction entities around the world. It involves an agreement in principle to share risk and to establish and promote partnership relationships. On the Big Dig, partnerships were used to improve schedule adherence, quality, safety, and performance, as well as to reduce risk, costs, claims, disputes, and litigation.

Partnering at the Big Dig was initially implemented in 1992, primarily on construction contracts, but its success in construction later led to its use in design contracts, community groups, and the development of internal and interagency partnerships. Almost 100 partnerships existed on the Big Dig based on contract values ranging from US$4 million to a half a billion. Though partnering is not always contractually required, on the Big Dig it was included in all construction contracts with durations of at least one year and a value of US$1 million or more (Daigle & Merlino, 1998). Partnering sessions were held on a regular basis to discuss the needs of the program, to resolve problems, and to improve controls. Partnering included leadership training, seminars, executive meetings, and other activities. The federal and state government officials and the contractor's project management team met regularly with an independent expert to assist in developing a single, integrated team. Through sharing knowledge, risk, and liability, partnering reduced the cost of contractor claims, increased the number of value-engineering savings proposals, and helped keep component projects on schedule.

14.6.6 Discussion

The integration of systems engineering functions and program management at the Big Dig enabled the technical and program decision makers to make more informed and consequently better decisions. Leadership across all disciplines was involved as component projects by their very nature were interdisciplinary. Decision making engaged many views and perceptions across the entire program from engineering and construction to project approvals and operations. A key to successful integration was the development of broad-based relationships and partnerships developed during the initiation stage of the effort. This fostered collaboration throughout the life of the program to make sure that the intended benefits of the program were delivered and sustained.

Organizational cohesion and organizational learning were strengthened through integrated risk and quality assurance, as well as a multilayered performance review process. An IPO was eventually adopted to unite engineering, construction, and program management. This extended to integrated project teams where project managers and systems engineers were held mutually accountable for each other's goals. The integration efforts were extended to include a "partnering process" that enabled positive and forward-looking problem solving and conflict resolution processes to reduce tensions amongst the program partners.

The actions taken in this example to increase integration included:

- Giving leaders shared roles (e.g., the engineering manager/deputy program manager) to encourage an integrated perspective.
- Directing project managers and engineers to work to shared goals with specific direction to take into account the other disciplines' perspective in decisions.
- Introducing an IPO and integrated team structures.
- Establishing comprehensive risk management and quality assurance integrated into the component projects.
- Integrating performance reviews that included overall technical compliance with scope and schedule specifications, start-up, testing and test data, and approval activities at several levels prior to the acceptance and payment of any contract.
- Providing rewards to the team rather than to individuals for innovation.
- Creating partnering provisions in contracts and having periodic partnering sessions to provide common awareness across the program.

14.7 Summary

These vignettes illustrate the development and implementation of actions to bring higher levels of integration between core engineering and management functions in organizations. They all employed practices and methods found in the Integration Framework and illustrate how those are implemented through change efforts. They also demonstrate that there is no "one-size-fits-all" approach to orchestrating successful change in engineering program organizations: At the very least, every situation is different, every organization is different, and every change pursues a different set of benefits.

In the first vignette, the challenge was the repeated technical failure of complex systems in a new and challenging technology area. The need for change was clear and urgent with each successive and costly mission failure and the inability of the program to deliver any tangible benefits. The implementation of a rigorous technical process by defining and integrating the chief systems engineer into the program organization structure provided essential information to the program management to improve the quality of decisions and coordination across the entire program. The program manager was therefore better able to understand and influence technical issues, including those at the subcontractor level. Mission success rates improved dramatically, and the organization demonstrated sustained change by the continued use of the practices by diffusing them into follow-on programs and through their impact on the development of the workforce.

In the second vignette, the challenge was a workforce that had limited exposure to and understanding of project and program management and systems engineering, but whose roles required that both be performed effectively. By widely deploying a multi-tiered training and certification process through a project management office and, eventually, a centralized training organization that crossed agency boundaries, professionals were able to gradually improve not only their understanding and skills associated with program management and systems engineering, but also tailor their application in their own programs and projects. The appreciation and application of both program management and systems engineering practices increased substantially as a result of the training.

In the third vignette, a specific software development method, Agile, was being applied, but with outcomes widely ranging from unquestioned success to disappointment. The cause was determined to be a misalignment between the program management organization and the technical functions. The company embarked on a number of change initiatives managed through an existing Lean Six Sigma improvement program infrastructure in the organization to transform how software was developed, including the roles and expectations of all those involved in the process, a focus on technical excellence and process discipline including definition of standard work, the development of a new mindset around collaboration and interaction, and the application of new metrics to evaluate performance. Not only did the quality and productivity improve significantly, but also the engagement of the employees and the climate of collaboration between management and technical functions was markedly improved and sustained as a result.

In the fourth vignette, company strategy required a new level of operating performance from the engineering organization. This translated into a division-wide formal change program that played out through a number of change projects. Top-down, large-scale transformation projects tackled strategic, central themes. Bottom-up initiatives provided processes and methods for enhancing value creation by individuals and teams. An outreach program encouraged participation by each member of the organization to achieve a new mindset around collaboration. Engineering productivity improved dramatically, but importantly the company avoided disruption during the global economic crisis, expanded its product line with no additional resources, and was able to achieve its strategic objectives.

In the fifth vignette, the technical and organizational complexity of the program meant that many of its core projects could not have been successful without using a more integrated operating approach. The program increased integration through the implementation of joint roles, integrated risk and quality assurance programs, and multilayered performance review processes. An integrated project organization structure was implemented, which was extended to integrated project teams where project managers and systems engineers were held mutually accountable for each other's goals. These approaches were extended to program partners as well. The success of the initial application of these approaches was so compelling that they were eventually applied across most aspects of the program.

These vignettes were selected because they demonstrate a diverse set of challenges and approaches to improving integration and collaboration across management and technical functions, and across different business sectors and settings. Across the vignettes, one sees significant differences in the degree of urgency to complete the change, the scope of the change effort, and the path taken. Nevertheless, each illustrates a deliberate, systematic approach to improving elements of integration in each organization. In some cases, the efforts were formally designated as change and improvement programs within the organization with commensurate status and resources. The specific objectives and elements of each effort were tailored to address the specific challenges the organization faced; but, nevertheless, some elements of the Integration Framework can be seen in all the cases. All demonstrate how these principles were successfully applied across a range of organizational and program settings.

14.8 Discussion Questions

1. Which vignette best relates the challenges to integration that you have experienced in your own workplace? What specific elements of the vignette are most relevant to your situation?

2. Which elements of the Integration Framework did you see employed most frequently in the vignettes? Were there any noteworthy missing examples where one or more of the principles was not applied?

3. Imagine that you have been asked to investigate options for improving the integration of program management and systems engineering in your organization.

Pick one of the vignettes as a model for the challenges before your organization. Identify the following:

a. What is the general situation of the organization and the particular integration challenge you face?

b. What principle(s) of integration would you propose applying to resolve the challenge? What aspects of this book can be used where?

c. How would you approach the implementation of these integration principles into your organization?

d. What challenges to implementation would you expect to encounter, both in the near term and the longer term?

14.9 References

Board on Infrastructure and the Constructed Environment. (2003). *Completing the Big Dig: Managing the final stages of Boston's Central Artery/Tunnel Project*. National Academy of Engineering, National Research Council, Transportation Research Board of the National Academies (National Academy), Committee for Review of the Project Management Practices Employed on the Boston Central Artery/Tunnel ("Big Dig"). Washington, DC: National Academies Press.

Central Artery/Tunnel Project (CA/T). (2001). *Revisions to resident engineer's manual*. Boston: Massachusetts Turnpike Authority.

Daigle, M. G., & Merlino, D. (1998). *Central Artery Tunnel Project Partnering Manual*. Boston: Massachusetts Highway Department.

Dweck, C. (2006). *Mindset: The new psychology of success*. New York: Random House.

Forsberg, K., Mooz, H., & Cotterman, H. (1996). *Visualizing project management*. Hoboken, NJ: John Wiley & Sons.

Greiman, V. (2013). *Megaproject management: Lessons on risk and project management from the Big Dig*. Hoboken, NJ: John Wiley & Sons.

International Council on Systems Engineering (INCOSE). (2015). *Systems engineering handbook: A guide for system life cycle processes and activities* (4th ed.). D. Walden, G. Roedler, K. Forsberg, R. Hamelin, T. Shortell (Eds.). Hoboken, NJ: John Wiley & Sons.

Project Management Institute (PMI). (2013). *A guide to the project management body of knowledge (PMBOK® Guide)* (5th ed.). Newtown Square, PA: Author.

Richards, M. (2003). Massachusetts Organization of State Engineers and Scientists (MOSES). Testimony before the Massachusetts State Legislature. Boston, MA.

Tobin, J. (2001). *Great projects: The epic story of the building of America, from the taming of the Mississippi to the invention of the Internet*. New York: Free Press.

Endnotes

1. Contributed by Stanley I. Weiss, consulting professor at Stanford University, University of California-Davis, Delft University of Technology, and National University of Singapore.

2. Contributed by Michael O'Brochta, President of Zozer, Inc.

3. Contributed by Tom Paider, Associate Vice President, IT Build Capability and Guru Vasudeva, Senior Vice President & CIO of Application & Data Services at Nationwide.

4. Contributed by Eric Rebentisch, Research Associate at the Massachusetts Institute of Technology and Josef Oehmen, Associate Professor at Technical University of Denmark. (Adapted from A Case Study on the Transformation of the Engineering Organization at BMW 2006-2012, Version 2.0. Massachusetts Institute of Technology, 2013. Copyright and all rights reserved. Material from this publication has been reproduced with the permission of MIT.)

5. Contributed by Virginia Greiman, Professor of Megaprojects and Planning at Boston University.

15

LEADING AN INTEGRATION CHANGE PROGRAM

15.1 Introduction

Having reviewed a number of the organizational challenges related to integrating program management and systems engineering, and read about the benefits, target outcomes, and efficiencies that can be realized from integrating these two disciplines, one may wonder how this can be directly applied and achieved in fast-moving, rapidly changing organizations. This chapter looks closely into the change management aspects of the effort to integrate program management and systems engineering; considers the unique characteristics of the change initiative required to achieve an integrated environment; and provides key guidance for leading such an initiative within a variety of organizational settings. This chapter references, elaborates, and expands upon the Integration Framework for program management and systems engineering described in Chapter 6 and illustrated in Figure 6-1. Chapter 13 serves as a starting point for the organizational change management thinking that must be present before, during, and after the execution of the integration program.

Before beginning, it may be beneficial to clarify the use of the terms "leader" and "organization" as presented in this chapter. Leaders are not only those who lead and direct the enterprise as a whole, but include component leaders, those who oversee a large share of an organization's resources such as finance, operations, product development, or division, region, and sector leaders. In this context, because they also influence, lead, and direct a large percentage of the organization's resources, program managers and chief systems engineers are included in this group. To differentiate them in the discussion, their roles are called out specifically. Organizational leaders will be qualified as such; systems engineers and program managers will be referred to collectively as program leaders, or identified in their specific roles.

The use of the term "organization" includes the concept that programs are organizations as well, and can function as unique, identifiable entities within the enterprise. With this in mind, references to "organization" refer to the enterprise as well as the individual programs underway within the enterprise.

15.2 Understanding the Work Ahead: The Organizational Context

Whether discussing a small business, a large multinational firm, a nonprofit, or a government organization, the foundational components and approach to implementing change remains surprisingly consistent. For instance, the framework and communications plans required for a change initiative within a small business are essentially the same as the framework and communications plans for a large, multinational organization, though the scale and the methods for performing these activities differ. Specifics such as identifying stakeholders and stakeholder groups and engaging them in the change process; determining stakeholder level of influence and authority; developing tailored communications to meet their specialized needs; and developing processes to deliver communications employing the most appropriate method, mode, and frequency will be composed of fundamentally the same elements regardless of the organization size or industry. Each will be tailored to meet the needs of the organization they serve, while the core elements remain functionally the same.

15.2.1 Managing Organizational Change

Whether the cause for concern has its roots in issues surfaced through interactions with employees, managers, senior managers, or executives, or perhaps from communication with external stakeholders, by the time business leaders begin seeking meaningful alternatives and solutions, the challenging issues that first inspired their investigative research have likely already taken a toll, leaving a significant and lasting impact on at least one part of the organization. It is this realization that causes the leader to act—responding with an increased sense of urgency. This realization that "something must be done" also places the leader in a difficult position. Suddenly becoming aware that "something within the organization must change" implies the notion that subtle, or in some cases obvious, signals that indicated the need for organizational change had been missed or misinterpreted at some point along the way.

When this occurs, it is important for the leader to pause and ponder the proper way forward. Leaders must carefully choose an approach for addressing change that will more likely foster success than failure, and must stand firm in the face of considerable organizational resistance in their commitment to achieve it. Additionally, to be successful at bringing about meaningful and lasting change, leaders must look forward toward positive structural change for the organization using facts and information about the existing conditions as a starting point while resisting the impulse to impose hastily conceived solutions, refraining from pushing for quick resolution, or looking backward into the current state seeking to identify the party or parties to whom responsibility for the existing troubled conditions can be assigned. As Pamela Erskine (2013) describes in her book *ITIL and Organizational Change*:

> [S]ome organizations foster such [negative] behavior by allowing leaders to blame team members, while failing to recognize a pattern which may relate to a leadership issue. Without accountability at the highest levels of the change initiative, it will be difficult to truly realize the desired outcomes.

Finding and assigning blame for organizational difficulty will not contribute to the creation of an atmosphere for change within the organization. In fact, doing so has quite the opposite effect. Assigning blame serves only to undermine the change leader, build mistrust, and silence open, creative problem solving; often driving team members away from seeking a more positive environment.

15.2.2 Selecting the Appropriate Way Forward

In response to the need for effective change, leaders will follow one of two similar but unique paths. One path is based on a decision to contract with outside consultants and experts who will be brought into the organization to identify key improvement opportunities, then design and lead the necessary organizational change. The alternate route is the selection of change agents and champions from within the organization who will be empowered to create the environment for change and will deliver on a commitment to make it happen. Selection of the latter path is based on the knowledge or an assumption that the necessary vision and talent is available within the organization.

It is important to note here that the individuals chosen to lead organizational change are vitally important to the overall success of the effort. Leading an active organization through transformational change is a complex and challenging initiative. A cultural change program, such as an initiative to integrate program management and systems engineering, will be elaborated within and across the organization over an extended period of time. These types of efforts are most often measured in years rather than months. The selection of change leaders for initiatives such as these, therefore, must be performed with studied and deliberate care. The leaders chosen for these initiatives must be perceived by stakeholders as inspirational, influential, persuasive, dynamic, and effective, or they face serious challenge leading the organization through difficult and extended transformational change.

Whether selecting change leaders from within or bringing them to the organization from the outside, both paths come with a unique set of benefits and challenges; a single aspect makes the selection of one over the other an important leadership decision—the sustainment of achieved improvements beyond the close of the program. Bringing consultants to an organization may accelerate initial progress toward the intended outcomes; however, consultants rarely remain with the organization to implement proposed changes and manage the sustainment of benefits. This means that a significant effort must be put into planning, performing, and monitoring the transition of change ownership and sustainment of benefits from the consultants to the leadership and employees of the organization (Kotter, 2012). Choosing change leaders and champions from within the organization may initially appear to be a slower approach as the organization orients itself to new leadership models, elevates and accepts new individual leaders, and clarifies the work ahead. As the change program progresses, however, the natural evolution and acceptance of new process norms requires little, if any, transition as the organization's structure and practice have already been prepared during the change program for ongoing benefits ownership and sustainment. The important difference is the near elimination of the transition effort for managing and sustaining improvements and benefits.

Selecting the most appropriate approach for integrating program management and systems engineering functions is derived from careful analysis of the existing organizational culture, structure, norms, and leadership. Whatever the case, either approach requires the committed involvement of the organization's leaders over an extended period of time (PMI, 2013a), as well as the steady hand of the chief systems engineer and program manager who will guide the organization's navigation through a number of important organizational change-enabling and transformational activities. Moreover, establishing and tracking a clear set of target benefits will provide direction and focus to the effort.

In the end, whether the organization chooses to implement change by calling upon experts from outside or draws upon leaders and change agents from within, many of the benefits of the change initiative may not be fully recognized or realized until after the conclusion of the program. Most importantly, real evidence of the impact of the organizational change will be seen in the ongoing and sustained operation of the organization. Certainly, there will be tangible improvements along the way while small wins and changes take hold, but true evidence of the success of a significant organizational change is witnessed in the day-to-day activities, culture, and performance of the organization over time (Garvin & Roberto, 2005). Is there a "new norm" for the way the organization operates—in its communications, practices, culture, and overall performance? Examples of observable changes include answers to the following questions:

- Are senior leaders typically engaged in supporting change activities—do they take on change-champion roles?
- How are decisions made 12 months after the close of the program? Are decisions collaboratively developed or has the organization reverted to the technical and program assignment for authority? How is authority and influence shared?
- Are the change leader, systems engineering, and program management roles clear and in use within the organization?
- How do systems engineers and program managers collaborate on work activities— are there fewer contentious arguments? How do these leaders resolve conflicts?
- How are ambiguity and uncertainty handled?
- How are missed targets dealt with and managed by the team?
- Do program team members typically and naturally conduct business and interact with each other in ways that are recognizably different from the way they conducted business prior to the change effort? Would the "old ways" of interacting, working, and conducting business seem foreign and unusual now? If not, then perhaps there is more work to do.

15.3 Planning for Change within the Organizational Context

The following sections examine the organizational context for implementing the Integration Framework for program management and systems engineering, elaborate the foundation upon which a change program will stand; and detail a five-part, success-enabling approach to implementing such a program. The sections highlight examples of successful and not-so-successful organizational change, specifically underscoring learnings and guidance, including an additional framework focused on meaningful measurements that allow one to bring about the successful integration of program management and systems engineering practice within organizations.

In the following discussion, organizational leaders within a fictitious organization have recognized that something is amiss. Defects and rework are a standard component of day-to-day operations. Throughput improvements seem to be slow in coming, product advancement is lagging, and there is a constant hum of discord between program management and systems engineering functions. Territorial battles for authority over strategic program direction and sophisticated technical decisions seem to be an accepted way of doing business, requiring regular executive intervention. These conditions have caught the attention of organization and program leadership, and they are eager to do something to improve the situation.

Embarking on an effort to integrate program management and systems engineering within a currently active organization is not a simple or trivial exercise. First and foremost, organizational leaders as well as program management and systems engineering leadership must recognize that this program, like any other program underway within the organization, is important to the organization's well-being and requires the same focused attention and commitment as other benefits-producing initiatives. A program designed to create change within an active organization can be as challenging as any program undertaken to produce complex products, systems, or components. If this is the case, where must the leaders responsible for the change program's target objectives begin?

Before answering that question, it will be helpful to clarify the makeup of the small leadership team that will be referred to over the remainder of the chapter. To be most effective, the change leadership team is typically composed of:

- **Executive Sponsor.** A member of the organization's executive team, this individual will be seen as the ultimate organizational champion for the initiative to integrate program management and systems engineering within the organization.
- **Program Manager.** The program manager will be charged with oversight and leadership of the change initiative from inception through conclusion and transition to those who will be responsible for sustainment of the outcomes, processes, and benefits generated by the program.
- **Systems Engineering Domain Leader(s).** The systems engineering domain leader brings deep technical experience and expertise to the program team, representing the organization's broad systems engineering environment. This individual is intimately aware of the typical interaction between systems engineering resources and other organizational entities including program managers, leads the systems engineering landscape across the organization, and can speak to the day-to-day operational culture of the organization's engineering resources. This individual is typically the most senior systems engineering executive present in the organization. In large and highly complex engineering organizations, this role may be represented by more than one individual if those systems engineering functions

are separate and uniquely grouped, such as mechanical, electrical, structural, and so on.

- **Program Management Domain Leader(s).** Program management domain leaders bring the unique challenges of business program leadership experience from across the organization to the leadership team. As in the case of the systems engineering domain leaders, individuals in this role are familiar with the day-to-day interactions of program managers and can accurately and fully represent the body of program management thinking from across the organization.
- **Governance Body.** These leaders are typically executive, decision-making members of the change program's governance team where they are joined by other organizational leaders who include partners and internal and external stakeholders. The governance team supports and guides the program and determines which program components (activities, projects, operational work) will be initiated, supported, modified, or retired. Extensive literature is available regarding the function and makeup of the governance team. Three informative references are *The Standard for Program Management* (PMI, 2013b), *Program Management* (Thiry, 2015), and *Governance of Portfolios, Programs, and Projects: A Practice Guide* (PMI, 2016).

15.3.1 Observing and Interviewing

To begin, if there is a suspicion among leaders that "something is amiss," and specifically that program management and systems engineering are not working together as well as they might, it may not be sufficient or effective for organizational leaders to simply act on that suspicion—implementing hastily conceived solutions intended to resolve whatever perceived issues there may be. When this does occur, frequently those impacted by top-down attempts such as these will ignore or reject the imposed solutions, sometimes immediately, sometimes after a trial period, citing leadership's lack of understanding of the "real" issues, or perhaps holding to a belief that leadership may be making changes to satisfy their own specific agenda or other "hidden" issues.

To be successful, those responsible for conducting the proposed integration program must be willing to invest the time necessary (Sirkin, Keenan, & Jackson, 2005) to fully assess the environment, and to establish, without bias or agenda, the true conditions and source of the trouble. This is a particularly important activity, for it allows the organization to step back from day-to-day operations to view the organization as an integrated whole, a living, functioning system made up of individuals and groups who are performing against the tasks before them. Additionally, the perceptions and strongly held beliefs that are illuminated and documented through observation can be used to form the baseline from which the program will be initiated. Documented observations will become particularly valuable when considering the metrics, measures, and indices that will be used to gauge the program's progress and success. This aspect is discussed at length in Section 15.3.5.

As the initial step of the program, observing day-to-day operations and talking with (interviewing) program leaders, stakeholders, team members, and other staff will have an additional immediate benefit—engagement. Speaking with program participants and listening intently while documenting their perceptions will let them know there is a serious attempt under way to fully understand the issues they face and will engage them in the definition of the problem long before there is an attempt to solve it.

Whether the effort is led by outside consultants or by leaders from within the organization, there must be a concerted attempt by all responsible parties to resist jumping to an early solution. The weakness of swiftly assessed problems and hastily implemented solutions is immediately sensed by the organization's employees as well as the program's team members and stakeholders. Engaging program leaders, team members, stakeholders, and staff in the definition of the organization's challenges will serve a number of functions. Approaching the challenge in this way will:

- Communicate that team members and stakeholders have a voice in defining the "real" issues.
- Surface the true state of the environment and the sentiment of those working within it.
- (May) uncover issues that were previously missed or misunderstood.
- Establish a clear baseline of conditions that will be used to focus the integration program's change management and process improvement activities.
- Signal that the initiative will not be based on a quick appraisal by a distant authority who will impose unstudied solutions on stakeholders.

Figure 15-1 illustrates the specific area of the Integration Framework addressed by observation and interviews with program management and systems engineering staff.

As an example, the research (Conforto, Rossi, Rebentisch, Oehmen, & Pacenza, 2013) suggests the definition of roles for the program manager and chief systems engineer are often not formally defined within organizations. Inquiring about the clarity of roles is a good place to begin observations and interviews. This issue serves as an example of the approach recommended for observation, discussion, and interviews that will address any and all issues for the organization.

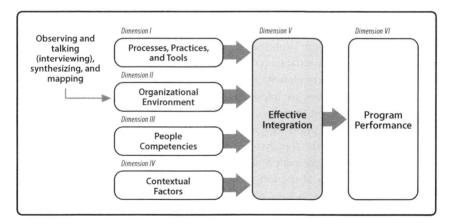

Figure 15-1: The dimension of the Integration Framework in view for initial engagement activities

The bulleted list of questions that follows is a nonexhaustive set of questions one may ask about the clarity of the program management and chief systems engineering roles.

- What is the *degree of clarity* that you perceive regarding the scope and authority of the program management role on your program? Of the chief systems engineering role in your program?
- Are both program management and systems engineering roles given equal support by leadership?
- Do you believe the program manager and chief systems engineer agree on the roles and responsibilities they each occupy?
- To what degree do the program manager and chief systems engineer collaborate on technical and nontechnical decisions that affect the program and your function?
- If there is conflict between the program manager and chief systems engineer, to what degree do you believe that conflict is based on the current definition and delineation of the program management and systems engineering roles rather than particular traits, behaviors, or characteristics of the individuals within them?
- Is there agreement among team members about recent decisions that have been made regarding the program?
- Is there agreement among other stakeholders about recent decisions that have been made regarding the program?
- Has the program manager or chief systems engineer explained the measures and metrics that are used to gauge the program's progress?
- If you had a magic wand that you could wave and one key aspect of the program would instantly improve, what would that be?

Responses to these and other questions and related information reflect the type of information that is collected and documented for use in developing the alternatives discussed in the next section.

15.3.2 Synthesizing, Sharing, and Mapping

The discussions may be directed at very specific program components and may address topics that are very different from the example presented above, or may be broad in scope and address concerns that span the entire program such as overall program communications or program component authorization. Regardless of the subject areas the observations and interviews are intended to address, the information must be tied to elements of the Integration Framework so the relevant issues can be easily articulated, grouped, communicated, prioritized, and, ultimately, understood.

Figure 15-2 presents the framework elements that must be present to achieve an integrated program management and systems engineering environment where the recognized characteristics of the program are: effective collaborative work, effective information sharing, and rapid and effective decision making.

The sample question set inquired about the perceived clarity of roles, responsibilities, and decision-making authority for the program management and systems engineering functions. This information is grouped and aligned with the key content in the

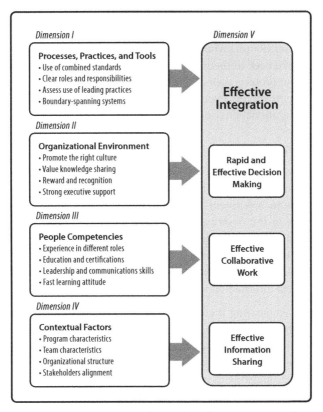

Figure 15-2: The four input dimensions that influence the effective integration dimension

processes, practices, and tools of the framework and represents an important element of the baseline that will be established for the change program itself. Other aspects of the processes, practices, and tools dimension could include tools and methods used in the program to deliver the benefits and may range from information infrastructure to analysis tools, and physical to virtual in nature.

15.3.2.1 Synthesizing

Various observations, interviews, and collected information can be grouped and aligned to one of the four framework dimensions shown on the left side of the Integration Framework, which leads to the effective integration dimension shown on the right.

When the observations, collected discussions, and interview information have been grouped, summarized, and aligned to the framework, the next step is to share the information with the various leaders and staff who contributed to the discussion.

This must be a delicately executed and carefully performed task, for it is the first step in generating trust for the change program and the people conducting it. The collected and summarized information will ultimately be shared broadly across the organization as a significant component of the baselining activity. Those who volunteer information through discussion and interview must feel the information accurately represents their views and perceptions. They must also believe the information will not be used to punish nor will it be used to discredit strongly held views and beliefs of the contributors. Contributors who volunteer information will likely expect to see this information reflected back to them in ways that accurately represent their comments and perceptions, but protects their anonymity and does not call them out individually or make reference to specific events. This aligns to Dimension II of the Integration Framework: Organizational Environment.

15.3.2.2 Sharing

Before sharing broadly, the collected information should be characterized as a set of objective conditions that can be seen as a reflection of the organization as a whole rather than an indictment of specific people, organizational components, or events. The intent of the observations, discussions, and interviews is to develop a set of de-identified comments and perceptions that form a generalized "statement of condition" for the organization, and to build trust within the organization that honest and direct feedback can be shared without the threat of sanction or fear of retaliation. Sharing the collected information serves many purposes during program start-up:

- **Validation.** First, sharing the collected information with those who provided it ensures that the observations, comments, and views collected and summarized are accurate. Honest feedback must be validated with those who originally contributed it before it is used for any other purpose. During this validation process, if modification and adjustments are necessary, those adjustments must be made and again validated before the information is shared more broadly. If differences remain between what individuals believe they have shared and what they see reflected back to them either directly or indirectly, there will be resistance to future attempts to engage them. This resistance may be rooted in a perception that the information is being used for a purpose other than what was stated and whether that perception is accurate or not (or if the differences are intentional or not), the facts will not matter. If this validation is not performed and differences remain, significant and lasting damage to the program will have been done.
- **Trust.** Sharing the information with the original contributors validates the information and demonstrates that the feedback will be used exclusively for the purpose of setting the organizational baseline and not as a vehicle for imposing sanctions and controls. This step also helps build trust between those who are collecting and summarizing information and leading the program and those who will participate in and be affected by the integration process. Creating trust is a cornerstone activity for the change program and its leaders, and must be kept in focus by the program manager, the chief systems engineer, and the organization's leadership. The change program's success or failure will balance on the degree of trust built and sustained between the change program's leaders and those who will participate in it.
- **Engagement.** Most importantly, sharing the information with the original contributors will engage them in the problem definition process and will set the tone for further dialog in the future. Clear, open, and honest communication among and across the program's participants is essential for the ongoing success of the program.

15.3.2.3 Mapping

After final review and acceptance by the original participants, the integration program's leaders will map the grouped and summarized information to the various dimensions of the Integration Framework. Linking issues identified through observation, discussion, and interview to dimensions of the framework will ground future discussions in a formal structure that will facilitate communications and will allow the organization to review, study, question, and "make sense" of the information as it is presented to them. This mapped information will make up the content for the initial communications and discussions held with the organizational leaders, program sponsors, program participants, and stakeholders.

15.3.3 Communications Planning: Presenting and Prioritizing Alternatives

Before embarking on an initiative that will bring about significant change to an organization such as an initiative to integrate program management and systems engineering, it will be important for the entire organization to understand the issues it faces as clearly as a few select individuals see them. Numerous failure scenarios have been documented where one part of an organization determined a significant organizational change was necessary and went about implementing change without communicating with and engaging other affected components of the organization.

In one example, organizational leaders from a multinational telecommunications company concluded it would be more efficient and financially advantageous to centralize all human resources and administrative operations. This meant that regional human resources and administrative support groups would have to relinquish current processes, methods, and systems that had been developed over many years to meet the needs of their existing local organizations, requiring them to adopt the central organization's "standard" processes while agreeing to tailor these processes only slightly for their local environments. This decision was made and implemented by the organization's four global business unit directors and appeared to have real merit when reviewed on paper. Unfortunately, these leaders misunderstood the impact of such a decision—misreading the very real likelihood of disruption to day-to-day operations. Additionally, they failed to clearly articulate the reasons behind their move, the intended benefits, or the processes that would be followed to make the change. This leadership team spent little time creating a shared sense of urgency within the organization about the need for change, claiming the need for centralization was "obvious to everyone." It was not. In addition to this, these leaders skipped the important initial step of engaging employees in discussion of the change and ignored or discounted valid protests from members of regional teams outside the headquarters organization. There were few influential members across the organization that supported this decision, most dutifully following what they believed to be failed and ill-conceived directives while quietly (and correctly) anticipating doom. The ensuing chaos not only stalled human resources and administrative functions across the enterprise, all organizational components that relied on human resources and administrative functions were affected, including sales, product development, service, and support. After 60 days, the initiative was brought to an abrupt halt by the organization's chief executive. Three of the four regional leaders were released over the next 60 days. It took nearly 16 months for the organization to recover.

To properly ground an important change initiative within an organization, those empowered to make it happen, including program management and systems engineering leaders, must do more than they believe they should do to ensure that the organization fully understands the need for the change. And they must equally communicate the consequences that will likely accompany inaction. To quote Sirkin, Keenan, and Jackson (2005), "when you feel you are talking-up a change initiative at least three times more than you need to, your managers will feel you are backing the transformation." With this statement in mind, individuals may wonder how, as members of the organization's leadership team, a program manager or chief systems engineer might go about communicating the need for change.

Having done the homework described in Section 15.3.1, organizational leaders are now prepared to embark on a broad communications campaign within the organization. This step addresses the first two of five key change-enabling activities: *Creating a sense of urgency*; and *Communicating the vision and alternatives*. Using John Kotter's (2012) eight-step change process as a starting point, one can group the steps into five foundational change-enabling activities as shown in Figure 15-3. Initial communications about the change program will be designed to address these first two elements.

As an organization prepares these first communications, the program's sponsors and leaders must acknowledge that all the work will not be accomplished in a single, sweeping action—and must design the communications as well as the program itself to address a set of prioritized program elements that will be addressed over time. Following prioritization, the program will begin with the most obvious, most beneficial, and, in some cases, easiest first. The prioritization process is further discussed in Section 15.3.5; however, the concept is highlighted here because it must be an element of the initial communications. If program stakeholders, including the organization's employees, perceive they will be asked to take on a virtual "mountain" of corrective actions, processes, and additional work over and above their day-to-day responsibilities, the mental image this creates can make it difficult for the organization's leaders to get beyond the first few communications without serious resistance.

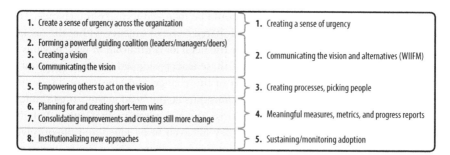

Figure 15-3: John Kotter's (2012) eight-step change process grouped into five change-enabling activities

There are a number of elements organizational leaders, including the program managers and chief systems engineers, must consider when planning how they will communicate what has been gathered about the current state of the organization. These include:

- **Leadership.** Selecting the right leader(s) who will deliver communications.
- **Delivery methods.** Selecting appropriate communications methods and modes such as stand-up presentations, round-table discussions, leadership "road shows," discussion forums, live training sessions, video presentations, email messages, published FAQs, a transformation program website, support center or help functions, progress tracking, and so on.
- **Messaging.** Refining the messaging to create a sense of urgency and communicate the forward-looking vision. Figure 15-4 is an example of the content to include in the messaging.
- **Frequency of communications.** Answer questions about the frequency of communications; define how often leaders deliver communications; how often others deliver communications; clarify who will deliver which communications.
- **Audience.** Anticipating and answering key question from stakeholders and employees such as those shown in Figure 15-5.

Creating a sense of urgency requires that communications are factual, accurate, and easily understood. Not everyone will be convinced, but the dual activities of establishing and reinforcing a trusting environment for communications and sharing unvarnished "truths" about the current conditions will begin laying the groundwork for more difficult activities ahead. There are two essential components of this communication: a detailed explanation of what is anticipated if no action is taken, and a high level "vision" of what the future can look like for the organization with a call to action.

Messaging Content

 These two lead to creating a sense of urgency:
- "These are current conditions"
- "This is what will happen if we don't act now"

 These lead to creating the vision:
- "To be successful, we will need everyone involved"
- "This is what success looks like"
- "We will prioritize the work"
- "We will measure and report progress openly"
- "When things don't go right, we will regroup, reevaluate, reprioritize, and move on"
- "We will reward achievement of target objectives"

Figure 15-4: Example of the messaging content

Audience Questions to Answer

- What's In It for Me? (WIIFM).
- How does this affect my work?
- What will you be doing and what will I have to do?
- Who else (which other organizations) will be part of the program?
- Is this in addition to what I'm already doing?
- How long will it take?
- What will happen if I don't go along with the plan?
- Will performance evaluation measures and systems be modified to reflect this?

Figure 15-5: Example of questions for which the audience will want answers

Referencing the scenario described earlier and using it as an example, information about the impact of these conditions must be gathered, articulated, and presented.

- **Defects and rework are a standard component of day-to-day operations.** The obvious impact to product quality, reliability, and sale-ability can be charted. Declining sales, increasing support costs, and increased overall production costs can be documented, graphed, and presented. Negative internal, employee-related metrics can also be linked to this condition where employee turnover increases, personal time off increases, documented complaints and challenges are on the rise, and so on.

- **Throughput improvements seem to be slow in coming, product advancement is lagging.** This is a serious condition and can be directly related to the organization's market position. An industry-leading organization does everything it can to avoid having its market share deteriorate. Lagging product advancement opens the door to competition and renders the organization vulnerable. This can be anticipated and the assumptions of the impact to the organization can be graphed in trend-lines with surprising, and sometimes frightening accuracy. The organization can ensure that the data used to create the trends are accurate, and can produce the data itself to reinforce this communication. Then, if there is a belief that the trends reflect a reasonable estimation of the future, the obvious impact to the organization is beyond refute.

- **There is a constant hum of discord between program management and systems engineering functions.** To highlight this issue, overall program performance is measured, detailed, and factually communicated. The impact of this type of disagreement can lead to extended schedules, incorrectly interpreted requirements, poorly derived solutions, flawed designs, and, ultimately, product failures.

Communicating detailed information such as this paints a stark and dismal picture for an organization. That is why it is particularly important for messages of this sort to be accompanied by a vision for a different future and a high-level plan for achieving it. Moreover, upon seeing and hearing this message, a majority of the organization's employees must perceive, or beyond that, believe, that there is a better future ahead, and must also feel they can be a meaningful part of creating that future. It will be the primary challenge of the organization's leaders to share this type of information in a way that enables a clear-minded understanding of the conditions while drawing a balance between the concerns and fear this communication creates and the energy and commitment for a different future that can be demonstrated in words and deeds. In their Harvard Business Review article, *Change Through Persuasion*, David A. Garvin and Michael Roberto (2005) describe an example of how one individual turned a failing merger between two leading hospitals into a rousing success, artfully creating a balance between a sense of urgency, value for the employees, and a new, better future for the merged organization.

Regardless of the size of the program or the organization, these communications elements must be carefully put in place before communications begin. In addition, change champions, those who will be visible representatives of the organization's commitment to support the program through to the end and who will lead the program through the entire duration of the effort, should be clearly identified and afforded as much authority to act as can be reasonably bestowed on the organization's most senior leaders.

15.3.4 Leaders and Decision Makers: Their Required Commitment and Involvement

Organizational communications are accomplished through verbal and nonverbal means. Most organizations focus on written, spoken, and visual communications and often ignore the behavior aspects of communication. Elaborate presentations and written communications are often prepared for the organization and are shared through emails, videos, discussions, training sessions, and live presentations. Organizational leaders, however, frequently downplay, misinterpret, or misunderstand the message that is delivered by the selection of the "who" of the communications. In organizational communications, employees can be quite perceptive and quick to assess a mismatch between words and deeds. For example, an urgent, impactful, organization-spanning message delivered by individuals who are perceived by the organization's employees as noninfluencers and nondecision makers, communicates that the urgency and importance of the message does not align with the actual behavior of the organization's leaders. If the issues being discussed are urgent and critically important to the organization's future and success, would not such a message be delivered by the organization's top leaders? In communicating key messages, selecting the right people to champion and deliver communications can be as important as—and in some cases more important than—the message itself.

As stated earlier, the commitment of organizational leaders to long-term engagement is critical to the success of a change program designed to integrate program management and systems engineering. With this in mind, securing various organizational leaders' commitment to the program from the beginning and throughout the duration of the program and beyond is a key factor for establishing the communications plan for the program. Ideally, it is these leaders who will champion the vision for the integrated organization. They are the advocates for the change that must take place, and communication planning is about helping them get their message across. Many of these leaders will be asked to deliver important communications throughout the life cycle of the program and, given that, they will be required to sustain their support and enthusiasm for the program's intended outcomes for the long term.

Additionally, these leaders will be seen as "standards bearers" for the program and will find it necessary to "walk the talk," so to speak, when conducting business. In effect, these leaders will be seen as "on stage" during any and all communications and interactions. Whether directly related to the change program or not, all behavior of a program leader will be seen as if it were related to the program in some way. A leader who verbally supports a change in outward communications, yet makes it difficult for anyone working within the program to find 30 minutes on the leader's calendar to discuss the program, is communicating one thing in words and another with behavior.

By the same token, an organizational leader who delivers an initial message for an important initiative and then delegates all future communications is effectively communicating that the initiative is not important enough for him or her to remain engaged. Employees are particularly adept at picking up these subtle yet revealing "communications." The consistency of the messaging and the sustained commitment of organizational leaders is critical to communicating a sense of urgency and building a lasting vision for the long term.

15.3.5 Building the Path for Change

Establishing a positive environment for change relies on the completion of the two elements detailed earlier: *Creating a sense of urgency* and *Communicating the vision and alternatives*. They are the foundation for trust, clarity of purpose, and support that will be required from the organization for the changes they are about to undertake. The next step will engage the program's participants, stakeholders, and leaders in creating the path forward for the program.

15.3.5.1 Prioritizing Initiatives

With the collected observation and interview information as a starting point, the change program's leaders will begin the process of prioritizing the various subelements and program components that will be conducted. This can be accomplished through facilitated discussions with program and component leads selected to oversee specific program components. Their selection is most often based on their abilities as leaders, as well as their experience, skill, and knowledge. (See also Chapter 10, "Developing Integration Competencies in People.") These facilitated discussions can lead to ranked prioritization of program activities and initiatives based on a numeric value assigned to two intersecting attributes, such as Overall Impact vs. Length of Time Required to Complete; Urgency vs. Availability of Resources; Impact vs. Ease of Implementation; etc. Figure 15-6, based on the work of Sirkin, Keenan, and Jackson (2005), illustrates how a priority matrix can be developed by assigning numeric values to the attributes

Impact vs. Resource Availability	Limited Impact X4	Moderate Impact X3	Significant Impact X2	Critical Impact X1
Resources Readily Available X1	4	3	2	1
Some, not all, Resources Readily Available X2	8	6	4	2
Few Resources Available X3	12	9	6	3
Resources must be Procured X4	16	12	8	4

☐ Take Action Now   ▨ Address Next   ▨ Wait, Reevaluate

Figure 15-6: Prioritization matrix example

(in this case Impact vs. Resource Availability), orienting them on the X and Y axes of a table and ranking the initiatives based on a total multiplied value for each.

This prioritization table shows how an organization can select initiatives to begin working by assigning actions to the value groupings. In this table initiatives with lower values will be given priority over those with higher values. This table also groups the values into three categories:

- Values 1–3: Take Action Now
- Values 4–7: Address Next
- Values 8–16: Wait, Reevaluate

The numeric values that make up the groupings can be adjusted to align with the specific environment and conditions of the organization. With these groupings established, initiatives can be placed in the cells (one initiative per cell) to establish priority. Evaluation of the initiatives is based on consideration of the two intersecting aspects.

As an example, using the focus issue presented earlier where there is a perception that program management and systems engineering roles are not clear, the prioritization team might consider the impact of such a condition as "Significant" or "Critical" to the organization's ongoing performance. If that is the case, then on the Y axis in the table shown in Figure 15-7, "Clarifying PM and SE Roles" could be placed in the Y axis cells. For the X axis, the prioritization team may agree that the resources for clarifying the roles might be present on the program team. If that is the case, the team could place "Clarifying PM and SE Roles" in the rows aligned with "Resources Readily Available." Multiplying the values for the related cells produces the values as described above. If one assumes that all initiatives with values between 1 and 3 will be prioritized, then "Clarifying PM and SE Roles" will be one of the first initiatives the team undertakes.

Impact vs. Resource Availability	Limited Impact: PM and SE Roles are Clear, Understood and Enforced X4	Moderate Impact: PM and SE Roles are Clear, but may not be Enforced X3	Significant Impact: PM and SE Roles are Loosely Defined X2	Critical Impact: PM and SE Roles have yet to be Defined X1
High Priority: Resources and Time are Available to Refine the Roles X1	4	3	2	1
Moderate Priority: Some Resources Available to Refine Role Definitions X2	8	6	4	2
Low Priority: Resources Available, but must be Oriented to the Work X3	12	9	6	3
Not a Priority: Resources must be Procured and Oriented to the Work X4	16	12	8	4

☐ Take Action Now ☐ Address Next ☐ Wait, Reevaluate

Figure 15-7: Prioritization table that reveals focus on clarifying program management and systems engineering roles

This will be continued for all the categories of input from observation and interview, resulting in a set of actions that will be addressed first, those that will be in line for action as soon as others are completed, and a grouping of actions that are on the "watch list" for reevaluation and future prioritization.

15.3.5.2 Measures, Metrics, and Reporting

Before beginning any change activity, however, meaningful measures and target metrics for each must be put in place and baselined so progress against improvement targets can be measured and reported. This is an essential part of the program management process. Program participants, stakeholders, and organizational leaders will want to know how the program is progressing, and they will not be satisfied with vague, subjective, or "soft" answers such as "we're making good progress" or "it appears we are doing better." Measures of improvement can and should be translated into meaningful numeric values that can be tracked, plotted, and reported. Baselining the current state will become the starting point for measurement.

To illustrate, one element of the initiative to integrate program management and systems engineering and one fictitious metric to measure progress will be used. If it is believed that there is little collaboration between program management and systems engineers, then one should be able to quantify the amount of collaboration that does exist between these two disciplines today. Perhaps collaborative decisions are reached by program managers and systems engineers only twice out of 10 opportunities for them to collaborate. That would mean collaboration is happening only 20% of the time. An improvement initiative might include a number of creative and interesting activities to encourage collaboration, and the improvement targets could be set for an early achievement number, a midterm target, and a final goal. For the purpose of illustration, these targets are arbitrarily set at 30%, 45%, and 60% respectively. For actual program initiatives, one would no doubt spend considerably more time aligning all improvement targets so that they are meaningful, realistic, and achievable.

Along with the metrics, the activity's measurement interval must be set. Sirkin, Keenan, and Jackson (2005) recommend that program measurement occur at two-month intervals or less. Their research has proven that regardless of the size of the program, review and measurement intervals that are longer than two months contribute to the underperformance risk of the program. So with the measures in place, the target improvement objectives clarified, and the measurement interval set, the work of the change activity can begin. As time passes, measurement of actual progress versus plan can be conducted and documented. The improvement points can be demonstrated over time in a graphical representation and adjustments to the program activity can be considered, if they are necessary.

Finally, relying on the communications guidance outlined above, all of this can be reported or shared visually with the program's participants, stakeholders, and leaders following each of the measurement intervals. This eliminates subjective or vague descriptions of program progress and establishes a clear means for communicating real results and achievement.

15.3.6 Achieving and Sustaining New Ways of Working

One of the most elusive aspects of change management programs, surprisingly, is not the achievement of target objectives and benefits, but rather sustaining changes and benefits once they have been achieved and delivered. Earlier, various examples of failed programs such as programs that begin with strong support and end with none; programs that fail to deliver intended outcomes and benefits; programs that are brought to a halt due to their negative impact on the sponsoring organization; programs that have been rendered unnecessary due to changing culture, technology, or laws were described. Looking carefully at some of these programs—even successful ones—reveals an interesting condition that is often overlooked: programs that initially succeed in bringing about intended changes are later found to be unsuccessful because the changes brought about by the program are not ingrained in the organization and the benefits that were achieved are not continuing to accrue. This has been observed many times in organizations where elaborate systems are developed and successfully implemented, only to have the systems sit idle from lack of use or applicability. Or, perhaps, a successful organizational change that has taken months and years to implement is reversed almost immediately after the change champion leaves the organization. Maybe new management takes over and does not believe the initiative has merit. Whatever the facts of the individual cases may be, the underlying cause for this can be traced to one of the most important components of the program—benefits sustainment.

Programs designed to bring about organizational change, such as an effort to integrate program management and systems engineering, are by their very nature disruptive. Old ways of working and communicating must be modified, tools and processes reconfigured, roles and responsibilities realigned, and systems that support all of this redesigned or replaced. These changes alone are enough to give pause to organizations considering such a structural change given the potential for extended disruption to "the way things work." Organizations that chose to take on this potentially disruptive change acknowledge the potential disorder and purposely create program components specifically designed to get the work done. Unfortunately, carefully considering and acting on modification to systems, processes, and tools will not be enough to ensure success. To make changes "stick" within the organization, and to ensure achieved benefits continue to deliver dividends beyond the end of the program, requires thoughtfully planned efforts to sustain them.

Thinking through the activities that will be undertaken to sustain benefits is not an add-on concept or an ancillary aspect of program management that can be casually addressed toward the end of a program. Quite the contrary, as discussed earlier, benefits sustainment is an important element of the benefits management plan that is at the core of program design. And the earlier in the program benefits sustainment activities are considered, the easier they will be to implement, and the more value they will ultimately deliver to the program's constituents.

When one considers the changes that will occur within an organization as part of a program designed to integrate program management and systems engineering, where *effective collaborative work, effective information sharing,* and *rapid and effective decision making* are the desired outcomes and will ultimately become the norm, one can easily envision a number of changes to organizational mores, resources, and "standards" that will be required to implement the necessary changes. Here are a few examples that relate directly to the desired outcomes. There are likely many more.

■ **Collaborative Work.** Organizations whose work is heavily oriented toward engineering activities typically create environments where technical resources (humans, systems, materials) are physically grouped together to enable them to work together seamlessly and easily. Business and business-related functions such as finance, procurement, human resources, administration, and program and project management are also routinely grouped together to enable them to easily share information and collaborate. Frequently, however, these two functions are not located in or near the same offices as senior executives. Engineering and program management functions may also not be physically located in the same room or on the same floor in a building; and, if they are, it is likely they are not both in the same building as the executives. Sometimes program management and systems engineering functions do not share the same building or the same office campus, or even the same city. Creating an environment where representatives from each of these functions (executive, technical, and business) are co-located so they can work together toward a common set of program goals, outcomes, and benefits may take considerable planning, effort, time, and funding.

- **Information Sharing.** Information and communications resources that support engineering functions are designed and tailored to facilitate easy access to information, plans, designs, processes, tools, etc. By the same token, the resources that support business and business-related functions are obtained, planned, integrated, and configured to support the unique needs of business functions. Seldom do these two functions share the same technology or knowledge-ware platforms. If they do, there are often duplicate sets of resources—one dedicated to the technical functions, the other created for business functions. If there is information sharing, it is often characterized by email, video content, and presentations shared over a low-tech information exchange facility. Information is often exchanged by sending it "over the wall" or presenting it from one function *to* the other. Transforming this to an environment where there is a shared common knowledge store that is easy to understand and navigate for both technical and program management resources, and establishing systems, physical environments, or forums for collaboration and information sharing is not only technically complex, but presents a number of significant social challenges as well.

- **Decision Making.** If technical and business decisions are traditionally divided between systems engineering and program management and sent to them respectively allowing each exclusive decision-making authority over issues within their domain, changing this to a practice where program management and systems engineering jointly consider, evaluate, and resolve decisions affecting programs for which they are responsible will be a substantial undertaking.

As discussed, organizations may determine that some or all of this will be required to transform their organization. Numerous examples identified cases where organizations have consciously acknowledged the time, effort, and resources necessary to take this on, and have stepped into the breach willingly only to find that after considerable expenditure of time, effort, and resources, the program fails to deliver the desired outcomes. Why does this occur with such regularity?

First, as outlined at the beginning of the chapter, all four input dimensions of the Integration Framework (shown in Figure 15-8) must be addressed by the program.

15.4 Putting the Four Input Dimensions for Change Together

The previous section discussed at length ways to create the organizational environment for integrating program management and systems engineering. It also elaborated the processes and constructs necessary for effectively communicating the current

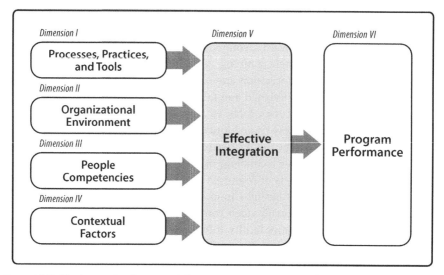

Figure 15-8: The Integration Framework for program management and systems engineering

conditions and future vision. Accompanying this dimension of the framework are the other three:

■ Processes, Practices, and Tools
■ People Competencies
■ Contextual Factors

And, the final answer to the question presented at the beginning of this section lies in the amount of benefits sustainment planning that is included in the program along with the obvious work that is described in the desired outcomes above. There are considerations for sustainment that accompany each of the desired outcomes, and these must become an integral part of the planning and performance of the program. In every case, the sustainment activity involves people. Here is the key message:

> To ensure intended changes take hold and become ingrained within the organization beyond the end of the program, and to ensure the benefits achieved by the program continue to accrue after the program has ended, the PEOPLE who will be responsible for carrying these activities forward must be identified; must acknowledge their roles and the daunting charge that accompanies them; and must be willing to carry out those roles.

This means that the program's leaders must identify upfront and throughout the program execution the future "owners" (leaders/champions) of the organizational models, processes, tools, communications, and related activities that will sustain the changes and benefits after the program has been completed, the consultants have been released, and the program's members and participants disbanded. Waiting until the end of the program to identify the future "sustainers of the new order" will put these individuals at a distinct disadvantage, as they will have little understanding of what went into defining their new roles or the unique aspects of these roles that will be required to carry them out. The future owners of the new environment, new ways of working, and new ways of making decisions must be identified early in the program's life cycle, must participate in the transformational program that brings about the changes, and must be willing to "carry the torch" into the future.

So now, when discussing the planning that must go into the program for integrating program management and systems engineering, one must consider the remaining three input factors for enabling the program, and must also identify the organizational leaders who will be responsible not only for delivering the initial program outcomes and benefits, but those who will carry the modified constructs of the organization into the future. In some cases, those leaders will be the very same key participants who perform the work of the program, in others the work will be transitioned to them. Transition of roles and responsibilities will occur when consultants are brought in to lead the effort initially but will not remain with the organization after it ends. Or perhaps "change leaders" will transition the new processes, tools, and approaches to "operational leaders" whose role and expertise is not in transformational change but that of operational excellence. Whatever the case, this critical component of the program cannot be discounted or ignored.

15.4.1 Processes, Practices, and Tools

To achieve the key factors of processes, practices, and tools, and reap the benefits they promise, program leaders must answer outstanding questions and consider a number of factors that will facilitate achieving them. For example, which processes must be modified to reduce friction between the organizations, reward the right behavior, and provide a platform for improved information sharing and decision making? The following are a few examples.

■ **Role delineation.** In a given organization, if it is agreed that program management and systems engineering roles are not clearly articulated, who will be responsible for modifying them? This cannot be accomplished without consulting a number of program managers and systems engineers within the organization, and ultimately the organization as a whole must come to some understanding of how these roles will work together in the future. Once established, these roles must then be incorporated into the operational functions within the organization so they can be used for recruiting, scope definition for the roles, and performance evaluation. Questions to be answered include:

❑ When these roles have been defined and accepted, who will be responsible for ensuring they become the norm for the organization?

❑ How will that happen?

❑ Who will be responsible for maintaining them and for ensuring they continue to reflect the necessary requirements and boundaries of the roles as the organization continues to evolve?

■ **Human resources systems.** If the roles and expectations of program managers and systems engineers are to be redefined, then the performance standards for these employees must also change. Old standards that encourage separation of duties and exclusive decision making must be replaced with performance objectives and measures that encourage and reward collaborative work, information sharing, and collaborative decision making. It will be impossible to achieve the intended objectives of the change program if employees are given a new set of objectives and measures that encourages collaboration, but performance and reward systems are structured in ways that encourage just the opposite. Questions to be answered include:

- ❏ Who are the individuals who will make these changes happen in back-office operational functions?
- ❏ Who are the individuals who will ensure these changes are made permanent and become the standard for performance beyond the end of the program?
- ❏ What people and systems will be used in the future to evaluate and reward performance?
- ❏ How will performance that does not align with the new standards be dealt with?

- ■ **Physical environment and supporting information systems.** Modifying the environment to encourage collaboration, sharing of information, and joint decision making is a costly and disruptive undertaking. Questions to be answered include:
  - ❏ Who will be responsible for laying out the various projects that will be conducted to make this happen?
  - ❏ Who will ensure those changes are made?
  - ❏ Who will continue to communicate the benefits of the new environment, ensuring the changes "stick" within the organization, and that employees do not revert back to the old ways of working?

- ■ **Tools and methods.** While a great deal of the communication and coordination to improve integration lies in the management domain, a significant portion of the benefits created by the program may result from activities that are primarily technical in nature. Work processes and methods and analytic tools play an important role in enabling greater collaboration and communication across discipline boundaries in the work of the program. In some instances, increased integration may require improvements to existing processes, practices, or tools. These improvements could in fact constitute major change programs in their own right, as was demonstrated in the BMW E-Division case study in Chapter 14. Questions to be answered include:
  - ❏ Who will determine whether existing tools and methods are structured so that integration is a natural outcome of work?
  - ❏ Who will be responsible for defining the various projects to upgrade or change the tools and methods to make this happen?
  - ❏ Who will provide the resources and support for major upgrades to tools and methods?
  - ❏ Who will be responsible for assessing and maintaining tools and methods to ensure that they continue to foster and enable integration over their life?

15.4.2 Organizational Environment

The previous sections of this chapter discussed a number of activities that contribute to creating the organizational climate for change. But creating the right climate for change will not be sufficient for the organization to reap the benefits of the change in the long term, allowing them to weave new ways of working into the fabric of the organization so that the new organizational environment becomes the recognized organizational standard. During the program, those influential thought leaders within the organization who will continue the themes of the change into the future must be identified. During and following the program they will be responsible for sustaining the positive outcomes of the program and will be the individuals who communicate and reinforce the trust that is developed, the clarity of the messaging that is communicated, and will be the visible examples of the organization's commitment to the ongoing sustainment of benefits and continuous evolution of the organization. Questions to be answered include:

- Who are the change champions for the organization now?
- Are they the same ones who will carry the message forward in the future?
- If not, how will the future leaders learn what they will be required to do to ensure the organizational environment is sustained and continues to improve?
- If the right leaders are not present in the organization, how will they be found and brought on board?
- How will their roles be articulated and how will their performance be measured?

Answers to these questions must be known long before the program's end.

15.4.3 People Competencies

Alignment of a number of physical and environmental factors must occur within an organization in order to achieve the target outcomes and benefits discussed. Included are the people who make up the organization now and in the future. If program management and systems engineering are not performing well together in the organization today, it is very likely the individuals in these roles possess certain abilities, knowledge, experience, and competencies that reflect a particular approach to the work. If a new way of working for program managers and systems engineers is the objective, it is very likely the people in these roles will have to adopt new ways of approaching the work and will be expected to acquire new interacting and interpersonal skills and competencies.

Collaborative work, effective information sharing, and rapid and effective decision making requires individuals who are skilled and confident about their respective domains, but are open to new ideas, collaborative and engaging by nature, and are eager to see more than a single view of a particular challenge. As described in the bullets on human resources systems, these new competencies and people skills must be incorporated into the role descriptions for program managers and systems engineers, performance and measurement systems should be aligned with them, role definitions for future leaders in these positions must include them, and staffing/employment processes updated to seek them out. Questions to be answered include:

- Who are the organizational leaders who will define the new competencies and leadership criteria?
- Who are the individuals who will measure and evaluate current leaders in these roles?

- How will future leaders be identified and brought on board?
- How will the roles be maintained and kept current?

15.4.4 Contextual Factors

Finally, program characteristics, team characteristics, organizational characteristics, and stakeholder engagement all impact how the program, program team, and the organization as a whole approach and evaluate delivery of outcomes and benefits. Changing some of these contextual factors may require adapting the organization's overarching strategy to include additional elements that enable increased integration between program management and systems engineering. It will be the responsibility of the change program's leaders along with the organization's executives to jointly bring together all of the work of the change initiative and guide its trajectory throughout the effort, from humble and sometimes challenging beginnings to a future that enables collaborative work, effective information sharing, and rapid and effective decision making. Questions to be considered include:

- Do the current product and service offerings have architectures and target markets that make integration across functions and programs easy or difficult?
- Do current approaches to team structure, governance, resourcing, and location enable collaborative work, effective information sharing, and rapid and effective decision making?
- Do the organizational structure, legal, and operational relationships with suppliers, partners and allies, and geographic location of operations enable or impede integration?

15.5 Practices to Consider

It is important for program managers to understand the unique characteristics of the systems engineering role—the concepts, approach, skills, and abilities. And it is likewise important for systems engineers to understand the practice of the program management role—the knowledge, competencies, business context, and approach. For a person in one of these roles understanding the requirements, knowledge, and nuances of the others' enables improved collaboration, sense making, trust development, communication, and overall performance.

Nothing replaces the value an individual brings to the table from years of practice and experience. Experienced practitioners achieve top performance through focused attention to continuous learning—building knowledge, developing and using tools and practices, and refining one's approach. To become a skilled practitioner, a program manager or systems engineer must spend many years developing, expanding, and honing their respective skills. When these experienced, skilled individuals are brought to bear in highly technical business settings, they are often, but not always, able to produce surprising, often unexpected improvement and progress.

There is also a creative side to these roles. Once the skills, knowledge, and experience are developed to a point where the practitioner can perform them consistently and perhaps effortlessly, practitioners are then able to use the other side of their brains—the creative side—to find inventive, novel, and game-changing ways to apply their skill.

15.5.1 Elements that Drive Success

There are eight key factors required for the success of a change initiative to integrate systems engineering and program management, or virtually any change program, in an organization.

■ Everyone involved and who will be affected must be shown the gravity of the current state. A sense of urgency must be universally acknowledged across the organization. As a component of this, alternatives for changing the organization must be evaluated for the contribution to the change (e.g., do nothing, make small improvements that will enable certain components to function better in the short term, focus on transforming the organization).

■ Senior leadership support and commitment for the long-term effort to integrate systems engineering and program management within the organization is a critical factor for change management success. This includes commitment from senior leadership to provide critical resources for implementation.

■ A clear set of target outcomes, ways of performing and interacting, ongoing performance targets, and indicators must be established at the start of the program.

■ Meaningful measures and metrics for gauging progress against targeted objectives must be established at the start of the initiative, and frequently reviewed during the life of the program.

■ Processes for monitoring and governing the change initiative must be established to provide a forum for regular review and adjustment of program components.

■ Clearly defined roles for both systems engineers and program managers are an essential ingredient to the integration of these roles within an organization. Delineation between the two roles is also essential.

■ Careful selection of the properly skilled individuals who will lead the change initiative.

■ Systems and technology solutions that support the integration of systems engineering and program management within the organization must be put in place or modified to support the initiative. Examples include performance appraisal and review systems, target objectives for individual performance that align with the transformation objectives, and review and reward intervals and criteria. Ecosystems that are unable to support the transformation must be redesigned or replaced.

15.5.2 No Shortcuts to Success

A number of factors that are present in successful change programs designed to achieve the desired outcomes of collaborative work, information sharing, and effective decision making, ultimately resulting in improved program performance have been reviewed. The dimensions of the Integration Framework and linked key program success-enabling activities to those dimensions have been articulated. A five-step process for developing and leading a change program within an organization was highlighted, and measures and metrics called out that will be used to gauge and communicate program success.

Initial research and experience that the framework and factors describe can deliver improved program performance and sustainable outcomes. Research, observation, and practice confirm that each of the dimensions of the framework and each of the steps outlined in the program success-enabling activities must be performed to achieve target objectives and benefits in complex programs. While various activities or components can be reordered, or perhaps the emphasis on particular elements of the framework can be increased or reduced, none of the elements of the framework nor the success-enabling activities can be skipped or ignored without direct impact to the program's likelihood for, or degree of success.

Referring to the Integration Framework or the five-step enabling activities, how would an integration change program succeed without the climate for change being established and communicated by influential leaders within the organization? Or, if the desired change climate had been effectively created, would the change program succeed without necessary modifications to roles and responsibilities, performance review and reward systems, communications processes, and employee engagement?

Instances where elements of the processes described and activities recommended have been skipped or eliminated to save time, effort, or resources, in other words, shortcutting the change management process, leads to failed programs or the inability of the organization to sustain the benefits initially achieved. And that failure can be directly tied to the absence of one of the dimensions of the Integration Framework or success-enabling activities.

While it may be tempting to shorten or reduce the scope of the change program in an attempt to achieve the program's intended benefits and desired outcomes more quickly or more easily, there are no meaningful shortcuts to achieving success in a program designed to integrate program management and systems engineering within an active organization. Each of the steps must be carefully understood, planned, performed, reviewed, reported, and repeated. Skipping change program steps or reducing scope inevitably will have a damaging effect on outcomes.

15.5.3 Shared Authority and Accountability

When considering and moving from a nonintegrated environment and culture to an integrated one, the end result should be shared authority and accountability between the program management and systems engineering functions to achieve the program's intended outcomes, enacted and empowered by the organization's leadership. The integrated program reflects this shared responsibility and accountability as both skill domains bring unique, complementary, and essential competencies to bear on the work and challenges of the program. In integrated program environments, the program manager and chief systems engineer collaborate effectively to move the program forward. When this is the case, the program manager and chief systems engineer view themselves as key partners who together share responsibility for the program's progress and outcome.

In nonintegrated program environments, the organizational culture reflects a characteristic division of labor, responsibility, and accountability where program management jealously defends its role as business overseer and decision maker while the systems engineering function protects its authoritative role as exclusive technical expertise and the decision point for all technical issues. In organizational environments such as these, program issues that arise are divided into technical and programmatic challenges. The issues are then assigned to the one domain with little communication or concern for the other. When technical issues are encountered, the systems engineering function maintains exclusive command authority over these decisions. When uncertainty, ambiguity, or scheduling, resource, and cost issues emerge the program management function is the "decider." Section 15.2 explained how this approach to managing complex programs can have a measurable negative impact on progress, productivity, quality, and the end result. A General Motors ignition problem that went on unchecked for 10 years and resulted in 124 verifiable deaths, and the NASA Challenger and Columbia disasters are disturbing examples of how this divided management approach, carried to the extreme, can create an organizational culture and behavior that is difficult to comprehend.

In integrated program management and systems engineering environments, program issues, challenges, and decisions are borne by both disciplines. Though technical issues may arise, the programmatic impact of these issues is also considered. Resolving technical challenges impacts not only the technological and engineering aspects of the program, but will be reflected with equal impact in changes to other, less-technical and nontechnical elements such as the program's overall trajectory and direction, intended benefits, schedule, cost, resources, design, quality, and ultimately, fitness for use. With this being the case, all technical issues are shared, analyzed, evaluated, and resolved jointly by the program manager and chief systems engineer.

By the same token, changes that affect the program's scope, schedule, cost, quality, intended benefits, and outcomes cannot be made without consideration of the impact to engineering. Changes that modify target outcomes, scope, add or eliminate program components, or lengthen or shorten the schedule have an immediate impact on the program's engineering functions. With a complex set of technical contributors, dependencies that exist between the delivery and integration of technical components must be reanalyzed, reconsidered, reenvisioned, or, in some cases, entirely scrapped to accommodate the requested changes. Given this interdependency, it is clear that program-affecting decisions are not exclusively technical or programmatic, but rather composite decisions that are considered and resolved jointly by the program's two leading domain experts—the program manager and chief systems engineer.

15.5.4 What Happens When Things Don't Go as Designed?

Even with the best possible planning completed, the most trusted leaders in place, and a strong plan to support and encourage change, sometimes things do not go as planned. What do successful organizations do? In organizations where an ability to effectively manage change is woven into the fabric of how they do business, the failure of certain components of the effort is a common occurrence. When this happens, the organization methodically reevaluates the various components of the program as described earlier in this chapter and sets about reprioritizing the work and the components to focus attention on weaker areas, strengthening its resolve to continually pursue the desired outcomes and benefits.

Organizations that successfully implement change over the long term repeat the processes outlined in this chapter on a cadence that focuses the entire organization on continual improvement. They build the required tools and processes, reinforce the positive climate for change, recruit and retain top talent, and infuse each effort with the capacity for continuous improvement.

15.6 Summary

To conclude this chapter and to summarize the discussion about the need to thoroughly consider the proper approach to the implementation of a change program that will integrate program management and systems engineering, the following list of key takeaways will help one navigate the organizational impact to people, processes, tools, and culture.

- Program managers and systems engineers each must understand the role of the other in a technical business setting and respect the unique skills, talent, experience, and contributions of the other.
- One role depends on the other for top team performance—they are not competitors for the same work, nor are they opponents working toward different objectives. Rather, they are partners and collaborators who work together, dependent on one another to deliver sustained top-team performance.
- Collaboration is built upon understanding of the others' role and trust in the others' ability to perform that role well.
- One must work to continuously improve one's own skill, knowledge, and experience.
- Leadership must create and sustain an environment where these roles are able to work together effectively.
- Picking meaningful metrics and monitoring achievement is a foundational component of change management success.
- Achievement and progress toward intended outcomes must be clearly measurable—and results against progress must be shared across the organization.
- Picking the right people and setting the tone is the role of the coach/leader.
- Communications is king. Continually communicating and reinforcing new ways of working, adjusting to performance information as it is occurring, and encouraging and rewarding good performance is required to change behavior.
- Developing a reward system that reinforces good behavior and discourages the wrong behavior is important to overall success.
- Strong, supportive, engaged leadership, continual communications, modeling and reinforcing good behavior, achieving small wins (early), creating and sustaining an environment with effective support systems up, down, and across the organization are essential elements for success.

15.7 References

Conforto, E. C., Rossi, M., Rebentisch, E., Oehmen, J., & Pacenza, M. (2013). *Survey report: Improving integration of program management and systems engineering*. Presented at the 23rd INCOSE Annual International Symposium, Philadelphia, USA. Retrieved from www.pmi.org/~/media/PDF/Business-Solutions/Lean-Enablers/PMI-INCOSE-MIT-Integration-Study.ashx

Erskine, P. (2013). *ITIL and organizational change*. Ely, England: IT Governance Publishing.

Garvin, D. A., & Roberto, M. (2005, February). Change through persuasion. *Harvard Business Review*.

Kotter, John P. (2012). *Leading change*. Cambridge, MA: Harvard Business Review Press.

Project Management Institute (PMI). (2013a). *Managing change in organizations: A practice guide*. Newtown Square, PA: Author.

Project Management Institute (PMI). (2013b). *The standard for program management* (3rd ed.). Newtown Square, PA: Author.

Project Management Institute (PMI). (2016). *Governance of portfolios, programs, and projects: A practice guide*. Newtown Square, PA: Author.

Sirkin, H. L., Keenan, P., & Jackson, A. (2005, October). The hard side of change management. *Harvard Business Review*.

Thiry, M. (2015). *Program management* (2nd ed.). England: Gower Publishing.

Part IV

A CALL TO ACTION

The factors that lead to better integration between program management and systems engineering may not all be within the influence of a specific program or organization. The book concludes with a discussion in Chapter 16 of factors that should be addressed beyond the immediate organization or program to improve integration. While summarizing key points in the book, Chapter 16 is forward-looking with a discussion of the implications of the overall message of increasing integration across a range of stakeholders, both within the organization and in the larger societal context.

The afterword represents an admonition to individual practitioners to reflect on the key messages of this book, identify a plan of action, and take action to create better integration between program management and systems engineering in their own sphere of influence. It also reflects upon some of the insights gained during the creation of this book and discusses some of those insights with a view toward future efforts to advance the knowledge and practice of integration.

16

CALLS TO ACTION

Transformational change often occurs during particularly turbulent periods in history. It may begin in small ways, but then expands as momentum builds and feeds on itself. Some might argue that key ingredients for a transformational stage are already heating up. Lyrics written 50 years ago illustrate the issues: "There's something happening here; what it is ain't exactly clear" (Stills, 1966). Corporate shareholders are challenging their organizations' leaders over strategies whose poor performance has weakened the companies. Taxpayers are revolting against higher taxes that persist despite lackluster public services and an unsustainable level of government waste and inefficiency. Many college graduates around the world have difficulty finding entry-level jobs in their fields, and new entrants to the workforce are challenged by cultures, systems, and roles that remain unchanged in a faster-paced, technology-enabled world. Despite talk of collaboration and alignment, workers in business and government remain siloed, unable to break through multiple layers of barriers based on role, function, and structure. In some cases, workers are simply accepting the status quo and no longer pushing for the kind of positive change that can turn average organizations into extraordinary ones.

In engineering programs, all of these elements exist today, but are more quickly reaching a boiling point. Government leaders are realizing that their portfolios of engineering programs are not sustainable for the long term as they currently function. Corporate leaders see the emergence of leaner, more adaptive companies as looming challenges to their market dominance. Neither business nor government can rely on a small cadre of exceptional leaders to sweep in and save them, particularly as large swaths of seasoned professionals plan to retire. Engineering degree programs are under pressure to deliver graduates who are ready to step into program teams and immediately start performing. Trade and professional societies find it challenging to keep pace with the external changes that are pressuring their members, and their members are finding other communities to meet those needs or are creating their own on the fly. So, the engineering program system is already in a state of transformational change aimed at addressing a future that will require professionals to immediately contribute to success while enabling sustainable program quality.

Rather than simply reacting to the pressure of external forces, leaders still have the opportunity to proactively drive change in engineering program performance. Program managers and chief systems engineers certainly have critical roles to play, but they alone cannot undertake or sustain such change on their own. Indeed, as this book has demonstrated, all system elements must actively participate in the transformation. The remainder of this chapter should not be construed as action items with specific assignments and timeframes, but rather as a means for further reflecting upon the issues raised within this book. This chapter looks specifically at five groups that can play a role in driving program management and systems engineering integration: academia, enterprise leaders, policymakers, professional societies, and researchers. Each of these groups has already contributed to some extent, but more remains to be done in furthering the effort to integrate deeply and fully systems engineering and program management.

16.1 Call to Action for Academia: Help Budding Professionals Learn to Adapt

Academic degrees are built upon the completion of a defined set of required courses, often originating from within areas of deep specialization. In the engineering discipline, there are four primary branches with almost 40 subspecialties, including systems engineering and engineering management (Hamilton, 2000). Around the world, there are thousands of degree-granting programs, although no accurate global figures exist. In the area of systems engineering, there are over 300 degree programs at the Baccalaureate, Master's, Doctoral, and Post-Doctoral levels (INCOSE, 2016a).

Anyone embracing a career involving technology must anticipate a lifetime of continuous learning beyond the achievement of academic degrees. Engineers of any specialization must maintain currency in their field. Systems engineers deal with technology and emergent properties of systems, requiring maintenance of systems engineering skills as well as awareness of the technical changes affecting their colleagues. The discipline of program management continues to evolve and it is incumbent on the program manager to remain current with developing practices. Both program managers and systems engineers must thrive on change—and work together to rise to the challenges of change.

For most of its history, project, program, and portfolio management have been interdisciplinary. Individuals who chose to move into those roles, or were placed into those roles, usually come with degrees in other fields such as engineering, business administration, or information technology. Starting in the late 1980s, academic curricula began to recognize and adopt project, program, and portfolio management as a unique field of study. In 2001, after recognizing the growing need for establishing quality educational standards in university programs offering academic awards in the field of study, the Project Management Institute created the Global Accreditation Center for Project Management Education Programs (GAC) as an independent academic accreditation body for accrediting university programs in project, program, and portfolio management (PMI, 2015). Since its establishment, the GAC has accredited more than 100 degree programs at the Baccalaureate, Master's, Doctoral, and Post-Doctoral levels (PMI, 2016a).

The mid-1990s also represented a watershed moment for engineering program accreditation, particularly in the United States. In 1996, the Accreditation Board for Engineering and Technology, Inc. (ABET) changed its accreditation requirements to include a broader array of professional skills beyond engineering, math, and science.

The changes recognized that engineering graduates needed to enter the workforce with a broader range of skills to compete effectively, specifically in such areas as communication, collaboration, problem solving, and ethics (ABET, 2006). These changes also opened the door for the inclusion of project management in undergraduate engineering curricula and program management in graduate- and doctoral-level programs. Just as graduate-level systems engineers are required to embrace program management principles, the technical demands are increasing beyond the classic systems engineering principles to include systems, systems thinking, and associated competencies.

> Modern design philosophies demand systems thinking in order to support the deep integration of technical systems and organizations are required to supply the types of services now expected. Systems engineering helps ensure that the system delivered is a coherent and effective solution to the system need (Pyster et al., 2012, Section 1.1).

The European Union began efforts to harmonize higher education approaches among Member States. The intention of the European Higher Education Area (EHEA) initiative is to remove barriers to educational equivalency that could obstruct workforce mobility while allowing Member States to retain national standards and practices. One research paper studying some of the impacts of the EHEA effort noted, "it is stressed that one of the measures necessary for achieving employability is developing transversal skills and competencies, such as communication and languages, the ability to handle information, to solve problems, to work in teams, and to lead social processes" (de los Rios, Cazorla, Diaz-Puente, & Yagüe, 2010). A separate study reinforced the need for the "transversal skills" (see Table 16-1) and specifically called out group work, project management, effective communication, and ongoing learning as main engineering competencies that students needed to develop (Rouvrais et al., 2006). Producing students with such capabilities was critical, the researcher noted, because "Today enterprises demand, more than experienced experts, [they expect] competent professionals" (de los Rios et al., 2010). So, as in the United States, Japan, Australia, and other countries around the world, many European colleges and universities have accelerated development of more interdisciplinary curricula to address workforce mobility and companies seeking more "ready-made" professionals.

The challenge for colleges and universities is to figure out how to incorporate these new skills into a curriculum that is already packed with required coursework. ABET did not provide clear guidance for effectively integrating the new criteria into existing

Table 16-1: Main competencies for engineering students	
Transversal Competencies	■ Interpersonal communications (group work, creativity) ■ Learning to learn ■ Oral communication (presentations, meetings) ■ Written communication (technical reports, argumentation techniques) ■ Project management
Scientific-technical Competencies	■ Designing (plan, write specifications) ■ Modelling (applying theoretical knowledge and methodologies) ■ Developing ■ Testing, assessing, and validating solutions ■ Interdisciplinary approach

Rouvrais et al., 2006. Reprinted by permission of Taylor & Francis Ltd, www.tandfonline.com

programs, leaving many universities struggling to meet the criteria (Banik, 2015). Lacking clear guidance or room to add more courses to their curricula, many schools have attempted to embed the new skills into the syllabi of their existing courses. For project management, a capstone course often represents the best vehicle for bridging between diverse sources of knowledge in undergraduate degree programs (Rebentisch, 2015). But some schools are taking more radical change approaches in response to the ABET standards.

The Department of Civil and Architectural Engineering at Tennessee State University has incorporated into its curriculum a project management course for civil engineers, architectural engineers, and construction engineers. The course focuses on the management and leadership capabilities required to successfully execute construction projects. A strong focus on management of stakeholders, cost, and schedule is balanced with addressing safety management, use of software tools, building and leading teams, and professional ethics (Banik, 2015).

The Electrical, Computer, Software, and Systems Engineering Department at Embry-Riddle Aeronautical University undertook efforts to integrate several graduate systems engineering and software engineering courses. The initiative also incorporated project management practices and software capabilities into the syllabus. Building an integrated program uncovered a key obstacle—there were no books presenting such an interdisciplinary approach. Babiceanu (2015) reported that faculty developed their course materials by integrating components from various publications, including:

- A Guide to the Project Management Body of Knowledge (PMBOK® Guide) (PMI, 2013)
- Systems Engineering Handbook (INCOSE, 2015)
- Systems Engineering Handbook (NASA, 2007)
- Guide to the Systems Engineering Body of Knowledge (SEBoK) (INCOSE, 2016b)
- Graduate Reference Curriculum for Systems Engineering (Pyster et al., 2012)
- Systems Engineering Competency Career Model (SECCM) (Whitcomb et al., 2015)
- Software Engineering Body of Knowledge (SWEBoK) (IEEE, 2014)

In designing the course, the faculty made an interesting observation:

> [T]he course materials are designed such that students gain an in-depth understanding of both the engineering project management and software project management areas. . . . Regardless of the registered students' software or computer engineering background, the project management process is fairly similar for both software and hardware systems development, so the need to reconcile the two views is not as acute as in the case of requirements engineering (Babiceanu, 2015).

The *Graduate Reference Curriculum for Systems Engineering* (GRCSE™) (Pyster et al., 2012) recognized the value of incorporating project management into engineering courses when they quote Pyster and Olwell (eds):

> SE [systems engineering] incorporates skill sets from many disciplines; including traditional engineering disciplines (electrical, mechanical, civil, etc.) as well as more management-focused disciplines (project management, program management, industrial engineering, etc.). It is important that systems engineers

possess basic knowledge related to these disciplines and also understand how SE is related to other disciplines. A student should be able to articulate how SE could and should interact with these disciplines and what common pitfalls may occur when these relationships are not properly managed. This is discussed in "Part 6: Related Disciplines" of the SEBoK (p. 18).

The GRCSE goes on to state:

> Given the increasing complexity of modern systems, it is imperative for graduates of SE programs to understand and appreciate the fundamental concepts of project management, their relationship with SE, and the ways in which complexity can be managed in projects. In addition to the general relationships, some disciplines, such as human factors, are now heavily entwined with systems. Human factors deals with complex systems that are generally operated and/or used by humans; in these systems, issues associated with usability and ergonomics play a major role in system success or failure (p. 18).

At the graduate and doctoral level, prospective students will find they have options. There are specific degree programs related to project, program, and portfolio management. In fact, most of the GAC-accredited programs are at the Master's and Doctoral level in project management. Prospective students will also find graduate and doctoral degrees in engineering with a concentration in project and/or program management.

The analysis of the research upon which this book is based confirmed roles and skills for engineering program leaders (program managers and chief systems engineers) that are consistent not only with traditional engineering education and training programs, but also with professional standards and certifications. This reinforces the notion that these roles are indeed part of functional disciplines based in specialized knowledge. While each of these domains has unique roles and skills, there are significant areas of overlapping or shared responsibility. Both program managers and chief systems engineers are viewed as jointly accountable for managing program and project risk, external supplier relations, quality management, and life cycle planning. In each of these areas, there are unique perspectives and analyses that each function brings to the shared responsibility. Nevertheless, successful integration may not be so much in the accumulation of multiple analyses as it is the way in which one analysis or perspective informs the other, and ultimately shapes the unified program-level approach. This suggests that the ability to synthesize integrated solutions from multiple perspectives is an important engineering leadership skill.

Whether through shared responsibilities or from the need to share knowledge derived from unique functional responsibilities, the respective functions require the ability to work together in an integrated fashion. The program manager claims that the most important skills for that role include leadership and stakeholder management (Conforto, Rossi, Rebentisch, Oehmen, & Pacenza, 2013). Combined, these suggest the ability to bring together diverse interests to embrace a common objective and work collaboratively. Chief systems engineers claimed that the most important skills for that role include systems thinking and requirements management, which suggests an ability to link overarching objectives to detailed elements in a holistic integrated perspective. Both program managers and chief systems engineers share communication as a key skill (Conforto et al., 2013). An educational or professional development program may not necessarily need to develop all of these skills in its students, but it should nevertheless strive to develop an understanding and appreciation of the different roles that are required in an integrated program leadership team.

Innovative engineering leadership education programs increasingly emphasize the introduction of more elements of life cycle processes and operations for engineered systems, including interpersonal skills and leadership. Yet they still may not address some of the important organizational and relational elements highlighted in this book, particularly, integration across functional and organizational boundaries—an important element of engineering program success. Unproductive tension between the program management and systems engineering disciplines results when integration of the disciplines is informal, ad hoc, or just ineffective. The roots of unproductive tension may ultimately lie with poorly defined roles and relationships in the program and organization. As engineering efforts become more integrated, and as relationships become more explicit and formally defined, the unproductive tension in organizations decreases. This suggests that organizational or program design may play a significant role in shaping the effectiveness of engineering efforts. While engineering students may learn a good deal about product design during the course of their education, they may not have much exposure to information about the design of organizations and the relationships they embody. These issues should be considered for addition in future engineering leadership curricula.

Academia should also consider whether there are better approaches for achieving true interdisciplinary education. The American Association of Colleges of Nursing presented a powerful definition of interdisciplinary education in its *Position on Interdisciplinary Education and Practice* (AACN, n.d.). It defined interdisciplinary education as:

> An educational approach in which two or more disciplines collaborate in the learning process with the goal of fostering interprofessional interactions that enhance the practice of each discipline. Such interdisciplinary education is based on mutual understanding and respect for the actual and potential contributions of the disciplines.

Current curricula "reengineering" activities are largely focused on fitting new content into existing curricula or, in the case of project, program, and portfolio management, developing specific degree programs in the field. At the undergraduate level, current approaches reinforce a siloed environment focused on a specific discipline that may incorporate elements from another discipline. At the graduate and doctoral levels, there may be more opportunity to achieve the objective of fostering interprofessional interactions, although engineering programs are likely to have a predominance of individuals with engineering undergraduate degrees. So how does the academic environment transform to become more interdisciplinary?

In their web resource post, *Interdisciplinary Approaches to Teaching*, Goldsmith, Hamilton, Hornsby, and Wells (n.d.) propose that faculty lead the change by doing the hard work required to build a truly interprofessional and interdisciplinary program. They advocate a model proposed by Allen Remko and James Welsh that empowers faculty to embrace their role as transformers.

The transformation that Goldsmith and colleagues (n.d.) propose is not just of the degree program, but of the individual faculty members themselves. The model requires that faculty members become interprofessional and interdisciplinary through their research, engagements with academic colleagues, and outreach to industry and government. According to Goldsmith and colleagues, only by living and embodying the transformation can faculties demonstrate to students the criticality of being interprofessional and interdisciplinary.

The Call to Action for academic institutions and faculty is to better position students for a competitive workforce by:

- Incorporating interdisciplinary practices, case studies, and related material into existing courses to the greatest extent possible
- Exposing students to more real-world engineering programs by bringing experienced professionals into the classroom and arranging for students to visit engineering program work sites
- Creating new courses in engineering program and project management or developing synergies with allied department's courses
- Establishing new degrees in engineering program management that fully integrate key skills and competencies from both domains

16.2 Call to Action for Enterprise: Build the Right Engine for Strategy Implementation

Enterprise leaders care about outcomes—the achievement of strategy or mission. Achieving outcomes requires that organizations have an engine that is capable of effectively implementing strategic objectives. One such approach is an "engine" with five, interlocking components:

- **Culture.** Culture reflects those behaviors and actions that are recognized. If a role is recognized as having a target on its back, like that of program manager or chief systems engineer, who in the organization will want that role? If individuals have to be told to work across silos, then collaboration in the organization is weak. So leaders must demonstrate the behaviors they expect their teams to mirror. They should also acknowledge when their teams exhibit the right behaviors and coach them when they do not.
- **Vision.** There must be a clear, obtainable objective that people can understand and direct their efforts to accomplish. They must understand the importance of the objective to the organization as well as their contribution to achieving the objective.
- **Talent.** Finding the right people with the right skills and those positive attributes that reflect an effective organizational culture is part of the talent component. In addition, good talent management must include ongoing professional development to ensure that the skills, competencies, and experience of the workforce remain leading-edge. And performance incentives should be layered to reward a range of accomplishments for teams as well as for individuals.

- **Capabilities.** The right people need capabilities that enable them to deliver their best performance on behalf of the organization. The methods, processes, and tools people use in their work should enable excellence by being tailored by and for the user community.
- **Leadership.** Regardless of an individual's formal role in the organization, the organization should build and encourage leadership at all levels to help staff engage with their work and with each other. Leadership must energize people to give their best effort, empower them with the appropriate authority, and enable them to build collaborative networks that deliver results for the organization.

Driving strategy implementation requires that these elements become constituents of a climate or ecosystem that enables integration to take place within the organization more readily. And it is the job of the leaders who are the stewards of this ecosystem to act to ensure that the ecosystem encourages and recognizes the importance of integration.

As has already been demonstrated, no effort is required to convince executive leaders that their organizations need to change. Culture is often pointed to as the most prominent cause of failure in programs and projects. In a study of CEOs, IBM (2008) identified the top challenges to successfully implementing strategic change. Corporate culture was mentioned as a challenge by half the respondents, second only to "changing mindsets and attitudes." Recognizing that need is keeping many of them awake at night along with two key questions:

- Is the organization capable of the change required?
- How does the organization manage and sustain the change initiative?

Most leaders believe that culture alone is the target of organizational change. In fact, Combe (2014) points out that there are three interlocking mechanisms that must work in tandem to effectively execute and sustain true organizational change: culture, commitment, and capacity.

Achieving the new mindset, to which systems engineering and program management must align practices in order to better enable collaboration and deliver greater value and customer satisfaction, is at the heart of the cultural change described in this book. It is imperative that executive leaders first model through their own actions, then hold program managers and chief systems engineers accountable for demonstrating the behaviors and attitudes that will embed the mindset within their teams. At the same time, the leadership also needs to ensure that other parts of the organization help to build and sustain the capacity necessary for the changes to take hold and become engrained in the new culture. But most importantly, executive leaders must hold themselves accountable to lead by example and make one of their primary jobs the mentoring of the next generation of enterprise leaders.

Talent management activities help support the right mindset, empower individuals to do their part, and sustain critical changes. For new employees, the proper orientation, mentoring, and coaching helps them adapt to the organization's environment, performance expectations, and cultural norms. Developing integrative training programs for team members from various disciplines helps them learn together, work together, and understand each other's contributions to the program or project.

Leveraging seasoned employees as coaches and mentors enables critical knowledge transfer about how:

- Real work gets done
- Barriers can be overcome
- Insight from experience and lessons learned avoids repetition of past mistakes

In the world of systems engineering and program management, there are solid examples of talent management programs created within organizations that focus on creating and sustaining an integrative and collaborative mindset. NASA's Academy of Project/Program and Engineering Leadership (APPEL) is one example. NASA (n.d.a) describes the program this way:

> The Academy's core curriculum offers a comprehensive, integrated approach to learning for NASA's technical workforce. The sequence of materials is designed to help participants expand their thinking to make connections among many systems engineering and project management principles and concepts, see the "big picture," and understand the context and interrelationships of the topics.
>
> This framework promotes the timely transfer of knowledge and skills into the work environment. Core courses range from the foundations of aerospace to advanced project management and systems engineering topics.

APPEL offers a broad range of courses designed to ensure that systems engineers and program managers understand vital elements of each other's disciplines and key points of integration so they are better able to communicate, collaborate, and deliver results. Educational programs target individuals at all levels, from new hires to seasoned professionals, and some "students" may ultimately become program instructors.

Beyond coursework, NASA Project Team Development Support provides coaching, workshops, and group sessions aimed at increasing a project's probability of success. Support is available to help program, project, and engineering leaders prepare their teams. It includes the availability of subject matter experts to support planning and scheduling, program control analysis, systems and integration support, risk management, and software management. And it features assessments to help uncover behavioral challenges that may ultimately affect team cohesion and performance.

As is often the case, NASA's APPEL evolved from major cultural gaps that led to small and large mission failures, including both the Challenger and Columbia space shuttle disasters. Those failures forced transformational change after loss of life. The post-disaster investigation found evidence of a persistent siloed culture that inhibited alignment of practices, effective communication, mutual respect, and collaboration. APPEL helps to sustain a changed mindset through its integrated mission focus and by indoctrinating staff members at all levels to the current, collaborative way of doing things. The culture change sustained by building the right capabilities within the team strengthens everyone's commitment to do what it takes for the program mission to succeed.

Besides effective talent management, another key capability that enables organizations to successfully execute their projects and programs is the establishment of methodologies. As explored in Chapter 8, a methodology and its related policies establish a system of practices, techniques, procedures, and rules used by a discipline to meet requirements and deliver value to stakeholders. Research shows that organizations with standardized practices, such as defined methodologies, perform better than those that do not, and they have higher rates of achieving their original business goals. Despite their value, many organizations do not utilize documented, aligned, and integrated methodologies (PMI, 2016b), instead relying on more ad hoc processes. Why? Because business process management and ongoing process improvement is often not valued by organizational leaders. For commercial organizations, such activities do not generate direct revenue, and are considered as operational overhead that the organization must bear. For government organizations, the resources, time, and expertise may not be available within the agency to support process development and improvement.

Within organizations that have established methodologies in place, appropriate elements of the processes, practices, and tools used by program managers and systems engineers must align in complementary ways and integrate at critical intersection points. For example, both program managers and systems engineers use risk management practices to identify and prepare to mitigate business, technical, supplier, and other risks that could impact the program. If project technical risks that could affect other projects and, ultimately, the success of the program are not visible to the program manager and chief systems engineer, program performance can be affected. Similarly, if business risks are not shared and clearly understood at all levels of the program, project managers and engineers could make decisions without fully understanding the implications of those decisions.

A study by MITRE Corporation Command and Control Center's Enterprise Systems Engineering Focus Group uncovered the importance of integrated engineering program capabilities. While focused specifically on evolving systems engineering approaches and techniques, the study looked at the system through an engineering program lens. In fact, "The objectives were clearly stated to improve program performance through the application of ESE (enterprise systems engineering)" (Crider & DeRosa, 2007). The study began by identifying key ESE processes: technical planning; enterprise architecture; capabilities-based engineering analysis; enterprise analysis and assessment; and strategic technical planning. Next, a series of case studies were developed to evaluate the application of the ESE processes to "tackle an existing enterprise challenge and/or fulfill a critical enterprise capability need" (Crider & DeRosa, 2007). The case studies reflected a range of programs and projects, including some that had already been completed. Participants included a broad range of engineering and project professionals.

The study found that the processes identified were sound and were being applied in various ways based on the unique aspects of the project or program. The most significant findings called out by Crider & DeRosa (2007) related to elements of building enterprise engineering program capabilities are:

■ Organizations need "to establish an enabling infrastructure (technical, business, operational) to achieve enterprise outcomes."

- Capabilities must extend beyond just technical skills and include such key leadership and business/strategy management skills as "Leadership, strategic vision, conflict management, balancing cooperation and competition, coalition building."
- Real-time lessons learned need to fuel improvement throughout the enterprise. Specifically, the study found that risk management practices of both program/ project management and systems engineering disciplines were insufficient for complex programs. In fact, some programs shifted from a "risk management" mindset to an "opportunity management" framework. The program team "built a successful [opportunity management] integration facility for their program. However, as it gained notoriety within the larger enterprise, they shifted its purpose and expanded it to become an enterprise resource."

These studies and examples clearly demonstrate that organizational leaders must embrace culture and capability development to effectively drive strategy and engagement. Organizational culture must value ongoing internal improvement and put resources and support structures in place to build, assess, and improve required capabilities. If the company values it and enables it to happen, engineering program teams will commit to sustaining it.

The Call to Action for organizational leaders is to enhance their organization's ability to effectively implement its strategies by:

- Being active shepherds of the organization's culture, demonstrating the right behaviors and enforcing the expectation that others will mirror those behaviors
- Ensuring that the organization enables integrative approaches that enhance value delivery to customers and realize strategic benefits for the company
- Contributing to engineering program team success by making timely decisions, removing roadblocks from the team's path, helping to build consensus, and keeping the team energized around the vision
- Ensuring that staff are actively developing themselves within and outside of the organization through internal knowledge-sharing networks, external scanning and scouting for leading practices at industry and professional events, and participation in research consortia

16.3 Call to Action for Policymakers: Refocus Oversight and Accountability in the Right Ways

There are two unique, but overlapping functions within government that, depending on the form of government, may be carried out by one or multiple entities. These functions have complementary roles to play in the transformation of government engineering program management capabilities:

- Policymakers—those who through legislation vehicles establish requirements for engineering program oversight, accountability, and controls.
- Government executive leaders—those who carry out public policy directives.

The Guide to Lean Enablers for Managing Engineering Programs (Oehman, 2012) outlined the challenges associated with driving improvements in engineering program performance within government. Those challenges have their roots in decisions and approaches adopted by policymakers and government executive leaders:

- Policymaker decisions and approaches
  - ❏ **Unstable funding environment.** Discontinuities and uncertainties in the funding of a program tend to cause instabilities with program staffing and subcontracts, and thus make efficient and effective program management more difficult.
  - ❏ **Policies demanding early subcontracting.** Some government programs have a policy-driven demand to subcontract many program management activities, even in the very early phases. These policies risk subcontracting of critical coordination and integration functions creating significant impediments to effective program planning and execution.
  - ❏ **Geographically dispersed subcontracting strategy (e.g., "made in 50 states").** Political forces create incentives for contractors of government-sponsored programs to subdivide program activities among as many states, provinces, or other jurisdictions as possible. This could contradict those enablers that demand efficient organizational structures in the program enterprise.
- Government executive leader decisions and approaches
  - ❏ **Program leadership rotation.** The personnel development policy, especially in the military services, might call for a regular rotation of the government-side program manager. This is contrary to maintaining clear and stable responsibility, accountability, and authority on both the customer and contractor sides. It also impacts having top leaders with deep program-specific business and systems engineering knowledge for the top program leadership.
  - ❏ **Lack of rigor in exercising known best practices.** Published government acquisition and program management guidelines and policies contain a large number of useful practices that support strong performance. However, those practices are not always fully implemented, a fact that is regularly identified in formal program audits and evaluations.
  - ❏ **Mismatch between contracting vehicle and risk profile.** The spectrum from fixed-price to cost-plus contracts creates specific incentives for behavior on the government and the contractor sides. Most importantly, it assigns the responsibilities for carrying cost risks driven, for example, by technology uncertainty or production inefficiencies between the parties. If the risk profile of a program is not aligned with the contracting vehicle and the incentives it creates, the resulting program environment will not be conducive to controlling cost.
  - ❏ **Promoting a bureaucracy of artifacts.** Risk aversion and the demand for oversight can create a culture and environment that keeps program and engineering leadership busy with documentation and administrative tasks, rather than focusing their efforts on performance and results.

The continued poor performance of many government engineering programs and tightening budgets is pushing policymakers and government executives to transform their thinking, particularly related to program management capabilities. In the United Kingdom, the Major Projects Authority (MPA) was established in 2011 with a mandate to oversee the government's portfolio of approximately 200 large programs and projects, totaling close to £500 billion in public funding. MPA manages a large number of engineering programs and projects covering transportation, infrastructure, technology systems, and military defense with its largest programs and projects within the Ministries of Defense and Health (Cabinet Office, 2015). Since its establishment, MPA has advanced development of government program and project management capabilities and expertise as well as the accountability of major project business owners. Its key accomplishments, as reported in the 2015 annual report, include:

- Transparency across the portfolio of the largest public sector programs and projects with measures tracking the likelihood of success and life cycle cost estimates.
- Moving some programs and projects to higher confidence levels of success. Troubled programs and projects are clearly identified and open to further evaluation and progression decisions.

MPA's leadership reflected the type of interdisciplinary perspective needed to transform engineering program performance. Tony Meggs, MPA's senior executive, brought significant experience as a business and technical leader in the private sector, including overseeing British Petroleum's technology, projects, and engineering functions. His deputy director, Steve Vine, was an experienced systems engineer.

In January 2016, MPA merged with Infrastructure U.K. (IUK). IUK, a division of Her Majesty's Treasury, was established in 2010 to support public sector capital investment in infrastructure and to develop financing schemes to encourage private sector investment in infrastructure. The new organization, the Infrastructure and Projects Authority (IPA), combines "government expertise in the financing, delivery and assurance of infrastructure projects" (Cabinet Office, n.d.). Meggs leads the new organization, and expectations are high that program and project performance will continue to improve.

In the United States, the 114th Congress passed legislation that focuses on building the federal government's program management capabilities. The legislation has several key components, including:

- The Office of Management and Budget, the executive agency responsible for oversight of agency performance, federal procurement, and financial management, is required to establish standards, policies, and guidelines for program/project management.
- The Office of Personnel Management is charged with developing a federal job series for program management professionals with requisite competencies, skills, and experience requirements.
- Each government agency is required to develop a five-year strategic plan for developing and improving its project and program management capabilities.
- Each agency is required to designate a program management improvement officer and to coordinate improvement efforts across agencies through an interagency council.

■ Ongoing reviews of the portfolio of government programs deemed high risk by government auditors, as well as requirements for individual government agencies to review their portfolios.

With regard to systems engineering, U.S. policymakers have received reports for over 16 years identifying opportunities to improve weapon systems acquisition programs through more effective use of systems engineering practices. In March 2001, the Government Accountability Office (GAO) reported to Congress that systems engineering, applied to weapon systems before product development began, reduced cost and delivered better results (GAO, 2001). The GAO noted that Department of Defense policy did not allow systems engineering application until after requirements were set. In June 2015, the GAO completed an analysis of 78 major defense program requirements (GAO, 2015). Again, the GAO cited the need for application of systems engineering within the programs. But this time, chiefs within the Department of Defense acknowledged not only the need for systems engineering, but also of stronger engineering program integration:

> Poor program outcomes can be traced to a culture in which the military services begin programs with unrealistic requirements, immature technologies, and overly optimistic cost and schedule estimates.... We presented our assessment of the requirements problem to current and former service chiefs and they generally agreed with it. Several service chiefs noted that more integration, collaboration, and communication during the requirements and acquisition processes needs to take place to ensure that trade-offs between desired capabilities and expected costs are made and that requirements are essential, technically feasible, and affordable before programs get underway.

The GAO also reported that the service chiefs felt that the government needed to improve its overall capabilities associated with systems engineering:

> Almost all of the service chiefs stated that there is a need to further enhance expertise within the government, and several specified expertise in systems engineering. Several service chiefs indicated that systems engineering capabilities are generally lacking in the requirements development process, and do not become available until after requirements are validated and an expensive and risky system development program is underway. Some service chiefs advocated that having systems engineering capabilities available to the military services during requirements development could help to ensure earlier assessment of requirements feasibility.

The chief's assessment suggests an opportunity for systems engineering improvement accountability legislation, similar to that for program management.

These are critical first steps in addressing program challenges and in enabling stronger performance. Given that in the United Kingdom, the United States, and many other countries, engineering programs targeting infrastructure, technology, security, and defense represent large percentages of their budgets, a similar focus is required to strengthen systems engineering capabilities, ensure stronger practice alignment, and enable collaboration.

The Call to Action for policymakers is to use its oversight and authorization powers to improve government engineering program management capabilities by:

- Holding agency or ministry leaders accountable for acting upon capability improvement opportunities uncovered in audit reports, particularly when those opportunities are not acted upon by the relevant agency or ministry
- Evaluating and changing government policies and practices that inhibit integrated approaches for managing engineering programs, such as acquisition and procurement laws and customary practices with their corresponding root causes
- Ensuring that the civil service has the right roles, skills, and capabilities to manage complex engineering programs, including support for ongoing learning and development for civil servants
- Acknowledging and promoting improvements achieved in engineering program performance

16.4 Call to Action for Industry and Professional Societies: Take an Interdisciplinary View

Trade and professional associations play a significant role in identifying and shaping effective practices that influence their organizational and practitioner members, particularly in the areas of standards and certifications.

In the field of systems engineering, the largest is the International Council on Systems Engineering (INCOSE). INCOSE is a not-for-profit membership organization founded in 1990 to share, promote, and advance systems engineering principles and concepts. INCOSE's members fill roles that range from student to senior practitioner and technical engineer to program and corporate management (Rebentisch, 2015). Many other engineering societies, such as IEEE, the American Society of Mechanical Engineers and the American Institute of Aeronautics and Astronautics, also have communities within their membership focused on systems engineering.

In the field of project, program, and portfolio management, the largest global professional organization is the Project Management Institute (PMI). PMI is a not-for-profit professional membership association founded in 1969. Other organizations associated with project and program management are the Project Management Association of Japan (PMAJ); and the International Project Management Association (IPMA).

One important method for advancing skills and roles for professionals is the promulgation of standards and certifications. Development of standards and certification is an important function that trade and professional associations advance on behalf of their members. In the standards area, there are several standards associated with program management and systems engineering, and even more relating to specific practices, such as risk management, configuration management, cost estimating, etc. A standard addresses the question, "What should we do?"

The most important international and commercial standards in the field of systems engineering are industry-spanning and include:

- Systems and Software Engineering—System Life Cycle Processes (ISO/IEC/IEEE 15288:2015)
- Systems and Software Engineering—Life Cycle Processes—Project Management (ISO/IEC/IEEE 16326:2009)
- Systems and Software Engineering—Software Life Cycle Processes (ISO/IEC 12207)

PMI publishes consensus-based standards detailing the widely accepted practices related to project and program management as:

- A Guide to the Project Management Body of Knowledge (PMBOK® Guide) (ANSI/PMI 99-001-2013)
- The Standard for Program Management (ANSI/PMI 08-002-2012)

Complementing these foundational standards are a range of practice standards, frameworks, and practice guides that further elaborate on specific project and program management practices and approaches.

With their large pool of professionals to serve as subject matter experts, trade and professional societies can tap their members' expertise to fill gaps in existing standards, particularly related to how the various standards connect and align with each other. Rather than promulgating more standards, membership organizations can develop guidelines, whitepapers, and other resources that help their members align the recommended practices in existing standards. Such activities would not only help to integrate practices, but could also help to establish a common technical language understood by both disciplines.

An important role of professional discipline communities is to increase the depth and specialization of knowledge within the community. Professional certifications provide an objective method for evaluating an individual's ability to apply knowledge and experience to real-life problems and challenges. Because the field of systems engineering is much smaller than the field of project management, other systems engineering certification processes tend to be associated with individual organizations. For instance, INCOSE offers the INCOSE ASEP (Associate), INCOSE CSEP (Certified), and INCOSE ESEP (Expert) certifications. The Object Management Group (OMG, n.d.a) describes itself as an international trade association that develops "enterprise integration standards for a wide range of technologies and an even wider range of industries." OMG's Certified Systems Modeling Professional™ is a four-tiered certification program that targets systems engineers utilizing Model-Based Systems Engineering practices (OMG, n.d.). Many universities that offer engineering degree programs also have certificate programs focused on systems engineering.

The list of program manager certifications in the much larger field of project management is more broad and diverse, as shown in Table 16-2.

Certifications and the requisite continuing professional development requirements for recertification encourage, enable, and reward increasing knowledge specialization and life-long learning. But increasing specialization carries the risk of creating greater distance between disciplines such as program management and systems engineering

Table 16-2: Project management professional credentials and certifications	
CAPM® (Certified Associate in Project Management)	PRINCE2 Foundation
PMP® (Project Management Professional)	PRINCE2 Practitioner
PgMP® (Program Management Professional)	IPMA Level A® (Certified Projects Director)
PfMP® (Portfolio Management Professional)	IPMA Level B® (Certified Senior Project Manager)
PMI-RMP® (PMI Risk Management Professional)	IPMA Level C® (Certified Project Manager)
PMI-SP® (PMI Scheduling Professional)	IPMA Level D® (Certified Project Management Associate)
PMI-ACP® (PMI Agile Certified Practitioner)	P2M (Project Management Specialist)
PMI-PBA® (PMI Professional in Business Analysis)	P2M (Project Manager Registered)
	P2M (Project Management Architect)

that must ultimately collaborate on complex programs. There is a growing concern that program managers and systems engineers view stakeholders' needs from within their own disciplinary perspectives, and as a result apply distinctly different approaches to the key work of engineering programs—managing the planning and implementation, defining the components and their interactions, building the components, and integrating the components. To mitigate this risk, there are opportunities for trade and professional societies to develop collaboratively educational programs and other activities that incorporate multidisciplinary perspectives, similar to NASA's APPEL program.

The Call to Action for industry and professional societies is to foster interdisciplinary integration by:

- Offering joint educational programs for practitioners through collaborative development of standards and guidelines that enable common practices and methods
- Collaborating on advocacy and educational efforts regarding the value of integration targeted to organizational leaders in business and government
- Facilitating collaborative research programs with the academic/research community, organizational leaders, and practitioners to identify leading practices for managing complex engineering programs

16.5 Call to Action for Researchers: Explore Interdisciplinary Systems

NASA's Apollo program achieved fame for landing a man on the moon and for the technological advances it delivered and enabled for the future. Its most impactful achievement, however, has received insufficient attention. Even NASA's own website and its treasure trove of documents fail to highlight its key legacy.

NASA's first administrator, Dr. T. Keith Glennan, immediately recognized the most critical risk to the Apollo Space Program. The inadequacy of systems, structures, culture, and practices to enable program management and technical leadership to effectively align their work and achieve performance objectives threatened to derail the program from the start. Glennan constructed NASA's program management capabilities in the late 1950s, borrowing from the experience of the armed forces and its contractors. Those capabilities solidified when U.S. Air Force Major General Samuel C. Phillips established a "program management office" that "centralized authority over design, engineering, procurement, testing, construction, manufacturing, spare parts, logistics, training, and operations" (NASA, n.d.b).

Glennan's official successor, James E. Webb, took Glennan's work to the next level. Webb realized he not only had to continue NASA's engineering program management transformation, he also had to influence future generations of program and project managers, systems engineers, and scientists to think, behave, and work differently. And academic researchers exploring research and development approaches were "not paying much attention to organizational variables or to innovation as a multistage, multiperson, complex process" (Roberts, 2007). Through partnerships with 13 of the leading engineering universities across the United States and with funding from NASA, Webb supported the establishment of management of technology (MOT) programs. The MOT programs targeted the education of future program leadership; but, more importantly, academic research focused on improving approaches for managing complex technical programs. Schools such as Massachusetts Institute of Technology (MIT), University of California at Berkeley, Vanderbilt University, Polytechnic Institute of New York University, Georgia Institute of Technology, and the University of New Mexico accepted the challenge. Collectively, the universities and NASA embarked on a relationship that spanned three decades and produced a broad range of research that is applied to today's engineering programs. NASA's assessment of the Apollo Space Program points out the significance of the MOT program:

> It may turn out that [the space program's] most valuable spin-off of all will be human rather than technological: better knowledge of how to plan, coordinate and monitor the multitudinous and varied activities of the organizations required to accomplish great social undertakings (NASA, n.d.).

From MIT's perspective, its MOT program "has changed the way the world thinks about innovation—how innovation is taught, how innovation is best employed in the real world, and the power of innovation to propel the transformation of products and business" (MIT Sloan, 2014, p. 8).

Eventually, the MOT programs shut down or evolved into other programs within the universities that had incubated them; and today there is scant information about available programs. But the need for rigorous research and insight into critical areas of engineering program management still remain, particularly in areas such as:

- Appropriate research methods for studying complex systems
- Understanding how diverse teams work, particularly management and engineering
- Complex systems development that combines both the technical and management system design
- A systems view of the dynamics of interdisciplinary efforts on complex projects and programs, particularly related to how individual roles and professional practices combine in a program environment to deliver results
- Effective practices, tools, and approaches for managing complex, adaptive engineering programs, especially related to risk management, cost management, and procurement models

Chettiparamb (2007) found that the above elements could benefit from insight utilizing evolving approaches in interdisciplinary research that can result in:

- Integrating existing frameworks and their associated practices, approaches, and methods
- Exploring the links in existing knowledge in such a way that completely new frameworks evolve and, in turn, establish new practices, approaches, and methods
- Expanding existing frameworks and their associated practices, approaches, and methods by incorporating knowledge from a more diverse range of fields

The great advantage that the research community offers is that it brings an objective viewpoint that helps to frame issues and opportunities in a way that does not get bogged down in interdisciplinary politics or turf battles. Coupling that objectivity within a multidisciplinary research team could produce groundbreaking insight and knowledge.

The Call to Action for researchers is to advance the body of knowledge associated with engineering program management by:

- Incentivizing research proposals focused on approaches for strengthening interdisciplinary team performance and improving effectiveness of engineering program performance
- Copying leading industrial practices by building multidisciplinary research teams to tackle big problems

16.6 References

Accreditation Board for Engineering and Technology (ABET). (2006). *Engineering change: A study of the impact of EC2000.* Retrieved from www.abet.org/wp-content/uploads/2015/04/EngineeringChange-executive-summary.pdf

American Association of Colleges of Nursing (AACN). (n.d). *Position on interdisciplinary education and practice.* Task Force on Interdisciplinary Education. Retrieved from www.aacn.nche.edu/publications/position/interdisciplinary-education-and-practice

Babiceanu, R. F. (2015, June). *Engineering project management graduate education in integrated software and systems engineering environments.* Presented at the American Society of Engineering Education Annual Conference, Seattle, Washington.

Banik, G. (2015, June). *Integration of project management course to satisfy ABET's requirements.* Presented at American Society for Engineering Education Annual Conference, Seattle, Washington.

Cabinet Office. (2015). *Major Projects Authority Annual Report 2014–15.* Retrieved from www.gov.uk/government/uploads/system/uploads/attachment_data/file/438333/Major_Projects_Authority_Annual_Report_2015.pdf

Cabinet Office. (n.d.). *New government body to help manage and deliver major projects for UK economy.* Retrieved from www.gov.uk/government/news/new-government-body-to-help-manage-and-deliver-major-projects-for-uk-economy

Chettiparamb, A. (2007). *Interdisciplinarity: A literature review.* Subject Centre for Languages, Linguistics and Area Studies, School of Humanities, University of

Southampton. The interdisciplinary teaching and learning group. Retrieved from www.llas.ac.uk/resourcedownloads/3219/interdisciplinarity_literature_review.pdf

Combe, M. (2014). *Change readiness: Focusing change management where it counts.* Retrieved from www.pmi.org/learning/~/media/PDF/Knowledge%20Center/Focusing-Change-Management-Where-it-Counts.ashx

Conforto, E. C., Rossi, M., Rebentisch, E., Oehmen, J., & Pacenza, M. (2013). *Survey report: Improving integration of program management and systems engineering.* Presented at the 23rd INCOSE Annual International Symposium, Philadelphia, PA. Retrieved from www.pmi.org/~/media/PDF/Business-Solutions/Lean-Enablers/PMI-INCOSE-MIT-Integration-Study.ashx

Crider, K. A., & DeRosa, J. K. (2007, April). *Findings of case studies in enterprise systems engineering.* MITRE Corporation.

Goldsmith, A. H., Hamilton, D., Hornsby, K., & Wells, D. (n.d.). *Interdisciplinary approaches to teaching* [web log post]. Retrieved from https://serc.carleton.edu/econ/interdisciplinary/how.html

Government Accountability Office (GAO). (2001). *Better matching of needs and resources will lead to better weapon systems outcomes.* Retrieved from www.gao.gov/assets/160/156905.pdf

Government Accountability Office (GAO). (2015). *Acquisition process: military service chiefs' concerns reflect need to better define requirements before programs start.* Retrieved from www.gao.gov/assets/680/670761.pdf

Hamilton, J. (2000, November). *The engineering profession.* Engineering Council: London. Retrieved from https://web.archive.org/web/20070810194330/http://www.engc.org.uk/documents/Hamilton.pdf

IBM. (2008). *Making change work: Continuing the enterprise of the future conversation.* Armonk, NY: IBM Corporation. Retrieved from http://www-935.ibm.com/services/us/gbs/bus/pdf/gbe03100-usen-03- making-change-work.pdf

IEEE Computer Society. (2014). *Software engineering body of knowledge (SWEBOK®).* P. Bourque, & Richard E. Fairley (Eds). Washington, DC: Author.

International Council on Systems Engineering (INCOSE). (2015). *Systems engineering handbook: A guide for system life cycle processes and activities,* (4th ed.). San Diego, CA: Author.

International Council on Systems Engineering and Systems Engineering Research Institute (INCOSE). (2016a). *2016 Worldwide directory of systems engineering and industrial engineering academic programs.* Retrieved from www.incose.org/docs/default-source/aboutse/se-academic-program-directory0231BA07E0A3.pdf?sfvrsn=18

International Council on Systems Engineering (INCOSE). (2016b). *Guide to the systems engineering body of knowledge (SEBoK),* v. 1.6. San Diego, CA: Author.

MIT Sloan. (2014). Joining NASA's orbit. *MIT Sloan. 8*(2). Retrieved from http://mitsloan.mit.edu/alumnimagazine/2014/spring-summer/pdf/MITSln_Smr14_LR_WithoutNotes.pdf

National Aeronautics and Space Administration (NASA). (n.d.a). Academy of Project/Program and Engineering Leadership web site, http://appel.nasa.gov/

National Aeronautics and Space Administration (NASA). (n.d.b). *Project Apollo: A retrospective analysis.* Retrieved from http://history.nasa.gov/Apollomon/Apollo.html

National Aeronautics and Space Administration (NASA). (2007). *Systems engineering handbook*. Washington, D.C.: Author.

Object Management Group (OMG). (n.d.a). *About OMG®*. Retrieved from www.omg .org/gettingstarted/gettingstartedindex.htm

Object Management Group. (n.d.b). *Show what you know*. Retrieved from www.omg .org/omg-certifications/

Oehmen, J. (Ed.). (2012). *The guide to lean enablers for managing engineering programs, version 1.0*. Cambridge, MA: Joint MIT-PMI-INCOSE Community of Practice on Lean in Program Management. URI: http://hdl.handle.net/1721.1/70495

Project Management Institute (PMI). (2013). *A guide to the project management body of knowledge (PMBOK® guide)*. Newtown Square, PA: Author.

Project Management Institute (PMI). (2015). *The handbook of accreditation for academic degrees and awards in project, program, and portfolio management and related programs—Fourth Edition*. Retrieved from www.pmi.org/~/media/PDF/Professional -Development/GAC_handbook_2015.ashx

Project Management Institute (PMI). (2016a). *Directory of accredited programs*. Retrieved from www.pmi.org/gac/directory-accredited-programs.aspx

Project Management Institute (PMI). (2016b). *Pulse of the Profession®, The high cost of low performance: How will you improve business results?* Retrieved from www.pmi.org/ learning/pulse.aspx

Pyster, A., Olwell, D. H., Ferris, T. L. J., Hutchison, N., Enck, S., Anthony, J., Henry, D., & Squires, A. (Eds.). (2012). *Graduate Reference Curriculum for Systems Engineering (GRCSE™)*. Hoboken, NJ, USA: Trustees of the Stevens Institute of Technology. Retrieved from http://bkcase.org/wp-content/uploads/2014/04/GRCSEv10_Final .pdf

Rebentisch, E. S. (2015, June). *Collaboration across linked disciplines: Skills and roles for integrating systems engineering and program management*. Presented at American Society for Engineering Education Annual Conference, Seattle, Washington.

Roberts, E. B. (2007). Managing invention and innovation. *Research-Technology Management, 50*(1). Retrieved from www.questia.com/library/journal/1P3-1200399851/ managing-invention-and-innovation

de los Rios, I., Cazorla, A., Diaz-Puente, J., & Yagüe, J. (2010). Project–based learning in engineering higher education: Two decades of teaching competences in real environments. *Procedia Social and Behavioral Sciences 2*, 1368–1378. Retrieved from www.academia.edu/11671597/Project_based_learning_in_engineering_higher _education_two_decades_of_teaching_competences_in_real_environments

Rouvrais, S., Ormrod, J., Landrac, J., Mallet, J., Gilliot, J-M., Thepaut, A., & Tremenbert, P. (2006). A mixed project-based learning framework: preparing and developing student competencies in a French Grande Ecole. *European Journal of Engineering Education 31*(1), 83–93. doi: 10.1080/03043790500429500

Stills, S. (1966). For What It's Worth [Recorded by Buffalo Springfield]. On *Buffalo Springfield* [Record], 1967. Hollywood, CA: Atco.

Whitcomb, C., Delgado, J., Khan, R., Alexander, J., White, C., Grambow, D., & Walter, P. (2015). *The department of the Navy systems engineering career competency model*. URI: http://hdl.handle.net/10945/4768

AFTERWORD: TOWARD AN INTEGRATED FUTURE

The Case for Integration

The basic premise of this book is that better program management and systems engineering integration, including more effective decision making, collaborative work, and information sharing, will lead to high-performing programs. The book addressed this in the three main parts:

- Part I made the case for why the reader should be concerned about integration between the program management and systems engineering disciplines.
- Part II described in greater detail what to do to increase integration between the program management and systems engineering disciplines.
- Part III addressed how to make integration a reality in programs by creating sustained change toward a new way of working together.

The findings from the program management and systems engineering integration research are documented in the book, making the case that this integration is important and there are a number of actions that can be taken to increase its impact in organizations.

New Insights Gained Along the Way

There is a saying, "You don't know what you know until you try to write it down." That was certainly confirmed during the course of writing this book. The underlying research findings revealed much about integration. The writing process quickly identified the areas that were not well-posed, relied on fuzzily defined concepts, or just lacked a sufficient knowledge base. A number of those gaps were filled along the way to the completed manuscript. Sources included published research by others or knowledge captured by practitioners specifically for this publication. In other cases, though, the information needed to close a knowledge gap could not be found.

For instance, there are numerous published reports documenting projects and their outcomes, including project management experiences and best practices. There are dramatically fewer published reports describing project management and systems engineering and how the two disciplines work together in the project. There are few published reports documenting programs and program management experiences and leading practices, particularly outside of the government programs sector. Beyond this book and its associated research activities, there was an extremely limited number of reports documenting how the program management and systems engineering disciplines work together on programs. Case study examples used in this book were repurposed and combined from other existing sources intended to demonstrate different points, or were created specifically for this work.

During the integration research interviews, each individual, almost to a person, had a different definition of integration than the next. None had formalized concepts or definitions of integration in use in their organizations, and certainly were not measuring it. A number of them were using practices or tools that led to more integrated efforts, but they were driven more by thoughtfully trying to avoid or mitigate self-inflicted problems than based on a formal understanding of the principles of integration. As discussed in the foreword, knowledge builds and evolves as people apply it in new ways to address challenges. As concepts mature, they become formally defined and standardized, and it becomes easier to transfer, replicate, and adapt them in new settings, and thus build new knowledge. The research experience showed that the understanding and formal application of the fundamentals of integration still are not very mature.

The research and writing of this book involved a very collaborative process, with practitioner experts from both the program management and systems engineering communities. A number of people were exposed to emerging research findings and in turn provided their perspectives on the findings. This included academic colleagues who offered ideas and suggestions during the course of the research, audience participants at conference presentations, and subject matter experts from both the program management and systems engineering communities who reviewed an early draft of the book manuscript. Overwhelmingly, the feedback was that integration between systems engineering and program management was an important issue to address, that it was not well-addressed by existing publications or practices, and that the emerging findings of the research rang true to the experience of the practitioner experts. This, they said, was a book that was urgently needed.

As a result of this feedback, many questions were answered and improvements were made in the manuscript. However, additional questions were raised in this process, some of which remain unanswered. The following is a sample of the questions that emerged from the review and writing phase of this effort.

- Are the principles and concepts of integration presented here universally applicable or are they unique to a certain program context and set of characteristics?
    - How can the integration concepts be tailored so that they can be applied successfully across a wide range of contexts and settings?
    - How do the size and scope of the program or organization affect the specific integration practices chosen and applied? Do some integration practices that work at one scale become suboptimal or even counterproductive at another?
    - Given the preponderance of evidence from a given setting (e.g., North America, aerospace, and large civil infrastructure), would the same findings be observed in examples from other national cultures and business sectors?
    - Would the same observations hold where other standards and professional organizations dominate the practice? How do others address integration, and do they have the same program behaviors related to poor integration between program management and systems engineering (or their equivalents) that are addressed here?
- How might organizations measure the extent to which their teams are integrated in order to target areas for improvement?
- How is the ongoing development of good practices (enhancing current practices), as well as the creation of emergent practices to deal with unique situations, addressed by the integration of program management and systems engineering?
- What are the respective roles of program managers and chief systems engineers in an integrated environment?
    - What roles do the program manager and chief systems engineer play, individually and together, in managing and realizing business benefits over the program's life cycle?
    - What is effective stakeholder engagement in the program domain? Where do the roles and responsibilities of program managers and chief systems engineers overlap related to stakeholders?
    - How is integration affected by turnover in program leadership roles, particularly when poor initial planning and decisions are inherited by the new leadership and cannot be undone? How does that impact the approach to integration that can be taken?
- What is the best way to manage talent for integrated operations?
    - How do organizations identify candidates, develop them through training, and build bench strength within their program management and systems engineering workforce?
    - What is the best career development strategy for integrated professionals? Is it necessarily the case that engineers must eventually become program managers, or can both be trained in how to do "integration" from within their respective discipline bases and roles?

❏ Both program management and systems engineering have a number of common roots and operate in generally the same environment. Yet they have different standards and means of professional progression. Would it be beneficial to create an integrated set of standards that encompass the essential elements of both disciplines or at least provide a "cross walk" between the two to enable the development of joint certifications for professionals?

■ Many of the problems associated with engineering program failures discussed in this book appear to be symptoms of underlying problems rather than the root causes of those problems. What are the root causes in engineering program failures?

Some of these questions might be raised because the research is still in an early stage where the concepts are still being refined and proven. A small number of studies cannot realistically be expected to answer all the questions that might arise in a complex organizational system. These issues are not fundamental, however, and can be addressed as more research is undertaken to answer questions such as these. Given the opportunity to both shape the practice of integration and to improve overall outcomes, hopefully some will be interested in expanding the knowledge base.

The Path Forward

The future of integration, it seems, is full of opportunity. The discussion and evidence presented in this book has hopefully inspired those with interest in improving program outcomes to work to improve program management and systems engineering integration. But where to start? There is no shortage of advice in this book on what to do:

■ Part II identified a number of actions, methods, and tools that if applied will encourage greater program management and systems engineering integration.

■ Part III identified a number of actions for making the changes necessary to increase integration and, importantly, the organizational climate and the human capital and talent base conducive to integration.

■ Part IV identified a number of actions for various program stakeholders to enable actions recommended in the previous parts.

Implementing these actions so that there is sustained improvement in the degree of program management and systems engineering integration could potentially stretch across years. Individual and institutional initiative and adaptiveness will carry the day as the integration playbook is still being written. Nevertheless, it is a course of action that will likely produce valuable returns based on the evidence seen so far.

It is also possible that even doing these things is only just beginning to scratch the surface or address the symptoms of why these two important disciplines in many cases do not work together as effectively as they could. The root causes of these conflicts may very well be related to "soft issues" explored in theory domains such as psychology, sociology, political science, political economy, and the like, rather than the immediate technical and management disciplines. Exploring these root causes will require longer-term, sustained effort in this area through research or other studies.

Regardless, a starting point on the path forward has been defined in various parts of this book. It may lose some definition a bit further out and could bend in a new direction at one point or another. The only way to know what lies next with any greater clarity is to begin the journey.

Good luck with your efforts to improve program management and systems engineering integration. And as you proceed, please share your experiences, your successes, and also your frustrations. The authors welcome the opportunity to learn from your experiences, but also to help share the lessons learned throughout the community of practitioners and researchers working in this important area.

GLOSSARY

Agile. A collective term that represents a comprehensive range of tools, techniques, methods, and practices applied to the management of projects with adaptive characteristics. While the term is largely associated with software development projects, Agile approaches can apply to any project. Agile approaches use short development cycles with frequent review and replanning meetings to coordinate project activities.

Benefits Management. See program benefits management.

Benefits. An outcome of actions, behaviors, products, or services that provide utility to the sponsoring organization as well as the program's intended beneficiaries.

Business Analysis. A practice for eliciting and defining project and program requirements that incorporates input from business owners to users with the objective of fully defining the requirements early in the project or program life cycle.

Business Case. The business case is developed to assess the program's balance between cost and benefit, and includes key parameters used to assess the objectives and constraints for the intended program.

Capability. The ability to do something or perform a specific task.

Change Agent. An early adopter of a proposed change who works to ensure the change is integrated into the organization in a sustainable way.

Change Champion. Anyone who sees the value to be gained by the change and works to promote the change within a sphere of influence. Often, the change champion does not have a role assigned, but is identified by the program team as a supporter who can influence others.

Change Management. A comprehensive, cyclic, and structured approach for transitioning individuals, groups, and organizations from a current state to a future state with intended business benefits. (Source: *Managing change in organizations: A practice guide*. Project Management Institute.)

Chief Systems Engineer. The role within a program that has the ultimate technical authority and accountability for the product or system being developed.

Collaboration. The result when a collective group of individuals work together closely, the contributions of all disciplines are valued, and information is shared openly.

Communications. In the program context, providing and maintaining clear visibility into all aspects of the program as it progresses so that all stakeholders, both internal and external, are presented with a single point of view of the details throughout the program life cycle and understand how any contribution they make fits within the whole.

Competency. An underlying characteristic of program management and systems engineering that includes a set of skills, attributes, and knowledge which results in effective performance. Competencies must be measurable and are fundamental to successful individual, team, and organizational performance.

Complex. The interactions between the parts of a system exhibit self-organization, where local interactions give rise to novel, nonlocal, emergent patterns. (Source: *Systems engineering handbook: A guide for system life cycle processes and activities* (4th ed.) International Council on Systems Engineering).

Complicated. The interactions between the many parts of a system are governed by fixed relationships. This allows reasonably reliable prediction. (Source: *Systems engineering handbook: A guide for system life cycle processes and activities* (4th ed.) International Council on Systems Engineering).

Configuration Management. A process for managing version control of requirements, specifications, and work.

Contextual Factors Dimension. The Integration Framework dimension that deals with multiple internal and external factors. It captures elements that may positively or negatively impact the integration performance in a given program and business context.

Cost-Benefit Analysis. A technique that compares actual or planned costs against the expected outcome, enabling the determination of value gained versus total resource invested.

Creative Tension. Tension is the stress that exists between what is and what is desired. It becomes creative when it produces ideas and solutions that may have not been considered had the tension not existed.

Culture. See organizational culture.

Current State. The existing organizational structure, processes, or activities as they exist at a point in time. The current state serves as a baseline against which the desired future state is compared producing a gap report that identifies required changes for achieving the future state.

Decision Theory. The process through which the human mind takes in information and formulates a response.

Discipline. A field of particular study that includes a common body of knowledge related to the work undertaken.

Effective Integration Dimension. The Integration Framework dimension that deals with the integration performance and its three key elements: rapid and effective decision making, effective collaborative work, and effective information sharing.

Emotional Intelligence. The capability that enables one to "tune in" to one's emotions and the emotional state of another and thereby adjust interactions relative to the situation.

Enterprise Environmental Factors. Changing circumstances and conditions outside the program's boundary, which may consist of corporate, environmental, and governmental variables that constrain the ability of a program to achieve its goals.

Enterprise. A complex, integrated, interdependent system of people, processes, and technology that creates value as determined by its key stakeholders.

Episodic Integration. Processes, practices, and tools applied at specific intervals within the life cycle of a program or project.

Framework. The structure or model that represents a theory, concept, system, or a set of interconnected elements.

Future State. The intended outcome and positioning of an organization at some future point in time, which is to be achieved through the execution of a portfolio of programs and projects.

Gate Reviews. Decision points in the program or project life cycle, usually after completing a phase, where the governance team reviews progress to plan and makes a go/recycle/no-go decision.

Governance. Systems and methods by which a program and its strategy are defined, authorized, monitored, and supported by its sponsoring organization. (Source: *The Standard for Program Management.* Project Management Institute.)

Hybrid Methodologies. The combination of principles, practices, techniques, and tools from different management approaches to develop a systematic process aimed to fit the management capability to the business context and needs and specific types of programs. The goal is to maximize program performance and product results, and allow the team to balance predictability with flexibility, reduce risks, and increase innovation in order to deliver better results to the business and added value to all stakeholders.

Improvisation. The practice of reacting while making and creating. Improvisation is linked with aspects of time and, particularly, pressure to achieve against a demanding or compressed timetable.

Incentives. The rewards for performing at or above a target level. Incentives may be tied to such things as delivering programs or projects ahead of schedule. They may also be used in behavior modification where certain positive behaviors are rewarded and negative or undesired behaviors are penalized.

Integrated Delivery. An approach that links people, systems, business structures, and practices into a process that fosters collaboration and trust.

Integrated Product and Process Development. An approach that uses multidisciplinary teams in design to jointly derive requirements and schedules with equal emphasis on product (i.e., design) and process (i.e., manufacturing) development. It is also referred to as simultaneous engineering or design-build.

Integrated Product Team. A linked framework for engaging program participants in order to avoid an individualized focus associated with program work and deliverables. The structure enables shared ownership and responsibility for the work produced.

Integrated Project Delivery (IPD). A project or program organizing approach that takes intentional action to ensure all organizational units affecting or affected by a program participate in the planning and delivery process. It is a useful tool that promotes integration between and across disciplines.

Integrated Project Organization (IPO). An approach for aligning staff from a program owner and a management consultant company under one integrated organizational structure.

Integration. Alignment of program management and systems engineering practices, tools and techniques, experience, and knowledge in a collaborative and systematic approach to increase team effectiveness toward achieving a common goal/objective in complex program development environments.

Integration Framework. The framework that illustrates how integration works in programs. The Integration Framework encompasses six dimensions: I) Process, practices and tools; II) Organizational environment; III) People competencies; IV) Contextual factors; V) Effective integration; and VI) Program performance.

Integration Index. A single variable that provides an overall score for the degree of integration achieved and represents all 17 variables associated with the Integration Framework.

Integration Performance. A measure that shows the level of integration within a program based on elements of the effective integration dimension of the Integration Framework.

Interdisciplinary Team. A group of diverse disciplines that come together and function interdependently as a whole to produce a shared outcome.

Iterative Development. A repeating approach to project work that utilizes short bursts of development activity followed by review and additional cycles of development to further enhance or modify outputs until required attributes are realized.

Leadership. A people-oriented competency focused on motivating and enabling individuals or teams to maximize their efforts to achieve desired outcomes.

Life Cycle. The span of activities related to program and project execution from initiation to closure of the initiative. The term is also used to define the stages through which a product moves from conception through implementation and eventually to retirement.

Measures of Effectiveness (MOE). Evaluation of the degree to which a system achieves its stated mission or operational objectives.

Measures of Performance (MOP). Evaluation of the physical and functional characteristics or attributes related to the system operation considering operational environment conditions.

Methodology. A documented approach for integrating interacting or interdependent practices, techniques, procedures, and rules to determine how best to plan, develop, control, and deliver a defined objective.

Mode-based Program Planning. A single model representing the relationships within a program to display its overall structure, relationships, and critical dependencies.

Obeya. A room where a cross-functional team meets to figuratively or literally break down the product completely and investigate changes to it in real time.

OODA Loop. A continuous cycle of observing, orienting, deciding, and acting (OODA) for decision making.

Organization. A collective reference to people, structures, and other assets assembled together to fulfill a mission by achieving a specific vision.

Organizational Agility. The ability of an organization to absorb changes or quickly adapt in response to internal or external factors, market conditions, customer demands and trends, competition, and technology evolution, as well as to cope with economic, environmental, political, and sociological shifts.

Organizational Culture. The collective values, philosophy, and practices of the organization's members as demonstrated in the behaviors and attitudes of the people in the organization.

Organizational Environment Dimension. An Integration Framework dimension related to elements of the organization context, structure, culture, and so on, primarily focused within the organization rather than on its external environment. Organizational Climate is a related concept. It defines those things that a company rewards, supports, and expects.

People Competencies Dimension. An Integration Framework dimension that deals with competencies among people, including experience, education, skills, abilities, and the like. Individual competence is generally recognized as the combination of knowledge, skills, and ability.

Perceptual Control Theory. When applied to teams, perceptual control theory is a three-step process where, once focused on a goal, the team talks about the goal daily to keep it at the forefront of team members' minds and reviews performance regularly to ensure information is shared.

Performance Indicators. A set of qualitative or quantitative variables used to monitor and evaluate planned goals and objectives.

Performance Measurement System. A clearly defined process for collecting, analyzing, and reporting program performance status to support decision-making across different levels of the organization.

Performance Metrics. The set of measures (management and technical) used to monitor, evaluate, and improve the efficiency, effectiveness, and results of a program. Management and technical metrics can be tangible and intangible.

Pervasive Integration. Processes, practices, and tools applied continuously throughout the life cycle of a project or program.

Portfolio Management. The centralized management of one or more portfolios of projects, programs and other activities to achieve strategic objectives. (Source: *The Standard for Portfolio Management*. Project Management Institute.)

Principles. A set of propositions and general rules that serve as the foundation of a management approach, method, or behavior.

Process Maturity. Formalized and managed processes that lead to more valuable and consistent outcomes.

Program. A group of related projects, subprograms, and program activities that are managed in a coordinated way to obtain benefits not available from managing them individually. (Source: *The PMI lexicon of project management terms*. Project Management Institute.)

Program Benefits Management. Program benefits management establishes the program architecture that maps how component projects will deliver the intended capabilities and outcomes to achieve the program benefits. It focuses program stakeholders on the outcomes and benefits to be provided by the various activities conducted during the program's duration. (Source: *The Standard for Program Management*. Project Management Institute.)

Program Kickoff Workshop. A meeting that brings together all key program stakeholders at the beginning of the program to gather insight and information and identify critical dependencies as early as possible before major decisions and commitments are made.

Program Life Cycle. The program life cycle spans the duration of the program and includes three major phases: program definition phase, program benefits delivery phase, and program closure phase. (Source: *The Standard for Program Management*. Project Management Institute.)

Program Manager. The role within a program that has the ultimate authority and accountability for realizing the overall program objectives and benefits.

Program Performance. Evaluation of the status of a program in terms of progress and results compared to a set of planned goals, objectives, and expectations. It is based on the evaluation of a set of performance indicators.

Program Performance Dimension. An Integration Framework dimension that measures the performance of the program in terms of schedule, budget, client satisfaction, and client requirements, and relates those outcomes to overall program benefits.

Program Performance Management. Defines the expected results to be realized by the program and how the program benefits will be achieved. See also performance measurement system and performance metrics.

Program Success Factors. A set of measurable outcomes that must be present or achieved in order for a program to be deemed successful.

Project. A temporary endeavor undertaken to create a unique product, service or result. (Source: *The PMI lexicon of project management terms*. Project Management Institute.)

Project Manager. The role within a project that has ultimate authority and accountability for the project deliverables.

Pulsed Product Integration and Iterative Development. Ongoing work to align product components into more complex components or into complete products that uses short cycles to create and deliver product increments, parts of the product, or other deliverables related to a program.

RACI. Acronym for Responsible, Accountable, Consulted, and Informed. It is a tool for categorizing the role of a stakeholder in a project or program and using the results to tailor communications.

Readiness Assessment. A measurement of the degree to which an organization is prepared to undertake a change. It evaluates organizational culture, structure, capacity, and processes among many other characteristics of the organization and its environment.

Requirements Management. The process by which the functionality or capability of the program or project output is ensured. The process begins with elicitation from stakeholders of needs and wants and progresses through documentation and validation for design, development, and delivery.

Risk Management. The identification and mediation of potential events that can affect the outcomes of a program or project.

Schedule Compliance Risk Assessment Methodology (SCRAM). An approach for identifying risks to meeting the program schedule. It can be used for the assessment and improvement of schedule risk compliance in projects and programs.

Set-based Design. An engineering process that evaluates a wide range of potential product features and systematically removes infeasible configurations in order to rapidly converge on the preferred solution.

Shared Space. The common functions, activities, and work shared between the systems engineer and the program manager with respect to technical management processes. It includes planning, assessment and control, decision management, risk management, configuration management, information management, measurement, and quality assurance.

Silo. See stovepipe mentality.

Sociotechnical System. A characterization of complex systems that acknowledges that both the people and the technology elements of the system are interdependent and influence each other. This perspective may be applied at multiple scales of activity, ranging from the design of individual or group work within organizations to the interactions between society's complex infrastructures and human behaviors.

Sponsor. The individual, often from the executive level, who is the ultimate organizational champion for the initiative within the organization and who is able to marshal resources as needed.

Stakeholder. An individual, group, or organization who may affect, be affected by, or perceive itself to be affected by a decision, activity, or outcome of a project, program, or portfolio. (Source: *A Guide to the Project Management Body of Knowledge (PMBOK® Guide)*. Project Management Institute.)

Standard. A documented statement that represents broadly accepted principles of what constitutes good practice or common guidelines. Standards address what needs to be done at a high level typically without specifying exactly how something is to be done.

Stovepipe Mentality. Pursuing work on a program by applying one's specialized knowledge and practices without regard to other potentially affected roles and functions. Sometimes referred to as working in a silo.

Strategy Implementation. The collective organizational effort to execute strategy by investing in the right initiatives to deliver desired business benefits.

System Dynamics Modeling. A simulation technique used to analyze complex and dynamic systems with multiple relationships between endogenous and exogenous elements.

System Life Cycle Stages. The progression of a system as the result of actions, performed and managed by people in organizations, using processes for execution of these actions. (Source: ISO/IEC/IEEE 15288:2015.)

System of Systems. An SOI [System of Interest] whose elements are managerially and/or operationally independent systems. These interoperating and/or integrated collections of constituent systems usually produce results unachievable by the individual systems alone. (Source: *Systems Engineering Handbook*. International Council on Systems Engineering.)

Systems Engineer. The role on a project or program team that applies the concept of systems engineering to the development of a product, service, capability, or outcome.

Systems Engineering. An interdisciplinary approach and means to enable the realization of successful systems. It focuses on defining customer needs and required functionality early in the development cycle, documenting requirements, then proceeding with design synthesis and system validation while considering the complete problem. (Source: www.incose.org. International Council on Systems Engineering.)

Systems Engineering Technical Review. A formal review and evaluation as to whether required systems engineering tasks have been satisfactorily completed prior to proceeding to the next stage of development.

Systems Thinking. The process by which one attempts to look at the whole rather than the individual parts to gain a better understanding of how the parts interact and are interdependent within the larger system.

Tailoring. The process of adapting and fitting processes and approaches to the specific needs of the organization and the project or program.

Teaming. The good of the whole is valued more than the individual disciplines that leads to accomplishing more than can be achieved by each discipline separately.

Technical Performance Measures (TPM). Attributes or characteristics of a system element according to the defined requirements or goals.

Transformational Change. A change implemented through programs that affects the way an organization conducts its business activities.

Uncertainty. The inability to predict or know an outcome due to influences that may be outside the control of the individual or system interacting with a system.

Unproductive Tension. A term used to describe any issue, situation, or behavior between individuals or teams that might negatively affect program performance by producing stress and conflict that works at cross purposes with program success.

Value Stream Map. A tool used to visualize the path or possible paths for accumulating value contributing to and building the intended program benefits.

Value. See benefits management.

Vee Model. A visualization method used to Break down the "problem to be solved" into a sequence of steps involving component activities, shown as a descending list on the left side of the Vee, and then reassembling as the components are completed ascending up the right side of the Vee.

Very Small Entity. A term used to define micro enterprises, or in some cases small projects, that interact with much larger organizations by contributing engineering expertise in highly specialized areas of technology.

Work Packages. Identifiable collections of tasks that may be developed sequentially or in parallel with other work activities before later combination into the whole of the deliverable.

Index

Printed and bound by CPI Group (UK) Ltd, Croydon, CR0 4YY

23/04/2025

14660930-0001